GUIDE TO FOOD STORAGE

Follow this guide for food storage, and you can be sure that what's in your freezer, refrigerator, and pantry is fresh-tasting and ready to cook.

IN THE FREEZER
(At –10° to 0° F)

DAIRY
Cheese, hard	3 months
Cheese, soft	2 weeks
Egg substitute	6 months
Egg whites	6 months
Egg yolks	8 months
Ice cream, sherbet	1 month

FRUITS AND VEGETABLES
Commercially frozen fruits	1 year
Commercially frozen vegetables	8 to 12 months

MEATS, POULTRY, AND SEAFOOD
Beef, Lamb, and Veal
Ground, uncooked, and all cuts, cooked	3 months
Roasts and steaks, uncooked	9 months

Pork
Ground, uncooked, and all cuts, cooked	3 months
Roasts and chops, uncooked	6 months

Poultry
All cuts, cooked	1 month
Boneless or bone-in pieces, uncooked	6 months

Seafood
Bass, perch, trout, and shellfish	3 months
Cod, flounder, and halibut	6 months

IN THE REFRIGERATOR
(At 34° to 40° F)

DAIRY
Buttermilk, low-fat	1 to 2 weeks
Cheese, grated Parmesan	1 year
Cheeses, Cheddar and Swiss	3 to 4 weeks
Cream cheese, ⅓-less-fat and reduced-fat	2 weeks
Eggs and egg substitute	1 month
Margarine	1 month

MEATS, POULTRY, AND SEAFOOD
Beef, Lamb, Pork, and Veal
Ground and stew meat, uncooked	1 to 2 days
Roasts, uncooked	2 to 4 days
Steaks and chops, uncooked	3 to 5 days

Chicken, Turkey, and Seafood
All cuts, uncooked	1 to 2 days

FRUITS AND VEGETABLES
Apples, beets, cabbage, carrots, celery, citrus fruits, eggplant, and parsnips	2 to 3 weeks
Apricots, berries, peaches, pears, plums, asparagus, cauliflower, cucumbers, mushrooms, okra, peas, peppers, salad greens, and summer squash	2 to 4 days
Corn, husked	1 day

IN THE PANTRY
Keep these at room temperature for six to 12 months.

BAKING AND COOKING STAPLES
Baking powder
Biscuit and baking mix
Broth, canned
Cooking spray
Honey
Mayonnaise, regular, light, and nonfat (unopened)
Milk, canned evaporated skimmed
Milk, nonfat dry powder
Mustard, prepared (unopened)
Oils, olive and vegetable
Pasta, dried
Peanut butter, reduced-fat
Rice, instant and regular
Salad dressings, bottled (unopened)
Seasoning sauces, bottled
Tuna, canned

FRUITS, LEGUMES, AND VEGETABLES
Fruits, canned
Legumes (beans, lentils, peas), dried or canned
Tomato products, canned
Vegetables, canned

Bananas Foster,
page 36

Sweet Curried Shrimp,
page 68

Café-Style Meat Loaf with
Browned Gravy, page 87,
and Garlic Mashed
Potatoes with Rosemary,
page 145

Rustic Corn Cakes with
Creamy Cumin Sauce,
page 79

Weight Watchers®

ANNUAL RECIPES
for SUCCESS

2002

Oxmoor House®

©2001 by Oxmoor House, Inc.
Book Division of Southern Progress Corporation
P.O. Box 2463, Birmingham, Alabama 35201

ISBN: 0-8487-2459-3
ISSN: 1526-1565
Printed in the United States of America
Second Printing 2002

Be sure to check with your health-care provider before making any changes in your diet.

Weight Watchers® is a registered trademark of Weight Watchers International, Inc., and is used under license by Healthy Living, Inc.

OXMOOR HOUSE, INC.
Editor-in-Chief: Nancy Fitzpatrick Wyatt
Executive Editor: Katherine M. Eakin
Art Director: Cynthia R. Cooper

WEIGHT WATCHERS® ANNUAL RECIPES
FOR SUCCESS 2002
Editor: Carolyn Land, R.D., L.D
Successes Editor: Patricia Wilens
Copy Editor: L. Amanda Owens
Editorial Assistant: Diane Rose
Editorial Interns: Lindsey Hanes, Megan Graves
Designer: Clare T. Minges
Director, Test Kitchens: Elizabeth Tyler Luckett
Assistant Director, Test Kitchens: Julie Christopher
Recipe Editor: Gayle Hays Sadler
Test Kitchens Staff: Jennifer Cofield; Gretchen Feldtman, R.D.;
    David Gallent; Ana Kelly; Jan A. Smith
Senior Photographer: Jim Bathie
Photographer: Brit Huckabay
Senior Photo Stylist: Kay Clarke
Photo Stylist: Ashley J. Wyatt
Publishing Systems Administrator: Rick Tucker
Director, Production and Distribution: Phillip Lee
Books Production Manager: Larry Hunter
Production Assistant: Faye Porter Bonner

CONTRIBUTORS
Indexer: Mary Ann Laurens
Recipe Development: Nancy Hughes, Jean Kressy, Marge Perry,
    Kathleen Royal Phillips, Eileen Runyan
Test Kitchens: Tamara Brown; Kate Wheeler, R.D.; Kelly Wilton

COVER: Brownie Sundae Pie, page 41
BACK COVER: Blackened Tuna with Orange-Zested Salsa, page 64

WE'RE HERE FOR YOU!

We at Oxmoor House are dedicated to serving you with reliable information that expands your imagination and enriches your life. We welcome your comments and suggestions. Please write to us at:

Oxmoor House, Inc.
Editor, Weight Watchers® Annual Recipes for Success
2100 Lakeshore Drive
Birmingham, AL 35209

To order additional copies of this publication or any others, call 1-205-445-6560.

For more books to enrich your life, visit
oxmoorhouse.com

CONTENTS

INTRODUCTION

Welcome 8

About Our Recipes 10

♈️

RECIPES

Appetizers & Beverages 11

Breads...18

Desserts 35

Fish & Shellfish 57

Meatless Main Dishes...............................73

Meats...86

Poultry..100

Salads 117

Sandwiches..126

Side Dishes...141

Soups & Stews 152

SUCCESSES

Step by Step...21

Fighting Back..28

A Name That Fits 45

A Healthful Hobby....................................52

Commitment for Life 89

Back in the Swing of Things 109

Changing Times 116

Home Free..133

It Runs in the Family 140

Making Time for Mom 157

WEEKLY MENU PLANNERS

Weeks 1-9.......................................164–181

♈️

General Recipe Index................182

POINTS® Recipe Index 189

Welcome!
Let this book be your guide to nourishing and nurturing a healthy, active lifestyle.

Healthy living is about more than being an ideal body weight or exercising four times a week. It's about maintaining a lifestyle that makes you happy—mentally and physically—whether that means five minutes of quiet time each day or training for and finishing a 5-K race. But keeping your life balanced isn't always easy.

We realize that you have enough to do each day without spending stressful hours in the kitchen. That's why we worked hard to make *Weight Watchers Annual Recipes for Success 2002* simple and enjoyable to use. This cookbook streamlines meals **(over 200 of the recipes take less than 20 minutes to prepare)** and ultimately gives you more time for the things that make you happiest! Throughout the book are handy, timesaving tips and step-by-step instructions to simplify recipe preparation. For your convenience, we've placed handy references in the front and back of the book, including:

- LOW-FAT INGREDIENT SUBSTITUTIONS
- VEGETABLE COOKING CHART
- GUIDE TO FOOD STORAGE
- METRIC EQUIVALENTS

CHOICES FOR EVERYONE
Weight Watchers Annual Recipes for Success 2002 makes it possible for you and your family to eat healthy, delicious meals. And with almost 500 new Weight Watchers recipes from which to choose, you're sure to find an array of dishes to tempt everyone from kids to vegetarians to meat-lovers.

You'll find recipes that you can't wait to try, such as Beef-and-Broccoli Stir-Fry (page 93), Buttery Tarragon Chicken (page 103), and Double Chocolate Bundt Cake (page 44).

NINE WEEKS OF MENUS
We've simplified meal planning by providing you with nine weeks of daily menus beginning on page 164. These menus are flexible, making it easy for you to adjust them to your personal tastes. Each day includes two or more one-serving recipe suggestions, with the **POINTS** values listed with each recipe and for each day. We've even planned in some quick snacks.

PICTURES OF HEALTH
You're not alone in your pursuit of a more healthful life. For motivation, you'll discover 10 inspiring success stories featuring people who have lost weight and kept it off through the Weight Watchers weight-loss program. For people like Rhonda Pigott (page 116), losing weight meant gaining self-esteem:

"I try to remember how I felt when I was overweight and how low my self-esteem was. You have to truly feel better about yourself when you're thin—that keeps me on track."

Stories like Rhonda's are scattered throughout the book for when you need extra motivation or willpower. Soon you, too, will have your own motivational story to share.

NUTRITION KNOW-HOW

Accurate information is an important tool in the pursuit of healthful living. So that you'll know where you stand nutritionally, you'll find guides with every recipe. Each recipe has a **POINTS** value calculated through the **POINTS**® Food System, an integral part of the new weight-loss program, Weight Watchers **Winning Points**. We've also included the diabetic exchanges for individuals who may have special dietary consider-ations, as well as a complete nutritional analysis (for more information, see "About Our Recipes" on page 10). Within each chapter you'll find the latest nutrition and health information that may address some of your concerns:

- *Is pasta fattening? (page 75)*
- *How do I know if I'm getting enough iron? (page 95)*
- *Why should I eat a meatless meal if I'm not a vegetarian? (page 84)*
- *Should I count my carbohydrates? (page 20)*

WE WANT TO HEAR ABOUT YOUR SUCCESS!

If you have a Weight Watchers weight-loss success story that you would like to share with us, please send a brief account of your personal experience to:

Weight Watchers Annual Recipes for Success
2100 Lakeshore Drive
Birmingham, AL 35209

Tell us your name, address, daytime telephone number, and E-mail address (if applicable). If possi-ble, please include before-and-after snapshots.

OUR FAVORITE RECIPES

We judge the merits of every recipe, and only the best make the cut. But a few have an indefinable quality that can only be described as the "yum factor." These recipes are so outstanding, they've become our personal favorites. We think they'll become yours and your family's as well.

- **Summer Berry Crisp (page 53).** Bake fresh berries under a buttery brown sugar-and-oat topping, and then add ice cream for a simply irresistible summer treat.

- **Angelic Tiramisu (page 39).** You'll shout hallelujah when you taste this heaven-sent coffee-flavored dessert.

- **Shrimp Po'boys with Remoulade Slaw (page 129).** Bring the tastes of New Orleans home with oven-fried shrimp topped with creamy slaw and served on toasty French bread.

- **Peanut Butter S'mores Bars (page 56).** Imagine a chewy peanut butter cookie loaded with chocolate, marshmallow, and peanuts that fits into your healthful meal plan. Sound too good to be true? Well, we've got the recipe for you!

- **Oatmeal Energy Bars (page 15).** Forget the pricey energy bars at health-food stores; create your own! Packed with fruit, oats, and peanut butter, these nutri-tious treats are sure to get you through your workouts.

- **Beer-Cheese Soup with Pretzel Croutons (page 153).** Warm up chilly football days with this rich velvety soup. The pretzel croutons are real crowd-pleasers.

- **Broccoli-and-Two Cheese Calzones (page 128).** Throw your family a curve on pizza night by serving calzones. Kids are guaranteed to eat up when their veggies are covered with cheese.

- **Fresh Corn-and-Basil Salad (page 119).** Save your best summer corn to mix with fresh basil and balsamic vinegar in this simple and delicious salad.

- **Beef Tenderloin with Marsala-Mushroom Sauce (page 93).** Simmer tenderloins in a rich sauce made with red wine, mushrooms, and butter. They're perfect for a romantic Valentine's meal or a dinner party.

About Our Recipes

♈♙♈

Weight Watchers Annual Recipes for Success 2002 gives you the nutrition facts you need. To make your life easier, we've provided the following useful information with every recipe:

- A number calculated through the **POINTS** Food System, an integral part of the **Winning Points** weight-loss program from Weight Watchers International, Inc.
- Diabetic exchange values for those who use them as a guide for planning meals
- A complete nutrient analysis per serving

POINTS FOOD SYSTEM

Every recipe in the book includes a number assigned through **POINTS** value. This system uses a formula based on the calorie, fat, and fiber content of the food. Foods with more calories and fat (like a slice of pepperoni pizza) receive high numbers, while fruits and vegetables receive low numbers. For more information about the **Winning Points** weight-loss program and the Weight Watchers meeting nearest you, call 1-800-651-6000.

DIABETIC EXCHANGES

Exchange values are provided for people who use them for calorie-controlled diets and for people with diabetes. All foods within a certain group contain approximately the same amount of nutrients and calories, so one serving of a food from a food group can be substituted or exchanged for one serving of any other item on the list. The food groups are starch, fruit, vegetable, milk, meat, and fat. The exchange values are based on the *Exchange Lists for Meal Planning* developed by the American Diabetes Association and The American Dietetic Association.

NUTRIENT ANALYSIS

Each recipe has a complete list of nutrients, including CAL (calories), PRO (protein), FAT (total fat), sat (saturated fat), CARB (carbohydrate), FIB (dietary fiber), CHOL (cholesterol), IRON, SOD (sodium), and CALC (calcium). Measurements are abbreviated g (grams) and mg (milligrams). Numbers are based on these assumptions:

- Unless otherwise indicated, meat, poultry, and fish refer to skinned, boned, and cooked servings.
- When we give a range for an ingredient (3 to 3½ cups flour, for instance), we calculate using the lesser amount.
- Some alcohol calories evaporate during heating; the analysis reflects that.
- Only the amount of marinade absorbed by the food is used in calculation.
- Garnishes and optional ingredients are not included in an analysis.

Nutritional values used in our calculations either come from The Food Processor, Version 7.5 (ESHA Research) or are provided by food manufacturers.

Appetizers & Beverages

ROASTED RED PEPPER DIP

Serve with crispy breadsticks and fresh vegetables.

2 (5½-ounce) bottles roasted red bell peppers, drained
1 tablespoon balsamic vinegar
¼ teaspoon salt
⅛ teaspoon ground red pepper
1 (8-ounce) tub light cream cheese, softened
1 garlic clove

1. Pat roasted peppers dry with paper towels.
2. Place all ingredients in a food processor; process until smooth, scraping sides of bowl if necessary. Cover and chill 2 hours. YIELD: 16 servings (serving size: 2 tablespoons).

POINTS: 1; EXCHANGE: ½ Fat;
PER SERVING: CAL 38 (59% from fat); PRO 1.6g;
FAT 2.3g (sat 1.6g); CARB 2g; FIB 0.1g;
CHOL 6.6mg; IRON 0.1mg; SOD 168mg;
CALC 20mg

SPINACH DIP WITH FETA

⅔ cup low-fat buttermilk
½ cup (2 ounces) crumbled feta cheese
½ cup fat-free sour cream
½ cup light mayonnaise
2 tablespoons chopped green onions (about 1)
¼ teaspoon salt
¼ teaspoon dried oregano
⅛ teaspoon pepper
1 (10-ounce) package frozen chopped spinach, thawed, drained, and squeezed dry

1. Place all ingredients in a food processor; pulse until blended. Serve with baked tortilla chips, carrot sticks, or pita wedges. YIELD: 18 servings (serving size: 2 tablespoons).

POINTS: 1; EXCHANGE: Free up to 2 tablespoons;
PER SERVING: CAL 34 (35% from fat); PRO 1.6g;
FAT 1.4g (sat 0.6g); CARB 4.2g; FIB 0.5g;
CHOL 4mg; IRON 0.4mg; SOD 156mg;
CALC 53mg

GOAT CHEESE-AND-ANCHOVY SPREAD

This is delicious as a spread on fresh baguette slices, as a dip with smoked salmon, or as a dressing on a veggie sandwich. Look for anchovy paste near the jarred pestos and tomato products in your grocery.

¼ cup (1 ounce) goat cheese, softened
2 tablespoons minced red onion
1 tablespoon fat-free sour cream
2 teaspoons anchovy paste
⅛ teaspoon pepper
1 (8-ounce) block fat-free cream cheese, softened

1. Place all ingredients in a food processor; process until smooth, scraping sides of bowl if necessary. YIELD: 12 servings (serving size: 2 tablespoons).

POINTS: 1; EXCHANGE: Free up to ¼ cup;
PER SERVING: CAL 26 (27% from fat); PRO 3.3g;
FAT 0.8g (sat 0.5g); CARB 1.5g; FIB 0g;
CHOL 2.7mg; IRON 0.1mg; SOD 113mg;
CALC 41mg

CARAMELIZED ONION-AND-WHITE BEAN SPREAD

Great as a topping on bagel or pita chips, this spread also makes a tasty substitute for traditional tomato sauce on your favorite homemade pizza.

Cooking spray
2 teaspoons olive oil
1½ cups chopped onion
½ teaspoon dried thyme
1 (19-ounce) can cannellini beans, rinsed and drained
¼ cup chicken or vegetable broth
1 tablespoon lemon juice
½ teaspoon bottled minced roasted garlic
¼ teaspoon salt
¼ teaspoon Worcestershire sauce
⅛ teaspoon freshly ground black pepper
Chopped fresh chives (optional)

1. Heat oil in a nonstick skillet coated with cooking spray over medium heat. Add onion and thyme; cook 10 minutes or until golden brown, stirring frequently.
2. Combine beans and next 6 ingredients in a food processor; add onion mixture, and pulse until coarsely pureed. Garnish with chives, if desired. YIELD: 16 servings (serving size: 2 tablespoons).

POINTS: 0; EXCHANGE: Free up to 2 tablespoons;
PER SERVING: CAL 38 (18% from fat); PRO 1.5g;
FAT 0.8g (sat 0.1g); CARB 6.1g; FIB 1.6g;
CHOL 0mg; IRON 0.5mg; SOD 123mg;
CALC 14mg

CAPONATA

(pictured on page 23)

In Italy, caponata is traditionally served as a salad, side dish, or relish. We suggest spooning it onto crostini—little toasts—and serving it as an appetizer.

2 teaspoons salt
1 (1-pound) eggplant, cut into
½-inch cubes
1 (14.5-ounce) can diced
tomatoes, undrained
2 tablespoons red wine vinegar
1 tablespoon capers, drained
2 teaspoons sugar
¾ teaspoon dried basil
¼ teaspoon salt
⅛ teaspoon pepper
1 tablespoon olive oil, divided
1 cup chopped onion
½ cup chopped celery
1 garlic clove, minced

1. Sprinkle salt over eggplant; stir well. Place eggplant in colander, and let stand 1 hour. Rinse well; drain.
2. Combine tomato and next 6 ingredients in a medium bowl; stir well, and set aside.
3. Heat 1½ teaspoons oil in a large nonstick skillet over medium–high heat. Add eggplant, and cook, stirring occasionally, 13 minutes or until tender. Transfer to a plate.
4. Add 1½ teaspoons oil to pan, and place over medium heat. Add onion and celery; cook, stirring occasionally, 4 minutes or until lightly browned. Add garlic; cook 1 minute. Add cooked eggplant and tomato mixture to pan; stir well. Cook 3 minutes or until thoroughly

heated. Serve at room temperature.
YIELD: 16 servings (serving size: ¼ cup).

POINTS: 0; **EXCHANGE:** 1 Vegetable; **PER SERVING:** CAL 26 (30% from fat); PRO 0.6g; FAT 0.9g (sat 0.1g); CARB 4.3g; FIB 1.3g; CHOL 0mg; IRON 0.2mg; SOD 309mg; CALC 9mg

PESTO CROSTINI WITH ROASTED PEPPER AND GOAT CHEESE

Using roasted red peppers in a jar makes these crostini quick and easy to prepare.

12 (½-inch-thick) slices diagonally cut French bread baguette
2 tablespoons commercial pesto, divided
1 cup bottled roasted red bell pepper, drained and thinly sliced
¼ cup (1 ounce) crumbled goat cheese

1. Preheat oven to 400°.
2. Place bread on an ungreased baking sheet; bake at 400° for 7 minutes, turning once.
3. Preheat broiler.
4. Spread each slice with ½ teaspoon pesto. Top evenly with roasted pepper and goat cheese. Broil 3 minutes or until lightly browned. YIELD: 12 servings (serving size: 1 crostino).

POINTS: 2; **EXCHANGES:** ½ Starch, 1 Fat; **PER SERVING:** CAL 68 (46% from fat); PRO 2.6g; FAT 3.5g (sat 1.2g); CARB 6.7g; FIB 0.6g; CHOL 3.5mg; IRON 0.6mg; SOD 161mg; CALC 53mg

BABA GHANOUSH WITH PITA CHIPS

Baba Ghanoush (bah-bah-gah-NOOSH) is a Middle Eastern dip typically made from eggplant, tahini, olive oil, and lemon juice. Look for tahini in the peanut butter or ethnic section of your grocery.

3 (6-inch) pitas, cut into 8 wedges
1 eggplant, cut in half lengthwise
(about 1 pound)
2 tablespoons tahini (sesame seed paste)
2 tablespoons lemon juice
1 tablespoon olive oil
¾ teaspoon salt
¼ teaspoon pepper

1. Preheat oven to 400°.
2. Place pita wedges in a single layer on a baking sheet. Bake at 400° for 9 minutes or until crisp and browned.
3. Pierce skin side of eggplant several times with a fork. Place cut side down on a baking sheet covered with aluminum foil. Bake at 400° for 25 minutes or until eggplant is tender when pierced with a fork. Remove eggplant from baking sheet, and cool.
4. Scoop out pulp with a spoon, and place pulp in a food processor. Add tahini and remaining ingredients; process until smooth, scraping down sides of bowl once. YIELD: 6 servings (serving size: ¼ cup dip and 4 pita wedges).

POINTS: 3; **EXCHANGES:** 1 Starch, 1 Vegetable, 1 Fat; **PER SERVING:** CAL 145 (32% from fat); PRO 4.1g; FAT 5.3g (sat 0.7g); CARB 21g; FIB 2.1g; CHOL 0mg; IRON 1.2mg; SOD 455mg; CALC 37mg

SWEDISH MEATBALLS

Serve extra meatballs on a bed of egg noodles for a quick dinner.

Cooking spray
1¼ pounds ground turkey
 ¾ cup soft rye breadcrumbs
    (about 2 [1-ounce] slices)
 ⅓ cup 1% low-fat milk
 2 tablespoons chopped fresh
    parsley
 2 tablespoons chopped green
    onions
 ½ teaspoon ground allspice
 ¼ teaspoon salt
 ¼ teaspoon freshly ground black
    pepper
 1 (14¼-ounce) can fat-free, less-
    sodium chicken broth, divided
 3 tablespoons all-purpose flour
 1 teaspoon lemon juice
 1 teaspoon dried dill
 ¼ teaspoon salt
 ¼ teaspoon freshly ground black
    pepper
 ½ cup reduced-fat sour cream

1. Preheat oven to 400°.
2. Line a baking sheet with foil, and coat the foil with cooking spray.
3. Combine turkey and next 7 ingredients in a large bowl. Shape into 36 (1-inch) meatballs, and place on a baking sheet. Bake at 400° for 15 to 17 minutes or until centers are no longer pink. Set aside, and keep warm.
4. Combine ½ cup chicken broth and 3 tablespoons flour; stir with a whisk until smooth.
5. Pour remaining broth into a large saucepan; bring to a boil. Slowly add flour mixture to broth, stirring constantly. Cook over medium heat until mixture thickens and returns

to a boil, stirring constantly. Add lemon juice and next 3 ingredients, stirring well.
6. Remove from heat, and stir in sour cream. Add meatballs, and stir gently. Cook over low heat until thoroughly heated. YIELD: 12 servings (serving size: 3 meatballs).

POINTS: 3; **EXCHANGES:** ½ Starch, 1 Lean Meat; **PER SERVING:** CAL 125 (36% from fat); PRO 10.9g; FAT 5g (sat 1.8g); CARB 8.2g; FIB 0.5g; CHOL 41mg; IRON 1mg; SOD 443mg; CALC 39mg

---

PARTY SHRIMP

(pictured on page 23)

To save time, purchase fresh steamed and peeled shrimp from your grocery.

 ⅓ cup finely chopped fresh parsley
 3 tablespoons finely chopped
    green onions
 3 tablespoons minced red onion
 2 tablespoons lemon juice
 1 tablespoon extra-virgin olive oil
 ¼ teaspoon salt
 ⅛ teaspoon ground red pepper
 1 pound large shrimp, cooked and
    peeled

1. Combine first 7 ingredients; add shrimp, tossing well. Cover and chill at least 3 hours. YIELD: 12 servings (serving size: approximately 3 shrimp).

POINTS: 1; **EXCHANGE:** ½ Very Lean Meat; **PER SERVING:** CAL 37 (36% from fat); PRO 5.1g; FAT 1.4g (sat 0.2g); CARB 0.6g; FIB 0.1g; CHOL 47mg; IRON 0.8mg; SOD 103mg; CALC 10mg

---

CHICKEN BITES WITH CREAMY PARMESAN DIP

This dip can also be used as a dressing for fresh greens.

 4 (4-ounce) skinless, boneless
    chicken breast halves
 ⅓ cup low-fat buttermilk
 ⅓ cup light mayonnaise
 ¼ cup (1 ounce) grated fresh
    Parmesan cheese
 ⅓ cup reduced-fat sour cream
 ½ cup low-fat buttermilk
 ¼ teaspoon salt
 ⅛ teaspoon pepper
 1 garlic clove, minced
 ½ cup Italian-seasoned
    breadcrumbs
Cooking spray

1. Cut each chicken breast half into 8 pieces. Combine chicken pieces and ⅓ cup buttermilk in a heavy-duty zip-top plastic bag; seal bag, and marinate in refrigerator 30 minutes.
2. Preheat oven to 425°.
3. To prepare dip, combine mayonnaise and next 6 ingredients in a small bowl.
4. Remove chicken from bag; discard marinade. Insert a wooden pick into each chicken piece. Dredge chicken in breadcrumbs. Place on a baking sheet coated with cooking spray. Coat breaded chicken with cooking spray. Bake at 425° for 10 minutes. Serve warm with dip. YIELD: 16 servings (serving size: 2 pieces chicken and 2 tablespoons dip).

POINTS: 2; **EXCHANGES:** ½ Starch, 1 Lean Meat; **PER SERVING:** CAL 80 (35% from fat); PRO 8.3g; FAT 3g (sat 1.1g); CARB 4.5g; FIB 0.2g; CHOL 21.5mg; IRON 0.4mg; SOD 242mg; CALC 50mg

MUSHROOM TARTLETS

2 (8-ounce) packages presliced
    mushrooms
Olive oil-flavored cooking spray
2 garlic cloves, minced
1 large shallot, chopped
⅓ cup (1⅓ ounces) shredded
    smoked Gouda cheese
2 teaspoons chopped fresh thyme
1 tablespoon lemon juice
½ teaspoon salt
¼ teaspoon pepper
2 (2.1-ounce) packages frozen
    miniature phyllo shells
Fresh thyme sprigs (optional)

1. Preheat oven to 350°.
2. Place mushrooms in a food
processor; pulse until minced.
3. Coat a large nonstick skillet with
cooking spray; place over medium
heat until hot. Add garlic and
shallot; sauté 3 minutes. Add mushrooms; cook, stirring frequently, 8 to
10 minutes or until mushrooms are
tender. Remove from heat; stir in
cheese and next 4 ingredients.
4. Fill each phyllo shell with
1 heaping teaspoon of mushroom
mixture. Place on a baking sheet;
coat with cooking spray. Bake at
350° for 10 to 12 minutes or until
phyllo shells are golden. Garnish
with thyme sprigs, if desired. YIELD:
30 servings (serving size: 1 tartlet).

POINTS: 0; EXCHANGE: ½ Vegetable;
PER SERVING: CAL 22 (27% from fat); PRO 1.1g;
FAT 0.7g (sat 0.3g); CARB 3.1g; FIB 0.3g;
CHOL 1.6mg; IRON 0.3mg; SOD 70mg;
CALC 13mg

CURRIED POPCORN

*For an even speedier variation,
combine the first 4 spices and add
to a bag of popped low-fat
microwave popcorn.*

2 teaspoons curry powder
1 teaspoon salt
1 teaspoon ground cumin
⅛ teaspoon ground red pepper
1 tablespoon canola oil
½ cup unpopped corn kernels

1. Combine first 4 ingredients in a
heavy-duty zip-top plastic bag, shaking well. Set aside.
2. Heat oil in a large Dutch oven
over medium-high heat. Add popcorn, stirring to coat. Reduce heat
to medium; cover and cook, shaking
constantly, until popping sound
stops.
3. Add popcorn to spice mixture,
and shake thoroughly. YIELD: 6 servings (serving size: 1½ cups).

POINTS: 1, EXCHANGES: 1 Starch, ½ Fat;
PER SERVING: CAL 84 (33% from fat); PRO 2.2g;
FAT 3.3g (sat 0.2g); CARB 12.6g; FIB 2.4g;
CHOL 0mg; IRON 0.7mg; SOD 389mg; CALC 6mg

A STICKY SITUATION

🍴

Spray the measuring cup with
cooking spray before measuring peanut butter. Getting the
peanut butter out of the cup will
be a much less sticky process.

OATMEAL ENERGY BARS

(pictured on page 22)
*Here's a quick, economical alternative
to the popular power and energy
bars. Low in fat but packed full of
carbohydrates, these bars are sure to
get you through your workout.*

¼ cup chilled butter or stick mar-
    garine, cut into small pieces
⅔ cup packed brown sugar
3 cups regular oats
1 cup raisins
½ cup dried cranberries
½ cup chopped dried apricots
1 teaspoon ground cinnamon
¼ teaspoon ground nutmeg
2 large egg whites, lightly beaten
½ cup chunky peanut butter
½ cup fat-free sweetened
    condensed milk
Cooking spray

1. Preheat oven to 350°.
2. Cut butter into brown sugar with
a pastry blender until crumbly. Stir
in oats and next 5 ingredients.
3. Combine egg whites, peanut butter, and condensed milk in a small
bowl; stir with a whisk until
smooth. Add egg mixture to oats,
and stir well.
4. Press mixture into a jelly-roll pan
coated with cooking spray. Bake
at 350° for 20 minutes; cool completely. Cut into 28 bars. YIELD:
28 servings (serving size: 1 bar).
NOTE: Bars can be stored in pan or
on a plate, covered.

POINTS: 3; EXCHANGES: 1½ Starch, ½ Fat;
PER SERVING: CAL 130 (25% from fat); PRO 3.4g;
FAT 3.9g (sat 1.1g); CARB 22.4g; FIB 1.9g;
CHOL 3.2mg; IRON 0.9mg; SOD 46mg;
CALC 30mg

WINE COOLERS

1 cup mixed juice blend (such as Ocean Spray's cranberry and Georgia peach fruit juice blend)
¾ cup dry white wine
¾ cup sugar-free, grapefruit-flavored soda (such as Fresca)
2 lime wedges

1. Combine juice, wine, and soda; stir well, and chill. To serve, pour over crushed ice. Squeeze lime wedge into each drink, and add wedges to glasses, if desired. YIELD: 2 servings (serving size: 1¼ cups).

POINTS: 3; **EXCHANGES:** ½ Starch, 1 Fruit; **PER SERVING:** CAL 140 (0% from fat); PRO 0.3g; FAT 0g (sat 0g); CARB 20.6g; FIB 0.1g; CHOL 0mg; IRON 0.5mg; SOD 7mg; CALC 19mg

LEMONY GINGERALE PUNCH

Perfect for a summer party, this beverage received top ratings in our test kitchens.

2 cups water
1 cup sugar
¼ cup grated peeled fresh ginger
1 cup lemon juice
1 (33.8-ounce) bottle club soda, chilled

1. Combine first 3 ingredients in a small saucepan; bring to a boil, stirring until sugar dissolves.
2. Cool completely; strain and discard ginger. Stir in lemon juice and club soda. Pour over ice. YIELD: 8 servings (serving size: 1 cup).

POINTS: 2; **EXCHANGES:** 2 Starch; **PER SERVING:** CAL 106 (0% from fat); PRO 0.2g; FAT 0g (sat 0g); CARB 28.1g; FIB 0.2g; CHOL 0mg; IRON 0.1mg; SOD 27mg; CALC 9mg

---

SMOOTHIE SMARTS

Quick, refreshing, and packed with nutrients, smoothies are a popular snack and meal substitute. Catering to this food trend, smoothie stores are popping up everywhere. However, store-bought smoothies can have lots of added products that could sabotage your weight loss and also your health. Here are some tips to help you pick a healthy smoothie:

• Look for smoothies made primarily with fruit and some low-fat yogurt or milk; avoid ones made with ice cream.

• Select a smoothie between 300 to 350 calories and under 5 grams of fat; ask for the nutrition facts if they are not posted.

• Say no to extras, such as added protein powders, herbs, vitamins, and so-called "fat-burners." None is proven to be safe or effective.

• Don't supersize your smoothie. Select a smaller smoothie to save extra calories.

PEACH FIZZ

(pictured on page 24)

1½ cups peach nectar
2 cups lime sparkling water
2 tablespoons sugar
1 tablespoon plus 1 teaspoon grenadine
4 peach slices
4 lime slices
4 fresh mint sprigs

1. Combine peach nectar and sparkling water in a 9-inch square baking pan. Freeze mixture 1 hour, scraping with a fork every 15 minutes to make a slushy mixture.
2. Wet top of each glass, and swirl in sugar. Add 1 teaspoon grenadine to each glass, and top with ¾ cup peach nectar mixture. Garnish each with a skewer of peach, lime, and mint. Serve immediately. YIELD: 4 servings (serving size: ¾ cup).

POINTS: 2; **EXCHANGES:** 2 Starch; **PER SERVING:** CAL 98 (0% from fat); PRO 0.4g; FAT 0g (sat 0g); CARB 25.6g; FIB 0.8g; CHOL 0mg; IRON 0.2mg; SOD 10mg; CALC 6mg

MANGO SMOOTHIE

(pictured on page 25)

1 banana, sliced
⅔ cup diced peeled mango (about 1 small)
⅔ cup strawberry low-fat yogurt
½ cup orange juice

1. Arrange sliced banana in a single layer on a baking sheet; freeze until firm (about 1 hour).
2. Combine banana and remaining ingredients in a blender; process until smooth. Serve immediately. YIELD: 2 servings (serving size: 1 cup).

POINTS: 3; **EXCHANGES:** 2 Fruit, 1 Skim Milk; **PER SERVING:** CAL 191 (6% from fat); PRO 4.5g; FAT 1.2g (sat 0.6g); CARB 42.8g; FIB 2.5g; CHOL 7.7mg; IRON 0.4mg; SOD 46mg; CALC 121mg

STRAWBERRY-BANANA SOY SMOOTHIE

(pictured on page 25)

Soy products are excellent sources of isoflavones, which are thought to prevent breast cancer and heart disease. Make sure to select a soy milk that is fortified with calcium.

2 cups fresh strawberries, stemmed and halved (about 10 strawberries)
1½ cups low-fat vanilla soy milk
1½ tablespoons honey
½ teaspoon vanilla extract
1 banana, sliced
1 cup frozen fat-free whipped topping, thawed
2 fresh mint sprigs (optional)

1. Combine first 5 ingredients in a blender, and process until smooth. Top each serving with ½ cup whipped topping; garnish with mint sprig, if desired. Serve immediately. **YIELD:** 2 servings (serving size: 2 cups).

POINTS: 3; **EXCHANGES:** 1 Starch, 1 Fruit, ½ Milk; **PER SERVING:** CAL 147 (7% from fat); PRO 2.3g; FAT 1.2g (sat 0.1g), CARB 32.4g, FIB 2.5g, CHOL 0mg; IRON 0.4mg; SOD 47mg; CALC 43mg

STRAWBERRY MILKSHAKE

3 cups vanilla low-fat ice cream or frozen yogurt
1 cup quartered fresh or frozen strawberries
½ cup 1% low-fat milk

1. Combine all ingredients in a blender; process until smooth. Serve immediately. **YIELD:** 4 servings (serving size: ¾ cup).

POINTS: 4; **EXCHANGES:** 1 Starch, 1 Fruit, 1 Milk; **PER SERVING:** CAL 197 (16% from fat); PRO 5.7g; FAT 3.4g (sat 1.7g); CARB 35g; FIB 2.7g; CHOL 8.7mg; IRON 0.4mg; SOD 84mg; CALC 196mg

FUDGY PEANUT BUTTER SHAKE

Warning: This rich shake is for true chocolate-lovers only! If chocolate fudge ice cream isn't at your grocery, substitute any fat-free chocolate ice cream or yogurt.

1 cup fat-free, no-sugar-added chocolate fudge ice cream (such as Edy's)
¾ cup low-fat chocolate milk
1 tablespoon reduced-fat peanut butter

1. Place ingredients in a blender; process until smooth. Serve immediately. **YIELD:** 2 servings (serving size: 1 cup).

POINTS: 4; **EXCHANGES:** 1½ Starch, 1 Skim Milk, ½ Fat; **PER SERVING:** CAL 200 (16% from fat); PRO 9.3g; FAT 3.6g (sat 1.1g); CARB 34.4g; FIB 2g; CHOL 2.7mg; IRON 0.7mg; SOD 161mg; CALC 191mg

MOCHA COCOA

1 cup 1% low-fat milk
1 tablespoon unsweetened cocoa
1 tablespoon sugar
½ teaspoon instant espresso or 1 teaspoon instant coffee granules

1. Pour milk into a microwave-safe container, and microwave at HIGH 1 to 2 minutes or until milk is hot, but not boiling.
2. Place cocoa, sugar, and coffee granules in a blender. Add milk, and process until blended. Pour into mug, and serve immediately. **YIELD:** 1 serving (serving size: 1 cup).

POINTS: 3; **EXCHANGES:** 1 Starch, 1 Skim Milk; **PER SERVING:** CAL 165 (17% from fat); PRO 9.2g; FAT 3.3g (sat 2.1g); CARB 27.4g; FIB 1.8g; CHOL 9.8mg; IRON 0.9mg; SOD 125mg; CALC 308

CAFFEINE BASICS

Worried about the effects caffeine in your morning coffee has? Caffeine is a mild stimulant to the body, but caffeinated beverages are considered safe for most people. In extreme amounts, caffeine can cause heart palpitations, high blood pressure, and constipation. However, if you drink caffeinated beverages on a regular basis, 2 to 3 servings per day are not likely to cause these side effects. Because caffeine does act as a diuretic, try to drink an additional glass of water for every caffeinated drink you consume.

Breads

HERB-AND-GARLIC BREADSTICKS

Thinly slicing the bread loaf gives these breadsticks their extra crunch.

1 (8-ounce) loaf sourdough bread
2 tablespoons extra-virgin olive oil
1½ teaspoons dried Italian seasoning
¼ teaspoon garlic powder

1. Preheat broiler.
2. Slice bread in half lengthwise. Slice each half into 8 long sticks.
3. Combine olive oil, Italian seasoning, and garlic powder in a small bowl. Brush breadsticks evenly with oil mixture; place on a baking sheet.
4. Broil 1 to 2 minutes or until lightly browned. Serve immediately. YIELD: 8 servings (serving size: 2 breadsticks).

POINTS: 2; EXCHANGES: 1 Starch, 1 Fat; PER SERVING: CAL 110 (36% from fat); PRO 2.5g; FAT 4.4g (sat 0.7g); CARB 15g; FIB 1g; CHOL 0mg; IRON 0.9mg; SOD 173mg; CALC 26mg

ROSEMARY-GARLIC BREADSTICKS

1 tablespoon extra-virgin olive oil
3 garlic cloves, minced
1 tablespoon minced fresh rosemary
½ teaspoon salt
1 (11-ounce) can soft breadstick dough

1. Preheat oven to 350°.
2. Heat oil in a small skillet over medium heat. Add garlic, and cook, stirring often, 1 to 2 minutes. Remove from heat, and stir in rosemary and salt.
3. Unroll dough, but do not separate into strips. Use a pastry brush to spread garlic mixture evenly across surface of dough. Working with each one at a time, tear breadsticks along the perforations, and twist each strip. Stretch slightly, and place on a baking sheet. Bake at 350° for 13 to 15 minutes or until golden. YIELD: 10 servings (serving size: 1 breadstick).

POINTS: 2; EXCHANGES: 1 Starch, ½ Fat; PER SERVING: CAL 102 (27% from fat); PRO 2.5g; FAT 3g (sat 0.2g); CARB 15.5g; FIB 0.4g; CHOL 0mg; IRON 0.9mg; SOD 326mg; CALC 2mg

MEDITERRANEAN PINWHEELS

½ cup boiling water
1 ounce sun-dried tomatoes (about 12)
16 pitted chopped kalamata olives
½ cup chopped fresh parsley
2 teaspoons dried basil
2 teaspoons dried oregano
1 garlic clove, minced
1 (10-ounce) can refrigerated pizza dough

1. Preheat oven to 425°.
2. Combine boiling water and tomatoes in a bowl; let stand 10 minutes or until soft. Drain and chop.
3. Stir together olives and next 4 ingredients. Add reserved tomato.
4. Roll dough into a 12 x 8-inch rectangle; spread evenly with olive mixture. Roll up dough, starting at long side and pressing firmly to eliminate air pockets; pinch seam to seal. Place on an ungreased baking sheet. Bake at 425° for 15 minutes or until lightly browned. Let stand 5 minutes. Cut into diagonal slices, using a serrated knife. Serve immediately. YIELD: 16 servings (serving size: 1 slice).

POINTS: 1; EXCHANGE: 1 Starch; PER SERVING: CAL 64 (24% from fat); PRO 2g; FAT 1.7g (sat 0.1g); CARB 10.1g; FIB 0.7g; CHOL 0mg; IRON 0.9mg; SOD 218mg; CALC 12mg

HERBED TOMATO FOCACCIA

(pictured on page 27)

Cooking spray
1 (11-ounce) can refrigerated French bread dough
2 teaspoons olive oil
2 garlic cloves, minced
1 teaspoon dried Italian seasoning
¼ teaspoon salt
¼ teaspoon pepper
2 plum tomatoes, very thinly sliced
⅓ cup (1⅓ ounces) grated fresh Parmesan cheese

1. Preheat oven to 375°.
2. Unroll dough onto a baking sheet coated with cooking spray. (Do not stretch dough.) Spread oil and garlic evenly over dough, using fingers.
3. Sprinkle dough with Italian seasoning, salt, and pepper. Top with a single layer of tomato slices.
4. Bake at 375° for 13 minutes; sprinkle with cheese. Bake 1 to 2 minutes or until cheese melts. Cut into 9 pieces. Serve immediately with soup or salad. YIELD: 9 servings (serving size: 1 piece).

POINTS: 2; EXCHANGES: 1 Starch, ½ Fat; PER SERVING: CAL 114 (26% from fat); PRO 4.5g; FAT 3.3g (sat 1.4g); CARB 16.1g; FIB 0.8g; CHOL 3mg; IRON 1mg; SOD 352mg; CALC 55mg

CHEDDAR-HERB ROLLS

½ (25-ounce) package homestyle
   roll dough (such as Rich's)
1 teaspoon dried thyme
1 teaspoon dried basil
1 teaspoon dried oregano
½ cup (2 ounces) reduced-fat
   shredded sharp Cheddar cheese
Cooking spray
1 large egg white
1 tablespoon water
1 tablespoon instant minced onion

1. Thaw dough according to package directions.
2. Combine thyme, basil, and
oregano.
3. Divide dough into 12 equal portions. Working with one portion at a
time (cover remaining portions to
keep dough from drying out), sprinkle ¼ teaspoon herb mixture and
2 teaspoons cheese over dough.
Knead dough to incorporate herbs
and cheese. Shape dough into a ball.
Place in a muffin cup or on a baking
sheet coated with cooking spray.
Repeat procedure with remaining
portions of dough, herbs, and
cheese. Let rise according to package
directions.
4. Preheat oven to 350°.
5. Combine egg white and water in
a bowl; stir well with a whisk. Brush
rolls with egg white mixture; sprinkle
evenly with minced onion. Bake at
350° for 13 minutes or until golden.
YIELD: 12 servings (serving size: 1 roll).
NOTE: To make cloverleaf rolls, after
incorporating herbs, divide each
portion of dough into 3 equal
pieces; roll each piece into a ball.

Place 3 balls in a muffin cup coated
with cooking spray. Repeat with
remaining portions of dough. Let
rise, and bake as directed.

POINTS: 2; **EXCHANGES:** 1 Starch, ½ Fat;
PER SERVING: CAL 100 (21% from fat);
PRO 4.6g; FAT 2.4g (sat 0.7g); CARB 15.7g;
FIB 1.1g; CHOL 3mg; IRON 1.3mg; SOD 210mg;
CALC 47mg

BANANA-BUTTERMILK
PANCAKES

(pictured on page 27)
These low-fat hotcakes are perfect for
a leisurely weekend breakfast.

1 cup all-purpose flour
1 tablespoon sugar
½ teaspoon baking soda
¼ teaspoon ground cinnamon
⅛ teaspoon salt
1 large egg
1 cup low-fat buttermilk
1 tablespoon butter or stick
   margarine, melted
⅔ cup mashed very ripe banana
   (about 1)
Cooking spray
½ cup maple syrup

1. Lightly spoon flour into a dry
measuring cup; level with a knife.
Combine flour and next 4 ingredients in a bowl. Combine egg,
buttermilk, and butter; add to dry
ingredients, stirring until smooth.
Stir in banana.
2. Spoon ¼ cup batter for each
pancake onto a hot griddle or skillet
coated with cooking spray. Turn
pancakes when tops are bubbly and

edges look cooked. Serve with
syrup. YIELD: 4 servings (serving size:
2 pancakes and 2 tablespoons syrup).

POINTS: 3; **EXCHANGES:** 2 Starch;
PER SERVING: CAL 169 (14% from fat); PRO 3.7g;
FAT 2.7g (sat 1.3g); CARB 33.1g; FIB 0.9g;
CHOL 32mg; IRON 1.1mg; SOD 172mg;
CALC 55mg

CARBOHYDRATE
CONCERNS

Counting carbohydrate grams
is a popular diet trend. People
have found that by limiting carbohydrates, they lose weight.
However, this drop on the
scale isn't from fat loss; it's
from loss of muscle and water.
Your body depends on carbohydrates as fuel to function
daily and, when deprived, will
break down lean tissue in
order to survive.

If you're eating a balanced
diet, there should be no need
to strictly monitor your carbohydrate intake, unless you have
diabetes. This means making
sure that 55% to 60% of your
total calorie intake is from a
wide variety of different carbohydrates (including breads,
fruits, and vegetables). Watch
for fat-free foods that may have
added carbohydrates. Too
many carbohydrates, just like
too much protein and fat, will
pack on the pounds and hinder
weight loss.

Step by Step

SANDRA O'REILLY • **HEIGHT** 5'2" • **BEFORE** 243 LBS. • **AFTER** 133 LBS.

Proudest Moment: "At my husband's office party, people kept asking him if he had remarried. He said, 'No, that's Sandy.' People said, 'Wow!' "

Sandra O'Reilly commutes to her office by train. At the station, she faces an immense flight of steps. For years she took the escalator. "I couldn't make it up those stairs," Sandra says of her former size-24, 243-pound self. After a lifetime of dieting and weight fluctuation, those stairs started to haunt her.

"I didn't feel good. I felt tired. My clothes were tight. My doctor recommended that I lose weight more times than I care to admit. I still couldn't make it up those stairs," she says.

So Sandra joined a Weight Watchers At Work program in January 1996, where she found moral support. "If you say, 'I'm hungry,' people there support you. Someone would say, 'You can do it.' During lunch nobody was eating the things you wanted and couldn't have," she says. The first week, Sandra lost 7 pounds.

Sandra continued to lose by changing her eating habits. She avoided junk food; added steamed vegetables, yogurt, and fruit; and drank eight glasses of water a day. She snacked on carrots and pretzels because they were easy to bring to the office.

Unlike the Weight Watchers she knew as a teenager, the **POINTS** plan was flexible, allowing Sandra to eat on the run (she often works 12-hour days, which she has plenty of stamina for now) or to indulge in a treat occasionally. "The plan allows a little of this and a little of that, so I can save room for six Hershey's Kisses every night as a reward," she says.

Sandra reached her goal weight of 141 pounds in August 1997, but kept losing until she got to 123 pounds. To maintain a healthy weight, Sandra still watches what she eats. For a flight to Florida, she took carrots for snacks. The vigilance was worth it, she says—she could wear a two-piece swimsuit.

When Sandra, now 46, began to lose weight, she started walking 30 minutes at lunch. She didn't love exercise at first, but she did like getting away from her desk. As she exercised more, it became easier. She liked feeling energetic and tried to find other ways to fit exercise into her day. She rode an

"The plan allows a little of this and a little of that, so I can save room for six Hershey's Kisses every night...."

exercise bike; then she began running three times a week, playing tennis, and exercising to tone her abdominal muscles. Now she can walk that flight of steps at the train station.

In the spring of 2001, Sandra acknowledged that she had gained 10 pounds since her lowest weight of 123. "At first I panicked," she says, "but really I feel healthier now." She believes in exercise, and walks every morning. "I enjoy being healthy and fit," she says. "Most of all, I love being able to wear fashionable clothing."

Oatmeal Energy Bars,
page 15

Caponata,
page 13

Party Shrimp,
page 14

Peach Fizz,
page 16

Strawberry-
Banana Soy
Smoothie, page 17

Mango Smoothie,
page 16

Buttermilk
Cornbread,
page 32

Cranberry-
Orange Scones,
page 31

Anadama
Raisin Bread,
page 34

Herbed Tomato Focaccia,
page 19

Banana-Buttermilk
Pancakes, page 20

27

Fighting Back

DAN BRAVERMAN • **HEIGHT** 5'10" • **BEFORE** 225 LBS. • **AFTER** 170 LBS.

Lesson Learned: "Losing weight was a psychological battle with myself. In the beginning, there didn't seem to be any help for me. Then I realized that all I had to do was help myself."

At 30, Dan Braverman was supposed to be at the top of his game. But he was unhappy. Things he once loved—taking long walks and ice skating in the park—weren't fun anymore. "I felt out of breath and exhausted," Dan says. "I felt older than my 30 years."

Dan had gained weight during his twenties, snacking at the office and enjoying his wife Kimberly's home cooking. "I ate everything in sight, and lots of it," he says. He was an emotional eater, turning to food when he was stressed or in a bad mood. "Finally, it dawned on me that my habits were all wrong," Dan says.

Kimberly signed him up for Weight Watchers, but he thought his situation was hopeless. "I was skeptical of the gimmicks out there," Dan says. But he saw turning 30 as a pivotal point in his life and wanted to take control. "Weight Watchers offered a systematic way for me to lose weight and gave me the opportunity to overhaul my attitude," he says.

Attending weekly meetings inspired Dan. He resolved to run on the treadmill at the gym every morning before work. "I used to work out once in a blue moon, but it exhausted me. This time, it was different," Dan says. He knew that physical activity would be key to losing weight, and he wanted to follow through on the commitment he'd made.

Soon workouts were a part of Dan's morning routine. "It's not fun to get up at 5:45, but I'd feel great when I finished," he says. "The more I did it, the more fun it was and the better I felt."

Dan reached his goal weight of 170 pounds within a few months. "I have more energy than ever," he says. His performance at work even improved. "I am confident now because I accomplished something I put my mind to," Dan says. His success inspired several associates, who followed his example and lost some pounds, too.

"The more I (exercised), the more fun it was and the better I felt."

Dan still enjoys Kimberly's cooking, which she bases on the POINTS plan. "Everything is better when you flavor foods with spices instead of butter," he says. "You actually taste the food." Kimberly learned along with Dan to eat smaller portions and to substitute low-fat condiments for high-fat ones. So instead of dressing a sandwich with mayonnaise, for example, they use mustard.

Maintaining his weight isn't always easy, and Dan admits he sometimes gains a few pounds. But he's conscientious about getting them off. And he stays in touch with his Weight Watchers group, checking in every six to eight weeks. Now, Dan can't imagine going back to his old habits. "I feel fantastic," he says. "I feel as if I have the energy to do anything."

Weight-loss results not typical.

HOT POPOVERS

Apricot Butter
   4 large egg whites
   1 cup fat-free milk
   1 cup all-purpose flour
   2 teaspoons sugar
   ¼ teaspoon salt
Butter-flavored cooking spray

1. Prepare Apricot Butter; set aside.
2. Preheat oven to 450°.
3. Combine egg whites and milk, stirring with a whisk until foamy. Lightly spoon flour into a dry measuring cup; level with a knife. Combine flour, sugar, and salt, stirring well with a whisk.
4. Coat a 12-cup muffin pan with cooking spray, and place in a 450° oven for 3 minutes.
5. Gradually stir flour mixture into egg mixture, stirring with a whisk just until blended. Remove muffin pan from oven. Divide batter evenly among hot cups.
6. Bake at 450° for 15 minutes. Reduce heat to 350°. (Do not remove popover cups from oven.) Bake an additional 20 minutes or until golden.
7. Serve popovers immediately with Apricot Butter, if desired. YIELD: 12 servings (serving size: 1 popover and 1 tablespoon Apricot Butter).

POINTS: 1; EXCHANGES: 1½ Starch;
PER SERVING: CAL 100 (14% from fat); PRO 3.3g;
FAT 1.6g (sat 1g); CARB 18.5g; FIB 0.3g; CHOL 5mg;
IRON 0.5mg; SOD 102mg; CALC 27mg

APRICOT BUTTER
   ½ cup apricot preserves
   3 tablespoons light butter, melted

1. Combine preserves and butter, stirring well. YIELD: ¾ cup (serving size: 1 tablespoon).

POINTS: 1; EXCHANGE: ½ Starch;
PER TABLESPOON: CAL 46 (27% from fat);
PRO 0.3g; FAT 1.5g (sat 1g); CARB 8.7g; FIB 0g;
CHOL 5mg; IRON 0mg; SOD 24mg; CALC 0mg

APPLE-GINGER MUFFINS

Don't let knobby fresh ginger scare you. Once peeled, fresh ginger grates easily and offers a spicy kick to these sweet muffins.

1¼ cups quick-cooking oats
   1 cup 1% low-fat milk
   ½ cup packed brown sugar
   3 tablespoons vegetable oil
   3 tablespoons honey
   1 teaspoon grated peeled fresh
     ginger
   1 large egg
   1 cup all-purpose flour
   ¼ cup whole wheat flour
1½ teaspoons baking powder
   ½ teaspoons baking soda
   ½ teaspoon salt
   1 cup diced peeled apple
Cooking spray
   2 teaspoons quick-cooking oats

1. Preheat oven to 400°.
2. Combine first 7 ingredients in a large bowl; stir with a whisk. Let stand 15 minutes.
3. Lightly spoon flours into dry measuring cups; level with a knife. Combine flours and next 3 ingredients in a large bowl; make a well in center of mixture. Add oat mixture to dry ingredients, stirring just until moist. Gently fold in apple.
4. Spoon batter into 12 muffin cups coated with cooking spray. Sprinkle 2 teaspoons oats over top of batter.
5. Bake at 400° for 18 to 20 minutes or until muffins spring back when touched. Serve warm. YIELD: 12 servings (serving size: 1 muffin).

POINTS: 4; EXCHANGES: 2 Starch, 1 Fat;
PER SERVING: CAL 181 (24% from fat); PRO 4g;
FAT 4.8g (sat 0.8g); CARB 31.3g; FIB 1.6g;
CHOL 19mg; IRON 1.3mg; SOD 230mg;
CALC 76mg

GRATING GINGER

Rub a piece of peeled ginger across the teeth of a ginger grater. A regular fine-toothed grater works well, too.

BLUEBERRY-BRAN MUFFINS

1½ cups shreds of wheat bran cereal (such as All-Bran)
1¼ cups 1% low-fat milk
½ cup sugar
3 tablespoons vegetable oil
1 large egg
1 cup all-purpose flour
1 tablespoon baking powder
½ teaspoon salt
1 cup blueberries

1. Preheat oven to 400°.
2. Combine cereal and milk in a large bowl, stirring well. Let stand 10 minutes.
3. Add sugar, oil, and egg to cereal mixture; stir well.
4. Lightly spoon flour into a dry measuring cup; level with a knife. Combine flour, baking powder, and salt; add to cereal mixture, stirring just until moist. Gently fold in blueberries.
5. Place 12 paper liners in muffin cups; spoon batter into cups, filling three-fourths full. Bake at 400° for 18 to 20 minutes or until muffins spring back when touched. Remove from pans immediately; place on a wire rack. YIELD: 12 servings (serving size: 1 muffin).

POINTS: 3; **EXCHANGES:** 2 Starch, 1 Fat;
PER SERVING: CAL 145 (26% from fat);
PRO 3.5g; FAT 4.5g (sat 0.6g); CARB 25.5g;
FIB 3.1g; CHOL 19mg; IRON 1.9mg; SOD 254mg;
CALC 131mg

COUNTRY CORNBREAD MUFFINS WITH JALAPEÑOS

No time to stop and chop? Substitute 2 to 3 tablespoons of jarred chopped jalapeños for the fresh peppers.

1 cup all-purpose flour
¾ cup yellow cornmeal
2 tablespoons sugar
2 teaspoons baking powder
¾ teaspoon salt
¼ teaspoon baking soda
1¼ cups low-fat buttermilk
1 cup frozen whole-kernel corn, thawed
2 jalapeño peppers, seeded and finely chopped
1 large egg
Cooking spray
¼ cup yogurt-based spread (such as Brummel & Brown)

1. Preheat oven to 425°.
2. Lightly spoon flour into a dry measuring cup; level with a knife. Combine flour and next 5 ingredients in a bowl.
3. Combine buttermilk, corn, peppers, and egg. Add buttermilk mixture to flour mixture; stir just until moist.
4. Spoon batter into 12 muffin cups coated with cooking spray, filling three-fourths full. Bake at 425° for 15 to 17 minutes or until lightly browned. Remove from pans immediately; place on a wire rack. Serve warm with spread. YIELD: 12 servings (serving size: 1 muffin and 1 teaspoon spread).

POINTS: 3; **EXCHANGES:** 1½ Starch, ½ Fat;
PER SERVING: CAL 129 (18% from fat); PRO 3.7g;
FAT 2.6g (sat 0.7g); CARB 22.6g; FIB 0.9g;
CHOL 19mg; IRON 1.1mg; SOD 316mg;
CALC 78mg

CINNAMON-KISSED RASPBERRY MUFFINS

2 cups all-purpose flour
¾ cup sugar
1½ teaspoons grated orange rind
1 teaspoon baking powder
½ teaspoon baking soda
½ teaspoon salt
⅛ teaspoon ground cinnamon
¾ cup fat-free milk
1 tablespoon vegetable oil
1 teaspoon vanilla extract
1 (8-ounce) carton vanilla low-fat yogurt
1 large egg, lightly beaten
1½ cups raspberries
1 tablespoon all-purpose flour
Cooking spray
1 tablespoon sugar
⅛ teaspoon ground cinnamon

1. Preheat oven to 400°.
2. Lightly spoon 2 cups flour into dry measuring cups; level with a knife. Combine flour and next 6 ingredients in a bowl; stir well. Make a well in center of mixture. Combine milk, oil, vanilla, yogurt, and egg; add to dry ingredients, stirring just until moist.
3. Toss raspberries with 1 tablespoon flour; gently fold into batter.
4. Spoon batter into 18 muffin cups coated with cooking spray, filling three-fourths full. Combine 1 tablespoon sugar and ⅛ teaspoon cinnamon; sprinkle evenly over muffins. Bake muffins at 400° for 20 minutes or until golden. Remove from pans immediately; place on wire rack. YIELD: 18 servings (serving size: 1 muffin).

POINTS: 2; **EXCHANGES:** 1½ Starch;
PER SERVING: CAL 119 (10% from fat); PRO 2.9g;
FAT 1.4g (sat 0.3g); CARB 23.6g; FIB 1.1g;
CHOL 13mg; IRON 0.8mg; SOD 144mg;
CALC 56mg

MIXED FRUIT MUFFINS

By adding dried fruit and pecans to a muffin mix, you can create quick, hearty muffins packed with sweet fruit any time of year.

⅓ cup chopped pecans
1½ teaspoons ground cinnamon, divided
¾ cup water
½ cup dried cranberries
½ cup chopped dried apricots
1 (16.5-ounce) package low-fat blueberry muffin mix
1 large egg
Cooking spray

1. Preheat oven to 400°.
2. Combine pecans and ½ teaspoon cinnamon; mix well. Set aside.
3. Combine 1 teaspoon cinnamon and next 5 ingredients in a bowl, stirring just until moist.
4. Spoon batter into 12 muffin cups coated with cooking spray, filling two-thirds full. Sprinkle each with 1 teaspoon pecan mixture. Bake at 400° for 18 to 20 minutes or until lightly browned. Remove from pans immediately; place on a wire rack.
YIELD: 12 servings (serving size: 1 muffin).

POINTS: 4; **EXCHANGES:** 2 Starch, 1 Fruit, 1 Fat; **PER SERVING:** CAL 211 (20% from fat); PRO 2.9g; FAT 4.7g (sat 1.3g); CARB 40g; FIB 2.1g; CHOL 18mg; IRON 1.4mg; SOD 201mg; CALC 66mg

SWEET POTATO-BRAN MUFFINS

1 cup shreds of wheat bran cereal (such as All-Bran)
½ cup fat-free milk
1 cup all-purpose flour
⅔ cup packed brown sugar
1½ teaspoons baking powder
1½ teaspoons ground cinnamon
½ teaspoon baking soda
¼ teaspoon salt
¼ teaspoon ground nutmeg
⅛ teaspoon ground ginger
2 (4-ounce) jars pureed sweet potato (such as Gerber's)
⅓ cup maple syrup
1½ teaspoons vanilla extract
1 large egg
½ cup raisins
Cooking spray

1. Preheat oven to 400°.
2. Combine cereal and milk in a bowl; stir well, and let stand 5 minutes.
3. Lightly spoon flour into dry measuring cup; level with a knife. Stir together flour and next 7 ingredients in a large bowl. Add sweet potato and next 3 ingredients to cereal mixture; stir well. Add to dry ingredients, stirring just until moist. Stir in raisins.
4. Spoon batter into 12 muffin pans coated with cooking spray, filling three-fourths full. Bake at 400° for 25 minutes or until golden. Remove from pans immediately, and place on a wire rack. YIELD: 12 servings (serving size: 1 muffin).

POINTS: 3; **EXCHANGES:** 2 Starch, ½ Fruit; **PER SERVING:** CAL 163 (4% from fat); PRO 3g; FAT 0.8g (sat 0.2g); CARB 38.2g; FIB 2.6g; CHOL 18mg; IRON 1.9mg; SOD 194mg; CALC 93mg

CRANBERRY-ORANGE SCONES

(pictured on page 26)

2 cups all-purpose flour
2½ teaspoons baking powder
¼ teaspoon baking soda
¼ teaspoon salt
¼ cup sugar
3½ tablespoons chilled butter or stick margarine, cut into small pieces
¼ cup dried cranberries
2 teaspoons grated orange rind
½ cup low-fat buttermilk
1 large egg, lightly beaten
Cooking spray
1 teaspoon powdered sugar

1. Preheat oven to 375°.
2. Lightly spoon flour into dry measuring cups; level with a knife. Combine flour and next 4 ingredients in a bowl. Cut in butter with pastry blender or 2 knives until mixture resembles coarse meal. Stir in cranberries and rind. Add buttermilk and egg, stirring just until moist.
3. Turn dough out onto a lightly floured surface, and knead 15 times or until smooth.
4. Transfer dough to a baking sheet coated with cooking spray; pat into a 7-inch circle. Cut into 10 wedges, cutting to, but not through, bottom of dough. (Do not separate wedges.)
5. Bake at 375° for 20 to 22 minutes or until golden. Transfer scones to a wire rack; sift powdered sugar over top, and serve warm. YIELD: 10 servings (serving size: 1 scone).

POINTS: 4; **EXCHANGES:** 2 Starch, 1 Fat; **PER SERVING:** CAL 169 (26% from fat); PRO 3.7g; FAT 4.9g (sat 2.8g); CARB 27.5g; FIB 1g; CHOL 33mg; IRON 1.4mg; SOD 272mg; CALC 90mg

CINNAMON-RAISIN SCONES

    2 cups all-purpose flour
  ¼ cup sugar
1½ teaspoons baking powder
    1 teaspoon ground cinnamon
  ¼ teaspoon salt
  ¼ cup chilled butter or stick
      margarine, cut into small pieces
  ⅓ cup raisins
  ½ cup 1% low-fat milk
    1 large egg, lightly beaten
Cooking spray
    1 tablespoon 1% low-fat milk
    1 tablespoon cinnamon sugar

1. Preheat oven to 375°.
2. Lightly spoon flour into dry
measuring cups; level with a knife.
Combine flour and next 4 ingredients in a bowl; cut in butter with a
pastry blender or 2 knives until
mixture resembles coarse meal. Stir
in raisins.
3. Combine ½ cup milk and egg;
add to flour mixture, stirring just
until moist. (Dough will be sticky.)
4. Turn dough out onto a lightly
floured surface; knead lightly 4 or 5
times with floured hands. Pat dough
into a 7-inch circle on a baking
sheet coated with cooking spray. Cut
dough into 10 wedges, cutting to,
but not through, bottom of dough.
Brush with 1 tablespoon milk; sprinkle with cinnamon sugar.
5. Bake at 375° for 18 to 20 minutes
or until golden. Serve warm. **YIELD:**
10 servings (serving size: 1 scone).

POINTS: 4; **EXCHANGES:** 2 Starch, 1 Fat;
PER SERVING: CAL 185 (27% from fat); PRO 3.9g;
FAT 5.5g (sat 3.2g); CARB 30.3g; FIB 1.2g;
CHOL 34mg; IRON 1.5mg; SOD 193mg;
CALC 69mg

BUTTERMILK CORNBREAD

(pictured on page 25)

    2 tablespoons plus 1 teaspoon
      vegetable oil, divided
    1 cup yellow self-rising cornmeal
      mix
  ¾ cup finely chopped onion
  ½ cup low-fat buttermilk
  ¼ cup egg substitute
    1 (8¼-ounce) can cream-style corn

1. Preheat oven to 400°.
2. Coat a 9-inch cast iron skillet
with 1 teaspoon oil; place in oven
10 minutes.
3. Combine cornmeal mix and
onion in a medium bowl. Combine
buttermilk, 2 tablespoons oil, egg
substitute, and corn. Add to cornmeal
mixture, stirring just until moist.
Spoon batter into preheated pan.
Bake at 400° for 20 minutes or until
golden. Cut into 8 wedges. **YIELD:**
8 servings (serving size: 1 wedge).

POINTS: 3; **EXCHANGES:** 1 Starch, 1 Fat;
PER SERVING: CAL 128 (35% from fat); PRO 3.4g;
FAT 5.1g (sat 0.5g); CARB 17.9g; FIB 1.5g;
CHOL 1mg; IRON 1.1mg; SOD 320mg;
CALC 79mg

MASHING BANANAS

Bananas are sweeter and easier
to mash with a fork and blend
into a batter when overly ripe.

BANANA-DATE BREAD

1⅔ cups all-purpose flour
  ¾ teaspoon baking soda
  ¼ teaspoon salt
1⅓ cups mashed ripe banana
      (about 2)
  ¾ cup sugar
    2 tablespoons vegetable oil
    1 large egg
  ⅓ cup chopped dates
Cooking spray
    2 tablespoons brown sugar
    2 tablespoons all-purpose flour
  ¼ teaspoon ground cinnamon
    1 tablespoon plus 1 teaspoon
      chilled butter or stick
      margarine, cut into small pieces

1. Preheat oven to 350°.
2. Lightly spoon flour into dry measuring cups; level with a knife.
Combine flour, soda, and salt in a
bowl. Place banana and next 3
ingredients in a bowl; beat with a
mixer at medium speed until blended. Add flour mixture; stir just until
moist. Stir in dates. Pour batter into
an 8 x 4-inch loaf pan coated with
cooking spray.
3. Combine brown sugar, 2 tablespoons flour, and cinnamon in a small
bowl. Cut in butter with a pastry
blender until mixture resembles coarse
meal. Sprinkle evenly over batter.
4. Bake at 350° for 50 to 55 minutes
or until a wooden pick inserted in
center comes out clean. Cool in pan
on a wire rack 10 minutes; remove
from pan, and cool completely. **YIELD:** 1
loaf, 14 servings (serving size: 1 slice).

POINTS: 3; **EXCHANGES:** 2 Starch;
PER SERVING: CAL 171 (19% from fat); PRO 2.4g;
FAT 3.7g (sat 1.1g); CARB 33g; FIB 1.3g;
CHOL 18mg; IRON 1mg; SOD 126mg;
CALC 9mg

PUMPKIN-OAT BREAD WITH WALNUT STREUSEL TOPPING

Streusel Topping
1½ cups all-purpose flour
1 cup quick-cooking oats
¾ cup packed dark brown sugar
2 teaspoons baking powder
1 teaspoon ground cinnamon
½ teaspoon salt
¼ teaspoon baking soda
¼ teaspoon ground nutmeg
1 cup canned pumpkin
⅓ cup low-fat buttermilk
2 tablespoons vegetable oil
1 teaspoon vanilla extract
1 large egg, lightly beaten
Cooking spray

1. Prepare Streusel Topping; set aside.
2. Preheat oven to 350°.
3. Lightly spoon flour into dry measuring cups; level with a knife. Combine flour and next 7 ingredients in a medium bowl; make a well in center of mixture. Combine pumpkin and next 4 ingredients; add to flour mixture, stirring just until moist.
4. Spoon batter into an 8 x 4-inch loaf pan coated with cooking spray. Top with Streusel Topping; lightly spray topping with cooking spray.
5. Bake at 350° for 50 minutes or until a wooden pick inserted in center comes out clean. YIELD: 1 loaf, 16 servings (serving size: 1 slice).

STREUSEL TOPPING
3 tablespoons dark brown sugar
2 tablespoons all-purpose flour
¼ teaspoon ground nutmeg
¼ teaspoon ground cinnamon
1 tablespoon chilled butter
¼ cup chopped walnuts

1. Combine first 4 ingredients in a medium bowl; stir well with a whisk.
2. Cut in butter with a pastry blender or 2 knives until mixture resembles coarse meal. Stir in walnuts. YIELD: ½ cup.

POINTS: 3; **EXCHANGES:** 2 Starch, 1 Fat;
PER SERVING: CAL 169 (20% from fat); PRO 3.3g; FAT 3.8g (sat 0.9g); CARB 31.1g; FIB 1.4g; CHOL 16mg; IRON 3.7mg; SOD 131mg; CALC 75mg

WHOLE WHEAT ROLLS

2 packages dry yeast (about 4½ teaspoons)
½ cup warm water (100° to 110°)
2¼ cups all-purpose flour
2 cups whole wheat flour
1 (12-ounce) carton 2% low-fat cottage cheese
¼ cup packed brown sugar
3 tablespoons light butter, melted
2 large eggs
1 teaspoon salt
Cooking spray

1. Dissolve yeast in warm water in a large bowl; let stand 5 minutes.
2. Lightly spoon flours into dry measuring cups; level with a knife.
3. Place cottage cheese in a food processor; process 20 seconds or until smooth. Add brown sugar, butter, and eggs. Process just until blended. Stir cottage cheese mixture, whole wheat flour, and salt into yeast mixture. Stir in enough all-purpose flour to form a soft dough. Turn dough out onto a floured surface. Knead until smooth and elastic (about 10 minutes); add enough of remaining flour, one tablespoon at a time, to prevent dough from sticking to hands. (Dough will feel sticky.)
4. Place dough in a large bowl coated with cooking spray, turning to coat top. Cover and let rise in a warm place (85°), free from drafts, 45 minutes or until doubled in size. (Press 2 fingers into dough. If indentation remains, the dough has risen enough.)
5. Punch dough down; cover and let rest 5 minutes. Divide in thirds. Working with one portion at a time (cover remaining dough to keep from drying), shape each portion into 12 balls. Place balls in muffin cups coated with cooking spray. Repeat procedure with remaining two-thirds of dough.
6. Cover and let rise 30 minutes or until doubled in size.
7. Preheat oven to 375°.
8. Bake at 375° for 12 minutes or until golden. Immediately remove rolls from pans. YIELD: 36 servings (serving size: 1 roll).
NOTE: Dough balls may be frozen for 2 weeks. To prepare, place frozen balls in muffin cups. Let rise in a warm place (85°), free from drafts, 1 hour or until doubled in size. Bake as directed.

POINTS: 1; **EXCHANGE:** 1 Starch;
PER SERVING: CAL 79 (15% from fat); PRO 3.8g; FAT 1.3g (sat 0.6g); CARB 12.9g; FIB 1.2g; CHOL 14mg; IRON 0.8mg; SOD 113mg; CALC 11mg

CINNAMON SWIRL LOAF

1 large egg, separated
1 teaspoon water
1 package active dry yeast
¾ cup warm water (100° to 110°)
3 cups all-purpose flour
1½ tablespoons butter or stick
    margarine, melted
2 tablespoons honey
1¼ teaspoons salt
Cooking spray
1 tablespoon butter or stick
    margarine, melted
2 tablespoons sugar
1 teaspoon ground cinnamon

1. Combine egg yolk and 1 teaspoon water in a small bowl, stirring well with a whisk. Add 1 tablespoon yolk mixture to egg white, stirring well. Cover and chill remaining yolk mixture.
2. Combine yeast and warm water in a large bowl; let stand 5 minutes.
3. Lightly spoon flour into dry measuring cups; level with a knife. Stir 1 cup flour, egg white mixture, 1½ tablespoons butter, honey, and salt into yeast mixture; stir 1 to 2 minutes or until well-blended. Stir in 1¾ cups flour to form a stiff dough. Sprinkle work surface with remaining flour. Turn dough out onto floured surface, and knead until smooth and elastic (about 5 minutes).
4. Place dough in a large bowl coated with cooking spray, turning to coat top. Cover and let rise in a warm place (85°), free from drafts, 45 minutes or until doubled in size. (Press 2 fingers into dough. If indentation remains, the dough has risen enough.)
5. Punch dough down; turn out onto a lightly floured surface, and knead lightly 4 or 5 times. Roll dough into a 14 x 7-inch rectangle. Brush dough with 1 tablespoon melted butter. Combine sugar and cinnamon in a small bowl. Sprinkle dough with cinnamon mixture. Roll up rectangle tightly, starting at short side and pressing firmly to eliminate air pockets; pinch seam and ends to seal. Place dough, seam side down, in an 8 x 4-inch loaf pan coated with cooking spray. Cover and let rise in a warm place, free from drafts, 45 minutes or until doubled in size.
6. Preheat oven to 375°.
7. Gently brush top of loaf with chilled egg yolk mixture. Bake at 375° for 30 minutes or until loaf sounds hollow when tapped. Remove bread from pan immediately; cool on a wire rack. YIELD: 1 loaf, 12 servings (serving size: 1 slice).

POINTS: 3; **EXCHANGES:** 2 Starch, ½ Fat;
PER SERVING: CAL 162 (18% from fat); PRO 4g;
FAT 3.2g (sat 1.7g); CARB 29.3g; FIB 1.1g;
CHOL 24mg; IRON 1.6mg; SOD 273mg;
CALC 10mg

ANADAMA RAISIN BREAD

(pictured on page 26)
Anadama bread originated in New England. Traditional ingredients include cornmeal and molasses.

1 package active dry yeast
1 cup warm water (100° to 110°)
2¾ cups all-purpose flour
½ cup yellow cornmeal
½ cup raisins
¼ cup molasses
1½ teaspoons salt
1 teaspoon caraway seeds
Cooking spray

1. Combine yeast and warm water in a measuring cup; let stand 5 minutes.
2. Lightly spoon flour into dry measuring cups; level with a knife. Combine 1 cup flour and next 5 ingredients in a large bowl, stirring well. Add yeast mixture to flour mixture; beat with a mixer at medium speed 2 minutes or until smooth. Gradually add remaining flour to form a soft dough.
3. Turn dough out onto a lightly floured surface, and knead until smooth and elastic (about 10 minutes). Place dough in a large bowl coated with cooking spray, turning to coat top. Cover and let rise in a warm place (85°), free from drafts, 45 minutes or until doubled in size. (Press 2 fingers into dough. If indentation remains, the dough has risen enough.)
4. Punch dough down; turn dough out onto a lightly floured surface. Roll dough into a 12 x 7-inch rectangle. Roll up dough, starting at short side and pressing firmly to eliminate air pockets; pinch seam and ends to seal. Place roll, seam side down, in an 8 x 4-inch loaf pan coated with cooking spray. Cover and let rise in a warm place, free from drafts, 45 minutes or until doubled in size.
5. Preheat oven to 375°.
6. Bake at 375° for 35 minutes or until loaf sounds hollow when tapped. Remove bread from pan immediately; cool on a wire rack. YIELD: 1 loaf, 14 servings (serving size: 1 slice).

POINTS: 3; **EXCHANGES:** 2 Starch;
PER SERVING: CAL 167 (2% from fat); PRO 3.8g;
FAT 0.4g (sat 0.1g); CARB 37g; FIB 1.5g;
CHOL 0mg; IRON 2.2mg; SOD 296mg;
CALC 22mg

Desserts

APPLES WITH CARAMEL DIPPING SAUCE

½ cup fat-free caramel sundae syrup (such as Smucker's)
1 tablespoon fat-free milk
¼ teaspoon ground cinnamon
¼ teaspoon vanilla, butter, and nut flavoring or vanilla extract
¾ cup frozen fat-free whipped topping, thawed
4 cups Granny Smith or Red Delicious apple wedges (about 3 to 4 apples)

1. Combine first 4 ingredients; stir with a whisk until blended. Gently fold in whipped topping. Cover and chill. Serve with apple wedges. YIELD: 4 servings (serving size: 1 cup apple wedges and ¼ cup sauce).

POINTS: 3; EXCHANGES: 2 Starch, 1 Fruit; PER SERVING: CAL 175 (0% from fat); PRO 1.4g; FAT 0g (sat 0g); CARB 41.1g; FIB 1.8g; CHOL 0mg; IRON 0.2mg; SOD 120mg; CALC 31mg

FRUIT MEDLEY WITH ORANGE-YOGURT SAUCE

2 kiwifruit
2 cups strawberries, halved
2 navel oranges, peeled and sectioned
½ cup vanilla low-fat yogurt
1 tablespoon Grand Marnier or orange juice
Fresh mint sprigs (optional)

1. Peel kiwifruit; cut into ¼-inch slices. Cut slices in half.
2. Combine kiwifruit, strawberries, and orange sections in a bowl. Combine yogurt and liqueur, stirring well.

3. Spoon fruit mixture into 4 dessert bowls; drizzle 2 tablespoons dressing over fruit in each bowl. Garnish with mint sprigs, if desired. YIELD: 4 servings (serving size: 1 cup).

POINTS: 2; EXCHANGES: 1½ Fruit, 1 Skim Milk; PER SERVING: CAL 118 (6% from fat); PRO 3.1g; FAT 0.9g (sat 0.3g); CARB 24.8g; FIB 4.7g; CHOL 2mg; IRON 0.6mg; SOD 24mg; CALC 101mg

GRAPEFRUIT AMBROSIA COUPES

A coupe is any type of ice cream, frozen yogurt, or sherbet topped with fruit. Serving a grapefruit mixture over orange sherbet is a nice alternative to traditional ambrosia.

1 cup orange sherbet or sorbet
1 (26-ounce) jar pink grapefruit sections, drained
1 cup seedless red grape halves
4 teaspoons honey
4 teaspoons flaked coconut

1. Divide sherbet among 4 coupe dishes or other individual stemmed dessert dishes. Toss grapefruit and grapes in a bowl. Top each sherbet serving evenly with fruit. Drizzle each with 1 teaspoon honey, and sprinkle with 1 teaspoon coconut. YIELD: 4 servings (serving size: 1 dish).

POINTS: 3; EXCHANGES: 1½ Starch, 1 Fruit; PER SERVING: CAL 171 (9% from fat); PRO 1.7g; FAT 1.8g (sat 1.1g); CARB 40g; FIB 1g; CHOL 3mg; IRON 0.5mg; SOD 36mg; CALC 50mg

BANANAS FOSTER

(pictured on page 1)

¼ cup light butter
6 tablespoons packed brown sugar
1 teaspoon ground cinnamon
4 large bananas, sliced
¼ cup dark rum
2½ cups vanilla fat-free ice cream or frozen yogurt

1. Combine butter, brown sugar, and cinnamon in a large skillet over medium heat; cook, stirring constantly, until butter melts and sugar dissolves. Add banana; cook 2 minutes, coating slices in sugar mixture. Remove from heat.
2. Heat rum in a small saucepan over medium-low heat. Pour heated rum into one side of skillet. Ignite rum with a long match; let flames die down. Return to medium heat; cook 30 seconds, stirring gently to coat banana.
3. Place ½ cup ice cream in each of 5 goblets, and top with ½ cup banana mixture. Serve immediately. YIELD: 5 servings (serving size: ½ cup banana mixture and ½ cup ice cream).

POINTS: 6; EXCHANGES: 3 Starch, 1 Fruit, 1 Fat; PER SERVING: CAL 287 (16% from fat); PRO 4.8g; FAT 5.3g (sat 3.4g); CARB 57.5g; FIB 2.5g; CHOL 16mg; IRON 0.7mg; SOD 128mg; CALC 124mg

DEEP BUTTER-RUM SAUCE AND BANANAS

The sauce can be served over a variety of fruits, including strawberries, apples, pears, pineapple, or peaches.

⅓ cup fat-free evaporated milk
4 teaspoons cornstarch
½ cup packed brown sugar
¼ cup dark rum
¼ teaspoon salt
3 tablespoons yogurt-based spread (such as Brummel & Brown)
¼ teaspoon vanilla, butter, and nut flavoring or vanilla extract
4½ cups sliced banana (about 7)

1. Combine evaporated milk and cornstarch in a 2-quart saucepan, stirring well with a whisk until cornstarch dissolves. Add sugar, rum, and salt; stir well.
2. Place saucepan over medium-high heat; bring to a boil. Cook, stirring constantly, 2 minutes. Remove from heat; cool slightly. Add spread and flavoring; stir well. Serve over banana. YIELD: 6 servings (serving size: ¾ cup bananas and 2 tablespoons rum sauce).

POINTS: 4; **EXCHANGES:** 2 Starch, 1 Fruit, ½ Fat; **PER SERVING:** CAL 233 (11% from fat); PRO 2g; FAT 3g (sat 0.7g); CARB 46.6g; FIB 2.6g; CHOL 1mg; IRON 0.7mg; SOD 168mg; CALC 58mg

SPICED PEARS WITH CRANBERRIES

The juice and wine create a sweet syrup in this simple, elegant dessert.

3 firm, ripe Bartlett pears
1 cup cranberry juice
½ cup dry red wine
3 tablespoons sugar
1 tablespoon fresh lemon juice
5 whole cloves
1 (3-inch) cinnamon stick
½ cup dried cranberries

1. Peel pears, and remove cores. Cut each pear in half lengthwise.
2. Combine cranberry juice and next 5 ingredients in a large non-stick skillet. Add pears; bring to a boil. Cover, reduce heat, and simmer 20 minutes or until tender, turning once. Remove pear halves with a slotted spoon, reserving juice mixture in pan. Place pears in a serving dish.
3. Remove cinnamon sticks and whole cloves from pan; discard. Add cranberries. Bring to a boil, and reduce liquid by one-third. Pour syrup over pears; cool 20 minutes. YIELD: 6 servings (serving size: 1 pear half and ⅓ cup poaching liquid with cranberries).

POINTS: 3; **EXCHANGES:** 1 Starch, 2 Fruit; **PER SERVING:** CAL 194 (3% from fat); PRO 0.6g; FAT 0.8g (sat 0.1g); CARB 48.9g; FIB 3.9g; CHOL 0mg; IRON 0.6mg; SOD 4mg; CALC 20mg

VERY BERRY SHORTCAKE

1 (12-ounce) package frozen raspberries in light syrup, thawed
¼ cup sugar
1½ teaspoons butter or stick margarine
4 (½-inch-thick) slices fat-free pound cake (such as Entenmann's Fat-Free Golden Loaf)
1 cup vanilla fat-free ice cream or frozen yogurt
2 cups quartered strawberries

1. Add raspberries to food processor; process until smooth, scraping down sides if necessary. Place raspberries in a wire mesh strainer; press with back of spoon against sides of strainer to squeeze out juice. Discard pulp and seeds remaining in strainer. Combine raspberry puree and sugar in a small saucepan; bring to a boil over medium heat, stirring occasionally. Cover and chill.
2. Heat butter in a large nonstick skillet over medium heat. Add pound cake slices, and cook 2 minutes on each side or until golden. Cut each slice into 2 triangles.
3. Arrange 2 cake triangles on individual dessert plates. Top each serving with ice cream, strawberries, and raspberry puree. Serve immediately. YIELD: 4 servings (serving size: 2 cake triangles, ¼ cup raspberry puree, ¼ cup ice cream, and ½ cup strawberries).

POINTS: 5; **EXCHANGES:** 3 Starch, 1½ Fruit; **PER SERVING:** CAL 307 (5% from fat); PRO 4g; FAT 1.9g (sat 0.9g); CARB 71.4g; FIB 5.8g; CHOL 4mg; IRON 0.9mg; SOD 152mg; CALC 64mg

CHOCOLATE-RASPBERRY CRÊPES

(pictured on page 48)

⅓ cup all-purpose flour
⅓ cup fat-free milk
1 tablespoon cocoa
2 teaspoons brown sugar
1½ teaspoons vegetable oil
¼ teaspoon vanilla extract
⅛ teaspoon almond extract
1 large egg
1 cup raspberries
1 tablespoon Chambord
¾ cup (6 ounces) Neufchâtel
   cheese, softened
⅓ cup sifted powdered sugar
1 tablespoon fat-free milk
½ teaspoon vanilla extract
Butter-flavored cooking spray
4 teaspoons chocolate syrup

1. Lightly spoon flour into a dry measuring cup; level with a knife.
2. Combine flour and next 7 ingredients in a blender; process 1 minute and 15 seconds or until smooth, stopping once to scrape down sides. Cover and chill batter 1 hour.
3. Toss raspberries and Chambord gently in a small bowl. Cover and chill.
4. Beat Neufchâtel cheese and next 3 ingredients at high speed of a mixer 1 to 2 minutes or until creamy. Set aside.
5. Place an 8-inch crêpe pan or nonstick skillet over medium-high heat until hot. Coat with cooking spray. Remove pan from heat. Pour ¼ cup batter into pan; quickly tilt pan in all directions so that batter covers pan with a thin film. Cook about 1 minute.

6. Carefully lift edge of crêpe with a spatula to test for doneness. Crêpe is ready to turn when it can be shaken loose from pan and underside is lightly browned. Turn crêpe over, and cook 30 seconds on other side. Place crêpe on one of 4 individual serving dishes. Repeat procedure with remaining batter.
7. Spoon cheese mixture evenly onto center of crêpes. Bring 2 opposite sides to center of each crêpe, folding over filling. Place crêpes, seam side down, on serving plates. Spoon ¼ cup raspberry mixture over each crêpe, and drizzle each with 1 teaspoon chocolate syrup. YIELD: 4 servings (serving size: 1 crêpe).

POINTS: 6; **EXCHANGES:** 2 Starch, 1 Medium-Fat Meat, 1 Fat; **PER SERVING:** CAL 292 (40% from fat); PRO 9.6g; FAT 12.8g (sat 6.9g); CARB 32g; FIB 3.6g; CHOL 84mg; IRON 1.5mg; SOD 217mg; CALC 88mg

MAKING CRÊPES

Pour batter into center of pan; quickly tilt hot pan in all directions so that batter covers bottom before it starts to cook.

GREEK HONEY YOGURT

Until you try this dish, you won't believe how satisfying yogurt can be.

3 cups vanilla low-fat yogurt
4 teaspoons sliced almonds
¼ cup honey
Mint leaves (optional)

1. Place a colander in a medium bowl. Line colander with 4 layers of cheesecloth, allowing cheesecloth to extend over outside edges.
2. Spoon yogurt into colander. Cover loosely with plastic wrap; refrigerate 12 hours.
3. Place nuts in a dry skillet over medium-high heat. Toast the nuts, stirring constantly, about 3 minutes or until golden.
4. Spoon ½ cup drained yogurt into each of 4 serving dishes, and discard liquid. Top each bowl with 1 tablespoon honey and 1 teaspoon toasted almonds. Garnish with mint leaves, if desired. YIELD: 4 servings (serving size: ½ cup).
NOTE: Once yogurt is placed in serving dish, if there is any excess liquid, it can be removed by blotting gently with a paper towel.

POINTS: 5; **EXCHANGES:** 1 Starch, 2 Milk; **PER SERVING:** CAL 233 (12% from fat); PRO 9.5g; FAT 3.3g (sat 1.6g); CARB 43.2g; FIB 0.3g; CHOL 9mg; IRON 0.3mg; SOD 122mg; CALC 321mg

LIME TARTLETS

You can substitute orange or lemon juice for the lime juice in this recipe. Planning a party? An assortment of all three variations makes up a colorful dessert tray.

1 (2.1-ounce) package frozen mini phyllo dough shells, thawed
¼ cup fresh lime juice
1 large egg yolk
½ cup fat-free sweetened condensed milk
¼ teaspoon grated lime rind
5 tablespoons frozen reduced-calorie whipped topping, thawed
Lime zest (optional)
Mint springs (optional)

1. Preheat oven to 350°.
2. Bake phyllo shells at 350° for 5 minutes; set aside.
3. Heat lime juice in a small saucepan until hot.
4. Beat egg yolk with a mixer at medium speed 2 minutes. Gradually add lime juice, beating at low speed until blended. Return egg mixture to saucepan; cook over low heat, stirring constantly, 5 to 6 minutes or until thick and pale yellow. Stir in milk and lime rind.
5. Spoon filling evenly into phyllo shells. Cover and chill 1 hour.
6. Top each tartlet with 1 teaspoon whipped topping. Garnish with lime zest and mint sprigs, if desired. YIELD: 15 servings (serving size: 1 tartlet).

POINTS: 1; EXCHANGE: ½ Starch;
PER SERVING: CAL 49 (14% from fat); PRO 1.4g; FAT 0.8g (sat 0.3g); CARB 9.1g; FIB 0.1g; CHOL 15mg; IRON 0.2mg; SOD 31mg; CALC 31mg

BUTTERMILK PANNA COTTA WITH BLUEBERRY SAUCE

Panna cotta is a sweet Italian custard-like dessert. Served chilled with a fruit sauce, panna cotta is a deliciously cool ending to a summer meal.

2 envelopes unflavored gelatin
½ cup cold water
1½ cups low-fat buttermilk
¾ cup fat-free sour cream
⅔ cup fat-free sweetened condensed milk
1 pint blueberries
½ cup port wine
3 tablespoons sugar
¼ teaspoon salt

1. Sprinkle gelatin over cold water in a small saucepan; let stand 1 minute. Cook over low heat, stirring until gelatin dissolves, about 2 minutes.
2. Combine gelatin mixture, buttermilk, sour cream, and sweetened condensed milk in a large bowl; stir until smooth. Pour mixture evenly into 6 (6-ounce) custard cups or ramekins. Cover and chill 1 hour or until set.
3. Combine blueberries and remaining ingredients in a medium saucepan; bring to a boil. Reduce heat, and simmer 3 to 4 minutes or until slightly thick. Cover and chill.
4. To serve, unmold custard cups onto individual dessert dishes. Top with blueberry sauce. YIELD: 6 servings (1 panna cotta and ⅓ cup blueberry sauce).

POINTS: 4; EXCHANGES: 1½ Starch, ½ Fruit, 1 Skim Milk; PER SERVING: CAL 210 (5% from fat); PRO 9.4g; FAT 1.2g (sat 0g); CARB 40.2g; FIB 1.4g; CHOL 5mg; IRON 0.2mg; SOD 192mg; CALC 209mg

ANGELIC TIRAMISU

Almost too good to be true, this dessert is definitely heaven sent. For a slightly devilish twist, replace ¼ cup coffee with Kahlúa.

1 cup cold water
1 (14-ounce) can fat-free sweetened condensed milk
1 (1.4-ounce) package sugar-free vanilla instant pudding mix
1 (8-ounce) block ⅓-less-fat cream cheese, softened
1 (8-ounce) container frozen fat-free whipped topping, thawed
24 cake-style ladyfingers (2 [3-ounce] packages)
1 cup strong brewed coffee
1 tablespoon unsweetened cocoa

1. Combine first 3 ingredients in a large bowl; stir well with a whisk. Cover and chill 30 minutes.
2. Add cream cheese; beat with a mixer at medium speed until blended. Fold in whipped topping.
3. Split ladyfingers in half lengthwise. Arrange 16 halves in a single layer in an 8-inch square baking dish. Drizzle with ⅓ cup coffee. Spread one-third of pudding mixture evenly over ladyfingers. Repeat procedure twice with remaining ladyfingers, coffee, and pudding mixture. Cover and chill 8 hours. Sprinkle with cocoa. YIELD: 12 servings (serving size: about ¾ cup).

POINTS: 6; EXCHANGES: 3 Starch, 1 Fat; PER SERVING: CAL 302 (20% from fat); PRO 8.5g; FAT 6.7g (sat 3.6g); CARB 50.7g; FIB 0.6g; CHOL 98mg; IRON 1mg; SOD 229mg; CALC 155mg

Turkeyfoot Reading Center
Confluence, PA

STRAWBERRY-MERLOT ICE

(pictured on page 51)

2 cups Merlot or other dry red
    wine
1 cup white grape juice
    concentrate
1 (16-ounce) package frozen
    whole strawberries

1. Combine all ingredients in a
blender; process until smooth, stopping once to scrape down sides.
Pour mixture into a 13 x 9-inch
dish; cover and freeze at least
8 hours or until firm.
2. Remove mixture from freezer,
and scrape entire mixture with the
tines of a fork until fluffy. Serve
immediately, or spoon into a
freezer-safe container; cover and
freeze up to 1 month. YIELD: 12
servings (serving size: ½ cup).

POINTS: 2; EXCHANGE: 1 Fruit; PER SERVING:
CAL 98 (2% from fat); PRO 0.1g; FAT 0.3g (sat 0g);
CARB 18.2g; FIB 0.5g; CHOL 0mg; IRON 0.2mg;
SOD 10mg; CALC 9mg

MILK CHOCOLATE ICE CREAM

4 cups fat-free half-and-half
3 tablespoons unsweetened cocoa
1 (14-ounce) can fat-free
    sweetened condensed milk

1. Combine all ingredients in a large
bowl, stirring well with a whisk.
Cover and chill at least 8 hours.
2. Pour mixture into the freezer can
of an ice-cream freezer, and freeze
according to manufacturer's instructions. Spoon ice cream into a
freezer-safe container; cover and

freeze 2 hours or until firm. YIELD:
14 servings (serving size: ½ cup).

POINTS: 3; EXCHANGES: 2 Starch; PER SERVING:
CAL 157 (2% from fat); PRO 3.7g; FAT 0.2g
(sat 0.1g); CARB 31.0g; FIB 0.4g; CHOL 3mg;
IRON 0.2mg; SOD 110mg; CALC 157mg

FROZEN PEANUT BUTTER BRITTLE PIE

(pictured on page 48)
Prevent leftover peanut brittle from tempt-
ing you by freezing the extra, thawing
at room temperature when needed.

¼ cup light corn syrup
3 tablespoons creamy peanut butter
2 cups chocolate low-fat ice
    cream or yogurt, softened
1 (6-ounce) package reduced-fat
    graham cracker crust
2 tablespoons crushed peanut
    brittle, divided
2 cups vanilla low-fat ice cream,
    softened
8 tablespoons frozen fat-free
    whipped topping, thawed
4 teaspoons crushed peanut brittle

1. Combine corn syrup and peanut
butter in a small bowl.
2. Spoon chocolate ice cream into
crust; place in freezer 30 minutes.
Spread with half of peanut butter
mixture, and sprinkle with 1 tablespoon peanut brittle.
3. Spread vanilla ice cream over
peanut brittle; place in freezer 30
minutes. Spread with remaining
peanut butter mixture, and sprinkle
with 1 tablespoon peanut brittle.
Freeze 3 hours or until firm.
4. Place pie in refrigerator 20 minutes before serving to soften. Dollop
with whipped topping, and sprinkle

with 4 teaspoons crushed peanut
brittle. YIELD: 8 servings (serving size:
1 slice, 1 tablespoon whipped topping, and ½ teaspoon peanut brittle).

POINTS: 6; EXCHANGES: 3 Starch, 2 Fat;
PER SERVING: CAL 301 (28% from fat); PRO 6g;
FAT 9.4g (sat 2.3g); CARB 48.9g; FIB 2g;
CHOL 5mg; IRON 0.8mg; SOD 227mg;
CALC 103mg

FROZEN CHOCOLATE DECADENCE BROWNIES

(pictured on page 49)

1 (20.5-ounce) package low-fat
    brownie mix (such as Betty
    Crocker Sweet Rewards)
⅔ cup water
Cooking spray
1 (2.25-ounce) package sliced
    almonds
¾ cup seedless raspberry spread
    (such as Polaner All Fruit)
2 (1-pound) cans dark cherries in
    heavy syrup
4 cups chocolate low-fat ice
    cream, softened
1½ teaspoons instant coffee granules
1 (12-ounce) container frozen fat-
    free whipped topping, thawed

1. Preheat oven to 350°.
2. Stir together brownie mix and
water. Pour batter into a 13 x 9-inch
pan coated with cooking spray. Bake
at 350° for 20 to 25 minutes or
until a wooden pick inserted in
center comes out clean. Toast
almonds on rack below brownies
during last 5 minutes of baking.
Cool brownies and almonds completely on a wire rack.
3. Place raspberry spread in a bowl;
stir with a whisk until smooth.

Drain cherries, reserving 2 table-spoons juice; set juice aside. Rinse cherries; drain well. Add cherries to raspberry spread, stirring to coat.

4. Spread ice cream over brownies; spoon cherry mixture over ice cream.

5. Combine reserved cherry juice and coffee granules, stirring until coffee dissolves. Fold in whipped topping; spread over cherry mixture. Sprinkle with almonds. Cover and freeze at least 8 hours. YIELD: 24 servings (serving size: 1 square).

POINTS: 5; EXCHANGES: 3 Starch, ½ Fat;
PER SERVING: CAL 226 (12% from fat); PRO 3.6g;
FAT 3g (sat 0.4g); CARB 44.8g; FIB 1.3g;
CHOL 0mg; IRON 1.3mg; SOD 110mg;
CALC 34mg

BROWNIE SUNDAE PIE

(pictured on cover)

¼ cup butter, softened
¾ cup sugar
1 teaspoon vanilla extract
1 large egg
¾ cup all-purpose flour
⅓ cup unsweetened cocoa
¼ teaspoon baking powder
⅛ teaspoon salt
2 tablespoons fat-free milk
Cooking spray
3 cups strawberry fat-free frozen
  yogurt, softened
1½ cups frozen fat-free whipped
  topping, thawed
10 tablespoons chocolate syrup
10 maraschino cherries

1. Preheat oven to 350°.

2. Beat butter with a mixer at medium speed until light and fluffy. Add sugar, vanilla, and egg; beat until smooth.

3. Lightly spoon flour into a dry measuring cup; level with a knife. Combine flour, cocoa, baking powder, and salt. Add flour mixture, alternately with egg mixture and milk. (Batter will be very stiff.)

4. Transfer mixture to a 9-inch pieplate coated with cooking spray, spreading evenly on bottom.

5. Bake at 350° for 15 to 17 minutes or until a wooden pick inserted in center comes out clean. Cool completely on a wire rack.

6. Spoon yogurt into brownie crust, smoothing the top. Cover and freeze until firm.

7. Spread whipped topping over top of pie. Cover and freeze until firm.

8. Cut pie into 10 slices. Drizzle each slice of pie with 1 tablespoon chocolate syrup, and top with a cherry. YIELD: 10 servings (serving size: 1 slice).

POINTS: 6; EXCHANGES: 4 Starch, 1 Fat;
PER SERVING: CAL 305 (17% from fat); PRO 5.3g;
FAT 5.7g (sat 3.3g); CARB 57.4g; FIB 1.5g;
CHOL 34mg; IRON 1.2mg; SOD 160mg;
CALC 114mg

LEMON MERINGUE PIE

(pictured on page 47)

Cooking spray
½ (15-ounce) package refrigerated
  piecrust dough
1¾ cups sugar, divided
6 tablespoons cornstarch
1 cup water
⅓ cup fresh lemon juice
1 large egg yolk, lightly beaten
2 tablespoons light butter
¼ teaspoon grated lemon rind
4 large egg whites
¼ teaspoon cream of tartar

1. Preheat oven to 450°.

2. Fit dough into a 9-inch pieplate coated with cooking spray. Fold edges; flute. Pierce bottom and sides of dough with a fork. Place crust in freezer 10 minutes. Bake at 450° for 10 minutes or until lightly browned. Cool completely on a wire rack. Reduce temperature to 325°.

3. To prepare filling, combine 1¼ cups sugar and cornstarch in a medium nonaluminum saucepan. Stir in water and lemon juice. Bring to a boil over medium-high heat. Cook until thick and bubbly (about 2 minutes), stirring constantly with a whisk.

4. Gradually stir about one-fourth of hot cornstarch mixture into egg yolk, stirring constantly with a whisk; add to remaining cornstarch mixture, stirring constantly. Cook until thick and bubbly (about 1 minute), stirring constantly. Stir in butter and lemon rind. Pour mixture into prepared crust; cover surface with plastic wrap.

5. To prepare meringue, beat egg whites and cream of tartar with a mixer at high speed until foamy. Gradually add ½ cup sugar, 1 tablespoon at a time, beating until stiff peaks form. (Do not overbeat.)

6. Remove plastic wrap from filling; spread meringue evenly over filling, sealing to edge of crust. Bake at 325° for 25 minutes; cool on a wire rack 1 hour. Serve at room temperature. YIELD: 8 servings (serving size: 1 slice).

POINTS: 7; EXCHANGES: 4 Starch, 1 Fat;
PER SERVING: CAL 304 (21% from fat); PRO 3.1g;
FAT 7.3g (sat 2.9g); CARB 58.2g; FIB 0.3g;
CHOL 32mg; IRON 0.5mg; SOD 149mg;
CALC 9mg

PEACH PIE WITH SUGARED OAT TOPPING

(pictured on page 50)

½ (15-ounce) package refrigerated piecrusts
⅔ cup packed brown sugar, divided
3 tablespoons all-purpose flour
½ teaspoon ground cinnamon
7 cups peeled fresh peach slices or 2 (1-pound) bags frozen peach slices, thawed
½ cup regular oats
2 tablespoons light butter

1. Preheat oven to 425°.
2. Fit dough into a 9-inch pieplate. Fold edges under; flute.
3. Combine ⅓ cup brown sugar, flour, and cinnamon in a bowl. Sprinkle over peaches; toss gently. Spoon into crust.
4. Combine ⅓ cup brown sugar, oats, and butter; sprinkle over peach mixture. Bake at 425° for 10 minutes. Reduce oven temperature to 375°; shield edges of crust with foil, and bake an additional 25 minutes or until golden. Cool on a wire rack. YIELD: 8 servings (serving size: 1 slice).

POINTS: 6; **EXCHANGES:** 2½ Starch, 1 Fruit, 2 Fat; **PER SERVING:** CAL 296 (29% from fat); PRO 3.4g; FAT 9.8g (sat 2.2g); CARB 51.8g; FIB 3.8g; CHOL 5mg; IRON 1mg; SOD 178mg; CALC 33mg

WARM FRESH APPLE CAKE

¼ cup butter or stick margarine, softened
¾ cup packed brown sugar
1 large egg, lightly beaten
1½ cups all-purpose flour
1 teaspoon baking soda
1 teaspoon ground cinnamon
½ teaspoon salt
½ teaspoon ground nutmeg
2 medium Golden Delicious or Granny Smith apples, peeled and shredded
Cooking spray
¼ cup packed brown sugar
2 tablespoons chopped pecans

1. Preheat oven to 350°.
2. Beat butter with a mixer at medium speed until creamy; add ¾ cup brown sugar, beating well. Add egg, beating just until blended.
3. Lightly spoon flour into dry measuring cups; level with a knife. Combine flour and next 4 ingredients; gradually add to butter mixture. (Batter will be stiff.) Add apples, beating just until combined.
4. Spoon batter into an 8-inch square baking pan coated with cooking spray. Combine ¼ cup brown sugar and pecans; sprinkle over batter. Bake at 350° for 32 to 35 minutes or until a wooden pick inserted in center comes out clean. YIELD: 10 servings (serving size: 1 square).

POINTS: 5; **EXCHANGES:** 2½ Starch, 1 Fat; **PER SERVING:** CAL 225 (25% from fat); PRO 2.8g; FAT 6.5g (sat 3.2g); CARB 39.9g; FIB 1.3g; CHOL 34mg; IRON 1.5mg; SOD 304mg; CALC 30mg

FIG SPICE CAKE

¾ cup dried figs, finely chopped
3 tablespoons fresh orange juice
1 teaspoon grated orange rind
2 cups sifted cake flour
1 teaspoon baking powder
1 teaspoon ground cinnamon
½ teaspoon baking soda
½ teaspoon ground nutmeg
⅛ teaspoon salt
⅛ teaspoon ground allspice
1 cup packed brown sugar
1 cup low-fat buttermilk
¼ cup vegetable oil
2 large eggs, lightly beaten
Cooking spray
¾ cup sifted powdered sugar
½ teaspoon grated orange rind
4 teaspoons fresh orange juice

1. Preheat oven to 350°.
2. Combine first 3 ingredients in a small bowl; let stand while preparing cake batter.
3. Lightly spoon flour into dry measuring cups; level with a knife. Combine flour and next 6 ingredients. Combine brown sugar, buttermilk, oil, and eggs. Gradually add flour mixture to buttermilk mixture, beating with a mixer at low speed until blended. Stir in figs and any juices remaining in bowl.
4. Spoon batter into a 13 x 9-inch baking pan coated with cooking spray. Bake at 350° for 25 minutes or until a wooden pick inserted in center comes out clean. Cool completely in pan on a wire rack.
5. Combine powdered sugar, ½ teaspoon orange rind, and 4 teaspoons fresh orange juice.

Drizzle over cake. YIELD: 16 servings (serving size: 1 square).

POINTS: 4; EXCHANGES: 2 Starch, ½ Fruit, 1 Fat; PER SERVING: CAL 190 (21% from fat); PRO 2.7g; FAT 4.4g (sat 0.8g); CARB 36.1g; FIB 1.4g; CHOL 28mg; IRON 1.5mg; SOD 119mg; CALC 66mg

QUICK GINGERBREAD-PINEAPPLE CAKE

1 (15.25-ounce) can sliced pineapple in juice, undrained
1 tablespoon butter, melted
¼ cup packed brown sugar
1 (14.5-ounce) package ginger-bread cake and cookie mix
2 egg whites

1. Preheat oven to 350°.
2. Drain pineapple, reserving juice. Add enough water to juice to equal ¾ cup; set aside. Pat pineapple slices dry.
3. Coat a 9-inch round cake pan with melted butter; sprinkle with brown sugar. Arrange pineapple slices on top of brown sugar.
4. Combine pineapple juice mixture, cake mix, and egg whites; stir with a fork 1 minute. Pour batter into prepared cake pan.
5. Bake at 350° for 40 minutes or until a wooden pick inserted in center comes out clean. Cool in pan 5 minutes on a wire rack. Loosen cake from sides of pan, using a narrow metal spatula. Invert cake onto a serving plate. Cut into wedges. YIELD: 8 servings (serving size: 1 wedge).

POINTS: 6; EXCHANGES: 3 Starch, ½ Fruit, 1 Fat; PER SERVING: CAL 284 (22% from fat); PRO 4g; FAT 6.9g (sat 2.3g); CARB 52.4g; FIB 1.1g; CHOL 4mg; IRON 2.3mg; SOD 406mg; CALC 79mg

GLAZED LEMON LOAF CAKE

The sweetness and texture of this cake are similar to those of a traditional pound cake.

Cooking spray
1 tablespoon all-purpose flour
1¾ cups all-purpose flour
1 teaspoon baking powder
¼ teaspoon baking soda
⅛ teaspoon salt
5 tablespoons butter, softened
1 cup sugar
2 teaspoons grated lemon rind
1 teaspoon vanilla extract
1 large egg
2 large egg whites
1 (8-ounce) carton plain fat-free yogurt
3 tablespoons sugar
¼ cup fresh lemon juice

1. Preheat oven to 350°.
2. Coat bottom and sides of an 8-inch loaf pan with cooking spray; dust with 1 tablespoon flour, discarding any excess flour. Set aside.
3. Spoon 1¾ cups flour into dry measuring cups; level with a knife. Stir together flour, baking powder, baking soda, and salt.
4. Beat butter, sugar, lemon rind, vanilla, egg, and egg whites with a mixer at medium speed until smooth. Add flour mixture, alternately with yogurt and beginning and ending with flour mixture; beat well after each addition. Pour into prepared pan, spreading evenly.
5. Bake at 350° for 55 to 60 minutes or until a wooden pick inserted in center comes out clean. Place cake on wire rack.

6. Stir together 3 tablespoons sugar and lemon juice. Spoon mixture over hot cake. Cool 20 minutes. Remove from pan. Cool completely on wire rack. YIELD: 12 servings (serving size: 1 slice).

POINTS: 4; EXCHANGES: 2½ Starch, 1 Fat; PER SERVING: CAL 205 (23% from fat); PRO 3.9g; FAT 5.4g (sat 3.2g); CARB 36g; FIB 0.6g; CHOL 31mg; IRON 1mg; SOD 166mg; CALC 55mg

DESSERT DILEMMA

Many view their sweet tooth as their obstacle to successful weight loss. So, why even include a desserts chapter in a weight-loss cookbook? The answer has to do with balance and moderation. No foods are "good" or "bad"—some should just be consumed less frequently than others. Extremely restrictive diets that deny favorite foods may only intensify food cravings and make those foods even more irresistible. These feelings can lead to binges and overeating.

Every food can fit into the Weight Watchers plan—even desserts. The key is moderation and portion control. Make sure the slice of cake you cut is the actual suggested serving size. Also, be ready to fight the urge to eat more; don't let sweets sit out on the counter to tempt you. With moderation, indulging your sweet tooth periodically won't prevent weight loss; in fact, it may even help by lessening those destructive food cravings.

DOUBLE CHOCOLATE BUNDT CAKE

(pictured on page 46)

Cooking spray
  ½ cup unsweetened cocoa
  2 ounces sweet baking chocolate
  ½ cup boiling water
1½ cups granulated sugar
  ⅓ cup light butter, softened
  2 teaspoons vanilla extract
  2 large egg whites
  2 cups all-purpose flour
  2 teaspoons baking powder
  ½ teaspoon baking soda
  ½ teaspoon salt
  1 cup low-fat buttermilk
  1 teaspoon instant coffee granules
  1 ounce milk chocolate bar, melted (such as Hershey's)
  1 tablespoon fat-free milk
  ¼ cup powdered sugar
  2 teaspoons fat-free milk

1. Preheat oven to 325°.
2. Coat a 12-cup Bundt pan with cooking spray. Combine cocoa and baking chocolate in a small bowl; add boiling water, stirring until chocolate melts.
3. Beat granulated sugar and butter with a mixer at medium speed until well blended (about 5 minutes). Add vanilla and egg whites, 1 at a time, beating well after each addition. Lightly spoon flour into dry measuring cups; level with a knife. Combine flour and next 3 ingredients in a large bowl, stirring well with a whisk. Combine buttermilk and coffee granules, stirring until granules are dissolved. Add flour mixture to sugar mixture, alternating with buttermilk mixture, beginning and ending with flour mixture. Stir

in cocoa mixture. Spoon batter into prepared pan.
4. Bake at 325° for 1 hour or until a wooden pick inserted in center comes out clean. Cool 10 minutes; remove from pan. Cool on a wire rack.
5. To prepare glaze, combine melted chocolate bar and milk in a small bowl, stirring until smooth. Drizzle chocolate glaze over cake. Combine powdered sugar and milk in a small bowl, stirring well with a whisk. Drizzle glaze over cake. YIELD: 10 servings (serving size: 1 slice).

POINTS: 6; **EXCHANGES:** 4 Starch, 1 Fat; **PER SERVING:** CAL 316 (18% from fat); PRO 6.2g; FAT 6.7g (sat 4g); CARB 61.5g; FIB 2.2g; CHOL 12mg; IRON 1.9mg; SOD 360mg; CALC 110mg

MOLASSES ANGEL FOOD CAKE WITH LEMON SAUCE

(pictured on page 50)

Lemon Sauce
  1 cup sifted cake flour
  ½ cup packed brown sugar
  1 teaspoon ground ginger
  ½ teaspoon salt
 11 large egg whites
1¼ teaspoons cream of tartar
  ⅔ cup granulated sugar
  ¼ cup molasses
  1 teaspoon vanilla extract

1. Prepare Lemon Sauce; set aside.
2. Preheat oven to 350°.
3. Lightly spoon flour into a dry measuring cup; level with a knife. Sift together flour and next 3 ingredients.
4. Beat egg whites until foamy. Add cream of tartar; beat until soft peaks form. Add sugar, 2 tablespoons at a time, beating until stiff peaks form.

Slowly pour in molasses, beating egg white mixture until sugar dissolves. Fold in flour mixture over egg white mixture, ¼ cup at a time. Add vanilla.
5. Spoon batter into an ungreased 10-inch tube pan, spreading evenly. Break air pockets by cutting through batter with a knife. Bake at 350° for 35 to 38 minutes or until cake springs back when lightly touched. Invert cake pan; cool completely. Loosen cake from sides of pan, using a narrow metal spatula. Invert cake onto plate. Serve with Lemon Sauce. YIELD: 12 servings (serving size: 1 slice cake and 1 tablespoon sauce).

POINTS: 5; **EXCHANGES:** 3 Starch; **PER SERVING:** CAL 237 (9% from fat); PRO 5.6g; FAT 2.4g (sat 1.4g); CARB 48.9g; FIB 0.2g; CHOL 27mg; IRON 1.5mg; SOD 218mg; CALC 37mg

LEMON SAUCE

  ½ cup granulated sugar
  ¼ cup fat-free half-and-half
  1 large egg, lightly beaten
  3 tablespoons light butter or margarine
  2 tablespoons fresh lemon juice
  ½ teaspoon grated lemon rind

1. Combine first 3 ingredients in a small saucepan. Cook over medium heat until sugar dissolves, stirring constantly with a whisk. Add butter and lemon juice; cook over low heat, stirring constantly, just until mixture coats the back of a spoon (about 160°). Remove from heat; stir in lemon rind. Serve at room temperature or chilled. (Mixture thickens as it cools.) YIELD: ¾ cup.

POINTS: 1; **EXCHANGES:** ½ Starch, ½ Fat; **PER TABLESPOON:** CAL 55 (30% from fat); PRO 0.8g; FAT 1.9g (sat 1.1g); CARB 9.1g; FIB 0g; CHOL 23mg; IRON 0.1mg; SOD 28mg; CALC 6mg

A Name That Fits

LYDIA PRIEST • **HEIGHT** 5'8" • **BEFORE** 213 LBS. • **AFTER** 135 LBS.

Happiest moment: "On a silent retreat in July 1999, a woman came up to me and said she couldn't help talking—she had to tell me how beautiful I was. I'd never been called beautiful before."

Lydia Priest's grandchildren were the reason she joined Weight Watchers. "They called me Big Meema, and I didn't care for that," she explains. At the time, Lydia weighed 213 pounds. Then Lydia's health insurance company sent her a notice offering to pay for eight weeks of Weight Watchers.

"When I got there it was comforting to meet women my age who were all similarly overweight," says Lydia.

Lydia had steadily gained weight during her adult life. Although a glass of wine with dinner wasn't bad in and of itself, it relaxed Lydia's willpower and her portions steadily grew in size. "I'd say, 'I can eat those fries, and then I won't eat anything for three days.' Except, I'd never do it," she recalls. Lydia's Weight Watchers leader taught her how to make progress, not excuses.

"Meetings, exercise, and journal keeping are vital to keeping me on track."

As she kept an eye on what she ate, Lydia realized that when she baked for her grandchildren, she licked the bowl herself, consuming 15 calories per spoonful. She stopped that. Now, when she bakes, she fills the bowl with soapy water immediately so she won't lick it. Lydia also curbs her appetite by eating something every three hours, instead of three meals a day.

"I lost 5 pounds the first week and none the next two weeks," says Lydia. "It was good to go to meetings and learn that was normal." Lydia, who suffered a stroke at 30, had always eschewed exercise. The depression and self-consciousness she felt as a result of her disabilities kept her out of the gym. But the promise of weight loss was a strong motivator, so Lydia added exercise to her daily routine.

Her grandchildren soon saw the difference. "They changed my nickname to Meema," Lydia says. Then she lost even more weight. "Now it's Skinny Meema." And the name fits. A year after joining Weight Watchers, Lydia reached her goal weight. She rewarded herself with new clothes. "When I was fat, clothes didn't look good," she says. "Now I buy clothes at thrift stores and people say I look elegant."

But losing weight isn't just about looking good for Lydia. The charley horse she used to get in her leg at night is gone. She no longer has to stop to catch her breath and can't remember the last time she had heartburn.

Maintaining her weight isn't always easy. Lydia says, "Meetings, exercise, and journal keeping are vital to keeping me on track."

Lydia's contemplative walks help her think of ideas for poetry and have given her the confidence to write fiction. "If I can lose all of that weight, I can do more, even become a writer."

Double
Chocolate Bundt
Cake, page 44

Peanut Butter
S'mores Bars,
page 56

Lemon
Meringue Pie,
page 41

Frozen Peanut
Butter Brittle
Pie, page 40

Summer
Berry Crisp,
page 53

Chocolate
Raspberry Crêpes,
page 38

Frozen Chocolate
Decadence Brownies,
page 40

Brown Sugar
Icebox Cookies,
page 55

Molasses Angel
Food Cake with
Lemon Sauce,
page 44

Peach Pie with
Sugared Oat Topping,
page 42

Strawberry-
Merlot Ice,
page 40

A Healthful Hobby

KAREN SIMPSON • **HEIGHT** 5'6" • **BEFORE** 196 LBS. • **AFTER** 155 LBS.

Tip: "Our leader suggested that we find a hobby that would absorb our attention. For me, it was becoming more involved as a horse owner."

The festival of Kwanza is an occasion to set goals for the coming year and to think seriously about physical and spiritual well-being. In 1996, Karen Simpson vowed to accomplish two things she didn't think she could do: lose weight and buy a racehorse. "Both seemed impossible," Karen recalls. "Losing weight needed discipline I thought I didn't have, and owning a horse required money that wasn't in my budget."

Karen had dreamed about owning a horse since childhood. She surfed the Web and found an organization that offers partnership shares in racehorses. She also visited the Weight Watchers site. "When the scale neared 200 pounds, I had to do something," says Karen. "Like many African-Americans, I have a family history of diabetes and high blood pressure." Karen was resolved not to suffer the same fate.

Karen thinks she became overweight because she was bored. "I didn't have hobbies or anything to concentrate on. There were things I wanted to do, and I didn't do them," she says. "I became frustrated and ate instead." Through Weight Watchers, Karen learned to downsize the importance of food, making room for other passions. "It wasn't as hard as I thought it would be to change my thinking," says Karen. "I learned to refocus."

Becoming part owner of a 2-year-old filly motivated her to reach the weight-loss winner's circle. "Like a racehorse, I had to eat high-fiber grains and vegetables, drink all my water, and exercise."

Karen also made sure her diet had variety; she tried foods such as couscous and jícama and learned to prepare traditional foods with less fat. "I cooked collard greens using chicken broth and made sweet potatoes West African style, with juices of orange and lemon instead of sugar."

Karen also began walking, running, and cycling—"things I could just step outside and do," she says. "I felt better and had more energy.

> *"The pounds didn't come off fast, but the inches did."*

The pounds didn't come off fast, but the inches did. My clothes fit better."

Karen is enjoying her new perspective. "I learned how to lose weight," she says. "But more importantly, I learned that food isn't my life." The year 2000 was challenging for Karen. "Before, I would have overeaten," she says. "But I maintained my weight. The habits I learned in Weight Watchers served me well."

Weight-loss results not typical.

APPLE-BERRY COBBLER

Turbinado sugar adds a decorative, crystal effect to the cobbler because of its large, clear sugar granules.

1½ pounds Granny Smith apples, peeled and thinly sliced
2 cups fresh blackberries
¾ cup sugar
3 tablespoons cornstarch
1 tablespoon fresh lemon juice
1 teaspoon vanilla extract
¼ teaspoon ground cinnamon
Cooking spray
½ (15-ounce) package refrigerated piecrust
2 teaspoons fat-free milk
2 teaspoons turbinado sugar or granulated sugar

1. Preheat oven to 375°.
2. Combine first 7 ingredients in a large bowl. Spoon mixture into a 9-inch deep-dish pieplate coated with cooking spray.
3. Place piecrust on top of apple mixture. Fold edges under; flute. Cut 5 (1-inch) slits into top of pastry using a sharp knife. Brush top and edges of pie with milk; sprinkle with sugar. Bake at 375° for 40 minutes or until golden. Cool on a wire rack. YIELD: 8 servings (serving size: 1 slice).

POINTS: 4; **EXCHANGES:** 2 Starch, 1 Fruit, 1 Fat; **PER SERVING:** CAL 223 (21% from fat); PRO 1.1g; FAT 5.5g (sat 0.8g); CARB 43.9g; FIB 3.2g; CHOL 0mg; IRON 0.6mg; SOD 103mg; CALC 18mg

SUMMER BERRY CRISP

(pictured on page 48)
Most of the items in this recipe are sitting in your pantry.

2 cups fresh blueberries
2 cups halved strawberries
½ cup sugar
⅓ cup all-purpose flour
½ teaspoon ground nutmeg
½ teaspoon vanilla extract
⅛ teaspoon salt
Butter-flavored cooking spray
½ cup all-purpose flour
½ cup quick-cooking oats
⅓ cup sugar
⅓ cup packed brown sugar
½ teaspoon ground cinnamon
¼ cup chilled butter or stick margarine, cut into small pieces
2 cups vanilla fat-free ice cream

1. Preheat oven to 375°.
2. Combine first 7 ingredients in a medium bowl; toss well. Spoon into an 8-inch square baking dish coated with cooking spray.
3. Lightly spoon ½ cup flour into dry measuring cup; level with a knife. Combine flour, oats, ⅓ cup sugar, brown sugar, and cinnamon in a medium bowl; cut in butter with a pastry blender or 2 knives until mixture resembles coarse meal. Spoon over berry mixture; coat top with cooking spray.
4. Bake at 375° for 40 minutes or until topping is golden and filling is bubbly. Serve warm topped with ice cream. YIELD: 8 servings (serving size ½ cup crisp and ¼ cup ice cream).

POINTS: 6; **EXCHANGES:** 3 Starch, 1 Fruit, 1 Fat; **PER SERVING:** CAL 319 (19% from fat); PRO 4.2g; FAT 6.8g (sat 3.7g); CARB 62.5g; FIB 2.8g; CHOL 16mg; IRON 1.2mg; SOD 124mg; CALC 63mg

ALMOND-PEACH CRISP

Fresh peaches may be substituted for frozen. Use 2⅔ cups in place of the frozen package.

Butter-flavored cooking spray
1 (16-ounce) package frozen sliced peaches, thawed
¼ cup sugar
1 teaspoon vanilla extract
¼ cup unbleached flour
½ cup quick-cooking oats
¼ cup sugar
¼ cup packed brown sugar
1 teaspoon baking powder
1 teaspoon cinnamon
2 tablespoons reduced-calorie margarine
1 large egg white
¼ teaspoon almond extract
2 tablespoons sliced almonds

1. Preheat oven to 350°.
2. Coat an 8-inch square pan with cooking spray. Add peaches, and sprinkle with ¼ cup sugar and vanilla; stir gently.
3. Lightly spoon flour into a dry measuring cup; level with a knife. Combine flour and next 5 ingredients in a bowl; cut in margarine with a pastry blender until mixture is crumbly. Stir in egg white, almond extract, and sliced almonds. Dollop flour mixture over peach mixture. Coat lightly with cooking spray.
4. Bake at 350° for 45 minutes or until lightly golden. YIELD: 5 servings (serving size: ½ cup).

POINTS: 4; **EXCHANGES:** 2 Starch, 1 Fruit, 1 Fat; **PER SERVING:** CAL 219 (18% from fat); PRO 3.1g; FAT 4.4g (sat 0.7g); CARB 42g; FIB 1.4g; CHOL 0mg; IRON 1mg; SOD 168mg; CALC 81mg

CRUNCHY PEAR-BERRY GRANOLA CRISP

Using a granola cereal for the crisp's topping makes this a speedy dessert.

4 cups sliced peeled pear (about 3)
½ cup dried cranberries
3 tablespoons dark brown sugar
1 tablespoon cornstarch
1 tablespoon lemon juice
½ teaspoon vanilla extract
Butter-flavored cooking spray
2 cups low-fat granola cereal without raisins (such as Healthy Choice)

1. Preheat oven to 400°.
2. Combine first 6 ingredients in a large bowl; toss well. Spoon mixture into a 9-inch pieplate coated with cooking spray.
3. Top fruit mixture with granola; coat granola generously with cooking spray. Bake at 400° or until fruit is tender and topping is lightly browned. YIELD: 8 servings (serving size: ½ cup).

POINTS: 3; EXCHANGES: 2 Starch, 1 Fruit;
PER SERVING: CAL 184 (10% from fat); PRO 2.3g;
FAT 2.1g (sat 0.3g); CARB 41.3g; FIB 3.5g;
CHOL 0mg; IRON 1.2mg; SOD 62mg; CALC 23mg

SCANDINAVIAN RICE PUDDING WITH TOASTED ALMONDS

An easy way to toast almonds is to place them in a nonstick skillet over medium heat for 2 to 3 minutes or until lightly browned, stirring the nuts constantly.

2 cups cooked brown rice
2 cups 1% low-fat milk
1 large egg, lightly beaten
2 tablespoons sugar
2 teaspoons vanilla extract
½ teaspoon almond extract
¼ teaspoon salt
⅛ teaspoon ground cardamom
⅓ cup golden raisins
4 teaspoons sliced almonds, toasted

1. Combine rice and milk in a large saucepan; bring to a boil. Reduce heat, and simmer, uncovered, 10 minutes, stirring occasionally, until slightly thick.
2. Combine egg and next 5 ingredients. Stir about 1 cup hot rice mixture into egg mixture.
3. Add to remaining hot mixture in pan, and cook 5 minutes, stirring constantly, until mixture thickens. Stir in raisins. Sprinkle with almonds just before serving. Serve warm. YIELD: 5 servings (serving size: ½ cup).

POINTS: 4; EXCHANGES: 2 Starch, ½ Milk;
PER SERVING: CAL 208 (16% from fat); PRO 7.2g;
FAT 3.7g (sat 1.2g); CARB 36g; FIB 2g;
CHOL 46mg; IRON 0.8mg; SOD 184mg;
CALC 142mg

BREAD PUDDING WITH RUM-RAISIN CARAMEL SAUCE

Rum-Raisin Caramel Sauce
3 tablespoons light butter, melted
1 (10-ounce) French bread baguette, cut into 1-inch thick slices
1¾ cups 1% low-fat milk
1 cup sugar
1 tablespoon vanilla extract
1 (12-ounce) can evaporated fat-free milk
2 large eggs, lightly beaten
½ cup raisins
Cooking spray

1. Prepare Rum-Raisin Caramel Sauce; set aside.
2. Preheat oven to 350°.
3. Brush butter on one side of French bread slices; place bread, buttered side up, on a baking sheet. Bake at 350° for 10 minutes until lightly toasted. Cut into ½-inch cubes; set aside.
4. Combine 1% milk and next 4 ingredients in a large bowl; stir well with a whisk. Add bread and raisins to mixture, pressing gently to moisten; let stand 15 minutes. Spoon bread mixture into a 13 x 9-inch baking dish coated with cooking spray. Bake at 350° for 35 minutes or until set. Serve warm with Rum-Raisin Caramel Sauce. YIELD: 12 servings (serving size: about ½ cup pudding and 1 tablespoon sauce).

POINTS: 6; EXCHANGES: 3½ Starch, 1 Fat;
PER SERVING: CAL 283 (12% from fat); PRO 7.4g;
FAT 4g (sat 2g); CARB 52.4g; FIB 1.1g;
CHOL 47mg; IRON 1.1mg; SOD 250mg;
CALC 176mg

RUM-RAISIN CARAMEL SAUCE

⅓ cup evaporated fat-free milk
1 tablespoon cornstarch
½ cup packed brown sugar
¼ cup dark rum
2 tablespoons light butter
¼ cup raisins

1. Combine milk and cornstarch in a 2-quart saucepan, stirring well with a whisk until cornstarch dissolves. Add sugar and rum; stir well. Place pan over medium-high heat; bring to a boil. Cook, stirring constantly, 2 minutes. Remove from heat; cool slightly. Add butter and raisins; stir well. YIELD: ¾ cup.

POINTS: 1; **EXCHANGE:** 1 Starch;
PER TABLESPOON: CAL 66 (13% from fat);
PRO 0.7g; FAT 1g (sat 0.7g); CARB 12.8g; FIB 0.1g;
CHOL 4mg; IRON 0.2mg, SOD 25mg; CALC 27mg

THE SKINNY ON MILK

🍴🥄

Nothing's better with a dessert than a cold glass of milk. But what if you really don't care for skim milk? Because skim milk has no fat, it has a thinner consistency that some may think tastes watery. If you don't like skim milk, 1% fat milk is definitely your next best choice. Skim and 1% milks actually have the same amounts of protein, calcium, iron, and potassium. Their only difference is that 1% milk has slightly more fat, with 3 grams of fat per cup (while skim milk has 0 grams of fat per cup).

GINGERBREAD-RAISIN COOKIES

¾ cups all-purpose flour
½ teaspoon baking soda
1 teaspoon ground cinnamon
1 teaspoon ground ginger
⅛ teaspoon ground cloves
5 tablespoons stick margarine or butter, softened
½ cup sugar
⅓ cup packed dark brown sugar
3 tablespoons molasses
1 large egg
½ cup golden raisins
Cooking spray

1. Preheat oven to 350°.
2. Lightly spoon flour into dry measuring cups; level with a knife. Combine flour and next 4 ingredients, whisking well.
3. Place margarine, sugars, molasses, and egg in a large mixing bowl; beat with a mixer at medium speed until blended. Gradually stir in flour mixture and raisins.
4. Drop batter by rounded teaspoonfuls 1½ inches apart on baking sheets coated with cooking spray. Bake at 350° for 8 to 9 minutes or until lightly browned. Remove from baking sheets; cool completely on wire racks. YIELD: 39 cookies (serving size: 1 cookie).

POINTS: 1; **EXCHANGE:** ½ Starch; **PER SERVING:**
CAL 63 (24% from fat); PRO 0.8g; FAT 1.7g (sat 1g);
CARB 11.3g; FIB 0.3g; CHOL 9mg; IRON 0.4mg;
SOD 34mg; CALC 8mg

BROWN SUGAR ICEBOX COOKIES

(pictured on page 50)

1 cup all-purpose flour
¼ teaspoon baking soda
⅛ teaspoon salt
¼ cup stick margarine, softened
⅔ cup packed brown sugar
1 teaspoon vanilla extract
1 large egg white
Cooking spray

1. Combine first 3 ingredients in a bowl.
2. Beat margarine at medium speed of an electric mixer until light and fluffy. Gradually add sugar, beating until well blended. Add vanilla and egg white; beat well. Add flour mixture, and stir until well blended. Turn dough out onto wax paper; shape into a 6-inch log. Wrap log in wax paper; freeze 3 hours or until very firm.
3. Preheat oven to 350°.
4. Cut log into 24 (¼-inch) slices, and place slices 1 inch apart on a baking sheet coated with cooking spray. Bake at 350° for 8 to 10 minutes. Remove from sheet; cool on wire racks. YIELD: 2 dozen (serving size: 1 cookie).

POINTS: 1; **EXCHANGES:** ½ Starch, ½ Fat;
PER SERVING: CAL 60 (30% from fat); PRO 0.7g;
FAT 2g (sat 0.4g); CARB 10g; FIB 0.1g; CHOL 0mg;
IRON 0.4mg, SOD 52mg; CALC 7mg

ALMOND BISCOTTI

Biscotti is an Italian cookie that is baked as a loaf, sliced, and then baked again. Dip this extracrunchy cookie into coffee or warm milk.

¾ cup sugar
1 teaspoon vanilla extract
2 large eggs, lightly beaten
2 cups all-purpose flour
¾ cup slivered almonds, chopped and toasted
½ cup golden raisins
1¾ teaspoons baking powder
¼ teaspoon salt
Cooking spray

1. Preheat oven to 350°.
2. Combine sugar, vanilla, and eggs in a large bowl; stir well with a whisk. Lightly spoon flour into dry measuring cups; level with a knife. Combine flour and next 4 ingredients. Gradually add flour mixture to sugar mixture, beating with a mixer at low speed until a dry dough forms.
3. Turn dough out onto a lightly floured surface; knead lightly 7 or 8 times. Divide dough in half. Shape each portion into a 13-inch-long roll. Place rolls on a baking sheet coated with cooking spray; flatten to 1-inch thickness.
4. Bake at 350° for 20 minutes. Remove rolls from baking sheet; cool 10 minutes on a wire rack. Cut each roll into 18 (½-inch) slices. Place slices, cut sides down, on baking sheet.
5. Reduce oven temperature to 300°. Bake cookies 10 minutes. Turn cookies; bake an additional 10 minutes. Remove from baking sheet; cool completely on wire rack. YIELD: 3 dozen (serving size: 1 biscotto).

POINTS: 1; **EXCHANGE:** 1 Starch; **PER SERVING:** CAL 62 (17% from fat); PRO 1.5g; FAT 1.2g (sat 0.1g); CARB 11.6g; FIB 0.5g; CHOL 0mg; IRON 0.5mg; SOD 43mg; CALC 21mg

PEANUT BUTTER S'MORES BARS

(pictured on page 47)

1 cup packed brown sugar
½ cup reduced-fat peanut butter
2 tablespoons butter, softened
½ teaspoon vanilla extract
2 large egg whites
1½ cups self-rising flour
Cooking spray
1 (7-ounce) jar marshmallow creme
¼ cup chopped roasted peanuts
⅔ cup semisweet chocolate chips

1. Preheat oven to 350°.
2. Combine first 5 ingredients in a mixing bowl; beat with a mixer at medium speed until combined. Lightly spoon flour into dry measuring cups; level with a knife. Stir in flour.
3. Press mixture into a 13 x 9-inch pan coated with cooking spray. Spread marshmallow creme over dough. Sprinkle evenly with peanuts and chocolate chips.
4. Bake at 350° for 20 to 22 minutes or until lightly browned. Cool completely. YIELD: 28 servings (serving size: 1 bar).

POINTS: 3; **EXCHANGES:** 1½ Starch, 1 Fat; **PER SERVING:** CAL 135 (27% from fat); PRO 2.7g; FAT 4.3g (sat 1.6g); CARB 22.8g; FIB 0.8g; CHOL 2mg; IRON 0.7mg; SOD 138mg; CALC 34mg

RASPBERRY-LEMON SQUARES

¾ cup all-purpose flour
3 tablespoons sugar
⅛ teaspoon ground nutmeg
¼ cup butter or stick margarine
⅔ cup sugar
⅓ cup egg substitute
3 tablespoons fresh lemon juice
2 teaspoons grated lemon rind
¼ teaspoon baking powder
3 tablespoons seedless raspberry spread (such as Polaner All Fruit)
1 tablespoon powdered sugar

1. Preheat oven to 350°.
2. Lightly spoon flour into dry measuring cups; level with a knife. Combine flour, 3 tablespoons sugar, and nutmeg in a small bowl; cut in butter with a pastry blender or 2 knives until mixture resembles coarse meal. Firmly press mixture into bottom of an 8-inch square baking pan. Bake at 350° for 12 minutes.
3. While crust is baking, combine ⅔ cup sugar and next 4 ingredients, stirring with a whisk until blended. Remove crust from oven. Pour lemon mixture over warm crust.
4. Place fruit spread in a small microwave-safe bowl; microwave at HIGH 30 seconds or until melted. Drizzle over lemon mixture. Bake at 350° for 22 minutes or until very lightly browned around edges. Cool completely on a wire rack. Sift powdered sugar evenly over top. YIELD: 16 servings (serving size: 1 square).

POINTS: 2; **EXCHANGES:** 1 Starch, 1 Fat; **PER SERVING:** CAL 106 (26% from fat); FAT 3.1g (sat 1.8g); CARB 18.5g; FIB 0.2g; CHOL 8mg; IRON 0.5mg; SOD 46mg; CALC 10mg

Fish & Shellfish

PAN-SEARED SEA BASS WITH JALAPEÑO-LIME OIL

¾ teaspoon chili powder
½ teaspoon salt
½ teaspoon dried oregano
¼ teaspoon pepper
4 (6-ounce) sea bass fillets
½ teaspoon grated lime rind
3 tablespoons fresh lime juice
2 garlic cloves, minced
1 minced seeded jalapeño pepper
1½ tablespoons olive oil

1. Combine first 4 ingredients in a small bowl, stirring well. Rub evenly over fish. Cover and chill 10 minutes.
2. While fish chills, combine lime rind and lime juice in a small bowl; set aside. Combine garlic and jalapeño pepper in another small bowl; set aside.
3. Heat oil in a large nonstick skillet over high heat. Add fish; cook 6 minutes, turning often, or until fish flakes easily when tested with a fork and is brown on all sides. Place fish on serving platter.
4. Reduce heat to medium-high, and sauté garlic mixture 30 seconds. Remove from heat, and add lime juice mixture, stirring well; pour over fish. Serve immediately. YIELD: 4 servings (serving size: 1 fillet).

POINTS: 5; **EXCHANGES:** 4 Very Lean Meat, 1 Fat; **PER SERVING:** CAL 211 (37% from fat); PRO 30.4g; FAT 8.5g (sat 1.5g); CARB 1.8g; FIB 0.9g; CHOL 68mg; IRON 0.8mg; SOD 407mg; CALC 30mg

FLOUNDER FLORENTINE

Cooking spray
½ cup minced onion
2 garlic cloves, minced
1 (10-ounce) package frozen chopped spinach, thawed, drained, and squeezed dry
½ cup (4 ounces) tub-style light cream cheese
3 tablespoons grated fresh Parmesan cheese
2 tablespoons 1% low-fat milk
¼ teaspoon salt
¼ teaspoon black pepper
⅛ teaspoon ground red pepper
4 (6-ounce) flounder fillets

1. Heat a large nonstick skillet coated with cooking spray over medium heat. Add onion and garlic; sauté 3 minutes or until tender. Add spinach, and cook 1 minute.
2. Turn heat to low; add cream cheese and next 5 ingredients. Stir well; remove from heat.
3. Preheat oven to 350°.
4. Divide spinach mixture among fish fillets, spreading evenly over each and leaving a ¼-inch margin around edges.
5. Roll up each fillet, jelly-roll fashion, starting with the tail end, and secure with wooden picks.
6. Place fish in a 13 x 9-inch baking dish coated with cooking spray. Bake at 350° for 20 to 22 minutes or until fish flakes easily when tested with a fork. Serve immediately. YIELD: 4 servings (serving size: 1 fillet).

POINTS: 6; **EXCHANGES:** 1½ Vegetable, 4½ Very Lean Meat, ½ Medium-Fat Meat; **PER SERVING:** CAL 271 (30% from fat); PRO 38.4g; FAT 8.7g (sat 5g); CARB 7.7g; FIB 2.6g; CHOL 106mg; IRON 2mg; SOD 574mg; CALC 223mg

PECAN-CRUSTED GROUPER

¼ cup finely chopped pecans, toasted
2 tablespoons finely chopped onion
¾ teaspoon curry powder
¼ teaspoon salt
¼ teaspoon ground cumin
⅛ teaspoon ground red pepper
5 fat-free saltine crackers, crushed
1 garlic clove, minced
1 tablespoon butter, melted
½ teaspoon Worcestershire sauce
4 (6-ounce) grouper or perch fillets (½ inch thick)
Cooking spray

1. Preheat oven to 400°.
2. Combine first 8 ingredients in a bowl; stir well. Set aside. Combine melted butter and Worcestershire sauce.
3. Arrange fish on a jelly-roll pan coated with cooking spray. Spread ¾ teaspoon butter mixture on each fillet. Top with equal amounts of crust mixture, covering each piece entirely with crumbs.
4. Lightly coat tops of each fillet with cooking spray. Bake at 400° for 12 to 14 minutes or until fish flakes easily when tested with a fork. YIELD: 4 servings (serving size: 1 fillet).

POINTS: 6; **EXCHANGES:** ½ Starch, 5 Very Lean Meat, 1 Fat; **PER SERVING:** CAL 249 (36% from fat); PRO 33.1g; FAT 9.8g (sat 2.6g); CARB 6g; FIB 1.1g; CHOL 68mg; IRON 2.1mg; SOD 302mg; CALC 40mg

BREADED FISH ITALIAN STYLE

Tomato-Basil Relish
  4 (6-ounce) grouper or perch
    fillets (1 inch thick)
  ⅛ teaspoon salt
Cooking spray
  2 (1-ounce) slices white bread,
    toasted
  2 tablespoons chopped fresh basil
  1 tablespoon chopped fresh
    parsley
  1 tablespoon olive oil
  ¼ teaspoon salt
  ¼ teaspoon freshly ground black
    pepper
  2 garlic cloves, minced
  4 lemon wedges

1. Prepare Tomato-Basil Relish; set
aside.
2. Preheat oven to 425°.
3. Sprinkle fish with ⅛ teaspoon
salt; place on a baking sheet coated
with cooking spray.
4. Place bread in food processor;
process until coarsely ground.
Combine breadcrumbs, basil, and
next 5 ingredients in a small bowl.
Spoon breadcrumb mixture over
fish, pressing lightly to coat.
5. Bake at 425° for 15 minutes or
until fish flakes easily when tested
with a fork. Serve with Tomato-Basil
Relish and lemon wedges. YIELD:
4 servings (serving size: 1 fillet and
⅓ cup relish).

POINTS: 6; **EXCHANGES:** 1 Starch, 5 Very Lean
Meat, 1 Fat; **PER SERVING:** CAL 260 (32% from fat);
PRO 33.6g; FAT 9.1g (sat 1.3g); CARB 10.6g;
FIB 1.4g; CHOL 60mg; IRON 2.2mg; SOD 445mg;
CALC 51mg

TOMATO-BASIL RELISH
  1 tablespoon chopped fresh basil
  1 tablespoon olive oil
  1 tablespoon fresh lemon juice
  ¼ teaspoon freshly ground black
    pepper
  ⅛ teaspoon salt
  4 plum tomatoes, seeded and
    chopped
  1 garlic clove, minced

1. Combine all ingredients in a
bowl, tossing gently. YIELD: 4
servings (serving size: ⅓ cup).

QUICK FISH SUBSTITUTIONS

Can't find a particular fish?
Use this substitution list to
select another fish that has a
texture and flavor similar to the
one called for in the recipe.

Flounder: ocean perch,
orange roughy, sole

Grouper: halibut, sea bass,
snapper

Orange roughy: flounder, sole,
snapper, grouper

Perch: orange roughy, sole,
flounder

Salmon: swordfish, halibut,
trout, yellowtail tuna

Sea bass: grouper, halibut,
snapper

Snapper: sea bass, grouper,
redfish, pompano

HALIBUT FILLETS WITH TERIYAKI SAUCE

  ½ cup pineapple juice
  3 tablespoons low-sodium teriyaki
    sauce
  1 tablespoon honey
  ¾ teaspoon cornstarch
  ¼ teaspoon garlic powder
  ⅛ teaspoon ground red pepper
  2 tablespoons seasoned
    breadcrumbs
  4 (6-ounce) halibut fillets, skinned
    (about 1 inch thick)
  1 tablespoon vegetable oil

1. Combine first 6 ingredients in a
small bowl; stir well with a whisk.
2. Combine breadcrumbs and
halibut in a large zip-top plastic bag.
Seal and shake to coat.
3. Heat oil in a large nonstick skillet over medium heat. Add fish; cook
4 minutes on each side or until fish
flakes easily when tested with a fork.
Remove fish from pan; keep warm.
4. Add teriyaki mixture to pan.
Bring to a boil; cook, stirring constantly, 1 minute. Pour over fish.
YIELD: 4 servings (serving size:
1 fillet and 2 tablespoons sauce).

POINTS: 6; **EXCHANGES:** 1 Starch, 5 Very Lean
Meat; **PER SERVING:** CAL 280 (24% from fat);
PRO 36.9g; FAT 7.4g (sat 1.2g); CARB 14.1g;
FIB 0.1g; CHOL 80mg; IRON 1.9mg; SOD 304mg;
CALC 96mg

CAESAR MAHIMAHI

¼ cup plain fat-free yogurt
2 tablespoons grated Parmesan
  cheese
2 tablespoons fresh lemon juice
2 tablespoons low-fat buttermilk
1 tablespoon Dijon mustard
2 teaspoons Worcestershire sauce
2 teaspoons anchovy paste
¼ teaspoon pepper
6 garlic cloves, crushed
4 (6-ounce) mahimahi or other
  firm white fish fillets
Cooking spray

1. Combine first 9 ingredients, and
stir well with a whisk. Pour yogurt
mixture into a large zip-top plastic
bag, and add fish to bag. Seal and
marinate in refrigerator 20 minutes.
2. Prepare grill or broiler.
3. Remove fish from bag, reserving
marinade. Place fish on a grill rack
or broiler pan coated with cooking
spray, and cook 3 minutes on each
side or until fish flakes easily when
tested with a fork, basting frequently
with reserved marinade. YIELD: 4
servings (serving size: 1 fillet).

POINTS: 4; EXCHANGES: 4½ Very Lean Meat,
½ Skim Milk; PER SERVING: CAL 193 (14% from fat);
PRO 34.7g; FAT 3g (sat 0.8g); CARB 4.7g; FIB 0.1g;
CHOL 127mg; IRON 2.1mg; SOD 728mg;
CALC 84mg

GLAZED MAHIMAHI

3 tablespoons honey
3 tablespoons sherry vinegar
1 teaspoon minced peeled fresh
  ginger
4 garlic cloves, crushed
4 (6-ounce) mahimahi fillets
1½ teaspoons olive oil
¼ teaspoon salt
⅛ teaspoon freshly ground black
  pepper

1. Combine first 4 ingredients in a
shallow dish; stir well. Place fish in a
single layer over mixture in dish,
turning to coat. Cover and marinate
in refrigerator 20 minutes, turning
fish once. Remove fish from marinade, reserving marinade.
2. Heat oil in a nonstick skillet over
medium-high heat. Add fish, and
cook 6 minutes. Turn fish; sprinkle
with salt and pepper. Cook 3 minutes or until fish flakes easily when
tested with a fork. Remove from
pan; keep warm.
3. Add reserved marinade to pan;
cook over medium-high heat
1 minute, scraping pan to loosen
browned bits. Spoon glaze over fish.
YIELD: 4 servings (serving size:
1 fillet).

POINTS: 4; EXCHANGES: 1 Starch, 4½ Very Lean
Meat; PER SERVING: CAL 213 (12% from fat);
PRO 31.7g; FAT 2.9g (sat 0.6g); CARB 14.3g;
FIB 0.1g; CHOL 124mg; IRON 2.1mg;
SOD 297mg; CALC 33mg

OVEN-FRIED FISH

½ cup all-purpose flour
¼ teaspoon garlic powder
¼ teaspoon ground red pepper
¼ teaspoon black pepper
1 cup low-fat buttermilk
1 large egg
20 fat-free saltine crackers, coarsely
  crushed
1 teaspoon paprika
½ teaspoon salt, divided
4 (6-ounce) orange roughy fillets
2 tablespoons vegetable oil
4 lemon wedges

1. Preheat oven to 450°.
2. Combine first 4 ingredients in a
shallow bowl; stir well. Whisk
together buttermilk and egg in
another shallow bowl.
3. Combine cracker crumbs, paprika, and ¼ teaspoon salt on a small
platter.
4. Rinse fish; pat dry. Dredge fish in
flour mixture; then dip in buttermilk
mixture, and dredge in crumb
mixture.
5. Coat a jelly-roll pan evenly with
oil; place in oven 3 minutes or until
very hot. Remove pan from oven;
quickly place fish on pan.
6. Bake at 450° for 6 to 7 minutes on
each side or until fish flakes easily
when tested with a fork. Remove
from oven, and sprinkle with ¼ teaspoon salt. Serve immediately with
lemon wedges. YIELD: 4 servings (serving size: 1 fillet).

POINTS: 6; EXCHANGES: 1 Starch, 5 Very Lean
Meat, 1 Fat; PER SERVING: CAL 265 (31% from fat);
PRO 28.1g; FAT 8.9g (sat 1.1g); CARB 16.7g;
FIB 0.7g; CHOL 48mg; IRON 1.4mg; SOD 565mg;
CALC 70mg

CHILI-SEARED FISH WITH YUCATAN VEGETABLES

This colorful dish is full of zesty flavor and crisp vegetables. Try it rolled up in a whole wheat tortilla.

1 teaspoon seafood seasoning (such as Paul Prudhomme Seafood Magic)
½ teaspoon chili powder
4 (6-ounce) orange roughy fillets
Cooking spray
⅛ teaspoon salt
1 teaspoon olive oil
1 red bell pepper, thinly sliced
1 small onion, thinly sliced
1 cup frozen whole-kernel corn, thawed
2 tablespoons chopped fresh cilantro
2 limes, quartered

1. Combine seafood seasoning and chili powder in a small bowl. Rub mixture onto both sides of fish.
2. Heat a large nonstick skillet over medium-high heat. Coat fish with cooking spray. Add fish to pan; cook 3 minutes on each side or until fish flakes easily when tested with a fork. Place fish on a plate, sprinkle with salt, and keep warm.
3. Heat pan over high heat. Add oil, bell pepper, onion, and corn to pan. Sauté 3 minutes or until lightly browned. Stir in cilantro. Serve fish with corn mixture and limes. YIELD: 4 servings (serving size: 1 fillet and ⅓ cup corn mixture).

POINTS: 3; **EXCHANGES:** 2 Vegetable, 5 Very Lean Meat; **PER SERVING:** CAL 175 (14% from fat); PRO 25.9g; FAT 2.7g (sat 0.3g); CARB 12.2g; FIB 1.9g; CHOL 33mg; IRON 0.7mg; SOD 182mg; CALC 58mg

BROILED FISH WITH TAPENADE

A tapenade is a thick sauce made of olives, olive oil, herbs, and other seasonings.

¼ cup sliced sun-dried tomatoes, packed without oil
½ cup boiling water
8 kalamata olives, pitted and chopped
¼ cup chopped fresh parsley
1½ tablespoons chopped fresh basil
1 tablespoon red wine vinegar
1½ teaspoons olive oil
⅛ teaspoon salt
1 garlic clove, minced
Cooking spray
4 (6-ounce) orange roughy fillets (½ inch thick)
2 teaspoons olive oil
¼ teaspoon paprika
¼ teaspoon freshly ground black pepper

1. Combine tomatoes and water; let stand 10 minutes. Drain.
2. Combine olives and next 6 ingredients. Chop tomatoes; add to olive mixture. Stir well; set aside.
3. Preheat broiler.
4. Place fish on a baking sheet coated with cooking spray; drizzle with olive oil, and sprinkle with paprika and pepper. Broil 3 minutes. Top with olive mixture; broil 3 minutes or until fish flakes easily when tested with a fork. YIELD: 4 servings (1 fillet and about 1½ tablespoons tapenade).

POINTS: 4; **EXCHANGES:** 5 Very Lean Meat, 1 Fat; **PER SERVING:** CAL 179 (37% from fat); PRO 24.8g; FAT 7.2g (sat 0.8g); CARB 2.8g; FIB 0.6g; CHOL 33mg; IRON 0.9mg; SOD 350mg; CALC 63mg

GLAZED SALMON WITH FRESH GINGER

¼ cup thawed orange juice concentrate
2 tablespoons grated peeled fresh ginger
2 tablespoons dark brown sugar
2 tablespoons fresh lime juice
2 teaspoons low-sodium soy sauce
¼ teaspoon crushed red pepper
⅛ teaspoon salt
4 (6-ounce) salmon fillets (about 1 inch thick)
Cooking spray

1. Combine first 7 ingredients in a small bowl, stirring well. Set aside ¼ cup mixture.
2. Coat fish with cooking spray. Place a large nonstick skillet over medium-high heat until hot; add fish. Spoon 2 teaspoons orange juice mixture over each fillet; cook 4 minutes. Turn fish, and spoon an additional 2 teaspoons orange juice mixture over each fillet; cook 3 to 4 minutes or until fish flakes easily when tested with a fork.
3. Add reserved ¼ cup orange juice mixture to pan; place over medium heat, scraping pan to loosen browned bits. Cook 30 seconds or until sauce is slightly thick. Spoon sauce over fish. YIELD: 4 servings (serving size: 1 fillet).

POINTS: 7; **EXCHANGES:** 1 Starch, 5 Lean Meat; **PER SERVING:** CAL 301 (33% from fat); PRO 34.4g; FAT 10.9g (sat 1.7g); CARB 14.8g; FIB 0.3g; CHOL 94mg; IRON 1.6mg; SOD 251mg; CALC 33mg

SALMON WITH SWEET MANGO SALSA

1 (8-ounce) can pineapple tidbits in juice
1 peeled ripe mango, cut into ½-inch cubes
½ cup chopped red bell pepper
¼ cup finely chopped red onion
2 tablespoons chopped fresh cilantro
2 tablespoons fresh lime juice
1 tablespoon honey
1 finely chopped seeded jalapeño pepper
2 tablespoons brown sugar
1 teaspoon low-sodium soy sauce
Cooking spray
4 (6-ounce) salmon fillets, skinned
¼ teaspoon salt
¼ teaspoon cracked black pepper

1. Drain pineapple, reserving 3 tablespoons juice.
2. Combine pineapple, mango, and next 6 ingredients in a small bowl; chill.
3. Combine reserved 3 tablespoons pineapple juice with brown sugar and soy sauce. Set aside.
4. Preheat broiler.
5. Place salmon on broiler rack coated with cooking spray; brush with half of glaze. Sprinkle fish with salt and pepper. Broil 5 minutes; turn and brush with remaining glaze. Broil 5 minutes or until fish flakes easily when tested with a fork. Serve fish with salsa. YIELD: 4 servings (serving size: 1 fillet and ½ cup salsa).

NOTE: Serve salsa within 30 minutes for peak flavor. You can prepare the ingredients in advance, but don't combine them until 30 minutes before serving.

POINTS: 7; EXCHANGES: 1 Starch, 1 Fruit, 5 Lean Meat; PER SERVING: CAL 333 (29% from fat); PRO 33.4g; FAT 10.6g (sat 1.7g); CARB 26.1g; FIB 1.9g; CHOL 91mg; IRON 1.9mg; SOD 127mg; CALC 43mg

---

SNEAKY SALMON
🍴

Something as good as salmon must have a catch, right? One reason it tastes so good is because it's a high-fat fish. In fact, a typical salmon fillet gets about 46% of its calories from fat. So why make it part of your regular diet? The fat in salmon is monounsaturated and polyunsaturated, neither of which raises blood cholesterol levels. More important, salmon is full of omega-3 fats, a type of polyunsaturated fat that protects against heart disease. Salmon also has other bonuses: it's a great source of protein, vitamins E and B, iron, magnesium, and zinc. So don't let this fish's fat scare you away. Salmon makes a heart-healthy and diet-conscious addition to any meal.

SALMON-POTATO SALAD WITH LEMON-DILL DRESSING

(pictured on page 70)

8 small red potatoes
4 (6-ounce) salmon fillets, skinned
¼ teaspoon salt
¼ teaspoon black pepper
Cooking spray
¼ cup reduced-fat sour cream
¼ cup light mayonnaise
3 tablespoons chopped fresh dill
3 tablespoons finely minced red onion
3 tablespoons fresh lemon juice
1 teaspoon grated lemon rind
½ teaspoon salt
½ teaspoon freshly ground black pepper
1 cup fresh or frozen green peas, cooked
4 lemon wedges (optional)
Dill sprigs (optional)

1. Boil potatoes in water just until tender. Drain and place in ice water; drain well. Quarter potatoes; chill.
2. Preheat broiler.
3. Sprinkle fish evenly with ¼ teaspoon of salt and pepper; place on a broiler pan coated with cooking spray. Broil 5 minutes on each side or until fish flakes easily when tested with a fork. Let stand 10 minutes; chill.
4. Combine sour cream and next 7 ingredients in a small bowl. Cover and chill.
5. Place 1 fillet on each of 4 plates; add 8 potato quarters, and sprinkle

with ¼ cup green peas. Drizzle one-fourth of dressing over each; garnish with a lemon wedge and dill sprig, if desired. YIELD: 4 servings.

POINTS: 8; EXCHANGES: 1½ Starch, 5 Lean Meat, 1 Fat; PER SERVING: CAL 377 (33% from fat); PRO 38.2g; FAT 13.2g (sat 3.6g); CARB 23.4g; FIB 4.1g; CHOL 134mg; IRON 2.2mg; SOD 652mg; CALC 63mg

TARRAGON SNAPPER

2 tablespoons chopped fresh parsley
3 tablespoons light mayonnaise
1 tablespoon fresh lime juice
2 teaspoons olive oil
½ teaspoon dried tarragon
½ teaspoon Dijon mustard
¼ teaspoon salt
¼ teaspoon pepper
4 (6-ounce) red snapper fillets
Cooking spray

1. Preheat broiler.
2. Combine first 8 ingredients in a small bowl; set aside.
3. Place fish on a broiler pan coated with cooking spray, and broil 5 minutes. Turn fish; spread mayonnaise mixture over fish. Broil 5 to 7 minutes or until fish flakes easily when tested with a fork. YIELD: 4 servings (serving size: 1 fillet and 2 tablespoons sauce).

POINTS: 5; EXCHANGES: 5 Very Lean Meat, 2 Fat; PER SERVING: CAL 224 (35% from fat); PRO 33.7g; FAT 8.3g (sat 1.5g); CARB 1.5g; FIB 0.1g; CHOL 64mg; IRON 0.5mg; SOD 325mg; CALC 58mg

CREOLE BAKED SNAPPER

To decrease the spiciness of this dish, use a mild hot sauce such as Crystal Hot Sauce in place of the regular hot sauce.

1 tablespoon olive oil
½ cup chopped green bell pepper
½ cup chopped celery
½ cup chopped onion
½ teaspoon dried thyme
1¼ cups coarsely chopped tomato
¼ teaspoon salt
¼ teaspoon black pepper
2 garlic cloves, minced
2 teaspoons hot sauce
Cooking spray
4 (6-ounce) red snapper fillets
½ teaspoon Creole seasoning
¼ cup finely chopped fresh parsley

1. Preheat oven to 400°.
2. Heat oil in a large nonstick skillet over medium-high heat. Sauté bell pepper, celery, onion, and thyme 5 minutes or until onion just begins to brown. Stir in tomato and next 3 ingredients. Bring to a boil; cover, reduce heat, and simmer 2 minutes. Remove from heat. Stir in hot sauce.
3. Arrange fish in a single layer in a 13 x 9-inch baking dish coated with cooking spray. Sprinkle with Creole seasoning, and top with vegetables. Bake at 400° for 15 minutes or until fish flakes easily when tested with a fork. Sprinkle with parsley. YIELD: 4 servings (serving size: 1 fillet).

POINTS: 5; EXCHANGES: 1 Vegetable, 5 Very Lean Meat, 1 Fat; PER SERVING: CAL 224 (24% from fat); PRO 34.8g; FAT 5.9g (sat 1g); CARB 7g; FIB 1.9g; CHOL 60mg; IRON 1.2mg; SOD 329mg; CALC 76mg

GREEK SNAPPER

Olive oil-flavored cooking spray
¾ cup diced red onion
½ cup chopped green bell pepper
3 garlic cloves, minced
1 (14½-ounce) can chunky pasta-style tomatoes, undrained
3 tablespoons lemon juice
¾ teaspoon dried oregano
⅛ teaspoon freshly ground black pepper
4 (6-ounce) red snapper fillets
½ cup sliced pitted kalamata olives

1. Coat a large nonstick skillet with cooking spray; place over medium-high heat until hot. Add onion, bell pepper, and garlic; sauté until tender. Add tomatoes, lemon juice, oregano, and pepper; reduce heat, and simmer 2 minutes.
2. Add fish, spooning tomato mixture over fish. Cover and simmer 10 minutes; add olives. Cover and cook 4 minutes or until fish flakes easily when tested with a fork. YIELD: 4 servings (serving size: 1 fillet and ⅔ cup tomato mixture).

POINTS: 5; EXCHANGES: 3 Vegetable, 5 Very Lean Meat, 1 Fat; PER SERVING: CAL 268 (22% from fat); PRO 35.4g; FAT 6.5g (sat 1g); CARB 16.1g; FIB 2.8g; CHOL 60mg; IRON 1mg; SOD 784mg; CALC 90mg

CARIBBEAN MANGO TILAPIA

Tilapia (teh-LAH-pee-uh) is a farm-raised white fish with a delicate texture and sweet flavor.

4 seeded serrano chiles, seeded
3 garlic cloves, peeled
2 large shallots, peeled
2 cups chopped peeled mango
⅓ cup cider vinegar
¼ cup fresh orange juice
1 tablespoon chopped fresh or
    1 teaspoon dried thyme
2 teaspoons olive oil
4 (6-ounce) tilapia fillets
¼ teaspoon salt
Cooking spray

1. Combine first 3 ingredients in a food processor, and process until minced. Add mango and next 4 ingredients; process until smooth. Place mango mixture and fish in a zip-top plastic bag; seal and marinate in refrigerator 20 minutes. Remove fish from bag, reserving marinade. Pour reserved marinade into a small saucepan, and bring to a boil. Reduce heat, and simmer 5 minutes. Remove from heat.
2. Prepare grill or broiler.
3. Sprinkle fish with salt. Place fish on a grill rack or broiler pan coated with cooking spray. Cook 4 minutes on each side or until fish flakes easily when tested with a fork. Serve with mango sauce. YIELD: 4 servings (serving size: 1 fillet and ¼ cup mango sauce).

POINTS: 6; **EXCHANGES:** 1 Fruit, 4½ Very Lean Meat; **PER SERVING:** CAL 263 (23% from fat); PRO 32.7g; FAT 6.8g (sat 0.8g); CARB 19.3g; FIB 1.6g; CHOL 75mg; IRON 0.5mg; SOD 239mg; CALC 21mg

GRILLED TUNA STEAKS WITH HORSERADISH SAUCE

¼ cup Worcestershire sauce
2 tablespoons low-sodium soy sauce
1 tablespoon olive oil
1 teaspoon dried oregano
½ teaspoon freshly ground black pepper
2 garlic cloves, minced
4 (6-ounce) tuna steaks (about 1 inch thick)
½ cup reduced-fat sour cream
1½ teaspoons prepared horseradish
½ teaspoon salt
½ teaspoon Dijon mustard
¼ teaspoon Worcestershire sauce
Cooking spray

1. Combine first 6 ingredients in a large zip-top plastic bag. Add fish to bag; seal and marinate in refrigerator 1 hour, turning once.
2. Combine sour cream and next 4 ingredients in a small bowl; set aside.
3. Prepare grill.
4. Remove fish from marinade, reserving marinade. Place fish on grill rack coated with cooking spray; grill 6 minutes on each side or until fish is medium-rare or desired degree of doneness, basting frequently with reserved marinade. Serve with sour cream mixture. YIELD: 4 servings (serving size: 1 steak and 2 tablespoons sour cream mixture).

POINTS: 6; **EXCHANGES:** ½ Starch, 5 Very Lean Meat, 1 Fat; **PER SERVING:** CAL 268 (31% from fat); PRO 38.1g; FAT 8.8g (sat 3.4g); CARB 6.6g; FIB 0.4g; CHOL 92mg; IRON 3.3mg; SOD 864mg; CALC 127mg

BLACKENED TUNA WITH ORANGE-ZESTED SALSA

(pictured on page 69)

½ cup chopped yellow bell pepper
½ cup diced seeded tomato
¼ cup chopped green onions
2 tablespoons chopped fresh cilantro
1 tablespoon lime juice
1 teaspoon orange zest
2 teaspoons cider vinegar
¼ teaspoon salt
1 finely chopped seeded jalapeño pepper
2 teaspoons blackening seasoning
4 (6-ounce) tuna steaks (about 1 inch thick)
1 teaspoon vegetable oil

1. Combine first 9 ingredients in a small bowl; toss gently. Cover and chill 1 hour.
2. Sprinkle blackening seasoning on both sides of fish, pressing down firmly to allow seasoning to adhere.
3. Heat oil in a heavy-duty cast iron skillet over medium-high heat. Add fish, and cook 4 minutes on each side or until fish is medium-rare or desired degree of doneness. YIELD: 4 servings (1 tuna steak and ⅓ cup salsa).

POINTS: 4; **EXCHANGES:** 1 Vegetable, 5 Very Lean Meat; **PER SERVING:** CAL 194 (14% from fat); PRO 36.4g; FAT 2.9g (sat 0.6g); CARB 3.7g; FIB 1.1g; CHOL 77mg; IRON 2.3mg; SOD 399mg; CALC 52mg

GARLICKY CLAM-AND-MUSHROOM LINGUINE

6 ounces uncooked linguine
Cooking spray
1 (8-ounce) package presliced mushrooms
2 teaspoons olive oil
1 (6½-ounce) can chopped clams, undrained
1 teaspoon dried oregano
¼ teaspoon crushed red pepper
6 garlic cloves, minced
½ cup finely chopped green onions
⅓ cup chopped fresh parsley
⅓ cup grated Parmesan cheese
1 tablespoon olive oil
½ teaspoon salt
⅛ teaspoon freshly ground black pepper

1. Cook pasta according to package directions, omitting salt and fat; drain and keep warm.
2. Coat a large nonstick skillet with cooking spray; place over medium-high heat until hot. Add mushrooms, and cook 5 minutes or just until tender. Remove mushrooms from pan; keep warm.
3. Add 2 teaspoons olive oil to pan; add clams and next 3 ingredients, stirring often, until mixture comes to a boil. Reduce heat; add cooked mushrooms, onions, and parsley. Cook 2 minutes. Add pasta, Parmesan cheese, and remaining ingredients. Toss well. Serve immediately. YIELD: 4 servings (serving size: 1 cup).

POINTS: 6; EXCHANGES: 2 Starch, 1 Vegetable, 1 Lean Meat, 1 Fat; PER SERVING: CAL 303 (27% from fat); PRO 14.3g; FAT 9.2g (sat 2.5g); CARB 40.8g; FIB 3.7g; CHOL 14mg; IRON 3.5mg; SOD 647mg; CALC 147mg

INDIVIDUAL CRAB CASSEROLES

Cooking spray
1 cup finely chopped green bell pepper
½ cup finely chopped celery
½ cup finely chopped green onions
⅓ cup light mayonnaise
⅓ cup yogurt-based spread (such as Brummel & Brown)
¼ cup chopped fresh parsley
3 tablespoons Creole mustard
1 tablespoon fresh lemon juice
½ teaspoon Old Bay seasoning
½ teaspoon Worcestershire sauce
¼ teaspoon black pepper
⅛ teaspoon ground red pepper
1½ cups French bread breadcrumbs (about 2½ ounces bread), divided
1 pound lump crabmeat, drained and shell pieces removed

1. Preheat oven to 350°.
2. Coat a large nonstick skillet with cooking spray, and place over medium-high heat. Add bell pepper, celery, and onions; sauté 5 minutes or until vegetables are tender. Remove from heat.
3. Stir in mayonnaise and next 8 ingredients. Gently stir in ¾ cup breadcrumbs and crabmeat.
4. Spoon crabmeat mixture evenly into 6 gratin dishes coated with cooking spray; top each with 2 tablespoons breadcrumbs. Coat breadcrumbs with cooking spray. Bake at 350° for 20 minutes or until bubbly and lightly browned. YIELD: 6 servings (serving size: 1 gratin dish).
NOTE: If you don't have gratin dishes, use 6-ounce ramekins or custard cups. Bake at 350° for 28 minutes or until bubbly and lightly browned.

POINTS: 5; EXCHANGES: 1 Starch, 2 Very Lean Meat, 2 Fat; PER SERVING: CAL 210 (44% from fat); PRO 15.6g; FAT 10.2g (sat 2g); CARB 12g; FIB 2.4g; CHOL 63mg; IRON 1.4mg; SOD 617mg; CALC 97mg

MARYLAND CRAB CAKES

1 pound lump crabmeat, drained and shell pieces removed
1⅓ cups dry breadcrumbs
⅓ cup minced green onions
⅓ cup chopped fresh parsley
2 tablespoons lemon juice
1 tablespoon 2% reduced-fat milk
1 teaspoon hot sauce
½ teaspoon salt
¼ teaspoon pepper
4 large egg whites, lightly beaten
1⅓ cups dry breadcrumbs
2 tablespoons vegetable oil
Lemon wedges (optional)

1. Combine first 10 ingredients in a bowl. Divide mixture into 8 equal portions; shape each into a ½-inch-thick patty. Place breadcrumbs in a shallow dish; dredge patties in breadcrumbs.
2. Heat 1 tablespoon vegetable oil in a large nonstick skillet over medium-high heat. Add 4 patties, and cook 3 minutes. Carefully turn patties over; cook 3 minutes or until golden. Repeat procedure with remaining oil and patties. Serve with lemon wedges, if desired. YIELD: 4 servings (serving size: 2 crab cakes).

POINTS: 6; EXCHANGES: 1 Starch, 4 Very Lean Meat, 1 Fat; PER SERVING: CAL 282 (32% from fat); PRO 29.4g; FAT 10g (sat 1.8g); CARB 17.2g; FIB 1g; CHOL 114mg; IRON 2.2mg; SOD 830mg; CALC 162mg

OVEN-FRYING THE LOW-FAT WAY

To get a crispy fried texture, heat a small amount of oil in a jelly-roll pan before adding the oysters. This technique is also used for Oven-Fried Fish (page 60) and for Shrimp Po' Boys with Remoulade Slaw (page 129).

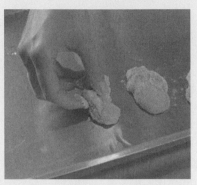

1. Pour oil onto a jelly-roll pan, tilting to coat. Place in oven for 3 minutes or until very hot.

2. Quickly place oysters on the hot oil, and return pan to oven.

CAJUN OVEN-FRIED OYSTERS WITH SPICY COCKTAIL SAUCE

(pictured on page 71)
To drain well, place oysters on paper towels for a few minutes before coating with cornmeal mixture.

½ cup ketchup
1 tablespoon prepared horseradish
1 teaspoon fresh lemon juice
½ teaspoon Worcestershire sauce
½ cup yellow cornmeal
1 teaspoon paprika
½ teaspoon salt
¼ teaspoon ground red pepper
¼ teaspoon black pepper
32 medium oysters, drained well
2 tablespoons vegetable oil
Lemon wedges (optional)

1. Preheat oven to 450°.
2. Combine ketchup and next 3 ingredients; set aside.
3. Combine cornmeal and next 4 ingredients in a bowl; stir well. Transfer to a plate. Add oysters in batches of 8; toss to coat completely.
4. Coat a jelly-roll pan evenly with oil; place in oven for 3 minutes or until very hot. Arrange oysters on pan in a single layer. Bake at 450° for 8 minutes; turn and bake an additional 8 minutes or until golden. Remove oysters from pan. Serve immediately with cocktail sauce. Garnish with lemon wedges, if desired. YIELD: 4 servings (serving size: 8 oysters and 2 tablespoons sauce).

POINTS: 5; **EXCHANGES:** 2 Starch, 1 Very Lean Meat, 2 Fat; **PER SERVING:** CAL 219 (37% from fat); PRO 7.8g; FAT 9.4g (sat 1.1g); CARB 27.5g; FIB 1.8g; CHOL 28mg; IRON 7.5mg; SOD 880mg; CALC 61mg

SEA SCALLOPS WITH LEMONY BUTTER SAUCE

1½ pounds sea scallops
½ teaspoon paprika
¼ teaspoon freshly ground black pepper
2 garlic cloves, minced
2 tablespoons butter
¼ cup dry white wine
2 tablespoons fresh lemon juice
¼ teaspoon salt
2 tablespoons chopped fresh flat-leaf parsley
6 cups hot cooked angel hair (about 12 ounces uncooked pasta)
Lemon wedges (optional)

1. Sprinkle scallops with paprika, pepper, and garlic.
2. Heat a large nonstick skillet over medium-high heat until hot. Melt 1 tablespoon butter in pan; add half of scallops. Cook scallops 2 minutes on each side. Transfer to a serving platter; keep warm. Repeat with remaining butter and scallops.
3. Add wine, lemon juice, and salt to pan; let simmer 30 seconds or until liquid is reduced to a glaze. Pour over scallops; sprinkle with parsley. Serve immediately on pasta. Garnish with lemon wedges, if desired. YIELD: 6 servings (approximately 4 scallops and 1 cup pasta).

POINTS: 7; **EXCHANGES:** 3 Starch, 3 Very Lean Meat, 1 Fat; **PER SERVING:** CAL 336 (16% from fat); PRO 25.9g; FAT 5.7g (sat 2.6g); CARB 43.5g; FIB 2.5g; CHOL 48mg; IRON 2.5mg; SOD 322mg; CALC 44mg

CUMIN SCALLOPS ON FIESTA RICE

(pictured on page 70)

1½ pounds sea scallops
1¼ cups water
⅛ teaspoon ground turmeric
½ cup uncooked long-grain rice
½ teaspoon salt, divided
1½ teaspoons ground cumin
⅛ teaspoon ground red pepper
⅛ teaspoon black pepper
1 tablespoon olive oil
½ cup finely chopped poblano chile pepper
2 tablespoons chopped fresh cilantro leaves
1 small tomato, seeded and diced
Lime wedges (optional)

1. Rinse scallops, and pat dry with paper towels to remove excess moisture.
2. Bring water to a boil in a 1½-quart saucepan over high heat; stir in turmeric and rice. Return to a boil; cover, reduce heat, and simmer 20 minutes.
3. Combine ¼ teaspoon salt, cumin, red pepper, and black pepper. Sprinkle cumin mixture over scallops; toss gently.
4. Heat ½ tablespoon olive oil in a large nonstick skillet, tilting pan to coat bottom. Add half of scallops; cook 2 minutes on each side or until browned. Remove scallops from pan; keep warm. Scrape off any residue in pan with a wooden spoon. Repeat procedure with remaining oil and scallops.
5. Add ¼ teaspoon salt, poblano pepper, cilantro, and tomato to cooked rice. Serve with lime wedges, if desired. YIELD: 4 servings (serving size: approximately 6 scallops and ⅔ cup rice).

POINTS: 7; **EXCHANGES:** 1½ Starch, 4 Very Lean Meat, 1 Fat; **PER SERVING:** CAL 301 (27% from fat); PRO 28.4g; FAT 8.9g (sat 1.4g); CARB 25.3g; FIB 1.1g; CHOL 51mg; IRON 2.1mg; SOD 593mg; CALC 58mg

SHRIMP REMOULADE

3 quarts water
2 tablespoons liquid shrimp and crab boil
1½ pounds medium shrimp
⅓ cup minced green onions
¼ cup plain nonfat yogurt
3 tablespoons Creole mustard
3 tablespoons light mayonnaise
1 tablespoon olive oil
¼ teaspoon dried tarragon
⅛ teaspoon salt

1. Combine water and crab boil in a Dutch oven; bring to a boil. Add shrimp; return to a boil, and cook 2 minutes. Remove from heat, and let stand 5 minutes. Drain and rinse with cold water. Peel and chill shrimp.
2. Combine onions and remaining ingredients in a small bowl, stirring well. Serve sauce with shrimp. YIELD: 4 servings (serving size: 3 ounces cooked shrimp and 2½ tablespoons sauce).

POINTS: 3; **EXCHANGES:** ½ Starch, 3 Very Lean Meat, 1 Fat; **PER SERVING:** CAL 144 (27% from fat); PRO 20.2g; FAT 4.1g (sat 0.9g); CARB 4.2g; FIB 1.4g; CHOL 181mg; IRON 3mg; SOD 485mg; CALC mg

MILD SHRIMP-AND-VEGETABLE CURRY

Cooking spray
2 finely chopped seeded jalapeño peppers
1 small green bell pepper, cut into thin strips
1 small onion, thinly sliced
1 pound tomatoes, coarsely chopped
¾ pound medium shrimp, peeled and deveined
¾ teaspoon salt
½ teaspoon curry powder
3 cups hot cooked long-grain rice

1. Coat a 12-inch skillet with cooking spray; place over medium-high heat until hot. Add jalapeño pepper, bell pepper, and onion; sauté 8 minutes or until onion is golden.
2. Add tomato and next 3 ingredients; bring to a boil. Cover, reduce heat, and simmer 8 to 10 minutes or until shrimp are done, stirring occasionally. Serve immediately over rice. YIELD: 3 servings (serving size: 1⅓ cups shrimp mixture and 1 cup rice).

POINTS: 7; **EXCHANGES:** 3 Starch, 4 Vegetable, 2 Very Lean Meat; **PER SERVING:** CAL 368 (5% from fat), PRO 23.7g; FAT 2.3g (sat 0.5g); CARB 63.6g; FIB 5g; CHOL 153mg; IRON 5.6mg; SOD 777mg; CALC 75mg

SWEET CURRIED SHRIMP

(pictured on page 2)

1½ pounds fresh medium shrimp
Cooking spray
 ½ cup diced sweet onion
1½ cups fat-free milk
 2 tablespoons all-purpose flour
 1 teaspoon sugar
 ½ teaspoon curry powder
 ¼ teaspoon salt
 ¼ teaspoon ground ginger
 ⅛ teaspoon ground red pepper
 ⅓ cup frozen green peas, thawed
2½ cups hot cooked long-grain rice
 ¼ cup roasted peanuts, chopped
 ½ cup chopped green onions

1. Peel shrimp; coat shrimp with cooking spray. Heat a nonstick skillet over medium heat; add shrimp, and cook 4 minutes or until shrimp are done, stirring constantly. Remove shrimp, and set aside.
2. Coat onion with cooking spray; increase heat to medium-high. Add onion, and cook 4 minutes or until lightly browned.
3. Whisk together milk and flour in a bowl. Add milk mixture, sugar, and next 4 ingredients to pan; cook 4 minutes or until mixture is slightly thickened, stirring constantly. Stir in shrimp, and cook until thoroughly heated. Stir peas into hot rice; serve shrimp over rice mixture. Garnish with peanuts and green onions. YIELD: 4 servings (1 cup shrimp mixture, ¾ cup rice, 2 tablespoons green onions, and 1 tablespoon peanuts).

POINTS: 6; **EXCHANGES:** *2 Starch, 1 Vegetable, 3 Very Lean Meat, 1 Fat;* **PER SERVING:** *CAL 311 (17% from fat); PRO 28.5g; FAT 5.9g (sat 1g); CARB 35.6g; FIB 2.7g; CHOL 184mg; IRON 3.7mg; SOD 604mg; CALC 167mg*

SHRIMP-AND-RED PEPPER STIR-FRY

 1 cup fat-free, less-sodium chicken broth
 1 tablespoon cornstarch
 3 tablespoons reduced-sodium soy sauce
1½ teaspoons sugar
 ½ teaspoon ground ginger
 ¼ teaspoon garlic powder
 ¼ teaspoon dried crushed red pepper
 2 teaspoons vegetable oil, divided
 ¾ pound medium shrimp, peeled and deveined
 1 large onion, cut into 8 wedges
 1 red bell pepper, cut into 1-inch pieces
 1 cup small broccoli florets
 4 cups hot cooked long-grain rice

1. Combine first 7 ingredients in a medium bowl; set aside.
2. Heat 1 teaspoon oil in a large skillet over high heat. Add shrimp, and sauté 3 minutes. Remove shrimp from pan; keep warm.
3. Add 1 teaspoon oil to pan. Add onion, bell pepper, and broccoli; sauté 4 minutes or until crisp-tender. Add broth mixture. Bring to a boil; reduce heat, and simmer, uncovered, 30 seconds, stirring constantly. Add shrimp; simmer 1 minute, stirring constantly. Remove from heat. Serve over rice. YIELD: 4 servings (serving size: 1 cup stir-fry and 1 cup rice).

POINTS: 7; **EXCHANGES:** *3½ Starch, 2 Vegetable, 1 Very Lean Meat;* **PER SERVING:** *CAL 346 (9% from fat); PRO 18g; FAT 3.6g (sat 0.5g); CARB 59.4g; FIB 3.5g; CHOL 97mg; IRON 4mg; SOD 730mg; CALC 62mg*

DELTA SHRIMP-AND-SAUSAGE JAMBALAYA

Cooking spray
 ½ pound turkey kielbasa sausage, sliced
1½ tablespoons olive oil
 2 cups chopped onion
1½ cups chopped green bell pepper
 ¾ cup chopped celery
 2 garlic cloves, minced
2½ cups fat-free, less-sodium chicken broth
 2 tablespoons tomato paste
 1 teaspoon hot sauce
 1 teaspoon Worcestershire sauce
 ½ teaspoon dried thyme
 ½ teaspoon dried oregano
 ¾ cup uncooked long-grain rice
 ½ pound large shrimp, peeled and deveined
 ½ cup chopped green onions

1. Coat a Dutch oven with cooking spray; place over medium-high heat until hot. Add sausage; sauté 4 minutes or until lightly browned. Drain on paper towels.
2. Add oil and next 4 ingredients to pan. Cook 8 minutes or until tender, stirring constantly. Add broth and next 5 ingredients. Bring to a boil; add rice. Return to a boil; cover, reduce heat, and simmer 22 minutes or until rice is tender.
3. Add shrimp and reserved sausage; cover and cook 3 minutes. Remove from heat; stir in green onions. Let stand 5 to 10 minutes. YIELD: 4 servings (serving size: 1½ cups).

POINTS: 7; **EXCHANGES:** *2½ Starch, 2 Vegetable, 1 Lean Meat, 1 Fat;* **PER SERVING:** *CAL 350 (19% from fat); PRO 20.5g; FAT 7.5g (sat 1.4g); CARB 49.3g; FIB 4.2g; CHOL 84mg; IRON 4.3mg; SOD 1023mg; CALC 82mg*

Blackened Tuna with
Orange-Zested
Salsa, page 64

Cumin Scallops on
Fiesta Rice, page 67

Salmon-Potato
Salad with Lemon-
Dill Dressing,
page 62

Skillet Roasted
Pepper Lasagna,
page 80

Cajun Oven-Fried Oysters
with Spicy Cocktail Sauce,
page 66

Chipotle Black Beans and Rice, page 75

Cheesy Soft Polenta with Roasted Vegetables, page 79

Meatless Main Dishes

CHEESY SPINACH-RICE SKILLET

2 jalapeño peppers
1 cup uncooked long-grain rice
1 teaspoon vegetable oil
1 cup chopped yellow onion
4 garlic cloves, minced
1 (10-ounce) package frozen chopped spinach, thawed, drained, and squeezed dry
1 cup evaporated fat-free milk
½ cup tub light cream cheese
¾ cup (3 ounces) reduced-fat shredded sharp Cheddar cheese
1 (14-ounce) can artichoke hearts, drained and chopped
¾ teaspoon salt
⅛ teaspoon black pepper

1. Remove and discard stems and seeds from jalapeño peppers; mince peppers, and set aside.
2. Cook rice according to package directions, omitting salt and fat.
3. Heat oil in a large nonstick skillet over medium-high heat. Add onion and garlic; sauté 5 minutes or until golden. Add spinach, minced pepper, and milk; stir to blend thoroughly. Bring to a boil; add cream cheese, and stir until cheese melts. Remove from heat.
4. Add rice, Cheddar cheese, artichokes, salt, and black pepper to spinach mixture; stir well. Place over medium heat; cover and cook 7 to 10 minutes, stirring twice, until mixture thickens slightly. YIELD: 4 servings (serving size: 1½ cups).

POINTS: 6; **EXCHANGES:** 2 Starch, 1 Vegetable, 1 Medium-Fat Meat, ½ Fat; **PER SERVING:** CAL 287 (22% from fat); PRO 14.1g; FAT 6.8g (sat 4g); CARB 41.2g; FIB 2.5g; CHOL 18mg; IRON 2.8mg; SOD 682mg; CALC 330mg

LENTILS-AND-BROWN RICE PILAF

2½ cups water
½ cup dried lentils
½ cup uncooked brown rice
Cooking spray
2 tablespoons olive oil
2 cups chopped yellow onion
¾ cup chopped red bell pepper
¾ cup chopped green bell pepper
1 (8-ounce) package mushrooms, quartered
4 garlic cloves, minced
½ cup chopped fresh parsley
1½ tablespoons low-sodium soy sauce
1½ tablespoons fresh lime juice
1 tablespoon Worcestershire sauce
¾ teaspoon salt
¼ teaspoon black pepper

1. Bring water to a boil in a saucepan. Add lentils and rice; return to a boil. Cover, reduce heat, and simmer 25 minutes or until rice is tender and liquid is almost absorbed. Remove from heat, and let stand 5 minutes or until liquid is absorbed.
2. Coat a large nonstick skillet with cooking spray; add oil, and place over medium-high heat. Add onion and peppers; sauté 2 minutes or until lightly browned. Reduce to medium-high heat; add mushrooms and garlic; sauté 4 minutes or until tender.
3. Add vegetables and remaining ingredients to lentils and rice. Let stand 15 minutes for flavors to blend. YIELD: 4 servings (serving size: 1¼ cups).

POINTS: 6; **EXCHANGES:** 2 Starch, 3 Vegetable, 1½ Fat; **PER SERVING:** CAL 301 (24% from fat); PRO 11.9g; FAT 8.2g (sat 1.2g); CARB 48g; FIB 10.2g; CHOL 0mg; IRON 4.3mg; SOD 683mg; CALC 68mg

GRILLED VEGETABLE PAELLA

1 red bell pepper
1 green bell pepper
2 small yellow squash, halved
Cooking spray
6 cups vegetable broth
½ teaspoon saffron threads, crushed
3 tablespoons olive oil
1 small red onion, quartered and sliced
3 garlic cloves, minced
1½ cups uncooked Arborio rice or other short-grain rice
4 plum tomatoes, chopped
1¼ cups frozen green peas, thawed
¼ teaspoon salt
¼ teaspoon paprika
⅛ teaspoon freshly ground black pepper
1 (10-ounce) package frozen artichoke quarters

1. Cut bell peppers in half lengthwise; discard seeds and membranes. Place pepper halves, skin sides up, on a baking sheet; flatten with hand.
2. Prepare grill. Place pepper halves and squash halves on grill rack coated with cooking spray; grill 5 minutes. Turn squash halves (do not turn pepper halves), and grill 5 minutes; remove peppers and squash from grill. (Peppers will be blackened.) Place peppers in a zip-top plastic bag; seal bag. Let stand 15 minutes. Peel peppers, and cut into 1-inch pieces. Cut squash into 1-inch pieces.
3. Bring broth and saffron to a simmer in a large saucepan. (Do not boil.) Keep warm over low heat.
4. Heat oil in a large Dutch oven over medium-high heat. Add onion; cook 3 minutes or until onion is

golden, stirring frequently. Add garlic and rice; cook 2 minutes, stirring frequently. Reduce heat to medium.
5. Stir in 2 cups broth mixture; cook 10 minutes or until liquid is nearly absorbed, stirring constantly. Add remaining broth mixture, ½ cup at a time, stirring constantly; cook until each portion of broth mixture is absorbed before adding the next (about 30 minutes total). Remove from heat. Add peppers, squash, tomato, and remaining ingredients during last 5 minutes of cooking time. Remove from heat; cover and let stand 5 minutes. YIELD: 6 servings (serving size: 2 cups).

POINTS: 7; EXCHANGES: 3½ Starch, 2½ Vegetable, 1½ Fat; **PER SERVING:** CAL 370 (22% from fat); PRO 8.5g; FAT 9.2g (sat 1.2g); CARB 64.1g; FIB 5.5g; CHOL 0mg; IRON 4.7mg; SOD 1132mg; CALC 42mg

PASTA MYTHS

🍴🍽️

You may have heard that pasta can quickly pack on pounds. But truth be told, pasta is not a fattening food. In fact, pasta contains almost no fat. The key to enjoying pasta while losing weight is learning to control portion sizes. Keep a measuring cup handy when serving up dinner plates; a ½-cup serving of pasta is around 100 calories and is one carbohydrate exchange. Choose marinaras or broth-based toppings rather than the higher fat Alfredo and cream-based sauces.

CHIPOTLE BLACK BEANS AND RICE

(pictured on page 72)

1⅓ cups uncooked long-grain rice
¾ teaspoon ground turmeric
2 teaspoons olive oil
¾ cup finely chopped onion
¼ teaspoon ground cumin
1 (15.5-ounce) can black beans, rinsed and drained
1 (14.5-ounce) can diced tomatoes, undrained
1 (4-ounce) can chopped green chiles
½ of 1 chipotle chili pepper in adobo sauce, finely chopped
½ teaspoon salt
¼ cup reduced-fat sour cream
¼ cup chopped fresh cilantro

1. Cook rice and turmeric in water according to rice package directions, omitting salt and fat.
2. Heat oil in a large nonstick skillet over medium heat. Add onion; sauté 2 minutes until tender.
3. Add cumin and next 4 ingredients. Bring to a boil; cover, reduce heat, and simmer 5 minutes. Remove from heat; stir in salt.
4. Top rice with bean mixture, sour cream, and cilantro. YIELD: 4 servings (serving size: 1 cup rice, 1 cup bean mixture, and 1 tablespoon sour cream).

POINTS: 8; **EXCHANGES:** 4 Starch, 2 Vegetable, 1 Fat; **PER SERVING:** CAL 394 (16% from fat); PRO 11.1g; FAT 7.1g (sat 2.8g); CARB 70.1g; FIB 7.4g; CHOL 16mg; IRON 4.9mg; SOD 902mg; CALC 116mg

KALAMATA-WHITE BEAN RICE

To pit olives, gently press the side of a chef's knife down onto each olive. The pit will easily separate from the olive.

1 teaspoon olive oil
2 cups seeded chopped red bell pepper (about 2 large)
1 cup chopped onion
2¼ cups water
1 cup long-grain rice
2 tablespoons chopped fresh basil
2 (16-ounce) cans navy beans, rinsed and drained
¼ cup lemon juice
¼ teaspoon salt
¼ teaspoon black pepper
25 kalamata olives, pitted and coarsely chopped
1 cup (4 ounces) crumbled feta cheese

1. Heat oil in a nonstick skillet over medium-high heat. Add bell pepper and onion; sauté 5 minutes or until tender.
2. Add water to pepper mixture; bring to a boil over medium-high heat. Stir in rice and basil. Bring to a boil. Cover, reduce heat, and simmer 18 to 20 minutes or until water is absorbed and rice is tender. Remove from heat.
3. Add beans and next 4 ingredients to rice; cover and let stand 5 minutes. Sprinkle with feta cheese. YIELD: 6 servings (serving size: 1⅓ cups).

POINTS: 7; **EXCHANGES:** 3 Starch, 2 Vegetable, ½ Medium-Fat Meat, 1 Fat; **PER SERVING:** CAL 369 (27% from fat); PRO 14g; FAT 11g (sat 4.5g); CARB 54.3g; FIB 6.7g; CHOL 22mg; IRON 3.4mg; SOD 837mg; CALC 193mg

CURRIED LENTILS AND CARROTS ON COUSCOUS

1 (14.5-ounce) can vegetable broth
½ cup dried lentils
⅓ cup chopped pecans
¾ cup water
½ cup uncooked couscous
1½ teaspoons vegetable oil
1¾ cups chopped carrot
1 cup chopped onion
1 garlic clove, minced
2 teaspoons sugar
¾ teaspoon curry powder
⅛ teaspoon salt

1. Bring vegetable broth to a boil in a saucepan. Stir in lentils; cover, reduce heat, and simmer 30 minutes or until tender. Drain lentils, reserving liquid. Set aside.
2. Place pecans in a large nonstick skillet; cook over medium heat, stirring constantly, 3 minutes or until toasted. Remove pecans from pan.
3. Bring ¾ cup water to a boil in a saucepan; gradually stir in couscous. Remove from heat; cover and let stand 5 minutes. Fluff with a fork. Cover and keep warm.
4. Heat a large nonstick skillet over medium-high heat; add oil. Add carrot and onion; sauté 8 minutes or until tender. Add garlic, and sauté 1 minute. Stir in sugar, curry powder, salt, and lentil liquid; cook 1 minute.
5. Spoon lentils over couscous, and top with carrot mixture. Sprinkle with pecans; serve immediately. YIELD: 4 servings (serving size: ½ cup couscous, ½ cup carrot, ⅓ cup lentils).

POINTS: 6; EXCHANGES: 2½ Starch, 1 Vegetable, ½ Very Lean Meat, 2 Fat; PER SERVING: CAL 296 (29% from fat); PRO 11.4g; FAT 9.9g (sat 0.8g); CARB 43.8g; FIB 9.5g; CHOL 0mg; IRON 3.1mg; SOD 550mg; CALC 50mg

RATATOUILLE WITH CHICKPEAS

1 tablespoon olive oil
1½ cups thinly sliced onion (about 1 large)
5 garlic cloves, minced
4 cups cubed eggplant (about ¾ pound)
2 cups cubed yellow squash
1¾ cups chopped green bell pepper
1 pound mushrooms, halved
1 (28-ounce) can diced tomatoes, undrained
1½ teaspoons salt
½ teaspoon black pepper
1 (15.5-ounce) can chickpeas (garbanzo beans), rinsed and drained
¼ cup chopped fresh basil or 1 tablespoon dried basil
6 cups hot cooked couscous

1. Heat oil in a Dutch oven over medium-high heat. Add onion and garlic; sauté 4 to 5 minutes or until onion is golden.
2. Add eggplant, squash, bell pepper, and mushrooms; sauté 5 minutes. Add tomatoes and next 3 ingredients; bring to a boil. Cover, reduce heat, and simmer 20 minutes or until vegetables are tender.
3. Stir in basil and cook, uncovered, 10 minutes or until some of the liquid has evaporated. Serve over couscous. YIELD: 6 servings (serving size: 1½ cups ratatouille and 1 cup couscous).

POINTS: 6; EXCHANGES: 3 Starch, 4 Vegetable; PER SERVING: CAL 334 (10% from fat); PRO 13g; FAT 4g (sat 0.4g); CARB 64.3g; FIB 10.5g; CHOL 0mg; IRON 3.1mg; SOD 817mg; CALC 81mg

SMOTHERED SQUASH AND PINTO BEANS

2 teaspoons olive oil
½ cup chopped onion
2 teaspoons minced seeded jalapeño pepper
2 garlic cloves, minced
1 cup sliced yellow squash
1 cup sliced zucchini
½ cup fresh corn kernels
1 (16-ounce) can pinto beans, drained
1 (14.5-ounce) can diced tomatoes, undrained
3 thyme sprigs
½ cup (2 ounces) shredded Monterey Jack cheese
2 cups hot cooked long-grain rice

1. Heat oil in a large skillet over medium-high heat. Add onion, jalapeño pepper, and garlic; sauté 2 minutes. Stir in squash and zucchini; sauté 2 minutes. Add corn and next 3 ingredients; cover, reduce heat, and simmer 10 minutes. Discard thyme; sprinkle with cheese. Serve over rice.
YIELD: 4 servings (serving size: 1 cup squash mixture and ½ cup rice).

POINTS: 7; EXCHANGES: 3 Starch, 2 Vegetable, 1 Lean Meat; PER SERVING: CAL 337 (20% from fat); PRO 13.7g; FAT 7.5g (sat 3.2g); CARB 55.2g; FIB 5.7g; CHOL 11mg; IRON 3.9mg; SOD 432mg; CALC 198mg

---

THE POWER OF BEANS

Incorporating beans into your diet may lower your body's levels of "bad" cholestreol. Studies have shown that a cup of beans per day increases "good" cholesterol by 9%.

MEXICAN TORTILLA CASSEROLE

1 teaspoon olive oil
1½ cups chopped onion
1 cup chopped yellow squash
1 (15-ounce) can kidney beans, drained
1 cup salsa
1½ teaspoons chili powder
1 teaspoon ground cumin
¾ teaspoon sugar
¼ teaspoon salt
1 (14.5-ounce) can Mexican-style stewed tomatoes, undrained
6 (6-inch) corn tortillas, cut in half
Cooking spray
1 (2.25-ounce) can sliced ripe olives, drained
2 tablespoons chopped fresh cilantro
1 cup (4 ounces) shredded Monterey Jack cheese
6 tablespoons reduced-fat sour cream

1. Preheat oven to 350°.
2. Heat oil in a large nonstick skillet over medium-high heat. Add onion and squash; sauté 5 minutes or until tender. Add beans and next 6 ingredients; bring to a boil. Reduce heat, and simmer, uncovered, 5 minutes or until thoroughly heated.
3. Arrange 6 tortilla halves in bottom of an 11 x 7-inch baking dish coated with cooking spray; top with half of tomato mixture. Sprinkle with olives and cilantro. Top with remaining 6 tortilla halves and tomato mixture.
4. Cover and bake at 350° for 20 minutes. Uncover and sprinkle with cheese; bake an additional 10 minutes. Top each serving with sour cream. YIELD: 6 servings (serving size: ⅙ of casserole and 1 tablespoon sour cream).

POINTS: 5; **EXCHANGES:** 1½ Starch, 3 Vegetable, 1 Medium-Fat Meat, 1 Fat; **PER SERVING:** CAL 270 (32% from fat); PRO 10.7g; FAT 9.8g (sat 4.5g); CARB 36.7g; FIB 7.2g; CHOL 22mg; IRON 2.2mg; SOD 809mg; CALC 227mg

SUCCOTASH QUESADILLAS

These vegetable-filled quesadillas make a quick and hearty meal or snack.

1 cup (4 ounces) reduced-fat shredded sharp Cheddar cheese
½ teaspoon cumin
¼ teaspoon salt
1 (15.25-ounce) can Mexican-style corn, drained
1 (10-ounce) package frozen lima beans
1 garlic clove, minced
6 (8-inch) flour tortillas
Cooking spray

1. Combine first 6 ingredients.
2. Heat a large skillet over medium heat until hot. Coat each tortilla on both sides with cooking spray. Place 1 tortilla in pan; spread ½ cup succotash mixture over tortilla. Fold in half, and cook 45 seconds on each side or until golden. Remove from pan, and keep warm. Repeat with remaining tortillas and succotash mixture. YIELD: 6 servings (serving size: 1 quesadilla).

POINTS: 5; **EXCHANGES:** 2 Starch, 1 Vegetable, 1 Medium-Fat Meat; **PER SERVING:** CAL 241 (22% from fat); PRO 14.9g; FAT 6.2g (sat 3.1g); CARB 33.7g; FIB 6.2g; CHOL 7mg; IRON 1mg; SOD 521mg; CALC 185mg

SPINACH-AND-BLACK BEAN QUESADILLAS

Cooking spray
1 teaspoon light butter
1 (10-ounce) package frozen chopped spinach, thawed, drained, and squeezed dry
1 (8-ounce) package presliced mushrooms
10 (8-inch) flour tortillas
5 tablespoons tub-style light cream cheese
1 (15-ounce) can black beans, rinsed and drained
¾ cup (3 ounces) reduced-fat shredded Monterey Jack cheese
½ cup reduced-fat sour cream

1. Place a large skillet coated with cooking spray over medium-high heat until hot. Add butter, spinach, and mushrooms; sauté until mushrooms are tender. Remove from heat.
2. Spread each of 5 tortillas with 1 tablespoon cream cheese; sprinkle evenly with spinach mixture, beans, and cheese. Top each with a tortilla.
3. Recoat pan with cooking spray; place over medium-high heat until hot. Carefully place 1 quesadilla in pan; cook 2 minutes on each side or until golden, pressing down with a spatula. Repeat procedure with remaining quesadillas, coating pan with cooking spray before adding each. Serve immediately with sour cream. YIELD: 5 servings (serving size: 1 quesadilla and 2 tablespoons sour cream).

POINTS: 8; **EXCHANGES:** 4 Starch, 1 Vegetable, 1 Medium-Fat Meat, ½ Fat; **PER SERVING:** CAL 402 (16% from fat); PRO 20.2g; FAT 7g (sat 4.4g); CARB 64.2g; FIB 7.2g; CHOL 23mg; IRON 5mg; SOD 1041mg; CALC 290mg

CHILI BEAN TOSTADA

Cooking spray
- ½ cup finely chopped onion
- 1 (16-ounce) can pinto beans, rinsed and drained
- ½ cup water
- 2 teaspoons chili powder
- 1 teaspoon ground cumin
- 1 teaspoon sugar
- 8 (6-inch) corn tortillas

Cooking spray
- 2 cups shredded iceberg lettuce
- 1 cup (4 ounces) reduced-fat shredded Cheddar cheese
- ¼ cup picante sauce or salsa
- ¼ cup reduced-fat sour cream

1. Preheat oven to 350°.
2. Heat a large nonstick skillet coated with cooking spray over medium-high heat. Add onion, and sauté 3 minutes or until tender. Add beans and next 4 ingredients; cook 5 minutes or until mixture thickens. Remove from heat; cover and keep warm.
3. Coat each side of tortillas lightly with cooking spray. Place on a baking sheet, overlapping if necessary. Bake at 350° for 4 minutes on each side or until lightly browned.
4. Place 2 tortillas, slightly overlapping, on each of 4 plates. Top evenly with beans, lettuce, cheese, picante sauce, and sour cream. YIELD: 4 servings (serving size: 2 tortillas, ⅓ cup beans, ½ cup lettuce, ¼ cup cheese, 1 tablespoon salsa, and 1 tablespoon sour cream).

POINTS: 6; **EXCHANGES:** 3 Starch, 1 Medium-Fat Meat, 1 Fat; **PER SERVING:** CAL 324 (26% from fat); PRO 15.6g; FAT 9.4g (sat 4.2g); CARB 44.8g; FIB 7.5g; CHOL 18mg; IRON 2.1mg; SOD 693mg; CALC 335mg

CORNBREAD-CRUSTED CHILE BEANS

- 1 teaspoon olive oil
- 1 cup chopped onion
- 1 (15-ounce) can light red kidney beans, rinsed and drained
- 1 teaspoon chili powder
- 1 teaspoon hot sauce
- ½ teaspoon ground cumin
- 1 (14.5-ounce) can chili-style diced tomatoes (such as Del Monte)
- 1 (4-ounce) can chopped green chiles
- 1 (8½-ounce) package cornbread mix (such as Jiffy)
- ½ cup (2 ounces) reduced-fat shredded sharp Cheddar cheese
- ⅓ cup fat-free milk
- 2 large egg whites

1. Preheat oven to 350°.
2. Heat oil in a 10-inch ovenproof nonstick skillet over medium-high heat. Add onion; sauté 5 minutes. Add kidney beans and next 5 ingredients; cook 5 minutes. Remove from heat.
3. Combine cornbread mix and remaining 3 ingredients; stir until blended. Spoon batter over bean mixture. Bake at 350° for 30 minutes. Cut into 4 equal wedges. YIELD: 4 servings (serving size: 1 wedge).

POINTS: 8; **EXCHANGES:** 4 Starch, 1 Vegetable, ½ Medium-Fat Meat, 1 Fat; **PER SERVING:** CAL 390 (20% from fat); PRO 14.3g; FAT 9g (sat 3.1g); CARB 66.6g; FIB 7.5g; CHOL 5mg; IRON 3.3mg; SOD 1264mg; CALC 324mg

CORN-AND-GREEN CHILE CASSEROLE

Cooking spray
- ⅔ cup finely chopped onion
- 1½ cups diced yellow squash
- 1½ cups (6 ounces) reduced-fat shredded sharp Cheddar cheese
- 1 cup frozen whole-kernel corn, thawed
- ½ cup yellow cornmeal
- 1 teaspoon baking powder
- ¼ teaspoon salt
- ¼ teaspoon pepper
- 1 (15-ounce) can cream-style corn
- 1 (4.5-ounce) can chopped green chiles, drained
- 4 large egg whites, lightly beaten
- 2 garlic cloves, minced
- 1 tablespoon finely chopped fresh cilantro (optional)

1. Preheat oven to 425°.
2. Heat a large nonstick skillet coated with cooking spray over medium-high heat. Add onion and squash; sauté 4 minutes or just until onion begins to brown. Remove from heat.
3. Stir in 1 cup cheese, corn, and next 8 ingredients. Place mixture in an 11 x 7-inch baking dish coated with cooking spray. Bake at 425° for 25 minutes or until center is set. Top with remaining ½ cup cheese. Bake an additional 5 minutes or until cheese melts. Garnish with cilantro, if desired. YIELD: 4 servings (serving size: ¼ of casserole).

POINTS: 7; **EXCHANGES:** 3 Starch, 1 Vegetable, 2 Medium-Fat Meat; **PER SERVING:** CAL 336 (20% from fat); PRO 21.2g; FAT 7.8g (sat 4.7g); CARB 50.4g; FIB 4.5g; CHOL 15mg; IRON 2.1mg; SOD 1030mg; CALC 480mg

CHEESY SOFT POLENTA WITH ROASTED VEGETABLES

(pictured on page 72)

To save time measuring, use four individual packets of plain instant grits, such as Quaker Original Flavor Instant Grits.

2 onions
2 yellow squash (about ½ pound)
2 zucchini (about ½ pound)
1 large red bell pepper, cut into
    1-inch pieces
2 teaspoons olive oil
¼ teaspoon salt
¼ teaspoon pepper
Cooking spray
2 cups water
1⅓ cups instant grits
¾ cup (3 ounces) reduced-fat
    shredded sharp Cheddar cheese
¼ cup evaporated fat-free milk
2 tablespoons yogurt-based spread
    (such as Brummel & Brown)
1 teaspoon ground cumin
1 teaspoon Worcestershire sauce
¾ teaspoon sugar
¼ teaspoon salt
⅛ teaspoon ground red pepper

1. Preheat oven to 450⁰.
2. Cut onions into eighths; separate layers. Cut yellow squash and zucchini in half lengthwise; cut each half into 2-inch pieces.
3. Place onion, squash, zucchini, bell pepper, olive oil, salt, and black pepper in a large bowl; toss well. Arrange vegetable mixture on a large baking sheet; coat vegetables with cooking spray. Bake vegetables at 450°, stirring twice, 12 to 14 minutes or until tender.
4. Bring water to a boil in a saucepan over high heat. Stir in grits, and remove from heat. Stir in cheese and remaining ingredients. Cover and keep warm.
5. Spoon grits onto plates, and top with vegetables. YIELD: 4 servings (serving size: ¾ cup grits and 1 cup vegetables).

POINTS: 5; *EXCHANGES:* 1½ Starch, 3 Vegetable, 1 Medium-Fat Meat, 1 Fat; **PER SERVING:** CAL 274 (28% from fat); PRO 12.3g; FAT 9g (sat 3.2g); CARB 39.6g; FIB 5.7g; CHOL 9mg; IRON 9.8mg; SOD 837mg; CALC 283mg

RUSTIC CORN CAKES WITH CREAMY CUMIN SAUCE

(pictured on page 4)

Creamy Cumin Sauce
Cooking spray
2 cups frozen whole-kernel corn,
    thawed
1 cup chopped zucchini
½ cup chopped red or green bell
    pepper
2 garlic cloves, minced
½ cup finely chopped green
    onions
¼ cup all-purpose flour
¾ cup yellow cornmeal
¾ teaspoon salt
¼ teaspoon fresh ground black
    pepper
⅛ teaspoon ground red pepper
⅓ cup low-fat mayonnaise
¼ cup chopped fresh cilantro
¼ cup fat-free milk
2 tablespoons lime juice
3 large egg whites
Lime wedges (optional)

1. Prepare Creamy Cumin Sauce; set aside.
2. Heat a large nonstick skillet coated with cooking spray over medium-high heat. Add corn and next 3 ingredients; cook 8 minutes or until tender. Stir in onions. Cool completely.
3. Lightly spoon flour into a dry measuring cup; level with a knife. Combine flour and next 4 ingredients in a large bowl. Combine vegetable mixture, mayonnaise, and next 4 ingredients; add to flour mixture, stirring until moist.
4. Heat a large nonstick skillet or nonstick griddle coated with cooking spray over medium-low heat. Spoon about ½ cup corn mixture onto skillet; flatten each patty to ½-inch thickness with a spatula. Cook 3 minutes on each side. Repeat procedure with remaining corn mixture. Serve with Creamy Cumin Sauce. Garnish with lime wedges, if desired. YIELD: 4 servings (serving size: 2 corn cakes and ¼ cup sauce).

CREAMY CUMIN SAUCE
1 tablespoon fresh lime juice
¼ teaspoon salt
¼ teaspoon ground cumin
¼ teaspoon chili powder
⅛ teaspoon ground red pepper
1 (8-ounce) carton reduced-fat
    sour cream

1. Combine all ingredients, stirring well. Cover and chill. YIELD: 1 cup.

POINTS: 7; *EXCHANGES:* 4 Starch, ½ Vegetable, 2 Fat; **PER SERVING:** CAL 372 (21% from fat); PRO 11.9g; FAT 9g (sat 4.5g); CARB 62.4g; FIB 4.6g; CHOL 29mg; IRON 2.2mg; SOD 860mg; CALC 131mg

SKILLET ROASTED PEPPER LASAGNA

(pictured on page 71)

Cooking spray
  1 cup chopped green bell pepper
  ½ cup chopped onion
  1 (7-ounce) jar bottled roasted red bell peppers, drained and chopped
  2 tablespoons chopped fresh basil
  2 garlic cloves, minced
  6 cooked lasagna noodles
  1½ cups bottled pasta sauce, divided
  1 cup 1% low-fat cottage cheese, divided
  1 (10-ounce) package frozen chopped spinach, thawed, drained, and squeezed dry, divided
  ¼ cup (1 ounce) grated fresh Parmesan cheese, divided
  1 cup (4 ounces) shredded part-skim mozzarella cheese

1. Preheat oven to 350°.
2. Place a large nonstick skillet coated with cooking spray over high heat. Add bell pepper and onion to skillet; sauté 3 minutes or until tender. Remove from heat; add red pepper, basil, and garlic.
3. Cut each lasagna noodle in half. Place 4 halves in bottom of an 11 x 7-inch baking dish coated with cooking spray. Top with ½ cup pasta sauce, ⅔ cup red pepper mixture, ½ cup cottage cheese, ⅓ cup spinach, and 1 tablespoon Parmesan cheese. Repeat layers one time. Top with remaining 4 noodles, ½ cup pasta sauce, ½ cup red pepper mixture, and mozzarella cheese.
4. Bake at 350° for 35 minutes. Sprinkle with remaining Parmesan cheese. Let stand 10 minutes before serving. YIELD: 4 servings (serving size: ¼ of casserole).

POINTS: 7; EXCHANGES: 2 Starch, 2 Vegetable, 2 Lean Meat; PER SERVING: CAL 335 (22% from fat); PRO 24g; FAT 8.2g (sat 4.8g); CARB 40.9g; FIB 3.9g; CHOL 23mg; IRON 2.7mg; SOD 924mg; CALC 380mg

VEGETABLE ALFREDO

  2 quarts water
  6 ounces uncooked egg noodles
  1 (16-ounce) package frozen broccoli, cauliflower, and carrots, thawed
  ½ cup (4 ounces) tub-style light cream cheese
  ¼ cup reduced-fat sour cream
  2 tablespoons fat-free milk
  1 teaspoon salt
  1 garlic clove, minced
  ¼ cup (1 ounce) grated fresh Parmesan cheese
  ¼ cup finely chopped green onions
Freshly ground black pepper

1. Bring 2 quarts water to a boil. Add noodles; cook 8 minutes. Add broccoli, cauliflower, and carrots; cook 3 minutes. Drain and keep warm.
2. Place cream cheese and next 4 ingredients in a food processor, and process until smooth.
3. Place pasta mixture in a large bowl. Add cream cheese mixture, and toss gently. Sprinkle with Parmesan cheese, onions, and pepper. YIELD: 4 servings (serving size: 1 cup).

POINTS: 6; EXCHANGES: 2 Starch, 1 Vegetable, ½ Medium-Fat Meat, 1 Fat; PER SERVING: CAL 290 (31% from fat); PRO 13.3g; FAT 10g (sat 5.9g); CARB 36.6g; FIB 4.5g; CHOL 60mg; IRON 2.4mg; SOD 886mg; CALC 208mg

MACARONI AND CHEESE WITH CARROTS AND ROASTED PEPPER

Cooking spray
  2 cups diced carrot (about 4)
  2 tablespoons all-purpose flour
  2 cups fat-free milk
  1¼ cups (5 ounces) reduced-fat shredded sharp Cheddar cheese
  2 tablespoons grated fresh Parmesan cheese
  ¼ teaspoon salt
  ⅛ teaspoon ground nutmeg
  ⅛ teaspoon pepper
  3 cups hot cooked elbow macaroni (about 1½ cups uncooked pasta)
  ½ cup diced roasted red bell pepper
  ¼ cup dry breadcrumbs

1. Preheat oven to 375°.
2. Coat a large saucepan with cooking spray; place over medium heat until hot. Add carrot; sauté 5 minutes. Place flour in a small bowl. Gradually add milk, stirring well with a whisk; add to carrot. Cook over medium heat 8 minutes, stirring constantly. Reduce heat to low. Add Cheddar cheese and next 4 ingredients; stir until cheese melts. Add macaroni and red bell pepper; stir well.
3. Spoon mixture into a 2-quart baking dish coated with cooking spray; sprinkle with breadcrumbs. Bake at 375° for 30 minutes. YIELD: 4 servings (serving size: 1½ cups).

POINTS: 7; EXCHANGES: 2½ Starch, 2 Vegetable, ½ Skim Milk, 2 Medium-Fat Meat; PER SERVING: CAL 378 (19% from fat); PRO 23.3g; FAT 8.1g (sat 4.7g); CARB 53.2g; FIB 4g; CHOL 18mg; IRON 2.6mg; SOD 722mg; CALC 556mg

QUICK PASTA SKILLET

Cooking spray
- 1 teaspoon olive oil
- 1 (8-ounce) package presliced mushrooms
- 1 cup chopped yellow onion
- ¾ cup chopped green bell pepper
- 1 teaspoon dried basil leaves
- ¼ teaspoon salt
- 2 garlic cloves, minced
- 1 (14-ounce) jar pizza sauce
- 4 cups hot cooked penne (about 2 cups uncooked tube-shaped pasta)
- 1½ cups (6 ounces) shredded part-skim mozzarella cheese

1. Preheat broiler.
2. Heat olive oil in a large nonstick skillet coated with cooking spray over medium-high heat. Add mushrooms; sauté 4 minutes. Add onion and next 4 ingredients; sauté 8 minutes or until vegetables are crisp-tender.
3. Add pizza sauce and pasta; cook 2 minutes, stirring constantly or until thoroughly heated and pasta is evenly coated with sauce. Remove from heat, and top with cheese.
4. Wrap handle of pan with foil; broil 1 minute or until cheese melts. **YIELD:** 4 servings (serving size: 1½ cups).

POINTS: 8; **EXCHANGES:** 3 Starch, 2 Vegetable, 1½ Medium-Fat Meat, ½ Fat; **PER SERVING:** CAL 385 (22% from fat); PRO 22g; FAT 9.6g (sat 5g); CARB 53g; FIB 5.3g; CHOL 23mg; IRON 4.1mg; SOD 652mg; CALC 342mg

WHITE BEAN AND WILTED SPINACH PENNE

- 8 ounces uncooked penne pasta
- 1 (10-ounce) package fresh spinach
- Olive oil-flavored cooking spray
- 2 (15-ounce) cans cannellini beans, rinsed and drained
- 1 cup chopped tomato
- ½ cup chopped fresh basil
- ¼ cup balsamic vinegar
- 1 tablespoon olive oil
- ½ teaspoon salt
- ½ teaspoon pepper
- ½ cup (2 ounces) freshly grated Parmesan cheese

1. Cook pasta according to package directions, omitting salt and fat. Drain well.
2. Remove coarse stems from spinach. Coat a Dutch oven with cooking spray. Place over medium heat until hot. Add spinach; sauté until it just begins to wilt. Add pasta, cannellini beans, and next 6 ingredients; toss gently. Sprinkle with cheese.
YIELD: 5 servings (serving size: 2 cups).

POINTS: 7; **EXCHANGES:** 3½ Starch, 1 Vegetable, ½ Medium-Fat Meat, 1 Fat; **PER SERVING:** CAL 361 (19% from fat); PRO 16.7g; FAT 7.7g (sat 2.7g); CARB 56g; FIB 8.2g; CHOL 9mg; IRON 5.4mg; SOD 746mg; CALC 273mg

---

SUPER SPINACH

Thanks to Popeye, we know to eat spinach for vitamins and minerals. However, many don't know that spinach also contains high levels of lutein—a phytochemical that protects the eyes from harmful ultraviolet rays.

FETA-AND-PENNE TOSS

- 6 ounces uncooked penne (tube-shaped pasta)
- Cooking spray
- 1 green bell pepper, cut into thin strips
- 1 large zucchini, quartered lengthwise and sliced
- 16 chopped pitted kalamata olives
- 1½ cups coarsely chopped seeded tomato
- ¼ cup finely chopped fresh parsley, divided
- 1 tablespoon chopped fresh basil
- ¼ teaspoon salt
- ¼ teaspoon dried crushed red pepper
- 1 (15-ounce) can cannellini beans, rinsed and drained
- 2 teaspoons olive oil
- ½ cup (2 ounces) crumbled feta cheese

1. Cook pasta according to package directions, omitting salt and fat. Drain well.
2. Heat a large nonstick skillet coated with cooking spray over medium heat. Add bell pepper and zucchini; sauté until crisp-tender.
3. Remove from heat; gently stir in olives, tomato, 3 tablespoons parsley, basil, and next 3 ingredients. Drizzle with oil. (Do not stir after adding oil). Cover and keep warm.
4. Drain pasta, and place in a large serving bowl. Top with zucchini mixture, crumbled feta cheese, and 1 tablespoon parsley. Toss well. **YIELD:** 4 servings (serving size: 1½ cups).

POINTS: 7; **EXCHANGES:** 2½ Starch, 2 Vegetable, ½ Medium-Fat Meat, 1½ Fat; **PER SERVING:** CAL 324 (29% from fat); PRO 11.2g; FAT 10.6g (sat 3.1g); CARB 46.8g; FIB 6.3g; CHOL 13mg; IRON 3.5mg; SOD 702mg; CALC 123mg

BROCCOLI ROTINI CASSEROLE

8 ounces uncooked rotini (corkscrew pasta)

4 cups broccoli florets

1 cup (4 ounces) reduced-fat shredded Cheddar cheese

½ cup reduced-fat sour cream

2 tablespoons fresh lemon juice

½ teaspoon salt

¼ teaspoon black pepper

⅛ teaspoon ground red pepper

1 (10-ounce) can condensed reduced-fat, reduced-sodium cream of mushroom soup

1 (4-ounce) jar sliced pimiento, drained

4 teaspoons grated fresh Parmesan cheese

1. Cook pasta according to package directions, omitting salt and fat. Cook 7 minutes or until "al dente"; add broccoli, and cook 3 minutes or until broccoli is crisp-tender. Drain well.

2. Combine Cheddar cheese and next 7 ingredients in a bowl, stirring well.

3. Return pasta to pan; add cheese mixture, stirring gently.

4. Cook over medium-low heat 5 minutes or until thoroughly heated. Sprinkle with Parmesan cheese. YIELD: 4 servings (serving size: 1⅔ cups).

POINTS: 8; EXCHANGES: 3 Starch, 1 Vegetable, 1 Medium-Fat Meat, 1 Fat; PER SERVING: CAL 374 (27% from fat); PRO 19.1g; FAT 11.5g (sat 6.5g); CARB 49.4g; FIB 3.8g; CHOL 33mg; IRON 2.7mg; SOD 844mg; CALC 428mg

HOT MONTEREY ZITI

¾ cup evaporated fat-free milk

2 tablespoons finely chopped green onions

1 tablespoon grated Parmesan cheese

1 teaspoon Dijon mustard

½ teaspoon salt

1 large egg white

1½ cups uncooked ziti (short tube-shaped pasta)

Cooking spray

¾ cup (3 ounces) shredded Monterey Jack cheese with jalapeño peppers

1. Preheat oven to 325°.

2. Combine first 6 ingredients in a small bowl; set aside.

3. Cook pasta according to package directions, omitting salt and fat. Drain well.

4. Place pasta in an 8-inch square baking dish coated with cooking spray. Pour egg mixture over pasta. Sprinkle with cheese. Bake, uncovered, at 325° for 20 to 23 minutes or until set. Cut into fourths. Serve immediately. YIELD: 4 servings (serving size: ¼ of casserole).

POINTS: 5; EXCHANGES: 1½ Starch, ½ Skim Milk, 1 Medium-Fat Meat; PER SERVING: CAL 250 (29% from fat); PRO 13.8g; FAT 8g (sat 4.9g); CARB 30g; FIB 1.2g; CHOL 28mg; IRON 1.2mg; SOD 571mg; CALC 302mg

BLACK BEAN-AND-CORN RAVIOLI WITH RED PEPPER SAUCE

1 cup fat-free black bean dip

½ cup frozen whole-kernel corn, thawed

¼ cup chopped green onions

2 tablespoons chopped fresh cilantro

½ teaspoon ground cumin

25 won ton wrappers

2 teaspoons cornstarch

Cooking spray

1 cup water

1 teaspoon olive oil

⅓ cup chopped green onions

3 garlic cloves, minced

½ cup vegetable broth

1 tablespoon red wine vinegar

2 teaspoons sugar

½ teaspoon salt

¼ teaspoon freshly ground black pepper

2 (7.25-ounce) bottles roasted red bell peppers, drained

10 tablespoons reduced-fat sour cream

1. Combine first 5 ingredients in a small bowl.

2. Working with one won ton wrapper at a time (cover remaining wrappers with a damp towel to keep them from drying), spoon 1 tablespoon bean mixture into center of each wrapper. Moisten edges of dough with water; bring 2 opposite corners together. Pinch edges together to seal, forming a triangle. Place ravioli on a large baking sheet sprinkled with cornstarch. Cover ravioli with a damp towel to keep them from drying.

3. Heat a large nonstick skillet coated with cooking spray over medium heat. Add ravioli, and cook 2 minutes on each side or until lightly browned. Add water; cover and cook 1 minute. Remove ravioli from pan with a slotted spoon; keep warm.

4. Heat oil in a large skillet over medium-high heat. Add onions and garlic; cook 3 minutes or until tender. Place onion mixture, broth, and next 5 ingredients in a food processor or blender; process until smooth. Return mixture to pan; cook over medium-high heat 3 minutes or until thoroughly heated. Serve ravioli with red pepper sauce and sour cream. YIELD: 5 servings (serving size: 5 ravioli, ½ cup sauce, and 2 tablespoons sour cream).

POINTS: 5; *EXCHANGES:* 2½ Starch, 1½ Vegetable, 1 Fat; **PER SERVING:** CAL 279 (19% from fat); PRO 10.4g; FAT 5.9g (sat 2.7g); CARB 45.1g; FIB 3.9g; CHOL 19mg; IRON 2.6mg; SOD 779mg; CALC 115mg

PEASANT SPINACH RAVIOLI

¾ cup 1% low-fat cottage cheese
2 teaspoons dried basil
¼ teaspoon ground nutmeg
1 (10-ounce) package chopped spinach, thawed, drained, and squeezed dry
1 large egg white, lightly beaten
1 garlic clove, minced
32 won ton wrappers
1 large egg white, lightly beaten
1 tablespoon cornstarch
4 quarts water
1⅓ cups low-fat marinara sauce
2 tablespoons grated fresh Parmesan cheese

1. Combine first 6 ingredients in medium bowl; set aside.

2. Working with 1 won ton wrapper at a time (cover remaining wrappers with a damp towel to keep them from drying), spoon about ½ tablespoon spinach mixture into center of each wrapper. Moisten edges of wrapper with egg white; bring 2 opposite corners together. Pinch edges together to seal, forming a triangle.

3. Place each wrapper on a baking sheet sprinkled with cornstarch Cover ravioli with a damp towel to keep them from drying.

4. Bring 4 quarts water just to a simmer in a large Dutch oven. Add 8 ravioli; cook 2 minutes, stirring once. Remove ravioli from pan with a slotted spoon; keep warm. Repeat procedure with remaining ravioli. Top ravioli with marinara sauce and Parmesan cheese. YIELD: 4 servings (serving size: 8 ravioli, ⅓ cup marinara sauce, 1½ teaspoons cheese).

POINTS: 5; *EXCHANGES:* 3 Starch, 1 Vegetable, 1 Lean Meat; **PER SERVING:** CAL 300 (8% from fat); PRO 18.2g; FAT 2.8g (sat 1.2g); CARB 51.4g; FIB 4.9g; CHOL 14mg; IRON 4.6mg; SOD 907mg; CALC 230mg

MAKING RAVIOLI

Ravioli is easy to prepare! After spooning mixture into center of a won ton wrapper, gently bring opposite corners together. Then pinch edges together to seal, forming a triangle.

FIRESIDE POTATOES AND VEGETABLES

Try serving this dish with scrambled eggs for brunch.

1½ pounds baking potatoes, cut into ½-inch cubes
Olive oil-flavored cooking spray
1 teaspoon olive oil
2 cups chopped onion
1⅓ cups chopped green bell pepper
1 teaspoon dried oregano
1 teaspoon paprika
1 (8-ounce) package presliced mushrooms
¼ cup water
½ cup chopped parsley
1¼ teaspoons salt
¼ teaspoon black pepper
1 cup (4 ounces) reduced-fat shredded sharp Cheddar cheese

1. Arrange potato in a vegetable steamer. Steam, covered, 10 to 12 minutes or just until tender.

2. Coat a 12-inch nonstick skillet with cooking spray; add oil. Place over medium-high heat until hot. Add onion and next 4 ingredients; sauté 6 to 8 minutes or until tender. Stir in water. Remove from heat; add potato, parsley, salt, and black pepper. Toss gently. Top with cheese; cover and let stand 5 minutes or until cheese melts. YIELD: 4 servings (serving size: 1¾ cups).

POINTS: 5; *EXCHANGES:* 2 Starch, 2 Vegetable, 1 Medium-Fat Meat; **PER SERVING:** CAL 260 (21% from fat); PRO 13.8g; FAT 6.3g (sat 3.3g); CARB 40.4g; FIB 5.4g; CHOL 10mg; IRON 2.3mg; SOD 943mg; CALC 298mg

YUKON GOLD-STUFFED PORTOBELLOS

4 medium Yukon gold potatoes
   (about 1¾ pounds), peeled and
   cut into 1-inch pieces
4 (5-inch) portobello mushroom
   caps
Olive oil-flavored cooking spray
⅛ teaspoon salt
⅛ teaspoon freshly ground black
   pepper
1 tablespoon light butter
4 garlic cloves, minced
½ cup fat-free milk
¾ teaspoon salt
¼ teaspoon freshly ground black
   pepper
4 (¾-ounce) slices provolone
   cheese
¼ cup chopped green onions
Freshly ground black pepper

1. Preheat oven to 450°.
2. Place potato in a saucepan; add
water to cover. Bring to boil: cover,
reduce heat, and simmer 20 minutes
or until tender. Drain.
3. Remove brown gills from undersides of mushrooms using a sharp
knife, if desired. Place mushroom
caps on a jelly-roll pan, stem side
down. Coat with cooking spray;
sprinkle with ⅛ teaspoon each
salt and pepper. Bake at 450° for
15 minutes, turning once.
4. Heat saucepan over medium heat
until hot. Add butter and garlic;
sauté 1 minute. Add milk, ¾ teaspoon salt, and ¼ teaspoon pepper;
stir well. Return potato to saucepan;
mash with a potato masher. Spoon
1 cup mashed potato onto each
mushroom cap. Top each with

1 slice cheese; sprinkle with onions.
Bake at 450° for 8 to 10 minutes or
until cheese melts. Sprinkle with
pepper. Serve immediately. YIELD: 4
servings (serving size: 1 stuffed
mushroom cap).

POINTS: 6; **EXCHANGES:** 3 Starch, ½ High-Fat
Meat, 1 Fat; **PER SERVING:** CAL 307 (24% from fat);
PRO 11.5g; FAT 7.8g (sat 4.5g); CARB 45.9g;
FIB 4.2g; CHOL 21mg; IRON 0.7mg; SOD 741mg;
CALC 205mg

SAUTÉED SPINACH WITH RUSTIC MASHED POTATOES

3 Yukon Gold potatoes, diced
   (about 2 pounds)
1 garlic clove
2 teaspoons olive oil
1½ cups chopped onion (about 1)
1 red bell pepper, seeded and
   diced
4 garlic cloves, minced
1 (10-ounce) package fresh
   spinach (about 4 cups)
¾ cup vegetable broth
¼ teaspoon crushed red pepper
½ cup 1% low-fat milk
1 tablespoon yogurt-based spread
   (such as Brummel & Brown)
¾ teaspoon salt
¼ teaspoon black pepper
6 tablespoons shredded Parmesan
   cheese

1. Place potato and 1 garlic clove in
a saucepan, and cover with water;
bring to a boil. Cover, reduce heat,
and simmer, 10 minutes or until
tender. Drain and set aside.
2. Heat oil in a large nonstick skillet
over medium-high heat. Add onion,

red bell pepper, and minced garlic;
sauté 5 minutes or until tender.
Add spinach, broth, and crushed red
pepper; cover and cook 3 minutes.
Stir well.
3. Add milk, spread, salt, and black
pepper to potato; beat with mixer
at medium speed for 1 minute or
until coarsely mashed. Serve spinach
mixture on top of mashed potato.
Sprinkle evenly with Parmesan
cheese. Yield: 4 servings (1 cup
potato and ⅔ cup spinach).

POINTS: 6; **EXCHANGES:** 3 Starch, 2 Vegetable,
1 Fat; **PER SERVING:** CAL 324 (18% from fat);
PRO 11.6g; FAT 6.7g (sat 2.2g); CARB 57.5g;
FIB 8.2g; CHOL 7mg; IRON 4.3mg; SOD 858mg;
CALC 251mg

MEATLESS MERITS

More and more people are
discovering the health benefits
of meat-free meals. In fact,
24% of American households
eat at least one or more meat-
free meals each week. Most
meatless meals have vegetables,
beans, grains, or soy (tofu)
as a base. These ingredients
give meatless dishes plenty of
cancer-preventing antioxidants
and fiber. People who follow
a meatless diet typically have
lower cholesterol levels, lower
body weights, and less of a risk
of cancer. Aside from the health
benefits, meatless dishes are
quick to prepare, economical,
and delicious.

VEGETARIAN COMFORT POT PIE

Cooking spray
1 (8-ounce) package presliced mushrooms
1 cup chopped red bell pepper
1¼ cups cubed peeled baking potato
1 cup frozen green peas, thawed
½ cup low-fat buttermilk
2 tablespoons chopped fresh parsley
¼ teaspoon salt
¼ teaspoon dried thyme
¼ teaspoon black pepper
1 (10.5-ounce) can condensed reduced-fat, reduced-sodium cream of mushroom soup
1 cup low-fat baking mix (such as reduced-fat Bisquick)
¾ cup low-fat buttermilk
1 large egg, lightly beaten

1. Preheat oven to 400°.
2. Heat a large nonstick skillet coated with cooking spray over medium heat. Add mushrooms and red bell pepper; sauté 8 minutes. Add potato and next 7 ingredients, stirring well. Spoon into an 11 x 7-inch baking dish.
3. Combine baking mix, buttermilk, and egg, stirring until moist. Spoon over vegetable mixture. Bake at 400° for 30 minutes or until golden. YIELD: 4 servings (serving size: ¼ of pie).

POINTS: 6; EXCHANGES: 3 Starch, 1 Vegetable, 1 Fat; PER SERVING: CAL 302 (17% from fat); PRO 11.8g; FAT 5.8g (sat 1.9g); CARB 51g; FIB 4.6g; CHOL 62mg; IRON 3mg; SOD 925mg; CALC 208mg

BOK CHOY-TOFU STIR-FRY

1 (14-ounce) package firm tofu
1 cup hot water
¼ cup low-sodium soy sauce
1½ tablespoons cornstarch
1 tablespoon sugar
1 teaspoon ground ginger
2 garlic cloves, minced
1 vegetable-flavored bouillon cube
3 tablespoons finely chopped unsalted, dry-roasted peanuts
2 teaspoons canola oil
Cooking spray
¾ cup thinly sliced carrot
¾ cup thinly sliced red bell pepper
4 cups coarsely chopped bok choy
½ (6-ounce) package frozen snow peas, thawed
3 cups hot cooked Chinese-style noodles or angel hair (about 6 ounces uncooked pasta)

1. Cut tofu into 1-inch cubes; drain for 5 minutes on paper towels.
2. Combine water and next 6 ingredients in a small bowl; stir until cornstarch is dissolved. Set aside.
3. Heat a nonstick skillet over medium-high heat. Add peanuts; cook 3 to 4 minutes or until lightly browned, stirring often. Set aside.
4. Heat oil in a large nonstick skillet over medium-high heat; arrange tofu in a single layer. Cook 5 minutes on each side or until lightly browned. Remove from skillet.
5. Coat pan with cooking spray. Add carrot, bell pepper, and bok choy; sauté 6 minutes or until white part of bok choy is crisp-tender. Increase heat to high; add tofu, peanuts, snow peas, and soy mixture. Bring to a boil; reduce heat, and simmer 1½ minutes or until slightly thick, stirring constantly. Serve over noodles. YIELD: 4 servings (serving size: 1 cup stir-fry and ¾ cup noodles).

POINTS: 7; EXCHANGES: 3 Starch, 2 Vegetable, 1 Medium-Fat Meat, ½ Fat; PER SERVING: CAL 340 (21% from fat); PRO 12.4g; FAT 8g (sat 1g); CARB 54.8g; FIB 3.4g; CHOL 0mg; IRON 2.7mg; SOD 782mg; CALC 130mg

CHEESY ZUCCHINI FRITTATA

½ cup (2 ounces) shredded part-skim mozzarella cheese
½ cup finely chopped green onions
¼ cup (1 ounce) grated fresh Parmesan cheese
¼ cup chopped fresh basil
¼ teaspoon black pepper
⅛ teaspoon salt
6 large egg whites
2 large eggs
1 teaspoon olive oil
1½ cups thinly sliced zucchini
½ cup chopped green bell pepper

1. Preheat oven to 475°.
2. Combine first 8 ingredients in a bowl; stir well with a whisk.
3. Heat oil in a nonstick skillet over medium-high heat. Add zucchini and bell pepper; sauté 5 minutes. Add egg mixture. Reduce heat to low; cook 5 minutes or until set around edges. Remove pan from heat.
4. Wrap handle of pan with foil. Bake at 475° for 8 minutes or until center is set. Cut into 4 wedges. YIELD: 4 servings (serving size: 1 wedge).

POINTS: 4; EXCHANGES: 1 Vegetable, 1 Very Lean Meat, 1 Medium-Fat Meat, ½ Fat; PER SERVING: CAL 155 (47% from fat); PRO 15.4g; FAT 8g (sat 3.7g); CARB 4.6g; FIB 1.3g; CHOL 119mg; IRON 0.8mg; SOD 381mg; CALC 215mg

Meats

BEEF, BEAN, AND VEGETABLE TACOS

2 teaspoons vegetable oil
1 small onion, chopped
1 small green bell pepper, seeded and chopped
½ pound ground round
1 cup frozen whole-kernel corn
1 (1.25-ounce) envelope 40%-less-sodium taco seasoning mix
1 (14.5-ounce) can chili-style tomatoes, drained
1 (16-ounce) can pinto beans, rinsed and drained
3 tablespoons chopped fresh cilantro
10 taco shells
2 cups chopped romaine lettuce
½ cup (2 ounces) reduced-fat shredded Cheddar cheese

1. Heat oil in a large nonstick skillet over medium-high heat. Add onion and pepper; sauté 3 minutes. Add beef, and cook until beef is browned and vegetables are tender, stirring to crumble meat.
2. Add corn, taco seasoning mix, tomatoes, and beans; bring to a boil, stirring occasionally. Reduce heat, and simmer, uncovered, 15 minutes or until mixture is slightly thick. Stir in cilantro.
3. Spoon ½ cup beef mixture into each taco shell; top evenly with lettuce and cheese. YIELD: 5 servings (serving size: 2 tacos).

POINTS: 7; **EXCHANGES:** 2 Starch, 2 Vegetable, 2 Medium-Fat Meat; **PER SERVING:** CAL 326 (26% from fat); PRO 19.6g; FAT 9.9g (sat 2.7g); CARB 42.9g; FIB 7.4g; CHOL 28mg; IRON 2.6mg; SOD 887mg; CALC 169mg

CAFÉ-STYLE MEAT LOAF WITH BROWNED GRAVY

(pictured on page 3)

½ cup finely chopped onion
½ cup finely chopped green bell pepper
½ cup regular oats
1 teaspoon dried oregano
2 teaspoons Worcestershire sauce
¼ teaspoon salt
¼ teaspoon black pepper
2 large egg whites
1 pound ground round
Cooking spray
Browned Gravy
2 tablespoons chopped fresh parsley (optional)

1. Preheat oven to 350°.
2. Combine first 8 ingredients in a large bowl; crumble beef over vegetable mixture, and stir until well-blended.
3. Shape beef mixture into an 8 x 4-inch loaf. Coat a rack and a shallow pan with cooking spray. Place meat loaf on rack in pan.
4. Bake at 350° for 55 minutes or until a thermometer registers 160°.
5. Prepare Browned Gravy.
6. Remove meat loaf from oven. Let stand 10 minutes. Cut into 8 slices. Serve with Browned Gravy. Sprinkle with parsley, if desired. YIELD: 4 servings (serving size: 2 slices meat loaf and ⅓ cup gravy).

BROWNED GRAVY

3 tablespoons all-purpose flour
1 (14½-ounce) can beef broth
⅛ teaspoon pepper
¼ cup evaporated fat-free milk
1 tablespoon reduced-calorie margarine

1. Place a large nonstick skillet over medium-high heat until hot. Add flour, and cook 6 to 8 minutes or until golden, stirring constantly.
2. Whisk in beef broth and pepper. Cook 8 to 10 minutes or until thickened, stirring often. Stir in milk; cook 2 minutes. Remove from heat; stir in margarine. Serve with Café-Style Meat Loaf. YIELD: 1⅓ cups (serving size: ⅓ cup).

POINTS: 5; **EXCHANGES:** 1 Starch, 1 Vegetable, 4 Lean Meat; **PER SERVING:** CAL 249 (24% from fat); PRO 31g; FAT 6.7g (sat 2g); CARB 17g; FIB 2g; CHOL 61mg; IRON 3.1mg; SOD 773mg; CALC 64mg

THE BONUSES OF BEEF

Red meat is not taboo in a healthy diet. In fact, lean beef fits easily into a healthful meal plan. Packed with nutrients, beef is a great source of protein, iron, niacin, zinc, and potassium. Although often thought to be full of fat and cholesterol, some cuts of beef are as lean as chicken. For the leanest cuts, look for the label "round" or "loin." Combine red meat with pasta or rice, bake it in a casserole, or use it in a stir-fry with vegetables to make a little meat go a long way.

MANDARIN BEEF STIR-FRY

Brown bean sauce can be found on the ethnic aisle at the grocery. Try serving this colorful dish over rice.

1 (1-pound) flank steak, trimmed and cut in half lengthwise
Cooking spray
5 cups broccoli florets
3 tablespoons water
¾ cup beef broth
1 tablespoon cornstarch
3 tablespoons spicy brown bean sauce (such as House of Tsang)
2 teaspoons minced peeled fresh ginger
1 teaspoon dark sesame oil
1 (11-ounce) can mandarin oranges, undrained

1. Cut steak diagonally across grain into thin slices. Heat a large nonstick skillet coated with cooking spray over medium-high heat. Add half of meat, and stir-fry 2 minutes; remove meat from pan, and keep warm. Repeat procedure with remaining meat. Add broccoli to pan; sprinkle with water. Cover and cook 3 minutes or until crisp-tender.
2. Combine broth and next 4 ingredients, stirring well with a whisk. Drain oranges, reserving ¼ cup liquid; stir liquid into broth mixture.
3. Add meat and broth mixture to broccoli; cook, stirring constantly, until thick. Gently stir in oranges. YIELD: 4 servings (serving size: 1½ cups stir-fry).

POINTS: 6; **EXCHANGES:** 1 Starch, 1 Vegetable, 3 Lean Meat; **PER SERVING:** CAL 294 (33% from fat); PRO 26.9g; FAT 10.4g (sat 4.1g); CARB 21.1g; FIB 2.4g; CHOL 59mg; IRON 3.2mg; SOD 529mg; CALC 54mg

GREEK STUFFED FLANK STEAK

½ cup finely chopped onion
Olive oil-flavored cooking spray
2 garlic cloves, minced
1 (10-ounce) package frozen chopped spinach, thawed, drained, and squeezed dry
⅓ cup (1⅓ ounces) crumbled feta cheese
2 tablespoons dry breadcrumbs
½ teaspoon salt
1 (1½-pound) flank steak, trimmed
½ teaspoon freshly ground pepper

1. Preheat oven to 425°.
2. Place a large nonstick skillet over medium-high heat; add onion. Coat onion with cooking spray, and sauté 5 minutes. Add garlic, and sauté 30 seconds. Remove from heat. Stir in spinach and next 3 ingredients.
3. Place steak between 2 sheets of heavy-duty plastic wrap; flatten to an even thickness using a meat mallet or rolling pin. Spread spinach mixture over beef, leaving a ½-inch margin around outside edges. Roll up beef, jelly-roll fashion, starting with 1 short side. Secure roll at 2-inch intervals with heavy string.
4. Place beef on broiler pan coated with cooking spray. Sprinkle beef with pepper; coat with cooking spray. Bake, uncovered, at 425° for 10 minutes. Reduce heat to 375°. Bake 25 minutes or to desired degree of doneness. Let stand 10 minutes. Remove string, and cut beef into 6 slices. YIELD: 6 servings (serving size: 1 slice).

POINTS: 5; **EXCHANGES:** 1 Vegetable, 3½ Lean Meat; **PER SERVING:** CAL 230 (43% from fat); PRO 26.7g; FAT 10.9g (sat 5.1g); CARB 5.4g; FIB 1.8g; CHOL 66mg; IRON 3.5mg; SOD 414mg; CALC 109mg

SIRLOIN STROGANOFF

(pictured on page 91)

1 pound boneless sirloin steak
Cooking spray
1½ cups chopped red onion
1 (8-ounce) package presliced mushrooms
2 tablespoons all-purpose flour
½ teaspoon salt
¼ teaspoon paprika
¼ teaspoon pepper
2 teaspoons vegetable oil
¾ cup beef broth
¾ cup fat-free sour cream
¼ cup chopped fresh parsley
2 cups hot cooked medium egg noodles (about 3 ounces uncooked pasta)

1. Trim fat from steak. Cut beef diagonally across grain into thin slices. Set aside.
2. Heat a large nonstick skillet coated with cooking spray over medium-high heat. Add onion; sauté 6 minutes. Add mushrooms; sauté 4 minutes or until tender.
3. Combine flour and next 3 ingredients in a bowl. Add beef, tossing to coat. Heat oil in pan over high heat. Add beef; sauté 6 minutes or until beef is done. Add reserved onion mixture and broth. Bring to a boil, reduce heat, and simmer 2 minutes or until sauce is thick. Remove from heat; stir in sour cream. Sprinkle with parsley. Serve over noodles. YIELD: 4 servings (serving size: 1 cup beef mixture and ½ cup noodles).

POINTS: 8; **EXCHANGES:** 2 Starch, 2 Vegetable, 3½ Lean Meat; **PER SERVING:** CAL 401 (26% from fat); PRO 35.5g; FAT 11.5g (sat 3.6g); CARB 38.2g; FIB 2.9g; CHOL 107mg; IRON 5.4mg; SOD 548mg; CALC 108mg

Commitment for Life

KAREN AGEMA • **HEIGHT** 5'7" • **BEFORE** 250 LBS. • **AFTER** 125 LBS.

Hint: "If you're hungry, then you're doing something wrong. Starving and bingeing, all or nothing doesn't work. You shouldn't ever feel deprived."

For most of her life, Karen Agema's weight was like a yo-yo—up and down, up and down. She tried all kinds of diets. But as she got older, there was a lot more up than down.

"I started dieting when I was 14," Karen says. Each time she lost weight, she gained it back plus more. Karen weighed 140 pounds at her wedding, but was up to 225 when her daughter, Erika, was born four years later. She went to Weight Watchers but quit just seven pounds from her goal. "I didn't believe I could maintain the weight, so I didn't try," Karen says.

It took a crisis to fix her resolve. Karen weighed 250 pounds when her marriage ended in divorce. "Everything was falling apart," Karen recalls. "I knew I had to take control of my life, for myself and for Erika. My weight was an obvious place to start."

Karen stuck it out this time, reaching her goal weight of 125 pounds in 18 months. (That's an average loss of 7 pounds a month.). What made this time different? "I just focused on gaining control of my eating," she says. "I couldn't control life, but I could control *this*. It was totally up to me."

"I'm an emotional eater," explains Karen, who used to eat whole bags of chips or a roll of cookie dough when she was upset. "I had to replace those bad habits with good ones, like walking. And I had to learn to forgive myself when I slip up—and keep going."

That attitude has helped Karen maintain her weight loss for nearly six years. It's not easy. As hard as it was to lose the weight, she says it can be just as hard to keep it off.

Karen did let down her guard for a while, until she discovered she had gained 15 pounds. "I freaked out, bought a big bag of candy, and ate the whole thing," Karen says. "That only made me feel worse." She vowed never to ignore her weight again. "Once you reach your goal, don't assume you no longer have a problem," she warns. "I know I'll have to watch my weight for the rest of my life."

> *"Once you reach your goal, don't assume you no longer have a problem."*

Now Karen finds other ways to feel better when she's upset, such as walking, attending a Weight Watchers meeting, or going out dancing with her boyfriend. When her dad had a heart attack in 2001, she did *not* turn to food for comfort.

Karen shares her commitment by leading Weight Watchers meetings, encouraging members to have realistic goals and to stay positive, no matter what the scale says. They know Karen shares their struggle. She admits, "I pray every day that I won't overeat, that I won't lose control. I'll never take that for granted again."

Fruit-Stuffed Pork
Tenderloin with
Orange-Mustard
Sauce, page 99

Beef Tenderloin
with Marsala-
Mushroom Sauce,
page 93

Sirloin
Stroganoff,
page 88

Beef-and-Broccoli
Stir-Fry, page 93

92

BEEF-AND-BROCCOLI STIR-FRY

(pictured on facing page)

1 pound boneless sirloin steak
1 cup beef broth
¼ cup low-sodium soy sauce
1 tablespoon cornstarch
2 teaspoons dark sesame oil, divided
1 tablespoon minced peeled fresh ginger
3 garlic cloves, minced
4 cups broccoli florets
2½ cups sliced onion (about 1)
1 cup thinly sliced carrot
6 cups hot cooked quick-cooking brown rice (such as Success)

1. Trim fat from steak. Cut beef diagonally across grain into very thin slices.
2. Combine broth, soy sauce, and cornstarch in a small bowl; stir with a whisk until blended.
3. Heat 1 teaspoon oil in a large nonstick skillet or wok over high heat. Add ginger and garlic; stir-fry 2 minutes. Add beef; stir-fry 5 minutes. Remove mixture from pan; keep warm. Add remaining 1 teaspoon oil; add broccoli, onion, and carrot. Sauté 7 minutes or until vegetables are crisp-tender. Return beef mixture to pan, and stir in cornstarch mixture; sauté 2 minutes or until thick and bubbly. Serve over rice. YIELD: 6 servings (serving size: 1 cup beef mixture and 1 cup rice).

POINTS: 8; EXCHANGES: 3 Starch, 2 Vegetable, 2 Very Lean Meat, 1 Fat; PER SERVING: CAL 402 (19% from fat); PRO 25.6g; FAT 8.3g (sat 2.5g); CARB 55.6g; FIB 6.3g; CHOL 51mg; IRON 3.4mg; SOD 609mg; CALC 64mg

SKILLET SIRLOIN WITH SWEET MARINADE

Combine ingredients in the morning, and let the meat marinate during the workday. Once dinnertime rolls around, you can have the main dish on the table in minutes.

1 pound boneless sirloin steak (¾ inch thick)
2 tablespoons dark brown sugar
3 tablespoons balsamic vinegar
1 tablespoon Worcestershire sauce
½ teaspoon salt
Cooking spray
½ cup beef broth

1. Combine first 5 ingredients in a large heavy-duty zip-top plastic bag. Seal bag; shake to coat. Marinate in refrigerator 8 hours.
2. Remove steak from marinade, reserving marinade. Heat a large skillet coated with cooking spray over high heat. Add beef, and cook 1 minute on each side or until browned. Reduce heat to medium-low; cook 4 minutes on each side or until done. Place beef on a platter; keep warm.
3. Increase heat to medium-high. Add reserved marinade and broth to pan; scrape pan to loosen browned bits. Bring to a boil; cook 4 minutes or until sauce is reduced to ¼ cup. Slice beef diagonally across grain into thin slices. Serve beef with sauce. YIELD: 4 servings (serving size: 3 ounces beef and 1 tablespoon sauce).

POINTS: 5; EXCHANGES: ½ Starch, 4 Lean Meat; PER SERVING: CAL 213 (31% from fat); PRO 26.5g; FAT 7g (sat 2.7g); CARB 9.3g; FIB 0g; CHOL 77mg; IRON 3.4mg; SOD 497mg; CALC 23mg

BEEF TENDERLOIN WITH MARSALA-MUSHROOM SAUCE

(pictured on page 90)

10 ounces shiitake mushrooms
4 (4-ounce) beef tenderloin steaks, trimmed
½ teaspoon pepper
¼ teaspoon salt
Cooking spray
1 teaspoon olive oil
¼ cup minced shallots
½ cup Marsala wine
¾ cups beef broth
½ teaspoon Dijon mustard
1 tablespoon light butter

1. Remove and discard stems from mushrooms; slice mushrooms.
2. Sprinkle steak with pepper and salt; coat with cooking spray. Heat a large nonstick skillet over high heat. Add beef; cook 3 to 4 minutes on each side or until desired degree of doneness. Place beef on a platter; keep warm.
3. Heat oil in pan over medium heat until hot; add shallots, and sauté 1 minute. Add sliced mushrooms; sauté 4 minutes or until tender. Add wine; bring to a boil, reduce heat, and simmer 2 minutes.
4. Add broth and Dijon mustard; boil 5 minutes or until liquid is reduced by half. Remove from heat. Add butter; stir until butter melts. Spoon sauce over beef. YIELD: 4 servings (serving size: 1 steak and ⅓ cup mushroom sauce).

POINTS: 5; EXCHANGES: 1 Vegetable, 3½ Lean Meat; PER SERVING: CAL 231 (41% from fat); PRO 26.3g; FAT 10.2g (sat 4.2g); CARB 6.4g; FIB 0.9g; CHOL 75mg; IRON 4.5mg; SOD 404mg; CALC 14mg

BEEF TENDERLOIN WITH HORSERADISH-MUSTARD CRUST

1¾ pounds beef tenderloin, trimmed
¼ teaspoon freshly ground black pepper
Cooking spray
1½ tablespoons Dijon mustard
1½ tablespoons prepared horseradish
1 cup French bread breadcrumbs
1 tablespoon chopped fresh parsley
2 teaspoons olive oil
⅛ teaspoon salt
⅛ teaspoon freshly ground pepper
2 garlic cloves, minced

1. Preheat oven to 400°.
2. Sprinkle tenderloin with pepper. Coat a large nonstick skillet with cooking spray; place over medium-high heat until hot. Add beef, and cook 10 minutes or until browned.
3. Combine mustard and horse-radish; spread onto beef. Combine breadcrumbs and remaining 5 ingre-dients; pat onto beef, pressing firmly. Coat beef with cooking spray. Insert meat thermometer into center of beef. Bake at 400° for 35 to 40 minutes or until temperature regis-ters 145° (medium-rare) to 160° (medium).
4. Place beef on a platter; cover with foil. Let stand 10 minutes before slicing. YIELD: 7 servings (serv-ing size: 3 ounces cooked beef).

POINTS: 5; **EXCHANGES:** ½ Starch, 3 Lean Meat;
PER SERVING: CAL 218 (43% from fat); PRO 24.8g;
FAT 10.3g (sat 3.4g); CARB 5.3g; FIB 0.5g;
CHOL 70mg; IRON 3.4mg; SOD 235mg;
CALC 21mg

SLOW-ROASTED BEEF AND GRAVY

1 teaspoon dried oregano
1 teaspoon paprika
½ teaspoon garlic powder
¼ teaspoon freshly ground black pepper
½ (2.6-ounce) package golden onion soup mix (such as Lipton Recipe Secrets)
Cooking spray
2 teaspoons olive oil
1¾ pounds eye-of-round roast, trimmed
1 cup water
⅓ cup dry red wine
2 tablespoons all-purpose flour
2 tablespoons water
2 tablespoons chopped fresh parsley

1. Combine first 5 ingredients; set aside.
2. Coat a Dutch oven with cooking spray; add oil. Place over medium-high heat until hot. Add beef, and cook 2 minutes on each side or until browned.
3. Sprinkle beef with soup mix mix-ture; add 1 cup water and wine to pan. Bring to a boil. Cover, reduce heat, and simmer 2 hours.
4. Place beef on a platter, reserving liquid in pan; cover beef with foil. Let stand 10 minutes before slicing.
5. Combine flour and 2 tablespoons water; add to cooking liquid. Simmer 8 to 10 minutes or until thick; add parsley. Serve over beef. YIELD: 7 servings (3 ounces cooked beef and ¼ cup gravy).

POINTS: 5; **EXCHANGE:** ½ Starch, 3 Lean Meat;
PER SERVING: CAL 207 (40% from fat); PRO 24.6g;
FAT 9.1g (sat 3.1g); CARB 5.7g; FIB 0.6g;
CHOL 60mg; IRON 2.1mg; SOD 512mg;
CALC 22mg

GLAZED VEAL CHOPS WITH GRAPES

4 (6-ounce) veal loin chops, trimmed
½ teaspoon salt
⅛ teaspoon pepper
1 teaspoon olive oil
¼ cup fresh orange juice
¼ cup balsamic vinegar
1 cup seedless red grapes, halved

1. Sprinkle veal with salt and pepper.
2. Heat oil in a large nonstick skillet over medium-high heat. Add veal; cook 7 to 8 minutes on each side or until done. Remove veal from pan; keep warm.
3. Add orange juice and vinegar to drippings; cook over medium heat 2 to 3 minutes, scraping pan to loosen browned bits. Return veal to pan; add grape halves, and cook 1 minute, turning veal to coat with sauce. Place veal on a serving platter. Pour sauce over veal. YIELD: 4 servings (serving size: 1 chop and ¼ cup sauce).

POINTS: 6; **EXCHANGES:** 1 Fruit, 4 Lean Meat;
PER SERVING: CAL 258 (34% from fat); PRO 30.5g;
FAT 9.6g (sat 2.5g); CARB 11.1g; FIB 0.5g;
CHOL 112mg; IRON 1.3mg; SOD 371mg;
CALC 40mg

MIDDLE EASTERN SWEET SPICED LAMB AND VEGETABLES

1 pound lean ground lamb
Cooking spray
1½ cups chopped onion
1 cup diced carrot
⅓ cup thinly sliced celery
½ teaspoon ground cinnamon
¼ teaspoon salt
¼ teaspoon ground allspice
¼ teaspoon ground nutmeg
¼ teaspoon ground cumin
⅛ teaspoon ground red pepper
1 (10-ounce) package yellow rice mix (such as Vigo)
2½ cups hot water
2 tablespoons chopped fresh mint
2 tablespoons pine nuts, toasted

1. Cook lamb in a large nonstick skillet over medium-high heat until lamb is browned, stirring to crumble. Drain in a colander.
2. Coat pan with cooking spray; place over medium heat until hot. Add onion, carrot, and celery; cook 8 to 10 minutes or until vegetables are tender. Add lamb, cinnamon, and next 6 ingredients to vegetable mixture; cook 1 minute, stirring frequently. Add water; bring to a boil. Cover, reduce heat, and simmer 20 to 25 minutes or until liquid is absorbed.
3. Place lamb mixture in a serving bowl; sprinkle with mint and pine nuts. YIELD: 6 servings (serving size: 1⅓ cups).

POINTS: 7; EXCHANGES: 2½ Starch, 1 Vegetable, 1½ Medium-Fat Meat, 1 Fat; PER SERVING: CAL 349 (30% from fat); PRO 18.4g; FAT 11.7g (sat 4.4g); CARB 42.8g; FIB 2.4g; CHOL 50mg; IRON 4mg; SOD 774mg; CALC 36mg

LAMB SHANKS ON LENTIL-SPINACH RAGOÛT

6 (1-pound) lamb shanks, trimmed
½ teaspoon pepper
¼ teaspoon salt
1 cup chopped onion
1 cup dry red wine
½ cup beef broth
4 carrots, scraped and sliced
2 celery stalks, sliced
1 (28-ounce) can no-salt-added diced tomatoes, undrained
1½ teaspoons dried rosemary leaves
2 bay leaves
3 slices center-cut bacon
2 (19-ounce) cans lentil soup (such as Progresso)
¾ cup tomato juice
1 tablespoon Dijon mustard
1 (10-ounce) package frozen chopped spinach, thawed and drained

1. Sprinkle lamb with pepper and salt. Heat an extra-large Dutch oven over medium-high heat. Add half of lamb; cook 3 minutes on each side or until browned. Remove from pan; set aside. Repeat with remaining lamb. Reduce heat to medium; add onion and next 4 ingredients. Cook 5 minutes, scraping pan to loosen browned bits. Add tomatoes, rosemary, and bay leaves. Return lamb to pan. Bring to a boil. Cover, reduce heat, and simmer 2 hours or until lamb is tender; discard bay leaves and liquid.
2. Cook bacon in a large nonstick skillet over medium-high heat until crisp. Remove bacon from pan, and crumble. Discard pan drippings. Add bacon, soup, and remaining 3 ingredients to pan. Simmer, uncovered, 30 minutes, stirring occasionally.
3. Serve lamb shanks on a bed of lentil ragoût. YIELD: 6 servings (serving size: 3 ounces cooked lamb and 1 cup ragoût).
NOTE: The discarded remaining braising liquid can be used to make a delicious soup; just skim the fat first.

POINTS: 5; EXCHANGES: 1 Starch, ½ Vegetable, 4 Lean Meat; PER SERVING: CAL 277 (26% from fat); PRO 31g; FAT 8.1g (sat 2.3g); CARB 19.9g; FIB 6.8g; CHOL 69mg; IRON 5.5mg; SOD 992mg; CALC 96mg

DON'T IGNORE IRON

Women of childbearing age need 15 milligrams of iron a day; during pregnancy and lactation, the need doubles! So how do you know if you're getting enough of this mineral that carries oxygen in the blood? If you are deficient, you'll probably feel tired and weak because your muscles are not able to get enough oxygen to work properly. You may also notice that you are more susceptible to colds and illness, as your immune system is not at its best.

Make a point to incorporate such iron-rich foods as fortified cereals, lean cuts of beef, beans, and fortified orange juice into your daily diet.

MEDITERRANEAN GRILLED LAMB

1½ pounds boneless leg of lamb, trimmed
¼ cup dry red wine
2 tablespoons chopped fresh rosemary
2 teaspoons olive oil
½ teaspoon salt
¼ teaspoon pepper
4 large garlic cloves, minced
Cooking spray

1. Slice lamb lengthwise, cutting to, but not through, other side. Open the halves, laying lamb flat. Slice each half lengthwise, cutting to, but not through, other side; open flat.
2. Combine wine and next 5 ingredients in a large heavy-duty zip-top plastic bag. Add lamb to bag; seal. Marinate in refrigerator 8 hours.
3. Prepare grill.
4. Remove lamb from bag, reserving marinade. Place reserved marinade in a small saucepan; bring to a boil. Boil 1 minute.
5. Place lamb on grill rack coated with cooking spray; cover and grill 20 minutes or until thermometer registers 145° (medium-rare) or to desired degree of doneness, turning and basting lamb once with reserved marinade. Let stand 10 minutes before slicing. YIELD: 6 servings (serving size: 3 ounces cooked lamb).

POINTS: 3; **EXCHANGES:** 2½ Lean Meat;
PER SERVING: CAL 121 (41% from fat); PRO 16.2g;
FAT 5.4g (sat 1.6g); CARB 1g; FIB 0.1g;
CHOL 50mg; IRON 1.3mg; SOD 233mg;
CALC 11mg

THYME PORK WITH APPLE-CHERRY COMPOTE

2 cups diced peeled Gala apple (about 2)
1 tablespoon fresh lemon juice
1 teaspoon chopped fresh thyme
¼ teaspoon salt
¼ teaspoon freshly ground black pepper
4 (4-ounce) boneless center-cut pork loin chops (about ½ inch thick)
Cooking spray
½ cup dry white wine
⅓ cup dried cherries
3 tablespoons brown sugar
⅛ teaspoon salt
⅛ teaspoon ground allspice
⅛ teaspoon ground cinnamon
1 tablespoon light butter

1. Toss apple with lemon juice; set aside.
2. Combine thyme, salt, and pepper. Sprinkle over pork. Coat a large nonstick skillet with cooking spray, and place over medium heat. Add pork, and cook 3 minutes on each side or until done. Remove pork from pan; keep warm.
3. Add wine to pan; simmer 1 minute. Add apple, cherries, and next 4 ingredients. Cover and cook 6 minutes over low heat. Uncover and cook 1 to 2 minutes or until mixture is thick. Stir in butter. Serve over pork. YIELD: 4 servings (1 pork chop and ⅓ cup compote).

POINTS: 6; **EXCHANGES:** 1 Starch, 1 Fruit, 3 Lean
Meat; **PER SERVING:** CAL 291 (23% from fat);
PRO 27.6g; FAT 7.4g (sat 2.9g); CARB 27.9g;
FIB 2.2g; CHOL 83mg; IRON 1.6mg; SOD 291mg;
CALC 39mg

PORK CHOPS WITH PLUM-BERRY SAUCE

4 (6-ounce) bone-in center cut pork chops (½ inch thick)
¼ teaspoon salt
¼ teaspoon pepper
Cooking spray
¼ cup minced shallots
1 cup beef consommé
2 tablespoons balsamic vinegar
½ teaspoon ground ginger
6 purple plums
2 tablespoons seedless blackberry spread (such as Polaner All Fruit)

1. Sprinkle pork with salt and pepper.
2. Heat a large nonstick skillet over medium-high heat until hot. Coat pork with cooking spray; add to pan. Cook 3 minutes on each side or until browned; remove from pan. Add shallots, and sauté until tender. Add consommé, vinegar, and ginger, stirring well. Cook, without stirring, over medium-high heat 5 minutes.
3. Remove pits from plums; slice plums.
4. Add fruit spread to pan, stirring until melted. Add pork to pan, and cook 5 minutes over medium-high heat or until done, turning once. Place pork on a serving platter. Add plums to sauce, and cook 3 minutes or until thoroughly heated. Spoon plum sauce over pork. YIELD: 4 servings (serving size: 1 chop and 1 cup sauce).

POINTS: 7; **EXCHANGES:** ½ Starch, 2 Fruit,
3½ Lean Meat; **PER SERVING:** CAL 337
(22% from fat); PRO 29.7g; FAT 8.5g (sat 2.8g);
CARB 36.8g; FIB 3.3g; CHOL 76mg; IRON 1.6mg;
SOD 614mg; CALC 35mg

PORK WITH SWEET CARAMELIZED ONIONS

½ teaspoon paprika
½ teaspoon ground cumin
¼ teaspoon pepper
⅛ teaspoon salt
4 (4-ounce) pork loin cutlets
  (¼-inch-thick)
1 teaspoon vegetable oil
1 pound Vidalia or other sweet
  onion, thinly sliced
1 tablespoon sugar
¼ teaspoon salt
1 teaspoon vegetable oil
¼ cup water

1. Combine paprika, cumin, pepper, and ⅛ teaspoon salt. Sprinkle evenly over pork.
2. Heat 1 teaspoon oil in a large nonstick skillet over high heat. Add onion, sugar, and ¼ teaspoon salt; cook 5 minutes or until browned. Remove from pan, and keep warm.
3. Reduce heat to medium-high; add 1 teaspoon oil. Add pork, and cook 1 minute. Turn pork, and add onion to pan. Add water, and cook 3 minutes or until pork is done.
YIELD: 4 servings (serving size: 1 cutlet and ¼ cup onions).
NOTE: If wafer-thin pork cutlets are not available, pound cutlets to ¼-inch thickness.

POINTS: 5; EXCHANGES: ½ Starch, 1 Vegetable, 3 Lean Meat; PER SERVING: CAL 223 (30% from fat); PRO 25.3g; FAT 7.3g (sat 1.9g); CARB 13.3g; FIB 2.2g; CHOL 71mg; IRON 1.4mg; SOD 280mg; CALC 41mg

FRUITED INDIAN-STYLE PORK

1 teaspoon turmeric
1 teaspoon ground coriander
1 teaspoon ground ginger
½ teaspoon ground cumin
¼ teaspoon crushed red pepper
2 teaspoons vegetable oil
4 (4-ounce) pork loin cutlets
Cooking spray
1 small onion, chopped
3 garlic cloves, finely chopped
1 cup fat-free, less-sodium
  chicken broth
½ cup dried cranberries
½ teaspoon salt
1 (8-ounce) can pineapple chunks
  in juice, drained
½ cup chopped tomato (about
  1 small)
3 cups cooked basmati rice

1. Place a large nonstick skillet over medium-high heat; add first 5 ingredients. Cook, stirring constantly, 1 minute or until fragrant. Remove from pan, and set aside.
2. Heat oil in same pan over medium-high heat. Add pork, and cook 2 minutes on each side or until pork is browned; place on a plate, and set aside.
3. Coat pan with cooking spray; place over medium-high heat until hot. Add onion and garlic; sauté 3 to 4 minutes or until tender. Add toasted spices, broth, cranberries, salt, and pineapple; stir constantly until mixture comes to a boil.
4. Return pork to pan; reduce heat, and simmer 15 minutes or until pork is tender. Stir in tomato, and cook 1 minute.
5. Place rice on each of 4 plates; top with pork cutlets and sauce.

YIELD: 4 servings (serving size: 1 cutlet, ¾ cup rice, and ½ cup sauce).

POINTS: 9; EXCHANGES: 2½ Starch, 1 Vegetable, 1 Fruit, 3 Lean Meat; PER SERVING: CAL 437 (20% from fat); PRO 29.4g; FAT 9.7g (sat 2.6g); CARB 56.8g; FIB 3.5g; CHOL 67mg; IRON 3.3mg; SOD 516mg; CALC 55mg

BRAISED PORK WITH GINGER-PEACH SAUCE

1 pound pork tenderloin,
  trimmed and cut into ½-inch
  medallions
½ teaspoon salt
⅛ teaspoon pepper
1 tablespoon olive oil
½ cup fat-free, less-sodium
  chicken broth
1 tablespoon chopped peeled
  fresh ginger
1 tablespoon Dijon mustard
⅓ cup peach jelly

1. Pound pork to ¼-inch thickness. Sprinkle evenly with salt and pepper.
2. Heat 1 teaspoon oil in a large nonstick skillet over high heat. Add pork, and cook 4 minutes on each side. Remove from pan. Repeat procedure with remaining oil and pork.
3. Add broth to pan, scraping pan to loosen browned bits. Add ginger, mustard, and jelly; cook 4 minutes or until thick. Add pork to pan; cook 1 minute or until thoroughly heated. YIELD: 4 servings (serving size: 2 medallions and 1 tablespoon sauce).

POINTS: 6; EXCHANGES: 1 Starch, 3 Lean Meat; PER SERVING: CAL 244 (29% from fat); PRO 24.6g; FAT 7.8g (sat 1.9g); CARB 19.5g; FIB 0.1g; CHOL 67mg; IRON 1.4mg; SOD 524mg; CALC 11mg

HERB-CRUSTED PORK WITH PINEAPPLE SAUCE

1 teaspoon dried thyme
1 teaspoon dried oregano
½ teaspoon salt
½ teaspoon ground coriander
½ teaspoon freshly ground black pepper
2 (¾-pound) pork tenderloins, trimmed
Cooking spray
1½ cups pineapple juice
4 teaspoons cornstarch
2 tablespoons spicy brown mustard

1. Prepare grill.
2. Combine first 5 ingredients in a small bowl. Rub mixture over pork. Insert a meat thermometer into thickest part of tenderloin, if desired.
3. Place tenderloins on grill rack coated with cooking spray; cover and grill 20 minutes or until meat thermometer registers 160°, turning occasionally.
4. Combine pineapple juice, cornstarch, and mustard in a small saucepan, stirring well with a whisk. Bring to a boil over medium heat. Cook, stirring constantly, 2 minutes or until thick.
5. Let pork stand 10 minutes before cutting into thin slices; serve pork with pineapple sauce. YIELD: 6 servings (3 ounces pork and 2 tablespoons sauce).

POINTS: 4; **EXCHANGES:** 1 Fruit, 3 Lean Meat; **PER SERVING:** CAL 193 (21% from fat); PRO 24.6g; FAT 4.3g (sat 1.4g); CARB 11.9g; FIB 1.1g; CHOL 67mg; IRON 1.8mg; SOD 322mg; CALC 31mg

ROAST PORK WITH LEMON-PEPPER CRUST

1 tablespoon grated lemon rind
1 teaspoon dried oregano
¾ teaspoon coarse-ground sea salt
½ teaspoon freshly ground black pepper
½ teaspoon olive oil
3 garlic cloves, minced
1 (1-pound) pork tenderloin, trimmed
Cooking spray

1. Preheat oven to 450°.
2. Combine first 6 ingredients. Spread mixture evenly over pork.
3. Place pork on a broiler pan coated with cooking spray. Insert a meat thermometer into thickest part of tenderloin.
4. Bake, uncovered, at 450° for 25 minutes or until thermometer registers 155°. Remove pork from oven, and cover with foil; let stand 10 minutes or until thermometer registers 160°. YIELD: 4 servings (serving size: 3 ounces pork).

POINTS: 3; **EXCHANGES:** 3 Lean Meat; **PER SERVING:** CAL 151 (29% from fat); PRO 24.2g; FAT 4.7g (sat 1.5g); CARB 1.4g; FIB 0.4g; CHOL 67mg; IRON 1.5mg; SOD 480mg; CALC 18mg

---

PORK PERKS

Packed with essential vitamins and minerals, pork is a smart choice in a healthful eating plan and is considered a lean meat. In fact, most trimmed cuts of pork, with the exception of ribs, are lean and some may even be extra lean. Good cuts to try are the tenderloin, loin roast, and sirloin or loin chops.

PORK ROAST WITH HOPPING JOHN STUFFING

2 slices bacon
2 cups chopped onion
1 cup chopped green bell pepper
4 garlic cloves, minced
4 cups chopped fresh spinach
3 cups hot cooked long-grain rice
½ cup chopped green onions
1 teaspoon Creole seasoning
1 teaspoon hot sauce
2 (15-ounce) cans black-eyed peas, rinsed and drained
2½ pounds boneless pork loin, trimmed
Cooking spray
½ teaspoon Creole seasoning
½ teaspoon black pepper

1. Cook bacon in a large skillet over medium-high heat until crisp. Remove bacon from pan, and crumble. Add onion, green pepper, and garlic to bacon drippings in pan; cook 5 minutes or until tender. Add spinach, and cook 1 minute or until spinach wilts. Stir in rice and next 4 ingredients. Keep warm.
2. Make a cut lengthwise down the center of pork, cutting to, but not through bottom. Starting from center cut, slice horizontally toward one side, stopping ½ inch from edge. Repeat on opposite side. Unfold each piece so it lies flat. Place between 2 sheets of heavy-duty plastic wrap. Flatten to ½-inch thickness, using a meat mallet or rolling pin.
3. Preheat oven to 375°.
4. Spoon 1½ cups rice mixture over pork, leaving a 1-inch margin. Roll pork, jelly-roll fashion, starting at short end. Secure with string at 1-inch intervals, and place, seam

side down, on a rack coated with cooking spray. Sprinkle with ½ teaspoon Creole seasoning and black pepper. Insert a meat thermometer into pork. Bake at 375° for 1 hour and 5 minutes or until meat thermometer registers 160°. Let stand 10 minutes before slicing. Serve with remaining rice mixture. YIELD: 10 servings (serving size: 3 ounces pork and about ⅔ cup rice mixture).

POINTS: 6; EXCHANGES: 2 Starch, ½ Vegetable, 3½ Lean Meat; PER SERVING: CAL 317 (21% from fat); PRO 31.1g; FAT 7.2g (sat 2.6g); CARB 30.8g; FIB 5.5g; CHOL 74mg; IRON 3.6mg; SOD 208mg; CALC 56mg

FRUIT-STUFFED PORK TENDERLOIN WITH ORANGE-MUSTARD SAUCE

(pictured on page 90)
Chinese five-spice powder is a mixture of ground cinnamon, cloves, fennel, anise, and peppercorns.

¼ cup dried apricots, chopped
¼ cup dried cranberries
¼ cup chopped dates
1 pound pork tenderloin, trimmed
1 tablespoon brown sugar
1 teaspoon garlic powder
1 teaspoon cumin
¼ teaspoon salt
¼ teaspoon Chinese five-spice powder
⅛ teaspoon ground red pepper
Cooking spray
½ cup fresh orange juice
2 tablespoons apricot spread
1 tablespoon brown sugar
½ teaspoon coarse grain mustard
⅛ teaspoon salt
1 teaspoon water
½ teaspoon cornstarch

1. Preheat oven to 400°.
2. Combine first 3 ingredients in a small bowl.
3. Make a slit lengthwise through center of pork, using a long, thin knife. Press fruit mixture into pork. Pat pork firmly to evenly distribute fruit mixture.
4. Combine brown sugar and next 5 ingredients in a small bowl. Rub spice mixture thoroughly on pork. Place pork in a 13 x 9-inch baking dish coated with cooking spray. Insert meat thermometer into the thickest part of pork. Bake at 400° for 35 to 40 minutes or until a meat thermometer registers 160°. Remove from oven, and let stand 5 minutes before slicing. Thinly slice pork into 12 pieces.
5. Combine orange juice, fruit spread, and brown sugar in a small nonstick skillet. Bring to a boil, and cook 2 to 3 minutes, stirring often. Add mustard and salt, stirring with a whisk. Combine water and cornstarch, stirring with a whisk to dissolve. Stir cornstarch mixture into sauce. YIELD: 4 servings (serving size: 3 slices pork and 3 tablespoons sauce).

POINTS: 5; EXCHANGES: 1 Starch, 1 Vegetable, 1 Fruit, 3 Lean Meat; PER SERVING: CAL 280 (14% from fat); PRO 25g; FAT 4.5g (sat 1.5g); CARB 35g; FIB 2.4g; CHOL 67mg; IRON 2.3mg; SOD 283mg; CALC 29mg

SKILLET HAM WITH SPICY PEACH SALSA

¼ cup packed brown sugar
½ teaspoon grated peeled fresh ginger
1 (16-ounce) package frozen sliced peaches, thawed
1 jalapeño pepper, seeded and minced
Cooking spray
4 (4-ounce) slices lean, reduced-sodium ham

1. Combine first 4 ingredients; set aside.
2. Coat a nonstick skillet with cooking spray; place over medium-high heat until hot. Add 2 slices of ham, and cook 3 minutes on each side. Remove from pan, and keep warm. Repeat process with remaining 2 slices of ham.
3. Add peach mixture to pan; cook 5 to 6 minutes, stirring frequently, or until peaches are thoroughly heated and liquid is syrupy.
4. Place 1 slice of ham on each of 4 plates; top each with ⅓ cup salsa. YIELD: 4 servings (1 slice ham and ⅓ cup salsa).

POINTS: 5; EXCHANGES: 1 Starch, 1 Fruit, 3 Lean Meat; PER SERVING: CAL 262 (22% from fat); PRO 24.5g; FAT 6.3g (sat 2.1g); CARB 25.8g; FIB 1.6g; CHOL 60mg; IRON 2mg; SOD 1104mg; CALC 21mg

Poultry

FARMHOUSE CHICKEN-AND-DRESSING CASSEROLE

1 teaspoon olive oil
1 cup chopped onion
¾ cup sliced celery
2 cups water
2 tablespoons yogurt-based spread (such as Brummel & Brown)
1 (10-ounce) can condensed reduced-fat, reduced-sodium cream of chicken soup, undiluted
1 (8-ounce) package cornbread stuffing (such as Pepperidge Farm)
½ teaspoon pepper
3 cups chopped roasted chicken breast
Cooking spray

1. Preheat oven to 350°.
2. Heat oil in a nonstick skillet over medium-high heat. Add onion and celery; sauté 4 minutes or until onion is golden.
3. Increase heat to high; add water. Bring to a boil, and cook 4 minutes or until celery is tender. Stir in spread until melted. Add soup, stuffing, and pepper. Remove from heat, and stir in chicken.
4. Place stuffing mixture in a 2-quart baking dish coated with cooking spray. Bake at 350° for 45 minutes or until top is golden. YIELD: 6 servings (serving size: ⅙ of casserole).

POINTS: 6; **EXCHANGES:** 2 Starch, 1 Vegetable, 3 Very Lean Meat, 1 Fat; **PER SERVING:** CAL 320 (20% from fat); PRO 27.5g; FAT 6.9g (sat 1.8g); CARB 35.5g; FIB 2.4g; CHOL 64mg; IRON 2.5mg; SOD 986mg; CALC 50mg

CHICKEN-AND-PASTA BAKE WITH BASIL

¼ cup all-purpose flour
2 cups 1% low-fat milk
1 cup (4 ounces) grated Asiago cheese
3 cups broccoli florets
4 cups hot cooked penne (tube-shaped pasta; about 8 ounces uncooked)
3 cups chopped roasted chicken breast
¼ cup chopped fresh basil
½ teaspoon freshly ground black pepper
¼ teaspoon salt
2 garlic cloves, minced
Cooking spray

1. Lightly spoon flour into a dry measuring cup; level with a knife. Place flour in a heavy saucepan; gradually add milk, stirring with a whisk until blended. Place over medium heat; cook until thick (about 8 minutes), stirring constantly. Remove from heat; add cheese, stirring until melted. Set aside.
2. Preheat oven to 350°.
3. Steam broccoli, covered, 4 minutes. Drain. Combine cheese sauce, broccoli, penne, and next 5 ingredients. Spoon into an 11 x 7-inch baking dish coated with cooking spray. Bake at 350° for 20 minutes or until bubbly. YIELD: 6 servings (serving size: ⅙ of casserole).

POINTS: 8; **EXCHANGES:** 2 Starch, 1 Vegetable, 4 Lean Meat; **PER SERVING:** CAL 375 (23% from fat); PRO 35.6g; FAT 9.3g (sat 4.7g); CARB 35.5g; FIB 2.4g; CHOL 80mg; IRON 2.7mg; SOD 250mg; CALC 321mg

SWEET-AND-SOUR CHICKEN

(pictured on page 110)

1 (15-ounce) can pineapple chunks in juice, undrained
1 tablespoon cornstarch
2 tablespoons low-sodium soy sauce
1 teaspoon brown sugar
¼ teaspoon crushed red pepper
2 teaspoons vegetable oil
1 pound chicken breast tenders
1 teaspoon minced peeled fresh ginger
1 cup red bell pepper strips
1 cup green bell pepper strips
3 garlic cloves, minced
2 cups hot cooked long-grain rice

1. Drain pineapple, reserving ⅔ cup juice. Combine cornstarch and soy sauce, stirring until cornstarch dissolves. Stir in reserved pineapple juice, brown sugar, and crushed red pepper.
2. Heat oil in a large nonstick skillet over medium-high heat. Add chicken and ginger; cook 3 minutes on each side or until chicken is browned. Add peppers and garlic; sauté 2 minutes.
3. Add cornstarch mixture; cook, stirring frequently, 3 minutes or until sauce thickens slightly. Add pineapple; cook 2 minutes. Serve over rice. YIELD: 4 servings (serving size: 1¼ cups of chicken and ½ cup cooked rice).

POINTS: 7; **EXCHANGES:** 2 Starch, 1 Vegetable, 1 Fruit, 3 Very Lean Meat; **PER SERVING:** CAL 352 (11% from fat); PRO 29.7g; FAT 4.1g (sat 0.6g); CARB 46.9g; FIB 2.9g; CHOL 66mg; IRON 2.6mg; SOD 389mg; CALC 33mg

BROILED TANDOORI CHICKEN

Traditional tandoori dishes get their name from being cooked in a tandoori oven. Used throughout India, a tandoori oven is made of clay and brick and withstands extremely high temperatures.

¼ cup chopped fresh cilantro
1 tablespoon paprika
1 tablespoon minced peeled fresh ginger
1 tablespoon fresh lemon juice
1½ teaspoons curry powder
½ teaspoon ground cumin
¼ teaspoon ground red pepper
1 (8-ounce) carton plain low-fat yogurt
1 garlic clove, minced
1 pound skinless, boneless chicken breasts, cut into 1-inch pieces
Cooking spray

1. Combine first 9 ingredients in a bowl. Stir in chicken; cover and marinate in refrigerator 30 minutes.
2. Preheat broiler.
3. Remove chicken from marinade, discarding marinade. Thread chicken evenly onto 4 (8-inch) skewers.
4. Place chicken on rack of broiler pan coated with cooking spray. Broil 6 minutes; turn skewers, and broil 6 minutes or until done. YIELD: 4 servings (serving size: 1 skewer).

POINTS: 3; **EXCHANGES:** 4 Very Lean Meat; **PER SERVING:** CAL 149 (13% from fat); PRO 28g; FAT 2.1g (sat 0.7g); CARB 3.3g; FIB 0.4g; CHOL 68mg; IRON 1.2mg; SOD 95mg; CALC 71mg

CREAMY CURRIED CHICKEN

¼ cup all-purpose flour
1 tablespoon curry powder
¾ teaspoon salt
½ teaspoon ground red pepper
1 tablespoon vegetable oil
1 pound skinless, boneless chicken breasts, cut into 1-inch pieces
1 cup chopped onion
2 cups fat-free milk
1 cup frozen sliced carrot
1 cup frozen green peas
½ cup chopped fresh cilantro
1 tablespoon fresh lime juice
1 teaspoon grated lime rind
2 cups hot cooked long-grain rice

1. Lightly spoon flour into a dry measuring cup; level with a knife. Combine flour and next 3 ingredients.
2. Heat oil in a large nonstick skillet over medium-high heat. Add chicken and onion; sauté 5 minutes or until chicken is beginning to brown.
3. Sprinkle flour mixture over chicken, stirring until chicken is thoroughly coated. Gradually add milk, stirring until smooth; add carrot. Bring to a boil; cover, reduce heat, and simmer 25 minutes, stirring occasionally.
4. Stir in peas. Bring to a boil; cover, reduce heat, and simmer 5 minutes. Remove from heat; stir in cilantro, lime juice, and lime rind. Serve immediately over rice.
YIELD: 4 servings (serving size: 1 cup chicken mixture and ½ cup rice).

POINTS: 8; **EXCHANGES:** 2 Starch, 2 Vegetable, ½ Skim Milk, 3 Very Lean Meat, ½ Fat; **PER SERVING:** CAL 394 (13% from fat); PRO 36.6g; FAT 5.7g (sat 0.8g); CARB 47.5g; FIB 4.6g; CHOL 68mg; IRON 3.5mg; SOD 638mg; CALC 209mg

SPICY CHIPOTLE CHICKEN-AND-PEPPER FAJITAS

2 teaspoons vegetable oil
1 pound skinless, boneless chicken breasts, cut into strips
1 (16-ounce) package frozen pepper stir-fry
3 garlic cloves, minced
1 cup diced tomato (about 2)
1 teaspoon dried oregano
½ teaspoon salt
1 canned chipotle chile in adobo sauce, chopped
8 (6.5-inch) flour tortillas
½ cup (2 ounces) shredded Monterey Jack cheese

1. Heat oil in a large nonstick skillet over medium-high heat. Add chicken and cook 6 minutes, stirring occasionally. Remove chicken.
2. Heat pan over medium-high heat. Add frozen pepper stir-fry and garlic; cook, stirring occasionally, 7 minutes or until softened. Stir in tomato, oregano, salt, chile pepper, and reserved chicken. Cook, stirring occasionally, 3 minutes or until chicken is done.
3. Heat tortillas according to package directions. Spoon chicken mixture evenly over each tortilla; sprinkle each with 1 tablespoon cheese. Fold bottom and sides of tortillas to center. YIELD: 4 servings (serving size: 2 fajitas).

POINTS: 8; **EXCHANGES:** 2 Starch, 2 Vegetable, 3½ Very Lean Meat, ½ Medium-Fat Meat, ½ Fat; **PER SERVING:** CAL 404 (21% from fat); PRO 37.2g; FAT 9.6g (sat 3.3g); CARB 41.6g; FIB 4.9g; CHOL 78mg; IRON 3.8mg; SOD 919mg; CALC 177mg

BUTTERY TARRAGON CHICKEN

(pictured on page 110)

4 (4-ounce) skinless, boneless
chicken breast halves
Butter-flavored cooking spray
2 tablespoons yogurt-based spread
(such as Brummel & Brown)
1 tablespoon minced fresh parsley
¼ teaspoon dried tarragon
⅛ teaspoon salt
4 cups cooked angel hair (about 8
ounces uncooked pasta)

1. Place a large nonstick skillet over
medium-high heat until hot. Coat
both sides of chicken with cooking
spray. Cook chicken 5 minutes on
each side or until done.
2. Combine spread and next 3
ingredients in a small bowl.
3. Place chicken on a serving platter; top evenly with spread mixture.
Serve immediately over pasta. YIELD:
4 servings (serving size: 1 chicken
breast half and 1 cup pasta).

POINTS: 7; **EXCHANGES:** 2½ Starch, 3 Very Lean
Meat, ½ Fat; **PER SERVING:** CAL 347 (14% from fat);
PRO 32.9g; FAT 5.1g (sat 1g); CARB 39.8g;
FIB 2.4g; CHOL 66mg; IRON 2.9mg; SOD 193mg;
CALC 25mg

SMOTHERED CHICKEN IN MUSHROOM RAGOÛT

1 teaspoon olive oil
4 (4-ounce) skinless, boneless
chicken breast halves
¼ teaspoon pepper
4 cups sliced cremini mushrooms
(about 8 ounces)
4 cups thinly sliced shiitake
mushroom caps (about 8 ounces)
2 cups chopped leek
⅓ cup dry white wine
⅓ cup fat-free, less-sodium
chicken broth
1 tablespoon sherry
¼ teaspoon salt
1 cup reduced-fat sour cream
2 cups hot cooked medium egg
noodles (about 3 ounces
uncooked noodles)
Chopped fresh parsley (optional)

1. Heat olive oil in a large nonstick
skillet over medium-high heat.
Sprinkle chicken evenly with pepper.
Add chicken to pan, and cook 6 minutes on each side. Remove from pan,
and keep warm.
2. Add mushrooms and leek to
pan; sauté 8 minutes. Return chick-
en to pan. Add wine, broth, sherry,
and salt; cook 2 minutes or until
chicken is done. Remove from heat;
stir in sour cream. Serve over noodles. Garnish with parsley, if desired.
YIELD: 4 servings (serving size: 1
chicken breast half, ¾ cup mushroom ragoût, and ½ cup noodles).

POINTS: 8; **EXCHANGES:** 2 Starch, 2 Vegetable,
3½ Very Lean Meat, 1 Fat; **PER SERVING:** CAL 383
(19% from fat); PRO 36.7g; FAT 7.8g (sat 3.8g);
CARB 39.6g; FIB 3.6g; CHOL 112mg; IRON 4.5mg;
SOD 381mg; CALC 131mg

CHICKEN CORDON BLEU

⅓ cup dry breadcrumbs
½ teaspoon caraway seeds
4 (4-ounce) skinless, boneless
chicken breast halves
2 ounces thinly sliced low-fat
deli ham
2 ounces thinly sliced Swiss
cheese
4 teaspoons Dijon mustard
Olive oil-flavored cooking spray

1. Preheat oven to 425°.
2. Combine breadcrumbs and
caraway seeds in a shallow dish.
Set aside.
3. Cut a horizontal slit through
thickest portion of each chicken
breast half to form a pocket; place
ham and cheese evenly into pockets.
4. Spread 1 teaspoon of mustard
over each chicken breast, coating
both sides. Dredge each breast in
breadcrumb mixture, pressing firmly
to coat. Coat lightly with cooking
spray.
5. Place chicken in a 13 x 9-inch
baking dish coated with cooking
spray. Bake, uncovered, at 425° for
22 to 25 minutes or until chicken is
done. Serve immediately. YIELD: 4
servings (serving size: 1 chicken
breast half).

POINTS: 5; **EXCHANGES:** ½ Starch, 4 Lean Meat,
½ High-Fat Meat; **PER SERVING:** CAL 239
(27% from fat); PRO 34.5g; FAT 7g (sat 3.3g);
CARB 7.8g; FIB 0.4g; CHOL 85mg; IRON 1.7mg;
SOD 517mg; CALC 179mg

CHICKEN KIEV

¼ cup yogurt-based spread (such as Brummel & Brown)
1 tablespoon finely chopped fresh parsley
1 tablespoon chopped fresh basil
1 garlic clove, minced
½ cup all-purpose flour
⅛ teaspoon salt
⅛ teaspoon pepper
¼ cup fat-free milk
2 large egg whites
½ cup dry breadcrumbs
¼ teaspoon salt
¼ teaspoon paprika
4 (4-ounce) skinless, boneless chicken breast halves
4 teaspoons fresh lemon juice
Cooking spray

1. Combine first 4 ingredients in a small bowl, stirring well. Shape into 4 balls; place on a small plate, and freeze 20 minutes or until firm.
2. Lightly spoon flour into a dry measuring cup; level with a knife. Combine flour, ⅛ teaspoon salt, and pepper in a shallow dish or plate.
3. Combine milk and egg whites in a small bowl; stir with a whisk until well-blended.
4. Combine breadcrumbs, ¼ teaspoon salt, and paprika in a shallow dish or plate.
5. Preheat oven to 425°.
6. Place each chicken breast half between 2 sheets of heavy-duty plastic wrap; flatten to ¼-inch thickness using a meat mallet or rolling pin.
7. Spoon 1 teaspoon lemon juice over 1 side of each chicken breast. Place 1 herb ball in center of each chicken breast. Fold long sides of chicken over herb ball; tuck in ends, and secure with wooden picks.

8. Working with 1 roll at a time, completely dust with flour mixture, shaking off any excess. Dip in milk mixture, and coat with breadcrumb mixture. Place on a baking sheet coated with cooking spray. Lightly coat each roll with cooking spray.
9. Bake at 425° for 20 to 25 minutes or until done. Remove wooden picks to serve. YIELD: 4 servings (serving size: 1 chicken roll).

POINTS: 6; EXCHANGES: 1½ Starch, 4 Very Lean Meat, 1 Fat; PER SERVING: CAL 297 (23% from fat); PRO 32g; FAT 7.3g (sat 1.6g); CARB 23.6g; FIB 0.9g; CHOL 66mg; IRON 2.5mg; SOD 535mg; CALC 70mg

GREEK CHICKEN WITH LEMON AND MINT

3 tablespoons grated lemon rind
3 tablespoons chopped fresh mint
1 tablespoon chopped fresh oregano
1½ tablespoons olive oil
½ teaspoon salt
½ teaspoon coarsely ground black pepper
3 garlic cloves, minced
4 (6-ounce) bone-in chicken breast halves

1. Preheat oven to 375°.
2. Combine first 7 ingredients in a small bowl. Spread mixture under skin of each chicken breast.
3. Bake chicken at 375° for 1 hour or until done. Remove and discard skin before eating. YIELD: 4 servings (serving size: 1 chicken breast half).

POINTS: 4; EXCHANGES: 4 Very Lean Meat, 1 Fat; PER SERVING: CAL 193 (39% from fat); PRO 26.7g; FAT 8.2g (sat 1.6g); CARB 2g; FIB 0.7g; CHOL 72mg; IRON 1.1mg; SOD 355mg; CALC 32mg

COQ AU VIN

This classic French dish makes a hearty one-dish meal on a cold winter night.

3 slices center-cut bacon
½ cup all-purpose flour
1 teaspoon salt, divided
½ teaspoon pepper
3½ pounds skinless chicken pieces
1 (14.5-ounce) can beef broth
1 teaspoon dried thyme
1 teaspoon dried rosemary
¼ pound small shallots (about 12)
8 garlic cloves
1 (16-ounce) package baby carrots
¾ pound small red potatoes, quartered (about 6)
1 (8-ounce) package whole mushrooms, stems removed
1 cup dry red wine
3 cups cooked hot long-grain rice

1. Cook bacon in a large skillet over medium heat until crisp; drain on paper towels, reserving 1 tablespoon drippings. Coarsely crumble bacon; set aside.
2. Lightly spoon flour into a dry measuring cup; level with a knife. Combine flour, ¾ teaspoon salt, and pepper in a large zip-top plastic bag. Add chicken; seal and shake well to coat.
3. Heat 1½ teaspoons bacon drippings in pan over medium-high heat until hot. Add half of chicken, shaking off excess flour. Cook 5 minutes on each side or until browned. Remove chicken from pan; place in a 13 x 9-inch baking dish. Repeat procedure with remaining 1½ teaspoons drippings and chicken; set aside.
4. Preheat oven to 350°.
5. Add broth and next 4 ingredients to pan; scrape pan to loosen

browned bits. Bring to a boil; cook 1 minute. Remove from heat.

6. Arrange carrot, potato, and mushrooms around chicken in baking dish; sprinkle vegetables with ¼ teaspoon salt. Pour broth mixture over chicken and vegetables. Cover and bake at 350° for 1 hour. Uncover and pour wine over chicken and vegetables; sprinkle with bacon. Cover and bake an additional 30 minutes or until chicken is done. Serve over rice. YIELD: 6 servings (serving size: 3 ounces cooked chicken, 1 cup potato mixture, and ½ cup rice).

POINTS: 9; **EXCHANGES:** 3 Starch, 2 Vegetable, 3 Lean Meat; **PER SERVING:** CAL 428 (20% from fat); PRO 31.2g; FAT 9.5g (sat 3.1g); CARB 53.4g; FIB 3.1g; CHOL 76mg; IRON 4.3mg; SOD 702mg; CALC 64mg

CHEATER'S DEEP-FLAVORED BARBECUED CHICKEN

(pictured on page 111)
Use foil in the bottom of the broiler pan to make cleanup easy.

¾ cup barbecue sauce
½ cup grape jelly
¼ cup low-sodium soy sauce
2 tablespoons cider vinegar
5 chicken drumsticks (about 1¼ pounds), skinned
5 chicken thighs (about 1½ pounds), skinned
Cooking spray

1. Preheat oven to 400°.
2. Combine first 4 ingredients in a medium saucepan. Bring to a boil; reduce heat, and simmer, uncovered, 40 minutes or until sauce measures 1 cup, stirring often.

3. Place chicken on rack of a broiler pan coated with cooking spray. Bake at 400° for 20 minutes. Remove from oven.
4. Preheat broiler.
5. Turn chicken; brush with ⅓ cup sauce. Broil 3 minutes. Repeat procedure 2 times or until glazed. YIELD: 6 servings (serving size: 1 thigh and 1 drumstick).

POINTS: 8; **EXCHANGES:** 2 Starch, 4 Lean Meat; **PER SERVING:** CAL 341 (28% from fat); PRO 33.3g; FAT 10.5g (sat 2.8g); CARB 28.4g; FIB 0.5g; CHOL 110mg; IRON 2mg; SOD 906mg; CALC 21mg

SKILLET MEXICAN CHICKEN

1 teaspoon olive oil
8 chicken drumsticks (about 2 pounds), skinned
1 cup finely chopped onion
1 (14.5-ounce) can diced tomatoes with Italian seasonings
¼ cup water
½ to 1 canned chipotle chile in adobo sauce, mashed

1. Heat oil in a large nonstick skillet over medium-high heat. Add chicken, and cook 5 minutes or until browned, turning often. Remove chicken.
2. Reduce heat to medium; add onion, and sauté 4 minutes or until just opaque.
3. Add tomatoes, water, and chile pepper to onion mixture; stir well. Bring sauce to a boil; add chicken, and spoon sauce over chicken to lightly coat. Cover, reduce heat, and simmer 50 to 55 minutes or until chicken is done, turning occasionally.
4. Place chicken on a serving platter, and spoon sauce over chicken. YIELD: 4 servings (serving size: 2 chicken legs and ¾ cup sauce).

POINTS: 5; **EXCHANGES:** 2 Vegetable, 4 Lean Meat; **PER SERVING:** CAL 248 (24% from fat); PRO 33.4g; FAT 6.4g (sat 1.5g); CARB 12.7g; FIB 1.7g; CHOL 117mg; IRON 3.2mg; SOD 681mg; CALC 90mg

POULTRY POSSIBILITIES

There are lots of lean poultry options from which to choose. Numbers are based on a cooked 3-ounce serving.

	POINTS	Calories	Fat (g)
Turkey, light meat, without skin	2	114	0.6
Cornish hen, without skin	3	114	3.3
Chicken breast, without skin	3	140	3.0
Chicken, dark meat, without skin	4	151	7.4
Turkey, dark meat, without skin	4	160	6.1
Duck breast, without skin	4	172	9.6
Goose, without skin	5	204	10.9

CHICKEN WITH LEMON, FIGS, AND OLIVES

¾ cup dry red wine
½ cup dried figs, quartered
⅓ cup chopped pitted kalamata olives
¼ cup lemon juice
2 tablespoons capers, drained
3 tablespoons honey
1 teaspoon ground cumin
½ teaspoon salt
½ teaspoon ground ginger
½ teaspoon ground cinnamon
⅛ teaspoon ground allspice
1 tablespoon olive oil
1¼ pounds skinless, boneless chicken thighs
1 (6.2-ounce) package long-grain and wild rice (such as Uncle Ben's)
5 lemon wedges (optional)

1. Combine first 11 ingredients; stir well, and set aside.
2. Heat oil in a large nonstick skillet over medium-high heat. Add chicken, and cook 8 minutes, turning to brown all sides. Remove chicken from pan; keep warm.
3. Add wine mixture to pan; scrape pan to loosen browned bits. Bring to a boil; cook 5 minutes. Add chicken to pan; cover and cook 10 minutes or until chicken is done. Serve with rice. Garnish with lemon wedges, if desired. **YIELD:** 5 servings (serving size: 3 ounces cooked chicken and ⅔ cup rice).

POINTS: 9; **EXCHANGES:** 2½ Starch, 1 Fruit, 3 Lean Meat, 1 Fat; **PER SERVING:** CAL 423 (25% from fat); PRO 27.2g; FAT 12.1g (sat 2.3g); CARB 53g; FIB 3.6g; CHOL 94mg; IRON 3.3mg; SOD 1031mg; CALC 82mg

LEMON-SAGE ROASTED CHICKEN AND VEGETABLES

1 (6-pound) roasting chicken
½ teaspoon salt
¼ teaspoon pepper
3 lemons, divided
¼ cup fresh sage leaves, divided
1 onion, thinly sliced and separated into rings
6 garlic cloves, halved
Cooking spray
6 red potatoes, unpeeled and quartered (1¼ pounds)
1 tablespoon brown sugar
1 teaspoon grated lemon rind
3 carrots, scraped and cut into 2-inch pieces
2 red onions, peeled and cut into sixths
2 large sweet potatoes, peeled and cut into sixths
1½ cups fat-free, less-sodium chicken broth
2 tablespoons all-purpose flour
1 tablespoon Dijon mustard
1 tablespoon fresh lemon juice

1. Preheat oven to 400°.
2. Trim excess fat from chicken. Remove giblets and neck; reserve for another use. Rinse chicken thoroughly under cold water, and pat dry with paper towels. Sprinkle chicken with salt and pepper.
3. Loosen skin from breast and drumsticks by inserting fingers and gently pushing between skin and meat. Thinly slice 1 lemon. Place slices and 3 tablespoons sage leaves between skin and meat of chicken. Halve 2 lemons; place in cavity of chicken. Insert meat thermometer into meaty part of thigh, making sure it does not touch bone.

4. Place remaining sage leaves, onion, and garlic in a large roasting pan coated with cooking spray. Place chicken in pan, breast side up. Combine potato and next 5 ingredients in a bowl; toss gently. Arrange vegetables in pan around chicken.
5. Bake chicken and vegetables, uncovered, at 400° for 15 minutes. Reduce heat to 350°; bake, uncovered, 1 hour and 30 minutes or until vegetables are tender and meat thermometer registers 180°. Remove vegetables from pan; keep warm. Transfer chicken to a serving platter; remove and discard skin, lemon slices, and sage. Remove and discard lemon halves from cavity. Set chicken aside; keep warm.
6. Add chicken broth to roasting pan. Cook over high heat, deglazing pan by scraping particles that cling to bottom; cook 5 minutes. Pour broth mixture through a wire-mesh strainer into a 1-cup liquid measuring cup, discarding onion, sage, and garlic. Skim fat from broth; add water to make 1 cup.
7. Combine flour and ¼ cup broth mixture in a small saucepan, stirring until smooth. Gradually add remaining broth mixture, stirring frequently. Cook over medium heat until thick and bubbly, stirring frequently. Stir in Dijon mustard.
8. Drizzle lemon juice over roasted vegetables. Arrange vegetables around chicken on a serving platter; serve with mustard mixture. **YIELD:** 12 servings (serving size: 3 ounces cooked chicken, 4 potato wedges, 1 sweet potato wedge, and 1 onion wedge).

POINTS: 5; **EXCHANGES:** 2 Starch, 3 Lean Meat; **PER SERVING:** CAL 272 (20% from fat); PRO 26.1g; FAT 6g (sat 1.6g); CARB 27.8g; FIB 3.3g; CHOL 71mg; IRON 2mg; SOD 285mg; CALC 49mg

GRILLED SPICE-RUBBED CORNISH HENS

(pictured on page 112)

    2 teaspoons dried mint flakes
    ½ teaspoon ground cumin
    ¼ teaspoon ground cinnamon
    ¼ teaspoon hot paprika
    ⅛ teaspoon ground nutmeg
    ½ teaspoon salt, divided
    3 garlic cloves, minced
    2 (1¼-pound) Cornish hens
    ¼ teaspoon pepper
Cooking spray

1. Combine first 5 ingredients, ¼ teaspoon salt, and garlic in a bowl.
2. Remove giblets and necks from hens. Rinse hens in cold water; pat dry. Split hens into halves; trim excess fat. Loosen skin from breasts and drumsticks by inserting fingers and gently pushing between skin and meat. Rub equal parts of spice mixture under loosened skin. Sprinkle hens with ¼ teaspoon salt and pepper.
3. Prepare grill.
4. Place chicken on grill rack coated with cooking spray; grill 10 minutes on each side or until juices run clear. Remove and discard skin.
YIELD: 4 servings (serving size: 3 ounces cooked chicken).

POINTS: 3; **EXCHANGES:** 3 Very Lean Meat; **PER SERVING:** CAL 121 (26% from fat); PRO 20.1g; FAT 3.4g (sat 0.9g); CARB 1.3g; FIB 0.4g; CHOL 90mg; IRON 1.1mg; SOD 346mg; CALC 24mg

TURKEY-VEGETABLE PARMESAN

(pictured on page 112)

    1 teaspoon olive oil
    1 cup chopped onion (about 1)
 1½ cups chopped green pepper
    2 garlic cloves, minced
    1 pound ground turkey breast
    1 (28-ounce) can diced tomatoes, drained
    1 (8-ounce) can tomato sauce with garlic and onion
    ½ teaspoon salt
    ¼ teaspoon black pepper
    2 zucchini, sliced
    3 cups hot cooked ziti (short tube-shaped pasta; about 6 ounces uncooked)
    3 tablespoons chopped fresh basil
    3 tablespoons grated Parmesan cheese

1. Heat oil in a nonstick skillet over medium-high heat. Add onion, green pepper, and garlic; sauté 7 minutes. Add turkey; cook until turkey is browned, stirring to crumble.
2. Add diced tomatoes, tomato sauce, salt, and black pepper. Bring to a boil; cover, reduce heat, and simmer 20 minutes, stirring occasionally.
3. Add zucchini; simmer 3 minutes. Add pasta and basil; return mixture to a boil. Remove from heat. Let stand 5 minutes. Sprinkle with cheese. YIELD: 5 servings (serving size: 1½ cups).

POINTS: 7; **EXCHANGES:** 1½ Starch, 3 Vegetable, 2 Lean Meat, 1 Fat; **PER SERVING:** CAL 347 (27% from fat); PRO 24.3g; FAT 10.3g (sat 3g); CARB 39.2g; FIB 5.1g; CHOL 75mg; IRON 3.4mg; SOD 728mg; CALC 107mg

TURKEY LO MEIN

One pound of boned, skinned chicken breast halves may be substituted for the turkey.

    6 ounces uncooked linguine
Cooking spray
 2½ teaspoons dark sesame oil
    1 pound turkey cutlets, cut into strips
    2 cups snow peas, trimmed
    1 cup red bell pepper strips
    1 cup broccoli florets
    ½ cup shredded carrot
    2 tablespoons chopped green onions
    1 teaspoon minced peeled fresh ginger
    ⅛ teaspoon crushed red pepper
    2 garlic cloves, crushed
    3 tablespoons low-sodium soy sauce

1. Cook pasta according to package directions, omitting salt and fat. Drain.
2. Coat a large nonstick skillet with cooking spray; add 1 teaspoon oil. Place over high heat. Add turkey, and stir-fry 5 minutes or until done. Add snow peas and next 7 ingredients; stir-fry 4 minutes. Add pasta and soy sauce; cook 2 minutes. Remove from heat; add remaining 1½ teaspoons oil, and toss well to coat. YIELD: 4 servings (serving size: 2 cups).

POINTS: 8; **EXCHANGES:** 2 Starch, 2 Vegetable, 3 Very Lean Meat, 1 Fat; **PER SERVING:** CAL 404 (23% from fat); PRO 33.1g; FAT 10g (sat 2.3g); CARB 43.8g; FIB 5.6g; CHOL 60mg; IRON 4.5mg; SOD 520mg; CALC 72mg

TURKEY WITH GOLDEN ONION GRAVY

2 teaspoons vegetable oil
1 (1-pound) turkey tenderloin, cut into bite-size pieces
1¼ cups thinly sliced onion
1 (8-ounce) package presliced mushrooms
½ cup water
1 tablespoon Dijon mustard
1 (10½-ounce) can beef broth
½ cup fat-free milk
1 tablespoon all-purpose flour
⅛ teaspoon pepper
5 cups hot cooked egg noodles (10 ounces uncooked)
Chopped fresh parsley (optional)

1. Heat oil in a large nonstick skillet over medium-high heat; add turkey. Sauté 6 minutes or until browned. Remove turkey from pan.
2. Add onion to pan; sauté 8 minutes. Add mushrooms; sauté 3 minutes or until tender. Add water, mustard, and broth; stir well. Return turkey to pan, and bring to a boil. Cover, reduce heat, and simmer 20 minutes.
3. Combine milk, flour, and pepper, stirring with a whisk. Add to turkey mixture. Simmer, stirring constantly, 2 minutes or until thick. Serve turkey and gravy over noodles. Garnish with parsley, if desired. YIELD: 5 servings (serving size: 1 cup turkey mixture and 1 cup noodles).

POINTS: 7; **EXCHANGES:** 2½ Starch, 1 Vegetable, 3 Lean Meat; **PER SERVING:** CAL 358 (20% from fat); PRO 29.2g; FAT 7.9g (sat 1.8g); CARB 41.9g; FIB 2.7g; CHOL 96mg; IRON 4.2mg; SOD 364mg; CALC 81mg

TURKEY SCALOPPINE WITH APRICOT-GINGER SAUCE

2 tablespoons all-purpose flour
¼ teaspoon salt
¼ teaspoon black pepper
1 (½-pound) turkey tenderloin, cut into strips
2 teaspoons vegetable oil
Cooking spray
1 cup green bell pepper strips
2 tablespoons minced shallots
1 teaspoon minced peeled fresh ginger
⅔ cup apricot nectar
⅔ cup fat-free, less-sodium chicken broth
1 tablespoon chopped dried apricots
1 tablespoon currants
2 teaspoons brown sugar
2 teaspoons balsamic vinegar

1. Combine first 4 ingredients in a large zip-top plastic bag; seal and shake to coat. Heat oil in a large nonstick skillet coated with cooking spray over medium-high heat. Add turkey mixture; stir-fry 3 minutes or until lightly browned. Remove from pan; keep warm.
2. Recoat pan with cooking spray; place over medium-high heat. Add bell pepper, shallots, and ginger; stir-fry 1½ minutes. Add nectar and remaining 5 ingredients; bring to a boil. Cook over medium heat 3 minutes or until slightly thick. Add turkey; cook 1 minute or until thoroughly heated. YIELD: 2 servings (serving size: 1¼ cups).

POINTS: 7; **EXCHANGES:** 1½ Starch, 1 Fruit, 3 Very Lean Meat, 1 Fat; **PER SERVING:** CAL 326 (24% from fat); PRO 27.2g; FAT 8.9g (sat 1.7g); CARB 35g; FIB 2.5g; CHOL 62mg; IRON 3mg; SOD 563mg; CALC 48mg

KICKED-UP RED BEANS AND RICE

Cooking spray
8 ounces smoked turkey kielbasa, sliced
2 teaspoons vegetable oil
1 cup chopped onion
1 cup chopped seeded poblano chile
¾ cup chopped celery
4 garlic cloves, minced
3 (15.8-ounce) cans red beans, rinsed and drained
1 cup water
1 tablespoon chopped fresh or 1 teaspoon dried oregano
1½ tablespoons chopped canned chipotle chile in adobo sauce
¼ teaspoon salt
2 (14½-ounce) cans diced tomatoes with garlic, basil, and oregano, undrained
1 (8-ounce) can no-salt-added tomato sauce
9 cups hot cooked rice

1. Place a Dutch oven coated with cooking spray over medium-high heat until hot. Add kielbasa; sauté 4 minutes or until lightly browned. Remove from pan.
2. Heat oil in pan over medium-high heat. Add onion and next 3 ingredients. Sauté 8 minutes or until tender. Stir in beans and next 6 ingredients. Bring to a boil; cover, reduce heat, and simmer 20 minutes. Serve red beans over hot cooked rice. YIELD: 9 servings (serving size: 1 cup beans and 1 cup rice).

POINTS: 7; **EXCHANGES:** 4 Starch, 2 Vegetable, ½ Lean Meat; **PER SERVING:** CAL 373 (8% from fat); PRO 13.8g; FAT 3.4g (sat 0.4g); CARB 72.3g; FIB 6.7g; CHOL 9mg; IRON 5.1mg; SOD 881mg; CALC 84mg

Back in the Swing of Things

JOHN LOWDER • **HEIGHT** 6'1" • **BEFORE** 340 LBS. • **AFTER** 216 LBS.

Tip: John joined a gym so he can take his walking regimen indoors during inclement weather.

John Lowder's doctor suggested that John could stand to lose a little weight, but the recommendation didn't do much good. Says John, "Doctors can advise you, but you have to decide for yourself." John, who loves to play golf, finally agreed with his doctor when he noticed it was getting more difficult to walk the course. As his weight soared to 340 pounds, John became depressed and even lost interest in some business deals. "I was concerned about the weight, but I didn't know what to do about it," he says.

Then John and his wife, Helen, read about a Weight Watchers At Work program at Helen's workplace. Inspired by the success of a co-worker, the couple signed up. Helen had a small amount of weight to lose, but John faced the daunting task of shedding more than 100 pounds. "I didn't put the weight on overnight," John says, "So I knew it wouldn't come off overnight."

"This isn't a diet; it's a lifestyle change."

Once John started the program, dogged determination took charge. After just one week he could run his hand around the inside of his waistband, and there was no looking back. He found it surprisingly easy to adopt new, healthful eating habits.

"I'm almost embarrassed to take credit, because I've eaten like a horse," he says. Many people associate weight loss with deprivation, but John found this wasn't the case. "This isn't a diet; it's a lifestyle change," he says. "I've changed my eating habits."

One change was adding more vegetables to his diet; he also started making healthful choices, such as grilled fish instead of a traditional steak-and-potato dinner. "It's amazing how my palate has changed. I used to eat green beans as a filler. Now I enjoy green beans."

Keeping a food journal has been helpful. In addition to writing down what he eats, John records his thoughts, exercise goals, and improved golf scores. "I'll probably do that for the rest of my life," reveals John.

Encouraged by early success, he began a walking regimen to improve his cardiovascular health. He progressed from 2 miles a day to 4 (sometimes 6), dropped more than 120 pounds, and feels like a young man. "I used to watch a lot of TV," he says, "but now I do more things outside." Whether he's working on a deal or hitting the links, John says he feels more confident. And while he's proud to have moved up from the senior to the championship tees, John says the biggest change is in his outlook. "I'm 57, and I don't view that as being old anymore."

109

Buttery Tarragon
Chicken, page 103

Sweet-and-
Sour Chicken,
page 101

Cheater's Deep-Flavored
Barbecue Chicken, page 105
and Coleslaw with Jalapeno
Mayonnaise, page 119

Turkey-Vegetable Parmesan, page 107

Grilled Spice-Rubbed Cornish Hens, page 107

Fresh Corn-and-
Basil Salad,
page 119

Grapefruit-and-Greens
Salad, page 118

Chicken Salad
with Asparagus,
page 124

Marinated Three-
Tomato Salad,
page 120

Fresh Fruit Salad
with Citrus-
Cilantro Dressing,
page 118

Changing Times

RHONDA PIGOTT • **HEIGHT** 5'7" • **BEFORE** 157 LBS. • **AFTER** 141 LBS.

Biggest Decision: Cutting her hair for the first time since high school symbolizes the lasting changes Rhonda has made.

To look at Rhonda Pigott's busy schedule today, you'd never guess that she once refused to go out. Embarrassed by the way she looked and afraid of gaining more weight, Rhonda avoided social engagements and family outings, particularly those held at restaurants.

In 1989, Rhonda struggled through a divorce and had to learn to balance single motherhood, her career, and a household. Rhonda had always come close to being overweight, but managed to keep the scale at a satisfactory number despite unhealthful habits. "I wouldn't eat until dinner, and that was the only meal I'd have all day," she says.

But when she remarried and settled into a new life, pounds started creeping on. "I'd worked to rebuild my self-esteem, and each extra pound knocked me down," she says.

She had gained only 15 pounds, but to Rhonda the weight was an albatross around her neck. She camouflaged the new weight with oversize jackets and big sweaters; not even her husband noticed. "But I was miserable," she remembers.

In June of 1997, Rhonda had gained two dress sizes and knew she could no longer ignore her weight. "I tried fad diets," she remembers. "But I wanted to change the person I imagined myself being once and for all." This time Rhonda wanted to do it right. So she joined Weight Watchers.

The accountability of weekly meetings was a real motivator for Rhonda. "I had tried to lose weight on my own for so long; I needed the regularity of a group meeting," she says. A month after joining, Rhonda recruited her mother. "We decided to reinforce each other's goals," Rhonda says.

At first, the weight came off slowly. But after a few months, her regimen of walking and adhering to the **POINTS** plan began to pay off. By November of that year, she had reached her goal weight. Rhonda and her mother, who lost 50 pounds, even convinced Rhonda's sister to give Weight Watchers a try.

"You have to truly feel better about yourself when you're thin—that keeps me on track."

Rhonda has maintained her goal weight for four years now, but she admits it's a daily struggle. "I try to remember how I felt when I was overweight and how low my self-esteem was," she says. "You have to truly feel better about yourself when you're thin—that keeps me on track."

Eating out is now one of the many ways Rhonda enjoys spending time with her family. "I slip up like everyone else," says Rhonda. "But the way I maintain my weight and lifestyle habits feels right for the first time."

Weight-loss results not typical.

Salads

FRESH FRUIT SALAD WITH CITRUS-CILANTRO DRESSING

(pictured on page 115)

2 cups pink grapefruit sections
  (about 2 large)
2 cups pineapple cubes
1⅓ cups sliced strawberries
1 cup orange sections (about 2)
1 cup seedless green grapes
⅓ cup orange juice
⅓ cup fresh lime juice
3 tablespoons finely chopped fresh
  cilantro
2 tablespoons honey

1. Combine first 5 ingredients in a large bowl; set aside. Combine orange juice and remaining ingredients. Pour mixture over fruit; toss gently. Cover and chill 1 hour. YIELD: 7 servings (serving size: 1 cup).

POINTS: 2; EXCHANGES: 2 Fruit; PER SERVING: CAL 106 (4% from fat); PRO 1.3g; FAT 0.6g (sat 0.1g); CARB 27.1g; FIB 3.1g; CHOL 0mg; IRON 0.5mg; SOD 2mg; CALC 31mg

FROZEN FRUIT SALAD

Serve this frozen salad as a refreshing summer dessert.

1¾ cups pineapple juice
⅓ cup thawed orange juice
  concentrate, undiluted
2 cups seedless green or red
  grapes, halved
2 cups sliced ripe banana (about 4)
2 cups chopped pineapple

1. Combine juices in a large bowl. Stir in remaining ingredients. Pour into a 13 x 9-inch baking dish.

Cover; freeze 4 hours or until firm. Let stand at room temperature 30 minutes or until slightly thawed. YIELD: 8 servings (serving size: 1 cup).

POINTS: 3; EXCHANGES: 2½ Fruit; PER SERVING: CAL 146 (4% from fat); PRO 1.3g; FAT 0.6g (sat 0.2g); CARB 36.4g; FIB 1.9g; CHOL 0mg; IRON 0.5mg; SOD 4mg; CALC 25mg

FIELD SALAD WITH MUSHROOMS AND FETA

6 cups gourmet salad greens
2 cups quartered mushrooms
½ cup (2 ounces) crumbled
  herbed feta cheese
3 tablespoons sun-dried tomato
  dressing (such as Kraft)

1. Combine first 3 ingredients in a large bowl. Sprinkle dressing over salad; toss to coat. YIELD: 4 servings (serving size: 1½ cups).

POINTS: 2; EXCHANGES: 1 Vegetable, 1 Fat; PER SERVING: CAL 86 (55% from fat); PRO 5g; FAT 5.8g (sat 2.3g); CARB 5.5g; FIB 2.3g; CHOL 10mg; IRON 1.5mg; SOD 322mg; CALC 88mg

GRAPEFRUIT-AND-GREENS SALAD

(pictured on page 113)

2 large grapefruit
1 cup thinly sliced red onion
1½ teaspoons fresh or ½ teaspoon
  dried thyme
¼ cup seasoned rice vinegar
1 tablespoon extra-virgin olive oil
1 tablespoon honey
1 teaspoon fennel seeds
¼ teaspoon salt
6 cups gourmet salad greens

1. Peel and section grapefruit to get 1½ cups sections, reserving 2 tablespoons grapefruit juice. Combine grapefruit, onion, and thyme in a large bowl.
2. Combine reserved grapefruit juice, vinegar, and next 4 ingredients; stir well with a whisk.
3. Add salad greens and dressing mixture to grapefruit mixture; toss well. Serve immediately. YIELD: 5 servings (serving size: 2 cups).

POINTS: 1; EXCHANGES: 1 Vegetable, ½ Fruit, ½ Fat; PER SERVING: CAL 86 (30% from fat); PRO 1.8g; FAT 3.1g (sat 0.4g); CARB 14.5g; FIB 3g; CHOL 0mg; IRON 1.2mg; SOD 135mg; CALC 56mg

SECTIONING CITRUS

1. To section an orange or grapefruit, first peel it with a paring knife, being sure to remove the white pith.

2. Holding fruit over a bowl to catch juices, slice between membrane and side of 1 segment with the knife blade.

BROCCOLI-AND-CAULIFLOWER SALAD WITH BLUE CHEESE DRESSING

Make this salad two to three hours ahead and then refrigerate to intensify the flavors.

1 (16-ounce) package fresh broccoli and cauliflower florets (such as River Ranch)
3 tablespoons low-fat mayonnaise
3 tablespoons low-fat buttermilk
2 tablespoons finely diced red onion
2 tablespoons crumbled blue cheese
¼ teaspoon salt
⅛ teaspoon freshly ground black pepper
1 tablespoon finely chopped fresh parsley

1. Steam broccoli and cauliflower, covered, 3 to 4 minutes or until crisp-tender. Rinse under cold water, and drain well. Set aside.
2. Combine mayonnaise, buttermilk, onion, blue cheese, salt, and pepper in a small bowl.
3. Combine broccoli and cauliflower with dressing in a large bowl. Sprinkle with parsley; stir well. YIELD: 4 servings (serving size: 1 cup).

POINTS: 1; **EXCHANGES:** 2 Vegetable, ½ Fat; **PER SERVING:** CAL 69 (26% from fat); PRO 4.1g; FAT 2.2g (sat 0.8g); CARB 10.2g; FIB 3.3g; CHOL 3mg; IRON 0.8mg; SOD 345mg; CALC 74mg

COLESLAW WITH JALAPEÑO MAYONNAISE

(pictured on page 111)
If you don't care for hot, spicy food, use the lower end of the range for jalapeños. To save time, buy the preshredded cabbage in the produce section of the grocery.

4 cups finely sliced green cabbage
⅔ cup frozen whole-kernel corn, thawed
½ cup shredded carrot
⅓ cup finely sliced red onion
¼ cup finely sliced red bell pepper
¼ cup finely sliced green bell pepper
¼ cup finely chopped fresh parsley
3 tablespoons finely chopped fresh cilantro
⅓ cup low-fat mayonnaise
⅓ cup fat-free sour cream
1 tablespoon sugar
1 tablespoon lime juice
¼ teaspoon salt
1 to 2 jalapeño peppers, seeded and minced

1. Combine first 8 ingredients in a large bowl; toss gently.
2. Combine mayonnaise and remaining 5 ingredients in a small bowl.
3. Add dressing to cabbage mixture, and toss gently. Cover and chill at least 3 hours. YIELD: 8 servings (serving size: ½ cup).

POINTS: 1; **EXCHANGES:** ½ Starch, 1 Vegetable; **PER SERVING:** CAL 62 (14% from fat); PRO 1.7g; FAT 1.1g (sat 0.1g); CARB 12.7g; FIB 1.7g; CHOL 1mg; IRON 0.5mg; SOD 185mg; CALC 39mg

FRENCH VINAIGRETTE SLAW

1 tablespoon extra-virgin olive oil
1 tablespoon cider vinegar
½ teaspoon salt
1 garlic clove, minced
2 beets
2 cups shredded red cabbage

1. Combine first 4 ingredients in a small bowl; set aside.
2. Peel beets under running water to prevent hands from staining; shred beets.
3. Combine cabbage and beets in a bowl; add oil mixture, and toss. Serve immediately. YIELD: 4 servings (serving size: ¾ cup).

POINTS: 1; **EXCHANGES:** 1 Vegetable, ½ Fat; **PER SERVING:** CAL 58 (57% from fat); PRO 1.1g; FAT 3.7g (sat 0.5g); CARB 6g; FIB 1.7g; CHOL 0mg; IRON 0.5mg; SOD 319mg; CALC 29mg

FRESH CORN-AND-BASIL SALAD

(pictured on page 113)

2¼ cups fresh corn kernels (about 4 ears)
1 cup thinly sliced fresh basil
1 tablespoon extra-virgin olive oil
1 tablespoon balsamic vinegar
½ teaspoon salt

1. Combine all ingredients, tossing well. YIELD: 4 servings (serving size: ½ cup).
NOTE: This no-cook recipe is best if made with fresh summer corn.

POINTS: 3; **EXCHANGES:** 1½ Starch, 1 Fat; **PER SERVING:** CAL 136 (28% from fat); PRO 3.4g; FAT 4.8g (sat 0.7g); CARB 24.2g; FIB 3g; CHOL 0mg; IRON 0.9mg; SOD 308mg; CALC 20mg

SLICED CUCUMBER SALAD

The English cucumber is ideal for this salad because it is seedless. Pickling or salad cucumbers may also be used.

2 cups thinly sliced peeled
   English cucumber
1 tablespoon minced fresh chives
2 teaspoons minced fresh cilantro
2 tablespoons rice vinegar
1 teaspoon sugar
⅛ teaspoon salt
⅛ teaspoon crushed red pepper

1. Combine cucumber, chives, and cilantro in a medium bowl. Combine vinegar and remaining 3 ingredients in a small bowl, stirring until sugar dissolves. Pour vinegar mixture over cucumber mixture; stir gently. YIELD: 4 servings (serving size: ½ cup).

POINTS: 0; **EXCHANGE:** Free up to 1 cup;
PER SERVING: CAL 12 (8% from fat); PRO 0.4g;
FAT 0.1g (sat 0g); CARB 2.6g; FIB 0.5g; CHOL 0mg;
IRON 0.1mg; SOD 74mg; CALC 9mg

CHUNKY POTATO SALAD

Easy and portable, this salad is perfect for a picnic, a cookout, or a potluck dinner.

⅓ cup low-fat mayonnaise
⅓ cup fat-free sour cream
2 tablespoons sweet pickle relish
1 teaspoon salt
⅛ teaspoon pepper
1 teaspoon Dijon mustard
4 cups cubed red potato
1 cup diced cucumber
½ cup diced celery
⅓ cup thinly sliced green onions
¼ cup chopped fresh basil
¼ cup chopped fresh parsley

1. Combine first 6 ingredients in a medium bowl; stir with a whisk.
2. Place potato and water to cover in a medium saucepan; bring to a boil. Reduce heat, and simmer, partially covered, 8 minutes or until tender; drain and cool slightly. Add cucumber and remaining 4 ingredients to potato. Add mayonnaise mixture, and stir gently. YIELD: 10 servings (serving size: ½ cup).

POINTS: 2; **EXCHANGES:** 1 Starch, ½ Fat;
PER SERVING: CAL 87 (29% from fat); PRO 1.6g;
FAT 2.9g (sat 0.5g); CARB 14.1g; FIB 1.1g;
CHOL 4mg; IRON 0.4mg; SOD 363mg;
CALC 23mg

TOMATILLO SALSA SALAD

This salad is a great dip for low-fat tortilla chips.

2 cups chopped tomatillos
   (about 12)
⅓ cup chopped fresh cilantro
¼ cup chopped green onions
½ teaspoon salt
½ teaspoon ground cumin
2 (4½-ounce) cans sliced ripe
   olives, drained and chopped
1 red bell pepper, chopped
1 (15-ounce) can black beans,
   rinsed and drained

1. Combine first 7 ingredients in a medium bowl, stirring well. Add beans, and toss gently. YIELD: 10 servings (serving size: ½ cup).

POINTS: 1; **EXCHANGES:** 2 Vegetables, 1 Fat;
PER SERVING: CAL 75 (50% from fat); PRO 1.9g;
FAT 4.3g (sat 0g); CARB 7.8g; FIB 2.4g; CHOL 0mg;
IRON 0.8mg; SOD 326mg; CALC 13mg

MARINATED THREE-TOMATO SALAD

(pictured on page 114)
Fresh herbs and white wine vinegar flavor this colorful salad.

2 cups halved red cherry
   tomatoes
2 cups halved yellow cherry
   tomatoes
½ cup chopped cucumber
½ cup chopped red onion
¼ cup white wine vinegar
1 tablespoon dried tomato
   sprinkles
1 tablespoon minced fresh basil
1 tablespoon minced fresh
   oregano
1 tablespoon olive oil
¼ teaspoon salt
¼ teaspoon pepper
1 garlic clove, minced
2 cups shredded romaine lettuce

1. Combine red and yellow tomatoes, cucumber, and onion in a large bowl.
2. Combine vinegar and next 7 ingredients in a small bowl; stir with a whisk until combined. Pour over tomato mixture, stirring gently to coat. Cover and chill 1 hour.
3. Divide shredded lettuce among 4 salad plates; spoon tomato mixture over lettuce. YIELD: 4 servings (serving size: ½ cup lettuce and 1 cup tomato mixture).

POINTS: 1; **EXCHANGES:** 2 Vegetable, 1 Fat;
PER SERVING: CAL 81 (41% from fat); PRO 2.4g;
FAT 4g (sat 0.6g); CARB 10.9g; FIB 2.8g;
CHOL 0mg; IRON 1.4mg; SOD 200mg;
CALC 31mg

MEXICAN BARLEY SALAD WITH BLACK BEANS AND CORN

2 cups water
¼ teaspoon salt
1 cup uncooked quick-cooking barley
1 cup frozen whole-kernel corn, thawed
1 cup canned black beans, rinsed and drained
½ cup finely chopped fresh cilantro
1 tablespoon extra-virgin olive oil
2 to 3 tablespoons fresh lime juice
½ teaspoon salt
¼ teaspoon ground cumin
1 poblano pepper, roasted, seeded, and chopped
5 lettuce leaves
10 tablespoons (2.5 ounces) shredded Monterey Jack cheese with jalapeño peppers

1. Bring water and salt to a boil in a medium saucepan. Add barley; cover, reduce heat, and simmer 10 minutes. Add corn (do not stir), cover, and cook 5 minutes or until barley is tender. Remove from heat, and let stand, covered, 5 minutes.
2. Transfer barley mixture to a large bowl. Add beans and next 6 ingredients; stir gently. Place lettuce leaves on 5 salad plates; spoon warm mixture onto lettuce leaves. Sprinkle each serving with cheese. YIELD: 5 servings (serving size: 1 cup and 2 tablespoons cheese).

POINTS: 6; EXCHANGES: 3 Starch, 1 Medium-Fat Meat, 1 Fat; PER SERVING: CAL 302 (25% from fat); PRO 11.7g; FAT 8.6g (sat 3.6g); CARB 46.7g; FIB 10.2g; CHOL 15mg; IRON 2.5mg; SOD 532mg; CALC 139mg

PANZANELLA

Ripe summer tomatoes greatly enhance this salad's flavor.

¼ cup chopped fresh basil
2 tablespoons chopped fresh parsley
2 tablespoons extra-virgin olive oil
2 tablespoons balsamic vinegar
¼ teaspoon freshly ground black pepper
1 garlic clove, minced
4 cups chopped tomato
½ cup thinly sliced red onion
6 cups French bread cubes, toasted

1. Combine first 6 ingredients in a large bowl. Add tomato and onion, and toss well. Cover and marinate at room temperature up to 2 hours.
2. Add bread; toss gently. Serve immediately. YIELD: 11 cups (serving size: 1 cup).

POINTS: 2; EXCHANGES: ½ Starch, 1 Vegetable, ½ Fat; PER SERVING: CAL 87 (33% from fat), PRO 2.2g; FAT 3.3g (sat 0.5g); CARB 12.7g; FIB 1.4g; CHOL 0mg; IRON 0.8mg; SOD 108mg; CALC 21mg

BULGUR WITH ZUCCHINI AND PEAS

1 cup uncooked bulgur
1 cup boiling water
¾ teaspoon salt, divided
1½ cups diced zucchini (about 1)
¾ cup frozen English peas, thawed
¼ cup minced fresh cilantro
3 tablespoons orange juice
3 tablespoons lime juice
1 tablespoon extra-virgin olive oil
⅛ teaspoon pepper

1. Combine bulgur, water, and ½ teaspoon salt in large bowl; let stand 20 minutes or until water is absorbed.
2. Add zucchini, ¼ teaspoon salt, peas, and remaining ingredients to bulgur; stir well. YIELD: 4 servings (serving size: 1 cup).

POINTS: 3; EXCHANGES: 2 Starch, 1 Vegetable, ½ Fat; PER SERVING: CAL 188 (19% from fat); PRO 6.4g; FAT 4.2g (sat 0.6g); CARB 34g; FIB 8.4g; CHOL 0mg; IRON 1.5mg; SOD 474mg; CALC 29mg

IS FRESH THE BEST?

You're trying to eat more vegetables, but is it best to eat fresh, frozen, or canned veggies? There's actually very little difference among the three choices. Fresh fruits and vegetables are often thought to be the best choice, but this depends on their harvest and how they are stored. If stored too long or improperly, they can lose nutrients. Because frozen and canned fruits and vegetables are usually processed and preserved at their peak, they may actually have slightly more nutrients, depending on the type of preservation process used. Processes that require higher temperatures can destroy nutrients. Since there's no straightforward answer, the best advice is to eat at least 5 servings of fruits and vegetables every day, whether fresh, frozen, or canned.

TABBOULEH WITH FETA

Feta cheese gives this classic Middle Eastern salad a twist. Serve with warm pita bread for a quick meal.

- ¾ cup uncooked bulgur
- 1¼ cups boiling water
- ¼ teaspoon salt
- 1½ cups chopped English cucumber
- 1 cup chopped plum tomato
- 1 cup finely chopped fresh parsley
- ½ cup finely chopped fresh mint
- ⅓ cup (1.3 ounces) crumbled feta cheese
- ¼ cup minced red onion
- 2 garlic cloves, minced
- 3 tablespoons fresh lemon juice
- 1½ tablespoons extra-virgin olive oil
- ¼ teaspoon freshly ground black pepper

1. Combine first 3 ingredients in a large bowl. Cover and let stand 30 minutes or until water is absorbed. Add cucumber and next 6 ingredients; mix gently.
2. Combine lemon juice, olive oil, and pepper in a small bowl; stir well with a whisk. Pour dressing over salad; toss gently to coat. Cover and chill at least 8 hours. YIELD: 5 servings (serving size: 1 cup).

POINTS: 3; **EXCHANGES:** 1 Starch, 1 Vegetable, 1 Fat; **PER SERVING:** CAL 160 (35% from fat); PRO 5.2g; FAT 6.7g (sat 2g); CARB 22.5g; FIB 5.8g; CHOL 8mg; IRON 2.7mg; SOD 231mg; CALC 96mg

ORZO WITH PESTO MAYONNAISE AND BROCCOLI

- ¾ cup uncooked orzo (rice-shaped pasta)
- 3 cups small broccoli florets
- ⅓ cup low-fat mayonnaise
- 3 tablespoons commercial pesto
- ½ teaspoon salt
- ⅛ teaspoon black pepper
- ⅓ cup diced red bell pepper

1. Cook orzo according to package directions, omitting salt and fat. Rinse and drain well.
2. Arrange broccoli in a steamer basket over boiling water. Cover and steam 3 minutes or until crisp-tender.
3. Combine mayonnaise and next 3 ingredients in a bowl, stirring well.
4. Combine orzo, broccoli, red pepper, and pesto mixture in a large bowl. Serve at room temperature.
YIELD: 6 servings (serving size: ⅔ cup).

POINTS: 3; **EXCHANGES:** 1 Starch, 2 Vegetable, 1 Fat; **PER SERVING:** CAL 165 (27% from fat); PRO 5.7g; FAT 5g (sat 1g); CARB 25g; FIB 2.1g; CHOL 3mg; IRON 1.6mg; SOD 389mg; CALC 78mg

PRIMAVERA PASTA SALAD

- 3 quarts water
- ½ teaspoon salt
- 8 ounces uncooked penne (tube-shaped pasta)
- ½ pound broccoli florets
- 1 cup sliced zucchini
- Cooking spray
- 1 (6-ounce) package sliced Canadian bacon, cut into ¼-inch strips
- ½ cup reduced-fat sour cream
- 2 tablespoons fat-free milk
- 2 cups grape tomatoes, halved
- 1 cup grated carrot
- ¾ teaspoon freshly ground black pepper
- 1 (7-ounce) jar roasted peppers, drained and cut into ½-inch strips
- ½ cup (2 ounces) grated fresh Parmesan cheese

1. Bring water and salt to a boil. Add pasta; cook 9 minutes. Add broccoli; cook 2 minutes. Add zucchini; cook 2 minutes. Drain; keep warm.
2. Place a large nonstick skillet coated with cooking spray over medium heat until hot. Add bacon, and sauté 3 minutes. Stir in sour cream and milk.
3. Combine pasta mixture, tomato, and next 3 ingredients. Add bacon mixture; toss well. Sprinkle with cheese. Serve chilled. YIELD: 6 servings (serving size: 2 cups).

POINTS: 6; **EXCHANGES:** 2 Starch, 2 Vegetable, 1 Lean Meat, 1 Fat; **PER SERVING:** CAL 292 (24% from fat); PRO 15.4g; FAT 8.1g (sat 4.1g); CARB 41.8g; FIB 7.2g; CHOL 32mg; IRON 1.8mg; SOD 812mg; CALC 210mg

WHITE BEAN-PASTA SALAD

3 cups cooked rotini or other
  corkscrew-shaped pasta
  (6 ounces uncooked pasta)
1½ cups diced tomato
1⅓ cups diced cucumber
½ cup coarsely chopped fresh basil
½ cup diced red bell pepper
¼ cup diced red onion
1 (15.5-ounce) can Great
  Northern beans or other white
  beans, rinsed and drained
1 cup fat-free Italian dressing
¼ teaspoon salt
⅛ teaspoon black pepper

1. Combine first 7 ingredients in a
large bowl, and toss gently. Add
dressing, salt, and black pepper; toss
gently. YIELD: 6 servings (serving size:
1⅓ cups).

POINTS: 3; **EXCHANGES:** 2 Starch, 1 Vegetable;
PER SERVING: CAL 174 (4% from fat); PRO 7.4g;
FAT 0.9g (sat 0.2g); CARB 35.9g; FIB 4.3g;
CHOL 0mg; IRON 2.1mg; SOD 705mg;
CALC 42mg

HURRY UP, WATER!

🍴

The most time-consuming part of
cooking pasta is waiting for the
big pot of water to boil. Here
are a couple of tips to help
speed up the process:

• Put the water on to boil as
soon as you come into the
kitchen.

• Cover the pot with a lid; this
traps the heat so that the water
boils faster.

TUNA-AND-WHITE BEAN SALAD

⅓ cup red wine vinegar
3 tablespoons olive oil
3 tablespoons fresh lemon juice
¼ teaspoon salt
¼ teaspoon freshly ground black
  pepper
2 teaspoons grated lemon rind
1 teaspoon Dijon mustard
1 teaspoon honey
1 garlic clove, minced
1 (19-ounce) can chickpeas
  (garbanzo beans), rinsed and
  drained
½ cup coarsely chopped fresh
  parsley
1 large red onion, thinly sliced
  and cut in quarters
1 (15-ounce) can cannellini
  beans, rinsed and drained
1 (12-ounce) can solid white tuna
  packed in water, rinsed and
  drained

1. Combine first 9 ingredients in a
small bowl; stir well with a whisk.
Set aside.
2. Combine chickpeas and remaining ingredients in a large bowl, tossing well.
3. Pour dressing over bean mixture,
and toss well. Cover and chill at least
3 hours. YIELD: 5 servings (serving
size: 1⅔ cups).

POINTS: 6; **EXCHANGES:** 1½ Starch, 1 Very Lean
Meat, 2 Fat; **PER SERVING:** CAL 268 (38% from fat);
PRO 17.5g; FAT 11.3g (sat 1.5g); CARB 24.4g;
FIB 5.8g; CHOL 21mg; IRON 2.8mg; SOD 369mg;
CALC 67mg

COCONUT-RICE SALAD WITH MANGO AND SHRIMP

5¾ cups water, divided
1 pound medium shrimp, peeled
  and deveined
¾ cup light coconut milk
1¼ cups uncooked long-grain rice
¼ teaspoon salt
2 cups cubed peeled ripe mango
  (about 2 large)
1 cup cubed seeded peeled
  cucumber
¼ cup chopped fresh cilantro
¼ cup thinly sliced green onions
¼ cup fresh lime juice
3 tablespoons chopped fresh mint
2 tablespoons minced seeded
  jalapeño pepper
½ teaspoon salt

1. Bring 4 cups water to a boil in a
large saucepan. Add shrimp; cook
1½ minutes or until done. Drain
and rinse with cold water. Cover
and chill.
2. Combine 1¾ cups water and
coconut milk in pan, and bring to a
boil. Add rice and ¼ teaspoon salt;
cover, reduce heat, and simmer
20 minutes or until liquid is
absorbed. Remove from heat, and
fluff with a fork. Spoon rice mixture
into a large bowl; cool.
3. Add shrimp, mango, and remaining ingredients to rice mixture, tossing well. Cover and chill. YIELD:
4 servings (serving size: 2 cups).

POINTS: 8; **EXCHANGES:** 3 Starch, 1 Fruit,
1 Vegetable, 2 Very Lean Meat; **PER SERVING:**
CAL 396 (10% from fat); PRO 22.4g; FAT 4.4g
(sat 2g); CARB 65.8g; FIB 2.6g; CHOL 130mg;
IRON 5mg; SOD 574mg; CALC 86mg

THAI BEEF SALAD

½ cup chopped fresh mint,
   divided
2 tablespoons minced onion
3 garlic cloves, minced
1 (1-pound) flank steak
1 (5-ounce) package Japanese
   soba noodles
⅓ cup fresh lime juice
1 tablespoon brown sugar
2 tablespoons reduced-sodium
   soy sauce
½ teaspoon salt
1 jalapeño pepper, minced
¼ cup chopped green onions
2 carrots, scraped and shredded
1 cucumber, peeled, seeded,
   and sliced
1 red bell pepper, thinly sliced
1 green bell pepper, thinly sliced
Cooking spray
4 cups shredded napa or savoy
   cabbage
¼ cups roasted peanuts, chopped

1. Combine ¼ cup mint, onion, and garlic; rub over steak. Cover and chill 30 minutes.
2. Preheat broiler.
3. Cook noodles according to package directions; drain and rinse under cold water. Drain well, and set aside.
4. Combine ¼ cup mint, lime juice, and next 4 ingredients in a large bowl; add noodles, and toss. Add green onions and next 4 ingredients; toss well.
5. Place steak on a broiler pan coated with cooking spray. Broil steak 7 minutes on each side or to desired degree of doneness. Let stand 5 minutes. Cut steak diagonally across grain into very thin slices. Add to noodle mixture; toss well. Divide cabbage evenly among 6 plates; top each plate of cabbage with noodle mixture. Sprinkle with peanuts.
YIELD: 6 servings (serving size: 1⅓ cups noodle mixture, ⅔ cup cabbage, and 2 teaspoons chopped peanuts).

POINTS: 6; EXCHANGES: 1½ Starch, 2 Vegetable, 2 Lean Meat, 1 Fat; PER SERVING: CAL 305 (29% from fat); PRO 22.4g; FAT 10.2g (sat 3.1g); CARB 32.5g; FIB 4.6g; CHOL 39mg; IRON 3.5mg; SOD 624mg; CALC 67mg

ASIAN NOODLE SALAD WITH CHICKEN AND SUGAR PEAS

1 tablespoon sugar
1 tablespoon reduced-fat peanut
   butter
2 tablespoons low-sodium soy sauce
2 tablespoons lime juice
1 teaspoon grated peeled fresh
   ginger
⅛ teaspoon crushed red pepper
2 teaspoons vegetable oil
1 teaspoon dark sesame oil
2½ cups trimmed sugar snap peas,
   cut in half diagonally
6 ounces uncooked Japanese soba
   noodles
1½ cups shredded cooked chicken
   breast
2 tablespoons chopped fresh
   cilantro
2 tablespoons chopped fresh parsley

1. Combine first 8 ingredients in a large bowl; stir with a whisk until blended.
2. Cook peas in boiling water 1 minute or just until crisp-tender. Drain and rinse with cold water; drain well.
3. Cook noodles according to package directions; drain and rinse under cold water. Drain well. Add noodles, peas, chicken, cilantro, and parsley to soy sauce mixture; toss well. YIELD: 4 servings (serving size: 1¼ cups).

POINTS: 7; EXCHANGES: 2½ Starch, 1 Vegetable, 2 Very Lean Meat, 1 Fat; PER SERVING: CAL 332 (19% from fat); PRO 25.9g; FAT 7.1g (sat 1.2g); CARB 43.4g; FIB 2.3g; CHOL 45mg; IRON 2.9mg; SOD 709mg; CALC 70mg

CHICKEN SALAD WITH ASPARAGUS

(pictured on page 114)

⅓ cup low-fat mayonnaise
3 tablespoons plain nonfat yogurt
1 teaspoon curry powder
¼ teaspoon salt
⅛ teaspoon pepper
1 teaspoon lemon juice
2½ cups (2-inch) sliced asparagus
   (about 1¾ pounds)
½ teaspoon salt
2 cups shredded cooked chicken
   breast
¼ cup thinly sliced radishes
2 tablespoons thinly sliced green
   onions
2 tablespoons finely chopped fresh
   cilantro
Boston lettuce leaves
12 cherry tomatoes, halved

1. Combine first 6 ingredients in a small bowl; set aside.
2. Boil asparagus in water and ½ teaspoon salt 2 minutes or until crisp-tender; drain. Plunge into ice water to stop cooking process; drain.
3. Combine asparagus, chicken, radishes, onions, and mayonnaise

mixture in a large bowl. Sprinkle with cilantro, and toss gently. Cover and chill.

4. Serve over lettuce leaves, and top each with 6 tomato halves. YIELD: 4 servings (serving size: 1¼ cups).

POINTS: 3; EXCHANGES: ½ Starch, 1 Vegetable, 2½ Very Lean Meat; **PER SERVING:** CAL 161 (21% from fat); PRO 20.1g; FAT 3.8g (sat 0.7g); CARB 12g; FIB 1.9g; CHOL 48mg; IRON 1.4mg; SOD 685mg; CALC 43mg

TURKEY WALDORF SALAD

Use leftover cooked turkey breast or poach fresh turkey cutlets for this salad.

¼ cup light mayonnaise
3 tablespoons fat-free sour cream
1 tablespoon lemon juice
¼ teaspoon salt
¼ teaspoon freshly ground black pepper
2 cups cubed Red Delicious apple (about ½ pound)
1½ cups cubed cooked turkey breast
1 cup seedless red grapes, halved
½ cup diced celery
2 tablespoons chopped walnuts, toasted
Lettuce leaves (optional)

1. Combine first 5 ingredients in a small bowl; stir with a whisk.
2. Combine apple, turkey, grapes, celery, and walnuts in a bowl. Stir in mayonnaise mixture; cover and chill. Serve on lettuce leaves, if desired. YIELD: 5 servings (serving size: 1 cup).

POINTS: 4; EXCHANGES: 1 Fruit, 2 Very Lean Meat, 1 Fat; **PER SERVING:** CAL 203 (38% from fat); PRO 15.2g; FAT 8.7g (sat 1.5g); CARB 17.1g; FIB 2.2g; CHOL 36mg; IRON 1mg; SOD 259mg; CALC 40mg

BLUE CHEESE DRESSING

¼ cup (1 ounce) crumbled blue cheese
⅓ cup light mayonnaise
⅓ cup low-fat buttermilk
1 tablespoon white wine vinegar
½ teaspoon salt
¼ teaspoon pepper
2 teaspoons prepared horseradish
1 teaspoon white Worcestershire sauce

1. Combine all ingredients in a bowl; stir well with a whisk. Cover and chill 1 hour. Serve with salad greens or fresh vegetables. YIELD: 9 servings (serving size: 2 tablespoons).

POINTS: 1; EXCHANGE: 1 Fat; **PER SERVING:** CAL 48 (77% from fat); PRO 1.2g; FAT 4.1g (sat 1.2g); CARB 1.6g; FIB 0.1g; CHOL 6mg; IRON 0.1mg; SOD 272mg; CALC 33mg

HONEY-MUSTARD DRESSING

¾ cup plain fat-free yogurt
¼ cup light mayonnaise
¼ cup honey
2 tablespoons Dijon mustard
2 tablespoons stone-ground mustard
1 tablespoon cider vinegar

1. Combine all ingredients in a bowl; stir well with a whisk until blended. Cover and chill. Serve with salad greens. YIELD: 11 servings (serving size: 2 tablespoons).

POINTS: 1; EXCHANGES: ½ Starch, ½ Fat; **PER SERVING:** CAL 57 (32% from fat); PRO 1.1g; FAT 2.1g (sat 0.3g); CARB 9g; FIB 0.4g; CHOL 2mg; IRON 0.2mg; SOD 165mg; CALC 28mg

CREAMY FETA DRESSING

1 garlic clove
⅓ cup light mayonnaise
¼ cup (1 ounce) crumbled feta cheese
⅓ cup reduced-fat sour cream
½ cup low-fat buttermilk
¼ teaspoon salt
⅛ teaspoon pepper

1. Drop garlic through food chute with food processor on; process until minced. Add mayonnaise and remaining ingredients. Process until well-blended, scraping sides of food processor bowl once. Cover and chill 1 hour. Serve with salad greens or summer tomatoes. YIELD: 8 servings (serving size: 2 tablespoons).

POINTS: 2; EXCHANGE: 1 Fat; **PER SERVING:** CAL 65 (76% from fat); PRO 1.5g; FAT 5.5g (sat 2.1g); CARB 2.4g; FIB 0g; CHOL 12mg; IRON 0.1mg; SOD 214mg; CALC 53mg

CITRUS VINAIGRETTE

¼ cup minced fresh basil
¾ cup thawed orange juice concentrate
½ cup water
3 tablespoons white wine vinegar
1½ tablespoons extra-virgin olive oil
1½ teaspoons minced fresh tarragon
1½ teaspoons Dijon mustard

1. Combine all ingredients; stir well with a whisk. Serve with salad greens or fruit. YIELD: 12 servings (serving size: 2 tablespoons).

POINTS: 1; EXCHANGES: ½ Fruit, ½ Fat; **PER SERVING:** CAL 44 (35% from fat); PRO 0.5g; FAT 1.8g (sat 0.2g); CARB 6.9g; FIB 0.2g; CHOL 0mg; IRON 0.1mg; SOD 17mg; CALC 9mg

Sandwiches

KALAMATA-CUCUMBER PARTY SANDWICHES

1 small cucumber
⅓ cup (3 ounces) ⅓-less-fat cream cheese
6 chopped pitted kalamata olives
1 garlic clove, minced
12 slices party-style pumpernickel bread

1. Cut ends from cucumber; score cucumber with a fork, leaving alternating strips of green and white. Slice very thinly.
2. Combine cream cheese, olives, and garlic; spread evenly on bread. Arrange 2 slices cucumber over olive spread. YIELD: 12 servings (serving size: 1 open-faced sandwich).

POINTS: 1; EXCHANGES: 1 Starch, ½ Medium-Fat Meat; PER SERVING: CAL 77 (29% from fat); PRO 3.7g; FAT 2.7g (sat 1.1g); CARB 11.1g; FIB 2g; CHOL 5mg; IRON 0.9mg; SOD 212mg; CALC 27mg

PREPARING PORTOBELLOS

To remove mushroom gills, hold cap in one hand, and gently scrape out gills with a spoon.

PORTOBELLO-AND-CARAMELIZED ONION SANDWICHES

These sandwiches will please everyone from burger-lovers to vegetarians.

½ tablespoon olive oil
3 cups thinly sliced onion
4 (4-inch) portobello mushroom caps
Cooking spray
2 tablespoons fat-free Italian dressing
1½ tablespoons low-sodium soy sauce
4 slices reduced-fat Swiss cheese
¼ teaspoon pepper
4 (2.4-ounce) Kaiser rolls

1. Heat oil in a large nonstick skillet over medium heat. Add onion; cook 15 to 20 minutes or until golden, stirring frequently.
2. Preheat broiler.
3. Remove brown gills from the undersides of mushrooms using a spoon; discard gills. Place mushrooms, cap side down, on baking sheet coated with cooking spray; broil 5 minutes.
4. Combine dressing and soy sauce. Brush mushrooms with mixture. Broil 5 minutes; turn and brush mushrooms with mixture. Broil 5 minutes or until mushrooms are tender. Top evenly with onions. Place 1 slice cheese over each, and sprinkle evenly with pepper. Broil 1 minute or until cheese melts.
5. Place mushrooms in rolls. YIELD: 4 servings (serving size: 1 sandwich).

POINTS: 6; EXCHANGES: 2 Starch, 2 Vegetable, 1 Medium-Fat Meat; PER SERVING: CAL 324 (25% from fat); PRO 17.1g; FAT 8.4g (sat 2.8g); CARB 38.4g; FIB 4.3g; CHOL 15mg; IRON 1.7mg; SOD 647mg; CALC 346mg

VEGGIE MELTS

These sandwiches taste great made with wheat or sourdough bread.

Cooking spray
2 teaspoons olive oil, divided
1 small green bell pepper, cut into strips
1 small red bell pepper, cut into strips
1 small onion, sliced
1 small zucchini, sliced
1 tablespoon salt-free Greek seasoning
8 (4-ounce) portobello mushrooms
1 teaspoon water
4 (3-ounce) wheat submarine rolls, split and toasted
4 slices reduced-fat provolone cheese

1. Coat a large skillet with cooking spray; add 1 teaspoon oil, and place over medium-high heat until hot. Add peppers, onion, and zucchini; sauté 3 minutes. Sprinkle with seasoning. Sauté until tender. Remove from pan.
2. Recoat pan with cooking spray. Heat pan over medium-high heat until hot; add 1 teaspoon oil. Add mushrooms, and cook 2 minutes on each side. Add water; cover and cook until tender. Add reserved vegetables to pan; stir well.
3. Arrange vegetables on bottom of rolls; top with cheese. Broil 1 minute or until cheese melts. Top with roll tops. YIELD: 4 servings (serving size: 1 sandwich).

POINTS: 6; EXCHANGES: 3 Starch, 1 Vegetable, 1 Lean Meat, ½ Fat; PER SERVING: CAL 323 (21% from fat); PRO 17g; FAT 7.9g (sat 2.3g); CARB 50.3g; FIB 6.5g; CHOL 5mg; IRON 3.2mg; SOD 581mg; CALC 276mg

BROCCOLI-AND-TWO CHEESE CALZONES

2 cups broccoli florets
1 teaspoon olive oil
½ cup chopped onion
2 garlic cloves, minced
1 (10-ounce) can refrigerated pizza dough
⅔ cup (2.6 ounces) preshredded part-skim mozzarella cheese
⅔ cup (2.6 ounces) reduced-fat shredded Cheddar cheese
1½ cups roasted garlic low-fat pasta sauce
1 teaspoon freshly ground black pepper

1. Preheat oven to 425°.
2. Steam broccoli, covered, 5 minutes or until tender; drain. Heat oil in a small nonstick skillet over medium-high heat. Add onion and garlic; sauté 3 minutes or until golden.
3. Roll pizza dough out; cut into 4 rectangles. Roll each rectangle to ⅛-inch thickness. Place ⅓ cup broccoli in center of each rectangle; top evenly with cheeses. Sprinkle with onion mixture. Spoon 2 tablespoons pasta sauce over onion mixture. Sprinkle evenly with pepper. Moisten edges of rectangles with water; bring opposite corners to center, pressing to seal.
4. Bake at 425° for 14 minutes or until golden. Serve with remaining sauce. YIELD: 4 calzones (serving size: 1 calzone and ¼ cup pasta sauce).

POINTS: 7; **EXCHANGES:** 3 Starch, 1 Vegetable, 2 Medium-Fat Meat; **PER SERVING:** CAL 351 (25% from fat); PRO 19.1g; FAT 9.8g (sat 4.1g); CARB 47g; FIB 4.8g; CHOL 18mg; IRON 2.5mg; SOD 999mg; CALC 329mg

CURRIED EGG SALAD SANDWICHES

Using some of the boiled egg yolks gives this salad mixture a creamy texture and rich flavor, much as a full-fat egg salad would have.

6 hard-cooked large eggs
1 tablespoon finely chopped red onion
1 tablespoon sweet pickle relish
3 tablespoons low-fat mayonnaise
¼ teaspoon salt
¼ teaspoon ground curry
⅛ teaspoon freshly ground black pepper
4 leaves green leaf lettuce
4 English muffins, split and toasted

1. Cut eggs in half lengthwise, removing yolks. Reserve 4 egg yolks for another use. Chop whites and remaining 2 yolks. Combine egg, onion, and relish in a small bowl.
2. Combine mayonnaise, salt, curry, and pepper; add to egg mixture.
3. Place 1 lettuce leaf on the bottom half of each English muffin. Spoon one-third egg salad over leaves, and top with remaining muffin halves. YIELD: 4 servings (serving size: 1 sandwich).

POINTS: 4; **EXCHANGES:** 2 Starch, 1 Lean Meat, 1 Fat; **PER SERVING:** CAL 211 (17% from fat); PRO 11.9g; FAT 3.9g (sat 0.8g); CARB 31.6g; FIB 2.3g; CHOL 106mg; IRON 1.6mg; SOD 618mg; CALC 100mg

FRIED EGG SANDWICHES WITH TOASTED MUSTARD SEED AÏOLI

Toasted Mustard Seed Aïoli
1 cup egg substitute
¼ teaspoon salt
¼ teaspoon freshly ground black pepper
4 teaspoons light butter
4 (2-ounce) bagels, split and toasted
8 thin tomato slices
16 large fresh spinach leaves

1. Prepare Toasted Mustard Seed Aïoli; set aside.
2. Combine egg substitute, salt, and pepper. Place a small skillet over medium heat until hot. Add 1 teaspoon butter to pan; pour ¼ cup egg mixture in center of pan. Do not stir. Cook until almost set; turn egg, and cook 30 seconds. Remove from heat, and keep warm. Repeat with remaining butter and egg mixture.
3. Spread 1 tablespoon Toasted Mustard Seed Aïoli on bottom half of each bagel; add cooked egg, and top each evenly with tomato and spinach. Top with remaining bagel half. YIELD: 4 servings (serving size: 1 bagel sandwich and 1 tablespoon aïoli).

POINTS: 5; **EXCHANGES:** 2 Starch, 1 Vegetable, 1 Very Lean Meat, 1 Fat; **PER SERVING:** CAL 274 (22% from fat); PRO 15.7g; FAT 6.7g (sat 1.9g); CARB 38g; FIB 2.9g; CHOL 7mg; IRON 4.7mg; SOD 756mg; CALC 127mg

TOASTED MUSTARD SEED AÏOLI

2 teaspoons mustard seeds
1 garlic clove
¼ cup low-fat mayonnaise

1. Place mustard seeds in a small skillet; cover and place over medium heat 2 minutes or until seeds start to pop. Remove from heat; let stand 5 minutes. Place seeds in a mini-food processor, and process 2 minutes; add garlic, and process until minced. Add mayonnaise, and process until smooth. YIELD: ¼ cup.

POINTS: 1; EXCHANGE: ½ Starch; PER TABLESPOON: CAL 35 (39% from fat); PRO 0.5g; FAT 1.5g (sat 0g); CARB 4.9g; FIB 0.3g; CHOL 0mg; IRON 0.2mg; SOD 140mg; CALC 11mg

SMOKED SALMON-AND-WATERCRESS SANDWICHES

½ cup (4 ounces) ⅓-less-fat cream cheese, softened
1 teaspoon Dijon mustard
⅛ to ¼ teaspoon pepper
1 tablespoon capers
24 (1.1-ounce) slices marble rye bread (such as Pepperidge Farm)
5 ounces thinly sliced smoked salmon
1 cup chopped trimmed watercress

1. Combine first 3 ingredients; stir with a whisk until smooth. Stir in capers.
2. Cut each piece of bread with a 3-inch round cutter; spread about 2 teaspoons cheese mixture on 12 rounds. Top evenly with salmon and watercress. Place remaining 12 bread rounds on top of watercress. YIELD: 12 sandwiches (serving size: 1 sandwich).

POINTS: 2; EXCHANGES: 1 Starch, ½ Fat; PER SERVING: CAL 96 (31% from fat); PRO 5.4g; FAT 3.3g (sat 1.5g); CARB 11.2g; FIB 0.8g; CHOL 9mg; IRON 0.9mg; SOD 469mg; CALC 26mg

SHRIMP PO'BOYS WITH REMOULADE SLAW

(pictured on page 136)
Make sure to get the oil on the jelly-roll pan very hot before adding the shrimp. The hotter the oil, the better the shrimp fry.

2 tablespoons chopped green onions
1 tablespoon chopped fresh parsley
1½ tablespoons sweet pickle relish
1 tablespoon Creole mustard
2 tablespoons light mayonnaise
2 tablespoons white wine vinegar
¼ teaspoon salt
2½ cups packaged cabbage-and-carrot coleslaw
1¼ pounds jumbo shrimp
3 garlic cloves, minced
3 tablespoons yellow cornmeal
2 teaspoons all-purpose flour
½ teaspoon salt
¼ teaspoon ground red pepper
2 tablespoons peanut oil
3 (3-ounce) submarine rolls, split

1. Preheat oven to 450°.
2. Combine first 7 ingredients. Pour over slaw; toss gently to coat. Set aside.
3. Peel and devein shrimp. Combine shrimp and garlic in a large zip-top plastic bag; shake to coat. Combine cornmeal and next 3 ingredients in a medium bowl. Add to shrimp; shake until well-coated.
4. Coat a jelly-roll pan evenly with oil; place in oven for 3 minutes or until very hot. Arrange shrimp on pan in a single layer. Bake at 450° for 3 minutes; turn and bake an additional 1 minute or until golden. Remove shrimp from pan.

5. Spoon slaw mixture evenly over bottom halves of rolls; top each with 4 shrimp. Cover with top halves of rolls. YIELD: 6 servings (serving size: ½ sandwich).

POINTS: 5; EXCHANGES: 2 Starch, 2 Very Lean Meat, 1 Fat; PER SERVING: CAL 253 (29% from fat); PRO 18.3g; FAT 8.3g (sat 1.8g); CARB 27.2g; FIB 2.3g; CHOL 129mg; IRON 4mg; SOD 724mg; CALC 77mg

ROAST BEEF SANDWICHES WITH HORSERADISH CREAM

8 (1-ounce) slices rye bread
1½ tablespoons low-fat sour cream
1½ tablespoons fat-free mayonnaise
2 teaspoons prepared horseradish
½ pound thinly sliced deli roast beef
2 ounces reduced-fat Jarlsburg cheese or reduced-fat Swiss cheese, thinly sliced
4 green lettuce leaves
8 small tomato slices

1. Preheat oven to 450°.
2. Arrange bread on a jelly-roll pan. Bake at 450° for 5 minutes or until golden.
3. Stir together sour cream, mayonnaise, and horseradish; spread evenly on toasted bread. Top with roast beef, cheese, lettuce, and tomato. Top with remaining bread slices. Cut in half diagonally. YIELD: 4 servings (serving size: 1 sandwich).

POINTS: 5; EXCHANGES: 2 Starch, 2 Lean Meat; PER SERVING: CAL 273 (23% from fat); PRO 19.6g; FAT 6.9g (sat 3.4g); CARB 32.5g; FIB 3.9g; CHOL 34mg; IRON 2.7mg; SOD 876mg; CALC 184mg

STUFFED BLUE CHEESE BURGERS

(pictured on page 135)

1 pound ground round
¼ cup (1 ounce) crumbled blue
　cheese
1 teaspoon olive oil
1 large sweet onion, thinly sliced
　and separated into rings
2 cups presliced mushrooms
⅛ teaspoon salt
⅛ teaspoon pepper
Cooking spray
4 (2.4-ounce) Kaiser rolls
4 teaspoons creamy mustard blend
　(such as Dijonnaise)

1. Divide beef into 4 equal portions.
Roll each portion into a ball; make a
pocket in the side of each ball, and
insert 1 tablespoon blue cheese. Roll
back into a ball, and flatten into a
3½-inch pattie. Cover and chill.
2. Prepare grill.
3. Heat oil in a large nonstick skillet
over medium–high heat. Add onion,
and sauté 12 to 14 minutes or until
golden. Add mushrooms; sauté until
tender and liquid is absorbed. Add salt
and pepper. Set aside, and keep warm.
4. Place patties on grill rack coated
with cooking spray; grill, covered,
6 minutes on each side or until done.
5. Place pattie on bottom half of
roll; top each with ¼ cup onion
mixture. Spread 1 teaspoon mustard
on cut side of remaining roll halves.
Cover burgers with roll tops. YIELD: 4
servings (serving size: 1 sandwich).

POINTS: 7; EXCHANGES: 1½ Starch, 1 Vegetable,
3½ Lean Meat; PER SERVING: CAL 342
(27% from fat); PRO 31.4g; FAT 10.3g (sat 3.3g);
CARB 31g; FIB 2g; CHOL 66mg; IRON 3.7mg;
SOD 568mg; CALC 76mg

MEATBALL SUBS

¾ pound ground round
¼ cup minced onion
2 tablespoons chopped fresh basil
2 tablespoons dry breadcrumbs
2 tablespoons 1% low-fat milk
¼ teaspoon salt
¼ teaspoon pepper
1 garlic clove, minced
Cooking spray
2 cups low-fat three-cheese pasta
　sauce (such as Sutter Home)
4 (2½-ounce) hoagie rolls (such
　as Cobblestone Mills), unsliced
2 tablespoons finely chopped
　red onion
½ cup (2 ounces) preshredded
　part-skim mozzarella cheese

1. Preheat oven to 400°.
2. Combine first 8 ingredients in a
bowl. Shape into 24 meatballs.
3. Arrange meatballs evenly on a
jelly-roll pan coated with cooking
spray. Bake at 400° for 20 minutes
or until done. Turn oven up to 450°.
4. Combine meatballs and pasta
sauce in a medium saucepan. Place
over low heat until sauce is warm,
stirring often. Keep warm.
5. Hollow out center of each hoagie
roll. (Reserve soft bread for another
use.) Spoon 6 meatballs into each
roll. Spoon sauce evenly over meatballs. Top each sandwich with onion
and 2 tablespoons mozzarella cheese.
6. Arrange sandwiches evenly on a
baking sheet. Bake at 450° for 5
minutes or until cheese melts. YIELD: 4
servings (serving size: 1 hoagie roll).

POINTS: 7; EXCHANGES: 2 Starch, 3 Lean Meat;
PER SERVING: CAL 344 (25% from fat); PRO 29.3g;
FAT 9.4g (sat 1.5g); CARB 27.5g; FIB 3.8g;
CHOL 46mg; IRON 1.8mg; SOD 190mg;
CALC 19mg

GRILLED STEAK WRAPS WITH AVOCADO PICADILLO

(pictured on page 136)

Avocado Picadillo
½ pound flank steak
1 tablespoon salt-free fajita or
　Mexican seasoning
2 medium poblano peppers,
　halved and seeded
1 red bell pepper, halved and
　seeded
1 yellow bell pepper, halved and
　seeded
3 tablespoons fresh lime juice
2 tablespoons chopped fresh
　cilantro
2 teaspoons olive oil
½ teaspoon freshly ground black
　pepper
Cooking spray
1 teaspoon olive oil
1 large onion, sliced
6 (10-inch) fat-free flour tortillas
6 tablespoons fat-free sour cream
¾ cup reduced-fat shredded
　Cheddar cheese

1. Prepare Avocado Picadillo; cover
and chill.
2. Rub both sides of meat with
fajita seasoning; place in a large zip-
top plastic bag, and marinate in
refrigerator at least 8 hours.
3. Place peppers in a zip-top plastic
bag. Stir together lime juice and
next 3 ingredients; pour over
peppers. Marinate in refrigerator at
least 2 hours.
4. Prepare grill.
5. Place meat and peppers (skin
sides down) on grill rack coated
with cooking spray; grill, covered, 12
minutes. Remove peppers, and place

in a zip-top plastic bag 10 minutes. Turn meat, and grill 10 minutes or until desired degree of doneness. Let stand 5 minutes. Cut meat diagonally across grain into thin slices. Remove skins from peppers, and cut peppers into strips.

6. Heat oil in a large nonstick skillet over medium heat. Add onion; sauté 15 minutes or until lightly browned.

7. Heat tortillas according to package directions.

8. Divide meat and vegetables evenly among tortillas. Top each tortilla with 1 tablespoon sour cream, 2½ tablespoons Avocado Picadillo, and 2 tablespoons cheese; roll up. **YIELD:** 6 servings (serving size: 1 wrap).

POINTS: 6; **EXCHANGES:** 2 Starch, 2 Vegetable, 1 Medium-Fat Meat, 1 Fat; **PER SERVING:** CAL 314 (29% from fat); PRO 17.4g; FAT 10.5g (sat 3.6g); CARB 38.9g; FIB 4.5g; CHOL 26mg; IRON 2.5mg; SOD 579mg; CALC 149mg

AVOCADO PICADILLO

½ cup finely chopped ripe avocado
½ cup finely chopped plum tomato
2 tablespoons finely chopped green onions
1 tablespoon fresh lime juice
¼ teaspoon salt
⅛ teaspoon freshly ground black pepper
2 garlic cloves, pressed

1. Stir together all ingredients. Cover and chill. **YIELD:** 1 cup.

CHIPOTLE-GLAZED PORK SANDWICHES

1 (1-pound) pork tenderloin, trimmed
2 tablespoons chipotle hot sauce
2 tablespoons honey
2 tablespoons apple cider
2 teaspoons olive oil
1 large onion, sliced
1 small Granny Smith apple, peeled and thinly sliced
¼ teaspoon chipotle hot sauce
¼ teaspoon salt
Cooking spray
6 (2½-ounce) hoagie rolls

1. Place pork in a heavy-duty zip-top plastic bag. Add 2 tablespoons hot sauce, honey, and apple cider. Seal bag, and gently shake to coat. Marinate in refrigerator at least 8 hours. Drain, reserving marinade.

2. Heat oil in a large nonstick skillet. Add onion and apple; sauté 6 to 8 minutes or until tender. Stir in ¼ teaspoon hot sauce and salt.

3. Prepare grill.

4. Insert meat thermometer into thickest part of pork. Place pork on grill rack coated with cooking spray; grill 10 minutes on each side or until thermometer registers 160°. Remove from grill, and keep warm.

5. Boil reserved marinade in a small saucepan 1 minute.

6. Slice pork thinly, and place on bottom halves of rolls; top evenly with onion mixture and marinade. Cover with top halves of rolls. **YIELD:** 6 servings (serving size: 1 sandwich).

POINTS: 7; **EXCHANGES:** 3 Starch, 1 Vegetable, 2 Lean Meat; **PER SERVING:** CAL 344 (17% from fat); PRO 23.5g; FAT 6.9g (sat 2.2g); CARB 50.8g; FIB 3.4g; CHOL 45mg; IRON 3.7mg; SOD 594mg; CALC 74mg

HOMEMADE CHICKEN SALAD SANDWICHES

(pictured on page 137)

1 pound skinless chicken breast halves
½ teaspoon freshly ground black pepper
3 celery stalks, halved
3 rosemary sprigs
3 thyme sprigs
¾ cup seedless red grapes, halved
2 tablespoons chopped pecans, toasted
½ cup light mayonnaise
2 tablespoons coarse ground mustard
2 teaspoons salt-free Greek seasoning
4 curly leaf lettuce leaves
8 (0.66-ounce) slices light oatmeal bread

1. Combine first 5 ingredients in a large saucepan; add water to cover. Bring to a boil; cover, reduce heat, and simmer 30 minutes or until chicken is tender. Drain; remove chicken, and cool. Discard liquid.

2. Remove meat from bones; coarsely chop chicken. Combine chicken, grapes, and pecans in a bowl. Stir mayonnaise, mustard, and seasoning into chicken mixture. Cover and chill.

3. Place lettuce on each of 4 bread slices; top each with ¾ cup chicken salad and remaining bread slice. **YIELD:** 4 sandwiches (serving size: 1 sandwich).

POINTS: 6; **EXCHANGES:** 2 Starch, ½ Fruit, 2½ Very Lean Meat, 1 Fat; **PER SERVING:** CAL 305 (20% from fat); PRO 26.8g; FAT 6.8g (sat 0.5g); CARB 34.1g; FIB 5.1g; CHOL 53mg; IRON 2.1mg; SOD 666mg; CALC 59mg

OPEN-FACED MEDITERRANEAN GRILLED CHICKEN SANDWICHES

(pictured on page 134)

4 (4-ounce) skinless, boneless chicken breast halves
½ cup plus 1 tablespoon sun-dried tomato dressing (such as Kraft), divided
Olive oil-flavored cooking spray
4 slices reduced-fat provolone cheese (such as Sargento Light Deli Style)
4 (1½-ounce) slices Italian or French bread
1½ cups shredded romaine lettuce
2 plum tomatoes, thinly sliced
2 teaspoons chopped fresh basil
¼ teaspoon freshly ground black pepper

1. Place each chicken breast half between 2 sheets of heavy-duty plastic wrap; flatten to ½-inch thickness, using a meat mallet or rolling pin. Combine chicken breast halves and ½ cup dressing in a heavy-duty zip-top plastic bag; seal bag securely, and marinate in refrigerator at least 8 hours.
2. Prepare grill.
3. Remove chicken from marinade, discarding marinade. Place chicken on grill rack coated with cooking spray; grill, covered, 4 minutes on each side or until done. Top with cheese, and grill 1 minute or until cheese melts. Coat bread with cooking spray; grill, covered, 1 minute on each side or until toasted.
4. Toss lettuce with 1 tablespoon dressing. Top bread slices evenly with lettuce and tomato. Place a chicken breast over each. Sprinkle with basil and pepper. Serve immediately.
YIELD: 4 servings (serving size: 1 open-faced sandwich).

POINTS: 6; **EXCHANGES:** 1 Starch, 1 Vegetable, 4 Very Lean Meat, 1 Fat; **PER SERVING:** CAL 305 (26% from fat); PRO 35.6g; FAT 8.8g (sat 2.2g); CARB 19.7g; FIB 1.7g; CHOL 71mg; IRON 2.2mg; SOD 602mg; CALC 199mg

TURKEY-AND-CHUTNEY PITA WRAPS

(pictured on page 134)
Going on a picnic or need a new lunchbox idea? These rolls pack easily and travel well.

2 honey whole wheat pita wraps or 12-inch whole wheat flour tortillas
⅓ cup tub-style light cream cheese
3 tablespoons cranberry chutney (such as Major Grey)
½ pound lean deli cooked turkey breast, thinly sliced
1 cup alfalfa sprouts

1. Spread pita wraps with cream cheese to within ½ inch of edge. Top evenly with chutney, turkey, and sprouts, spreading to within 1 inch of edge.
2. Roll up each pita wrap tightly, pressing gently to hold together. Cut each in half. **YIELD:** 4 servings (serving size: ½ wrap).

POINTS: 6; **EXCHANGES:** 2 Starch, 1 Vegetable, 1 Very Lean Meat, ½ Medium-Fat Meat, 1 Fat; **PER SERVING:** CAL 273 (39% from fat); PRO 16.3g; FAT 6.7g (sat 3.4g); CARB 37.4g; FIB 2.2g; CHOL 31mg; IRON 1.4mg; SOD 799mg; CALC 105mg

TURKEY COBB SANDWICHES

½ cup (2 ounces) reduced-fat shredded Cheddar cheese
⅓ cup fat-free mayonnaise
¼ cup (1 ounce) crumbled blue cheese
¼ teaspoon freshly ground black pepper
1 green onion, thinly sliced
4 leaves green leaf lettuce
8 (0.66-ounce) slices light white bread, lightly toasted
12 large watercress sprigs, trimmed
¼ pound thinly sliced smoked deli turkey
4 slices 40%-less-fat bacon (such as Gwaltney's), cooked and halved
8 thin slices tomato

1. Combine first 5 ingredients in a small bowl, stirring well.
2. Place lettuce leaves on 4 slices bread; top evenly with watercress. Layer turkey, bacon, and tomato evenly on watercress. Spread mayonnaise mixture evenly on remaining slices of bread; top sandwiches with bread.
3. Slice sandwiches in half diagonally, using a wooden pick to hold each half together. **YIELD:** 4 servings (serving size: 1 sandwich).

POINTS: 5; **EXCHANGES:** 2 Starch, 1 Lean Meat, 1 Medium-Fat Meat, ½ Fat; **PER SERVING:** CAL 231 (30% from fat); PRO 17.5g; FAT 8.2g (sat 3.7g); CARB 25.4g; FIB 5.6g; CHOL 28mg; IRON 2.1mg; SOD 987mg; CALC 223mg

Home Free

LINDA DOWNHOUR • **HEIGHT** 5'5" • **BEFORE** 245 LBS. • **AFTER** 140 LBS.

Hint: When you're losing weight, don't use food as a reward. Reward yourself with a new pair of jeans or a shirt instead.

When her two daughters left home in 1991, Linda Downhour, 48, filled her empty nest with chocolate. "I ate junk food, and chocolate—anything chocolate." It didn't stop there. At fast-food restaurants, she'd eat the biggest cheeseburger on the menu, usually with a large order of fries. "Then I'd come home and eat a bag of potato chips."

In a few years, Linda gained 100 pounds, and lost her self-esteem. She had little energy, and her joints were in constant pain. "In the evenings, I would lie on the couch," Linda recalls. "I'd try to get up, but I ached all over."

Finally, in an effort to be healthier, Linda began a walking regimen. She began with a mile every day. She soon felt better but wasn't seeing the progress she wanted. She had to change her eating habits.

Linda joined Weight Watchers in September 1997 and began to cook more wisely. "Now I steam vegetables. I don't fry anything. I grill meat or bake it. And though it's not part of the Weight Watchers program, I weigh and measure—I really watch portion size."

Linda found keeping a food journal very helpful. "If I try to keep track in my head, I forget, and end up eating more than I should." And she learned how to eat healthier at fast-food restaurants. "I get a grilled chicken sandwich with lettuce and tomato,

no mayonnaise. Sometimes I'll get a small bowl of chili or a plain baked potato with a salad."

Linda is fully committed to her walking program. She slowly increased her distance and now walks 5 or 6 miles most days of the week. "I walk 1 or 2 miles in the morning and usually 4 miles in the evening," she says. "We live in a rural community with lots of farmland. It's a wonderful area for walking."

With all that walking and a more healthful approach to cooking, the weight began to melt away. By September 1998, about a year after she joined Weight Watchers, Linda had lost more than 100 pounds.

"I feel so much better now. I have tons of energy." She even wrote a poem to tell us about her success:

I can cross my legs, my joints don't ache,
and that's not all for heaven's sake.
My necklace seems longer;
my rings are made smaller.
Some people think I even look taller.

"I weigh and measure—
I really watch portion size."

Linda's family is proud of her healthful lifestyle and her new, slender self. But by spring of 2001, Linda found she'd gained back a few pounds. She continues to attend Weight Watchers meetings when she can. "It's hard," she admits, "but I've got to keep at it."

Turkey-and-Chutney Pita Wraps, page 132

Open-Faced Mediterranean Grilled Chicken Sandwiches, page 132

Stuffed Blue
Cheese Burgers,
page 130

Shrimp Po' Boys
with Remoulade
Slaw, page 129

Grilled Steak
Wraps with
Avocado Picadillo,
page 130

Homemade Chicken
Salad Sandwiches,
page 131

Zucchini-and-
Corn Sauté,
page 148

Confetti
Couscous,
page 149

Roasted Fall
Vegetables,
page 149

Asian Vegetable
Stir-Fry, page 148

Scalloped Potatoes
with Spinach and
Cheese, page 146

It Runs in the Family

BEVERLY ANGLIN • **HEIGHT** 5'7" • **BEFORE** 220 LBS. • **AFTER** 138 LBS.

Hint: "Don't put limits on yourself. All my life, people said, 'You're big-boned, you'll never be small.' I believed it, but it wasn't true."

Beverly Anglin's parents grew up during the hard times of the Depression, so they didn't want their children to go without. "Feeding us was my mother's way of showing love," says Beverly. Sometimes love took the form of fried chicken, biscuits, and gravy. Other times it was cakes and pies. "She's a great traditional Southern cook," Beverly says of her mother.

By age 6, Beverly was already overweight, and she stayed that way through adolescence and into adulthood. Then one day about 12 years ago, Beverly saw a home video that changed her life. "There was a shot of this overweight woman taken from the back," she recalls. "When she turned around, I realized—oh, my gosh—it's me."

Beverly weighed more than 220 pounds then and was a size 22. "Over the next six years, I went on a number of diet plans, and I lost a total of 54 pounds," she says. "But the diets weren't healthful, and they didn't stress a lifetime eating plan." None of them helped her lose "that final 20 pounds."

But meeting and marrying a health-conscious former Green Beret did. "We went backpacking and jogging, but I was still eating fattening foods, and I was still shopping in plus-size stores, just as I had been all my life," Beverly says. "My husband was concerned about my weight because he was concerned about my health. But no matter what I weighed, he gave me unconditional love. That's very motivating."

With her husband's support and the encouragement of a friend, Beverly joined a Weight Watchers program. "I was surprised by the freedom the program allows," she says. "I'm actually eating more now than I did before." And she's eating better. "I never ate breakfast in the past and just had a snack for lunch," Beverly explains, "but I would eat the whole kitchen when I got home. Now, I eat three meals a day, plus a snack. The difference is I eat balanced meals with lots of fruits and vegetables, and I drink lots of water."

Beverly joined a gym and works out twice a week with a personal trainer. She takes an aerobics class or walks two miles several times a week. "Now that I have lost that final 20 pounds, I have more confidence, and I take more risks," she says. "Now I feel good about going to a pool party. In the past, that sort of thing was intimidating."

"I'm actually eating more now than I did before."

In 2001, Beverly is successfully maintaining her goal weight. "My husband jokes that he sees less and less of me nowadays," she says. "But he's not complaining. Now, I believe I can look good and feel fit for life."

Side Dishes

VALENCIA ARTICHOKES

¼ cup low-fat sour cream
¼ cup plain low-fat yogurt
2 tablespoons orange juice
1 teaspoon chopped fresh
   dill
½ teaspoon honey
¼ teaspoon grated orange rind
2 artichokes (about
   1¼ pounds)
1 teaspoon grated orange rind
⅛ teaspoon salt

1. Combine first 6 ingredients in a small bowl. Cover and chill.
2. Cut off stems of artichokes; remove bottom leaves. Trim about ½ inch from tops of artichokes. Place artichokes, stem ends down, in a large Dutch oven filled two-thirds with water. Add 1 teaspoon orange rind and salt; bring to a boil. Cover, reduce heat, and simmer 40 minutes or until a leaf near the center of each artichoke pulls out easily.
3. Place artichokes in a large ice-filled bowl; cool. Place artichokes, stem sides up, on a rack to drain. Remove tough outer leaves and small inner leaves from artichokes; discard. Serve with yogurt dip. YIELD: 2 servings (serving size: 2 tablespoons dip and 1 artichoke).
NOTE: Store remaining yogurt dip in refrigerator.

POINTS: 1; **EXCHANGES:** ½ Starch, 2 Vegetable, ½ Fat; **PER SERVING:** CAL 100 (21% from fat); PRO 4.6g; FAT 2.3g (sat 1.3g); CARB 18.3g; FIB 6.5g; CHOL 7mg; IRON 2.2mg; SOD 263mg; CALC 107mg

LEMON ROASTED ASPARAGUS

40 asparagus spears (about 1 pound)
Cooking spray
2 teaspoons olive oil
2 tablespoons finely chopped fresh cilantro
2 teaspoons fresh lemon juice
½ teaspoon salt
½ teaspoon grated lemon rind
¼ teaspoon pepper

1. Preheat oven to 450°.
2. Snap off tough ends of asparagus. Place asparagus on a jelly-roll pan coated with cooking spray. Drizzle with oil, turning to coat.
3. Bake at 450° for 8 to 10 minutes or until asparagus is tender, shaking pan often to roast asparagus evenly. Sprinkle remaining ingredients over asparagus. YIELD: 5 servings (serving size: 8 spears).

POINTS: 0; **EXCHANGE:** 1 Vegetable; **PER SERVING:** CAL 28 (37% from fat); PRO 1.9g; FAT 1.4g (sat 0.2g); CARB 3.3g; FIB 1.2g; CHOL 0mg; IRON 0.6mg; SOD 154mg; CALC 16mg

PREPARING ASPARAGUS

Gently snap off the tough end of asparagus where it seems to break naturally.

STIR-FRIED ASPARAGUS AND CARROTS

1 teaspoon vegetable oil
2 cups (1½-inch) diagonally cut asparagus
1 cup (¼-inch) julienne-cut carrot
⅓ cup sliced water chestnuts, drained, rinsed, and halved
2 teaspoons low-sodium soy sauce
1 tablespoon minced fresh cilantro
½ teaspoon sugar
½ teaspoon sesame oil

1. Heat oil in a large nonstick skillet over medium-high heat. Add asparagus, carrot, and water chestnuts. Cook 7 minutes or until vegetables are crisp-tender, stirring occasionally.
2. Add soy sauce and remaining ingredients, stirring well. YIELD: 4 servings (serving size: ½ cup).

POINTS: 1; **EXCHANGES:** 2 Vegetable, ½ Fat; **PER SERVING:** CAL 65 (25% from fat); PRO 2.3g; FAT 2g (sat 0.2g); CARB 11.2g; FIB 4.1g; CHOL 0mg; IRON 10.3mg; SOD 117mg; CALC 24mg

BUTTERY BABY LIMAS WITH TARRAGON MUSTARD

1¼ cups water
1 (10-ounce) package frozen baby lima beans, thawed
2 tablespoons yogurt-based spread (such as Brummel & Brown)
1 tablespoon Dijon mustard
¼ teaspoon salt
¼ teaspoon dried tarragon leaves
⅛ teaspoon pepper

1. Bring water to a boil in a small saucepan; add beans. Cover and simmer 8 minutes. Drain well. Add yogurt-based spread and remaining ingredients to beans; stir well. YIELD: 5 servings (serving size: ⅓ cup).

POINTS: 1; **EXCHANGES:** 1 Starch, ½ Fat; **PER SERVING:** CAL 85 (25% from fat); PRO 4.2g; FAT 2.5g (sat 0.5g); CARB 12g; FIB 3.6g; CHOL 0mg; IRON 1.3mg; SOD 245mg; CALC 22mg

ROASTED BEETS AND SWEET POTATOES

    1 tablespoon olive oil
    ⅛ teaspoon salt
 1½ teaspoons balsamic vinegar
 1¼ pounds beets, peeled and cut
       into 1-inch cubes (about 3)
    1 large peeled sweet potato, cut
       into 1-inch cubes
 Cooking spray

1. Preheat oven to 425°.
2. Combine first 3 ingredients in a large bowl. Add beets and sweet potato, stirring well.
3. Line a baking sheet with foil; coat foil with cooking spray. Place vegetable mixture in a single layer on prepared pan.
4. Bake 35 minutes or until potato is tender, stirring after 25 minutes. Serve immediately. YIELD: 4 servings (serving size: 1 cup).

POINTS: 3; **EXCHANGES:** 1½ Starch, 2 Vegetable; **PER SERVING:** CAL 176 (19% from fat); PRO 3.5g; FAT 3.9g (sat 0.6g); CARB 33.4g; FIB 5g; CHOL 0mg; IRON 1.5mg; SOD 181mg; CALC 39mg

BROCCOLI WITH ALMOND-BREADCRUMB TOPPING

    6 cups chopped broccoli
    ⅓ cup dry breadcrumbs
    2 tablespoons grated Parmesan
       cheese
    2 tablespoons finely chopped
       almonds
    1 teaspoon dried basil
    1 teaspoon dried oregano
    ¼ teaspoon salt
    ¼ teaspoon pepper

1. Preheat oven to 450°.
2. Cook broccoli in boiling water 2 minutes, and drain. Rinse with cold water; drain well. Place broccoli in an 11 x 7-inch baking dish.
3. Combine breadcrumbs and remaining 6 ingredients; sprinkle breadcrumb mixture over broccoli. Bake at 450° for 15 minutes or until breadcrumbs are golden brown. YIELD: 8 servings (serving size: ¾ cup).

POINTS: 3; **EXCHANGES:** 1 Starch, ½ Medium-Fat Meat; **PER SERVING:** CAL 52 (29% from fat); PRO 3.4g; FAT 1.7g (sat 0.4g); CARB 7.3g; FIB 2.5g; CHOL 1mg; IRON 1.1mg; SOD 153mg; CALC 69mg

---

BRAVO FOR BROCCOLI

🍴

Broccoli may just be the perfect vegetable. Loaded with the antioxidants beta-carotene and Vitamin C, it protects against cancer. It's also a great choice for women of child-bearing age because of its high folic acid content, which promotes proper neural tube formation in a fetus. Broccoli's high fiber also keeps digestion smooth and cholesterol levels down. And to top it off, broccoli is one of the few vegetables available all year.

OLD-WORLD CABBAGE AND ONIONS WITH BACON

To shred cabbage, start by slicing the head into fourths; remove core of each wedge. Then turn over and thinly slice into shreds using a sharp knife.

    2 slices bacon
    1 cup thinly sliced Vidalia or
       other sweet onion
    5 cups shredded cabbage
    1 teaspoon sugar
    ¼ teaspoon salt
    ⅛ teaspoon pepper

1. Cook bacon in a large nonstick skillet over medium-high heat until crisp; remove bacon from pan, reserving 1 tablespoon drippings in pan. Crumble bacon.
2. Add onion to hot drippings; sauté 5 minutes or until tender. Add cabbage and sugar; sauté 10 minutes. Stir in reserved bacon, salt, and pepper; remove from heat. Cover; let stand 2 minutes. YIELD: 4 servings (serving size: ½ cup).

POINTS: 2; **EXCHANGES:** 2 Vegetable, 1 Fat; **PER SERVING:** CAL 83 (50% from fat); PRO 2.6g; FAT 4.9g (sat 2g); CARB 8.4g; FIB 2.6g; CHOL 7mg; IRON 0.6mg; SOD 245mg; CALC 48mg

CABBAGE AND CARROTS PARMESAN

1½ teaspoons light butter
4 cups finely sliced napa
   (Chinese) cabbage
1 cup freshly shredded carrot
2 tablespoons grated fresh
   Parmesan cheese
¼ teaspoon salt
⅛ teaspoon pepper
1 teaspoon lemon juice

1. Melt butter in a large nonstick skillet over medium heat. Add cabbage and carrot; cover and cook 5 minutes, stirring once. Remove from heat; add cheese and remaining ingredients, and stir well. Serve immediately. YIELD: 3 servings (serving size: ½ cup).

POINTS: 1; **EXCHANGES:** 2 Vegetable, ½ Fat; **PER SERVING:** CAL 69 (28% from fat); PRO 4.2g; FAT 2.4g (sat 1.5g); CARB 9.8g; FIB 4g; CHOL 7mg; IRON 0.6mg; SOD 322mg; CALC 100mg

GINGERED CARROTS AND PEAS

1½ teaspoons butter
3 cups (¼-inch) julienne-cut
   carrot (about 1 pound)
3 tablespoons dark brown sugar
½ cup frozen peas, thawed
½ teaspoon grated peeled fresh
   ginger
¼ teaspoon salt
⅛ teaspoon pepper

1. Melt butter in a large nonstick skillet over medium heat. Add carrot

and sugar; stir well. Reduce heat to medium-low; cook, covered, 15 minutes or until carrot is tender, stirring occasionally. Add peas, ginger, salt, and pepper; cook 1 minute or until thoroughly heated. YIELD: 4 servings (serving size: ½ cup).

POINTS: 2; **EXCHANGES:** 1½ Starch, 1 Vegetable, ½ Fat; **PER SERVING:** CAL 111 (13% from fat); PRO 2.1g; FAT 1.7g (sat 0.9g); CARB 23.2g; FIB 4g; CHOL 4mg; IRON 1mg; SOD 221mg; CALC 42mg

CAULIFLOWER PUTTANESCA

2 teaspoons olive oil
⅓ cup diced onion
⅓ cup chopped green bell pepper
1 garlic clove, minced
1 (14½-ounce) can diced
   tomatoes, undrained
¼ cup water
1 tablespoon chopped pitted
   kalamata olives
1 tablespoon red wine vinegar
1 teaspoon sugar
1 teaspoon capers
2 teaspoons tomato paste
⅛ teaspoon black pepper
4½ cups cauliflower florets

1. Heat oil in a large nonstick skillet over medium heat. Add onion and green bell pepper; sauté 6 minutes or until tender. Add garlic; cook 30 seconds. Add tomatoes and next 7 ingredients; stir well. Bring to a boil; reduce heat, and simmer, uncovered, 10 minutes or until thick. Keep warm.

2. Steam cauliflower 4 minutes or until crisp-tender. Spoon cauliflower onto serving plates; top with sauce. YIELD: 6 servings (serving size: ⅔ cup cauliflower and ⅓ cup sauce).

POINTS: 1; **EXCHANGES:** 2 Vegetable, ½ Fat; **PER SERVING:** CAL 66 (29% from fat); PRO 2.6g; FAT 2.3g (sat 0.3g); CARB 10.4g; FIB 3.6g; CHOL 0mg; IRON 0.7mg; SOD 167mg; CALC 34mg

BALSAMIC ROASTED ONIONS

3 large sweet onions (about
   1¾ pounds)
Cooking spray
¼ cup balsamic vinegar
1 tablespoon olive oil
1 teaspoon dried thyme
½ teaspoon dried basil
¼ teaspoon salt
⅛ teaspoon pepper

1. Preheat oven to 450°.
2. Peel onions, leaving roots intact; cut each onion into 6 wedges.
3. Place onion wedges in an 11 x 7-inch baking dish coated with cooking spray. Combine vinegar and remaining ingredients; pour over onion wedges, tossing gently to coat. Cover; bake at 450° for 25 minutes. Uncover; bake 45 minutes or until tender. YIELD: 6 servings (serving size: 1 cup).

POINTS: 1; **EXCHANGES:** 2 Vegetable, ½ Fat; **PER SERVING:** CAL 72 (33% from fat); PRO 1.6g; FAT 2.6g (sat 0.4g); CARB 11.8g; FIB 2.5g; CHOL 0mg; IRON 0.7mg; SOD 102mg; CALC 33mg

ROASTED PEPPERS AND CORN

2 cups water
½ teaspoon turmeric
1 cup dry long-grain parboiled
 rice (such as Uncle Ben's)
Cooking spray
1 cup chopped red bell pepper
1 cup chopped green bell pepper
1 cup frozen whole-kernel corn
½ cup chopped onion
¾ cup (3 ounces) reduced-fat
 shredded sharp Cheddar cheese
1 tablespoon yogurt-based spread
 (such as Brummel & Brown)
½ teaspoon salt
½ teaspoon ground cumin
⅛ teaspoon pepper

1. Preheat oven to 425°.
2. Bring water and turmeric to a
boil in a medium saucepan. Add
rice; cover, reduce heat, and simmer
20 minutes or until liquid is
absorbed.
3. Arrange peppers, corn, and onion
in a single layer on a baking sheet
coated with cooking spray. Coat
vegetables with cooking spray. Bake
at 425° for 20 minutes or until
vegetables begin to brown.
4. Spoon vegetables into a large
bowl. Add rice, cheese, and remaining ingredients; toss well. **YIELD:**
5½ cups (serving size: ½ cup).

POINTS: 2; **EXCHANGES:** 1 Starch, 1 Vegetable,
½ Fat; **PER SERVING:** CAL 116 (16% from fat);
PRO 4.4g; FAT 2.1g (sat 1g); CARB 20.5g; FIB 1.3g;
CHOL 3mg; IRON 1mg; SOD 172mg; CALC 86mg

GARLIC MASHED POTATOES WITH ROSEMARY

(pictured on page 3)

1 pound baking potatoes, peeled
 and coarsely chopped
2 teaspoons olive oil, divided
4 garlic cloves, minced
1½ teaspoons chopped fresh
 rosemary
½ cup fat-free half-and-half
¾ teaspoon salt
¼ teaspoon pepper

1. Place potatoes in a large
saucepan, and cover with cold water.
Bring to a boil; cover, reduce heat,
and simmer 15 minutes or until tender. Drain; wipe pan dry.
2. Heat 1 teaspoon oil in saucepan
over medium-high heat until hot.
Add garlic and rosemary; cook 3
minutes, stirring often.
3. Add drained potatoes, 1 teaspoon
oil, half-and-half, salt, and pepper to
garlic mixture. Place over low heat,
and mash with a potato masher.
YIELD: 3 servings (serving size: 1 cup).

POINTS: 3; **EXCHANGES:** 2 Starch, ½ Fat;
PER SERVING: CAL 182 (17% from fat); PRO 2.8g;
FAT 3.3g (sat 0.5g); CARB 33.3g; FIB 2.8g;
CHOL 0mg; IRON 1.6mg; SOD 631mg;
CALC 47mg

HASH-BROWN CASSEROLE

1 cup thinly sliced green onions
1 cup (4 ounces) shredded
 reduced-fat Cheddar cheese
2 tablespoons margarine, melted
¼ teaspoon pepper
1 (32-ounce) package frozen
 Southern-style hash brown
 potatoes, thawed
1 (16-ounce) carton fat-free sour
 cream
1 (10¾-ounce) can condensed
 reduced-fat, reduced-sodium
 cream of mushroom soup,
 undiluted
Cooking spray
½ teaspoon paprika

1. Preheat oven to 350°.
2. Combine first 7 ingredients in a
large bowl; spoon into a 13 x 9-inch
baking dish coated with cooking
spray. Sprinkle with paprika. Bake at
350° for 1 hour or until bubbly.
YIELD: 9 servings (serving size: 1 cup).

POINTS: 3; **EXCHANGES:** 1 Starch, ½ Medium-Fat
Meat; **PER SERVING:** CAL 146 (27% from fat);
PRO 6.7g; FAT 4.3g (sat 1.5g); CARB 17.8g;
FIB 0.7g; CHOL 8mg; IRON 0.7mg; SOD 224mg;
CALC 105mg

FRESH OR DRIED—YOU PICK!

Here's a quick tip if you don't
have a fresh herb that a recipe
calls for: Substitute one teaspoon
of dried herb for each tablespoon of fresh chopped herb.

SCALLOPED POTATOES WITH SPINACH AND CHEESE

(pictured on page 139)

2 pounds peeled Yukon Gold potatoes, cut into ⅛-inch slices
1¼ cups 1% low-fat milk
1 cup fat-free, less-sodium chicken broth
3 tablespoons all-purpose flour
½ teaspoon salt
⅛ teaspoon pepper
Dash of nutmeg
Cooking spray
2 teaspoons butter
2 cups sliced Vidalia or other sweet onion
1 cup (4 ounces) reduced-fat shredded sharp Cheddar cheese
1 (10-ounce) package frozen chopped spinach, thawed and squeezed dry
3 tablespoons grated Parmesan cheese

1. Preheat oven to 450°.
2. Place potato slices in a large saucepan, and cover with water. Bring to a boil; reduce heat, and simmer, uncovered, 6 minutes or until tender. Drain well; set aside.
3. Combine milk and next 5 ingredients in a medium bowl, stirring with a whisk until blended.
4. Melt butter in a large nonstick skillet coated with cooking spray over medium-high heat. Add onion; sauté 7 minutes or until golden. Reduce heat to medium. Gradually add milk mixture, stirring with a whisk until blended. Cook 5 minutes or until thick and bubbly; stirring constantly with a wooden spoon. Add cheese, stirring until cheese melts. Remove from heat.
5. Arrange half of potato slices in an 11 x 7-inch baking dish coated with cooking spray. Top with half of spinach and half of cheese sauce. Repeat with remaining potato, spinach, and sauce. Sprinkle with Parmesan cheese. Bake at 450° for 15 to 18 minutes or until golden and bubbly. YIELD: 8 servings (serving size: 1 cup).

POINTS: 4; EXCHANGES: 1½ Starch, 1 Vegetable, ½ Medium-Fat Meat, ½ Fat; PER SERVING: CAL 191 (21% from fat); PRO 10.1g; FAT 4.6g (sat 2.9g); CARB 28.6g; FIB 3.5g; CHOL 11mg; IRON 1.3mg; SOD 429mg; CALC 260mg

GARLIC- AND GREEN ONION-STUFFED POTATOES

3 large baking potatoes (about 2¼ pounds)
1 cup sliced green onions
5 garlic cloves, minced
Butter-flavored cooking spray
1 (8-ounce) carton low-fat sour cream
¾ teaspoon salt
¼ teaspoon pepper
3 tablespoons grated Parmesan cheese

1. Preheat oven to 450°.
2. Pierce potatoes with a fork, and bake at 450° for 1 hour or until done; cool slightly. Reduce oven to 350°.
3. Place a nonstick skillet over medium-high heat until hot. Coat onions and garlic with cooking spray; add to pan and sauté 5 minutes or until tender. Remove from heat.
4. Cut each potato in half lengthwise; scoop out pulp, leaving a ¼-inch shell. Mash pulp with a potato masher. Add onion mixture, sour cream, salt, and pepper to pulp.
5. Spoon potato mixture into shells; sprinkle evenly with Parmesan cheese. Place stuffed potatoes on a baking sheet; bake at 350° for 15 minutes or until thoroughly heated. YIELD: 6 servings (serving size: 1 potato half).

POINTS: 4; EXCHANGES: 3 Starch, 1 Fat; PER SERVING: CAL 218 (14% from fat); PRO 5.9g; FAT 3.5g (sat 2.5g); CARB 42g; FIB 4.1g; CHOL 15mg; IRON 2mg; SOD 400mg; CALC 111mg

WHIPPED SPICED SWEET POTATOES

1 pound peeled sweet potatoes, cut into 1-inch cubes
¼ cup packed brown sugar
2 tablespoons light butter
½ teaspoon ground cinnamon
⅛ teaspoon salt
⅛ teaspoon ground allspice
1 teaspoon vanilla extract

1. Steam sweet potato, covered, 10 minutes or until tender.
2. Place potato in a medium bowl. Beat potatoes with a mixer at high speed until smooth. Add brown sugar and remaining ingredients, beating well. YIELD: 5 servings (serving size: ½ cup).

POINTS: 3; EXCHANGES: 2 Starch, ½ Fat; PER SERVING: CAL 151 (15% from fat); PRO 1.8g; FAT 2.7g (sat 1.7g); CARB 31g; FIB 1.6g; CHOL 8mg; IRON 0.7mg; SOD 101mg; CALC 29mg

BAKED TOMATOES TAPENADE

½ cup pitted kalamata olives, chopped
2 teaspoons capers
2 teaspoons olive oil
1 teaspoon balsamic vinegar
½ teaspoon lemon juice
1 garlic clove, minced
Cooking spray
2 (10-ounce) tomatoes, sliced in half horizontally

1. Preheat oven to 400°.
2. Combine first 6 ingredients. Arrange tomato halves on a baking sheet coated with cooking spray. Bake at 400° for 6 minutes. Remove from oven. Top evenly with olive mixture. Bake at 400° for 6 minutes. YIELD: 4 servings (serving size: 1 tomato half).

POINTS: 3; EXCHANGES: 2 Vegetable, 1½ Fat; **PER SERVING:** CAL 110 (63% from fat); PRO 1.6g; FAT 8.2g (sat 1g); CARB 9.1g; FIB 1.8g; CHOL 0mg; IRON 0.8mg; SOD 392mg; CALC 17mg

---

TOMATO TIPS

There's more to tomatoes than just their juicy freshness and bright red color. Tomatoes are packed full of good-for-you nutrients and are a very low-calorie food. One medium tomato can provide up to 20% of your daily recommended vitamin A and 40% of your daily recommended vitamin C, while packing in only about 30 calories. In addition to being a good source of soluble fiber and potassium, the tomato has been shown to reduce the incidence of several cancers.

SPINACH- AND FETA-STUFFED TOMATOES

4 large tomatoes (about 8 ounces each)
Cooking spray
1 cup chopped onion
1 (10-ounce) package frozen chopped spinach, thawed, drained, and squeezed dry
1 cup cooked couscous
2 teaspoons chopped fresh rosemary
¼ teaspoon salt
¼ teaspoon pepper
¾ cup (3 ounces) crumbled feta cheese,

1. Preheat oven to 350°.
2. Cut top off each tomato. Scoop out pulp, leaving shells intact. Chop and reserve ¾ cup pulp. Discard tops and remaining pulp, or save pulp for another use. Invert tomato shells on paper towels; let stand 30 minutes.
3. Place a large nonstick skillet coated with cooking spray over medium heat until hot. Add onion and sauté 5 minutes or until tender. Add tomato pulp, spinach, couscous, rosemary, salt, and pepper; cook 2 minutes or until thoroughly heated. Remove from heat, and stir in feta cheese.
4. Spoon about ¾ cup filling into each tomato shell. Place tomatoes into an 8-inch square baking dish coated with cooking spray. Bake at 350° for 25 minutes or until thoroughly heated. YIELD: 4 servings (serving size: 1 tomato).

POINTS: 3; EXCHANGES: ½ Starch, 4 Vegetable, 1 Fat; **PER SERVING:** CAL 184 (26% from fat); PRO 9.1g; FAT 5.7g (sat 3.4g); CARB 27.8g; FIB 6.1g; CHOL 19mg; IRON 2.9mg; SOD 459mg; CALC 209mg

---

STEWED CHARD WITH TOMATOES AND ROASTED GARLIC

Fresh chopped and stemmed spinach can be substituted for the Swiss chard.

12 cups coarsely chopped Swiss chard (about 2 bunches)
⅓ cup water
2 teaspoons olive oil
½ cup chopped onion
1 (14.5-ounce) can roasted garlic-flavored diced tomatoes, undrained
1 teaspoon sugar
¼ teaspoon salt
⅛ teaspoon pepper
2 teaspoons red wine vinegar

1. Rinse chard, drain slightly, and place in a large Dutch oven. Add ⅓ cup water. Cover and cook over medium heat 16 minutes or until tender, stirring occasionally. Drain well.
2. Heat oil in a large nonstick skillet over medium-high heat; add onion, and cook 4 minutes or until tender, stirring occasionally. Stir in diced tomato and next 3 ingredients. Bring to a boil; reduce heat, and cook, uncovered, 5 minutes or until slightly thick, stirring occasionally.
3. Stir in chard. Bring to a boil; cover, reduce heat, and simmer 5 minutes. Stir in vinegar. YIELD: 7 servings (serving size: ½ cup).

POINTS: 1; EXCHANGES: 2 Vegetable; **PER SERVING:** CAL 53 (23% from fat); PRO 1.9g; FAT 1.5g (sat 0.2g); CARB 9.1g; FIB 1.8g; CHOL 0mg; IRON 1.7mg; SOD 505mg; CALC 68mg

STUFFED ZUCCHINI AND YELLOW SQUASH

To save time, packaged angel hair cole slaw may be substituted for the shredded green cabbage.

2 zucchini, halved lengthwise (about 6 ounces each)
2 yellow squash, halved lengthwise (about 6 ounces each)
Cooking spray
2 cups shredded green cabbage
1 cup finely chopped onion
1 cup finely chopped green bell pepper
1 teaspoon dried oregano
2 garlic cloves, minced
Dash of crushed red pepper
2 (1-ounce) slices whole wheat or seedless rye bread
¾ cup (3 ounces) shredded part-skim mozzarella cheese
¼ cup chopped fresh parsley
2 tablespoons Parmesan cheese
½ teaspoon salt
⅛ teaspoon black pepper

1. Preheat oven to 350°.
2. Scoop pulp out of zucchini and yellow squash, leaving a ¼-inch shell. Place squash and zucchini shells on a baking sheet, and set aside. Coarsely chop pulp.
3. Coat a large nonstick skillet with cooking spray; place over medium-high heat. Add pulp, cabbage, and next 5 ingredients. Cook 10 minutes or until liquid is absorbed and vegetables are tender, stirring constantly. Remove from heat.
4. Place bread in a food processor; pulse 5 to 7 times or until coarse crumbs form.
5. Add breadcrumbs, cheese, and remaining ingredients to vegetable mixture; stir well. Spoon vegetable mixture evenly into squash and zucchini shells, pressing firmly.
6. Bake at 350° for 25 to 30 minutes or until shells are tender. YIELD: 4 servings (serving size: 1 squash half and 1 zucchini half).

POINTS: 3; EXCHANGES: ½ Starch, 3 Vegetable, 1 Medium-Fat Meat; **PER SERVING:** CAL 171 (28% from fat); PRO 12.4g; FAT 5.7g (sat 3g); CARB 20.7g; FIB 4.9g; CHOL 14mg; IRON 2.1mg; SOD 545mg; CALC 277mg

ZUCCHINI-AND-CORN SAUTÉ

(pictured on page 137)

2 teaspoons olive oil
4 cups (½-inch) diced zucchini (about 1 pound)
1 cup fresh corn kernels or 1 cup frozen corn kernels, thawed
2 tablespoons chopped fresh flat-leaf parsley
2 tablespoons thinly sliced green onions
¼ teaspoon salt
⅛ teaspoon pepper

1. Heat oil in a large nonstick skillet over medium-high heat. Add zucchini and corn; sauté 5 minutes or until zucchini is tender.
2. Add parsley and remaining ingredients, and stir well. Cook 1 minute or until thoroughly heated. YIELD: 7 servings (serving size: ½ cup).

POINTS: 1; EXCHANGE: ½ Starch; **PER SERVING:** CAL 39 (33% from fat); PRO 1.4g; FAT 1.6g (sat 0.2g); CARB 6.1g; FIB 1.4g; CHOL 0mg; IRON 0.4mg; SOD 89mg; CALC 11mg

ASIAN VEGETABLE STIR-FRY

(pictured on page 139)

2 tablespoons hoisin sauce
1 tablespoon low-sodium soy sauce
½ teaspoon cornstarch
1 jalapeño pepper, minced
1 pound asparagus
3 cups sugar snap peas, trimmed
1½ cups red bell pepper strips
1 cup chopped green onions (about 3)
2 teaspoons dark sesame oil
2 teaspoons minced peeled fresh ginger
¼ teaspoon salt
3 garlic cloves, minced
¼ cup chopped fresh cilantro

1. Combine first 4 ingredients in a small bowl; set aside. Snap off tough ends of asparagus; cut into 3-inch pieces, and place in a large bowl. Add peas, bell pepper, and onions; set aside.
2. Heat oil in a large nonstick skillet over medium-high heat. Add ginger, salt, and garlic; stir-fry 30 seconds. Add vegetable mixture; stir-fry 3 minutes.
3. Add hoisin sauce mixture; stir-fry 1 to 2 minutes or until thick and vegetables are crisp-tender. Remove from heat, and stir in cilantro. YIELD: 4 servings (serving size: 2 cups).

POINTS: 2; EXCHANGES: ½ Starch, 3 Vegetable, ½ Fat; **PER SERVING:** CAL 132 (18% from fat); PRO 5.5g; FAT 2.7g (sat 0.4g); CARB 21.3g; FIB 7.5g; CHOL 0mg; IRON 1.5mg; SOD 432mg; CALC 96mg

ROASTED FALL VEGETABLES

(pictured on page 138)

1½ pounds (½-inch) cubed peeled sweet potato
3 cups trimmed Brussels sprouts, halved (about 1 pound)
2 tablespoons olive oil
2 tablespoons balsamic vinegar
1 teaspoon dried thyme
½ teaspoon salt
¼ teaspoon freshly ground black pepper
4 garlic cloves, minced
1 large red onion, peeled and cut into 10 wedges
Cooking spray

1. Preheat oven to 450°.
2. Combine all ingredients except cooking spray in a large bowl; toss gently. Arrange vegetable mixture on a large broiler pan coated with cooking spray. Coat vegetable mixture with cooking spray. Bake at 450° for 35 to 40 minutes or until vegetables are tender and browned, turning once. YIELD: 6 servings (serving size: 1 cup).

POINTS: 3; **EXCHANGES:** 1½ Starch, 2 Vegetable, 1 Fat; **PER SERVING:** CAL 180 (19% from fat); PRO 4.7g; FAT 4.1g (sat 0.6g); CARB 33.6g; FIB 5.5g; CHOL 0mg; IRON 1.9mg; SOD 227mg; CALC 68mg

BARLEY PILAF WITH TOASTED ALMONDS AND RAISINS

2 teaspoons olive oil
½ cup chopped onion
2 cups fat-free, less-sodium chicken broth
1 cup uncooked quick-cooking barley
3 tablespoons sliced almonds, toasted
3 tablespoons golden raisins
2 tablespoons chopped fresh flat-leaf parsley
¼ teaspoon salt
⅛ teaspoon pepper

1. Heat oil in a 3-quart saucepan over medium heat. Add onion; cook 5 minutes, stirring occasionally. Add broth; bring to a boil. Add barley; cover, reduce heat, and simmer 15 minutes. Add almonds and remaining ingredients; stir well. Cover and let stand 5 minutes. YIELD: 6 servings (serving size: ½ cup).

POINTS: 3; **EXCHANGES:** 2 Starch, ½ Fat; **PER SERVING:** CAL 174 (18% from fat); PRO 5.4g; FAT 3.6g (sat 0.4g); CARB 31.8g; FIB 6g; CHOL 0mg; IRON 1.2mg; SOD 309mg; CALC 24mg

CONFETTI COUSCOUS

(pictured on page 138)

2 teaspoons olive oil
1 onion, chopped
4 garlic cloves, minced
1 red bell pepper, diced
1 green bell pepper, diced
1 yellow squash, diced
1 (5.8-ounce) package olive oil and garlic couscous
2 cups fat-free, less-sodium chicken broth
2 tablespoons pine nuts, toasted
½ cup chopped fresh basil
½ teaspoon freshly ground black pepper

1. Heat oil in a large nonstick skillet over medium-high heat; add onion and garlic. Cook 4 minutes, stirring occasionally, until golden. Add peppers and squash; cook 5 minutes, stirring occasionally, until vegetables are tender.
2. Cook couscous according to package directions, using chicken broth instead of water and omitting salt and fat. Stir in vegetable mixture, pine nuts, basil, and black pepper. YIELD: 8 servings (serving size: ⅔ cup).

POINTS: 2; **EXCHANGES:** 1 Starch, 1 Vegetable, ½ Fat; **PER SERVING:** CAL 125 (20% from fat); PRO 4.9g; FAT 2.9g (sat 0.4g); CARB 21.7g; FIB 2.6g; CHOL 0mg; IRON 0.9mg; SOD 334mg; CALC 27mg

GRATIN OF NOODLES AND MUSHROOMS

1 cup fat-free, less-sodium chicken broth
1 cup 1% low-fat milk
3 tablespoons all-purpose flour
½ teaspoon salt
⅛ teaspoon pepper
2 teaspoons butter
2 cups thinly sliced mushrooms
½ cup chopped onion
⅓ cup diced red bell pepper
1 garlic clove, minced
2 tablespoons grated Parmesan cheese
1 tablespoon dry sherry
3 cups hot cooked wide noodles
1 (1-ounce) slice white bread

1. Preheat oven to 450°.
2. Combine first 5 ingredients in a medium bowl; stir well with a whisk.
3. Melt butter in a large nonstick skillet over medium-high heat. Add mushrooms and next 3 ingredients; cook 6 minutes or until tender. Add milk mixture, and cook 6 minutes or until thick and bubbly, stirring constantly. Add Parmesan cheese and sherry; stir well. Remove from heat; add noodles, and stir gently.
4. Place bread in a food processor; pulse 10 times or until coarse crumbs form to measure ⅓ cup. Spoon mixture into a 10-inch gratin dish; sprinkle with breadcrumbs. Bake at 450° for 10 minutes. Let stand 10 minutes. YIELD: 8 servings (serving size: ½ cup).

POINTS: 3; **EXCHANGES:** 1½ Starch, ½ Fat;
PER SERVING: CAL 142 (18% from fat); PRO 6.2g;
FAT 2.9g (sat 1.3g); CARB 22.8g; FIB 1.4g;
CHOL 25mg; IRON 1.5mg; SOD 304mg;
CALC 76mg

LEMON BASMATI RICE WITH PINE NUTS

1 teaspoon canola oil
1 cup chopped onion
1 cup chopped celery
3 cups fat-free, less-sodium chicken broth
1½ cups uncooked brown basmati rice
¼ cup currants
¼ cup pine nuts, toasted
¼ teaspoon salt
¼ teaspoon pepper
1 teaspoon fresh lemon juice

1. Heat oil in a large saucepan over medium-high heat. Add onion and celery; sauté 5 minutes or until tender. Add broth, rice, and currants; bring to a boil. Cover, reduce heat, and simmer 55 minutes or until rice is tender and liquid is absorbed. Stir in pine nuts, salt, pepper, and lemon juice. YIELD: 10 servings (serving size: ½ cup).

POINTS: 3; **EXCHANGES:** 2 Starch, ½ Fat;
PER SERVING: CAL 149 (18% from fat); PRO 4.3g;
FAT 3g (sat 0.5g); CARB 26.9g; FIB 1.9g;
CHOL 0mg; IRON 1mg; SOD 258mg; CALC 22mg

BROWN RICE PILAF

1 teaspoon olive oil
½ cup diced carrot
⅓ cup diced celery
¼ cup chopped onion
1 cup uncooked long-grain brown rice
½ cup water
¼ teaspoon salt
⅛ teaspoon pepper
1 (14½-ounce) can fat-free, less-sodium chicken broth
¾ cup frozen peas, thawed
1½ to 2 tablespoons chopped fresh dill

1. Heat oil in a large saucepan over medium heat. Add carrot, celery, and onion; sauté 4 minutes or until tender. Add rice and next 4 ingredients; stir well. Bring to a boil; reduce heat, and simmer, covered, 45 minutes or until rice is tender.
2. Add peas, and stir gently. Remove from heat, and let stand 5 minutes. Add dill, and stir gently. YIELD: 6 servings (serving size: ½ cup).

POINTS: 3; **EXCHANGES:** 2 Starch;
PER SERVING: CAL 152 (11% from fat); PRO 4.9g;
FAT 1.8g (sat 0.3g); CARB 29.4g; FIB 3.4g;
CHOL 0mg; IRON 0.9mg; SOD 327mg;
CALC 25mg

CHOOSE THE RIGHT RICE

There are dozens of types of rice on the shelf, but is one better than another? It depends on what you're looking for. If speed is essential, try a converted or instant rice. If it's flavor you want, try a basmati or aromatic rice, such as Popcorn, Jasmine, or Texmati. An Italian risotto rice, such as arborio, offers a nice, creamy change. But if it's maximum health benefits you want, try a brown rice. All rices are high-carbohydrate, low-fat, low-sodium foods full of many B vitamins, but the fiber in brown rice gives it an edge. Its color comes from the whole rice grain and bran being intact; because of this, brown rice serves up 3 grams of fiber per cup, compared to other rices' 1 gram of fiber per cup.

VEGETABLE CREOLE RICE

Cooking spray
  1 teaspoon olive oil
  1 cup chopped onion
  1 cup chopped green bell pepper
  2 cups (½-inch) cubed peeled
    sweet potato
  4 garlic cloves, minced
  2 tablespoons tomato paste
  ½ teaspoon salt
  ½ teaspoon sugar
  ½ teaspoon dried oregano
  ½ teaspoon hot pepper sauce
  2 bay leaves
  2 (14.5-ounce) cans vegetable
    broth
  1 (14.5-ounce) can diced
    tomatoes, undrained
  1½ cups uncooked long-grain par-
    boiled rice (such as Uncle
    Ben's)
  ¼ cup chopped green onions
  1 (14.5-ounce) can light red
    beans, drained and rinsed

1. Heat oil in a large nonstick skillet
coated with cooking spray over
medium-high heat. Add onion and
bell pepper; sauté 8 minutes or until
tender. Add sweet potato and garlic;
sauté 1 to 2 minutes. Add tomato
paste and next 7 ingredients; stir
well. Bring to a boil; add rice.
Reduce heat; simmer, uncovered, 20
minutes or until rice is tender, stirring occasionally. Remove bay leaves.
2. Add green onions and beans; stir
gently. Cook over medium heat
until thoroughly heated. Serve
immediately. YIELD: 12 servings
(serving size: ¾ cup).

POINTS: 2; **EXCHANGES:** 2 Starch; **PER SERVING:**
CAL 142.7 (6% from fat); PRO 4.4g; FAT 1g
(sat 0.1g); CARB 29.4g; FIB 2.9g; CHOL 0mg;
IRON 1.5mg; SOD 499mg; CALC 34mg

VEGETABLE FRIED RICE

  1 teaspoon vegetable oil
  1 teaspoon dark sesame oil
  ⅔ cup thinly sliced celery
  1 cup trimmed snow peas
  3 cups cold cooked rice
  1 cup frozen peas and carrots,
    thawed
  ½ cup sliced green onions
  2 tablespoons chopped fresh basil
  3 tablespoons soy sauce
  1 tablespoon oyster sauce
  1 to 2 teaspoons grated peeled
    fresh ginger
  ¼ teaspoon pepper
Cooking spray
  1 large egg, beaten

1. Heat oils in a nonstick skillet over
medium-high heat. Add celery; stir-
fry 3 minutes. Add snow peas; stir-fry
1 minute. Add rice and next 7 ingredients; stir-fry 4 minutes. Transfer rice
mixture to serving bowl.
2. Coat pan with cooking spray;
place over medium-high heat until
hot. Add egg; stir-fry 1 minute. Stir
egg into rice mixture. YIELD: 8 servings (serving size: ½ cup).

POINTS: 2; **EXCHANGES:** 1 Starch, 1 Vegetable,
½ Fat; **PER SERVING:** CAL 121 (16% from fat);
PRO 4.3g; FAT 2.1g (sat 0.4g); CARB 20.9g;
FIB 1.7g; CHOL 27mg; IRON 1.4mg; SOD 392mg;
CALC 26mg

RISOTTO WITH LEEKS AND MUSHROOMS

  2 (14½-ounce) cans fat-free,
    less-sodium chicken broth
  2 teaspoons olive oil
  1½ cups thinly sliced leeks
  1½ cups presliced mushrooms
  1 cup uncooked Arborio rice
  3 tablespoons dry white wine
  ¼ teaspoon dried sage
  3 tablespoons grated Parmesan
    cheese
  ⅛ teaspoon pepper

1. Bring broth to a simmer in a
medium saucepan. (Do not boil.)
Keep warm over low heat.
2. Heat oil in a large saucepan over
medium heat. Add leeks and mushrooms; sauté 5 minutes or until leeks
are soft. Add rice; cook 1 minute,
stirring constantly. Stir in wine; cook
1 minute or until liquid is nearly
absorbed, stirring constantly. Add
sage and warm broth, ½ cup at a
time, stirring constantly until each
portion of broth is absorbed (about
24 minutes total). Stir in cheese and
pepper. YIELD: 6 servings (serving size:
⅔ cup).

POINTS: 4; **EXCHANGES:** 2 Starch, 1 Vegetable,
½ Fat; **PER SERVING:** CAL 195 (12% from fat);
PRO 6.6g; FAT 2.6g (sat 0.8g); CARB 34.7g;
FIB 1.3g; CHOL 2mg; IRON 1mg; SOD 438mg;
CALC 71mg

Soups & Stews

BERRY PATCH SOUP

(pictured on page 159)
Blend refrigerated leftovers with frozen banana slices to make a smoothie.

3 (16-ounce) packages frozen berry mix (strawberries, raspberries, blueberries, and blackberries), thawed
½ cup honey
¾ cup fat-free half-and-half
3 tablespoons Sauternes or other dessert white wine
11 tablespoons reduced-fat sour cream

1. Place one-third of berry mix in food processor or blender, and process until smooth. Strain pureed mixture through a sieve into a large bowl; discard pulp. Repeat procedure 2 times with remaining berry mix. Add honey, half-and-half, and wine to pureed mixture; stir well. Ladle soup into bowls. Dollop each with sour cream. YIELD: 11 servings (serving size: ½ cup soup and 1 tablespoon sour cream).
NOTE: 1 (16-ounce) package each of frozen strawberries, raspberries, and blueberries can be substituted for 3 (16-ounce) packages of frozen berry mix.

POINTS: 3; **EXCHANGES:** 1 Starch, 1 Fruit, ½ Fat; **PER SERVING:** CAL 149 (12% from fat); PRO 1.6g; FAT 1.9g (sat 1.2g); CARB 29.1g; FIB 2.7g; CHOL 8mg; IRON 0.7mg; SOD 26mg; CALC 55mg

BEER-CHEESE SOUP WITH PRETZEL CROUTONS

(pictured on page 158)

12 ounces light processed cheese, cubed (such as Velveeta Light)
2 cups fat-free half-and-half
1 (12-ounce) can light beer
1 garlic clove, minced
5 tablespoons all-purpose flour
½ cup water
¼ teaspoon ground red pepper
4 tablespoons chopped fresh chives
16 unsalted pretzel rounds (such as Paul Newman's)

1. Combine first 4 ingredients in a large saucepan; cook, uncovered, over medium-low heat, stirring frequently, until cheese melts.
2. Combine flour and water, stirring with a whisk; add to cheese mixture. Cover and cook over medium-low heat 15 minutes, stirring constantly, or until mixture is slightly thick. Stir in red pepper. Ladle into bowls; sprinkle with chives, and top with pretzels. YIELD: 8 servings (serving size: ⅔ cup soup and 2 pretzel rounds).

POINTS: 4; **EXCHANGES:** 1½ Starch, 1 Medium-Fat Meat; **PER SERVING:** CAL 182 (26% from fat); PRO 9.5g; FAT 4.8g (sat 3g); CARB 21.3g; FIB 0.2g; CHOL 18mg; IRON 0.3mg; SOD 759mg; CALC 289mg

CREAM OF CAULIFLOWER SOUP

1 tablespoon light butter
1½ cups chopped onion
2 pounds cauliflower, trimmed and coarsely chopped (about 4 cups)
3 cups fat-free, less-sodium chicken broth
½ teaspoon salt
¼ teaspoon pepper
2 thyme sprigs
1 cup fat-free half-and-half
2 tablespoons all-purpose flour
6 tablespoons reduced-fat shredded sharp Cheddar cheese

1. Melt butter in a 3-quart saucepan over medium heat; add onion, and cook 5 minutes, stirring constantly, until tender. Add cauliflower and next 4 ingredients. Bring to a boil; cover, reduce heat, and simmer 15 minutes or until cauliflower is very tender.
2. Combine half-and-half and flour, stirring with a whisk; add to cauliflower mixture. Bring to a boil; reduce heat, and simmer 2 minutes, stirring often. Remove and discard thyme. Cool 15 minutes.
3. Place half of cauliflower mixture in a food processor or blender; process until smooth. Pour pureed mixture into a large bowl; repeat procedure with remaining cauliflower mixture. Ladle into bowls; sprinkle each with cheese. YIELD: 6 servings (serving size: 1 cup soup and 1 tablespoon cheese).

POINTS: 2; **EXCHANGES:** ½ Starch, 1 Vegetable, ½ Medium-Fat Meat; **PER SERVING:** CAL 108 (23% from fat); PRO 6.4g; FAT 2.7g (sat 1.5g); CARB 13.9g; FIB 3.6g; CHOL 6mg; IRON 0.6mg; SOD 624mg; CALC 119mg

POTATO-AND-LEEK SOUP

4 cups cubed peeled baking
  potato (about 2 pounds)
4 slices reduced-sodium bacon
2 cups sliced leek (about 3)
2 garlic cloves, minced
½ cup tub-style light cream cheese
4 cups fat-free, less-sodium
  chicken broth
1 tablespoon all-purpose flour
1 cup fat-free half-and-half
2 tablespoons chopped fresh
  parsley
¾ teaspoon salt
½ teaspoon freshly ground black
  pepper

1. Place potato in a Dutch oven; add
water to cover. Bring to boil: cover,
reduce heat, and simmer 15 minutes
or until tender. Drain. Mash slightly
with a potato masher.
2. Cook bacon in a nonstick skillet
over medium heat until crisp.
Remove bacon from pan, reserving
2 tablespoons drippings; crumble.
Add leek and garlic to bacon drippings in pan; sauté 5 minutes.
3. Add leek mixture to potato; stir
in cream cheese until blended. Add
broth and flour, stirring well with a
whisk. Bring to a boil. Reduce heat,
and simmer, uncovered, 5 minutes.
Add half-and-half and remaining
3 ingredients; stir well. Sprinkle with
bacon. YIELD: 6 servings (serving size:
1½ cups).

POINTS: 4; EXCHANGES: 2 Starch, 1 Vegetable,
1 Medium-Fat Meat; PER SERVING: CAL 229
(20% from fat); PRO 8.7g; FAT 5g (sat 2.9g);
CARB 35g; FIB 2.7g; CHOL 14mg; IRON 1.9mg;
SOD 920mg; CALC 86mg

BUTTERNUT SQUASH-AND-CARAMELIZED ONION SOUP WITH PESTO

(pictured on page 160)

1 butternut squash (about
  1¾ pounds), halved lengthwise
2 teaspoons olive oil
3 cups sliced Vidalia or other
  sweet onion (about 1 large)
½ cup Sauternes or other dessert
  white wine
2 (14½-ounce) cans fat-free,
  less-sodium chicken broth
2 tablespoons commercial pesto

1. Preheat oven to 375°.
2. Place butternut squash, cut side
down, in a baking dish. Pour water
to depth of ½ inch. Bake at 375° for
45 minutes or until very tender.
Scoop out pulp; set aside.
3. Heat oil in a large skillet over
medium heat. Add onion; cook
30 minutes or until golden brown,
stirring frequently. Stir in wine and
chicken broth. Bring to a boil; cover,
reduce heat, and simmer 10 minutes
or until onion is tender. Cool 5
minutes.
4. Place half of onion mixture and
half of squash in a blender; process at
low speed until smooth. Return
soup to pan; repeat procedure with
remaining squash and onion. Bring
to a boil; reduce heat, and simmer,
uncovered, 5 minutes or until thoroughly heated. Ladle into bowls;
spoon 1 teaspoon pesto into center
of each bowl. Swirl soup and pesto
together using the tip of a knife.

YIELD: 6 servings (serving size: ¾ cup
soup and 1 teaspoon pesto).

POINTS: 2; EXCHANGES: 3 Vegetable, 1 Fat;
PER SERVING: CAL 104 (32% from fat); PRO 4.2g;
FAT 4g (sat 0.9g); CARB 14.8g; FIB 3.5g;
CHOL 2mg; IRON 0.9mg; SOD 421mg;
CALC 83mg

POSOLE WITH SUMMER SQUASH

1 tablespoon vegetable oil
1 large onion, halved lengthwise
  and sliced
3 zucchini, coarsely chopped
1 (29-ounce) can Mexican-style
  hominy, undrained
¼ teaspoon salt
¼ teaspoon pepper
1 (14½-ounce) can fat-free,
  less-sodium chicken broth
3 (4-ounce) cans whole green
  chiles, undrained and coarsely
  chopped
⅓ cup fresh lime juice (about
  1½ limes)

1. Heat oil in a Dutch oven over
medium-high heat. Add onion and
zucchini; sauté 5 minutes or until
onion is tender. Stir in hominy and
next 4 ingredients. Bring to a boil;
cover, reduce heat, and simmer 15
minutes. Uncover; remove from
heat, and stir in lime juice. YIELD: 8
servings (serving size: 1 cup).

POINTS: 1; EXCHANGES: ½ Starch, 1½ Vegetable,
½ Fat; PER SERVING: CAL 96 (22% from fat);
PRO 3.5g; FAT 2.3g (sat 0.2g); CARB 15.2g;
FIB 6.5g; CHOL 0mg; IRON 1.4mg; SOD 530mg;
CALC 30mg

TORTELLINI FAGIOLI

(pictured on page 160)

Cooking spray
- ½ cup chopped green bell pepper
- 2 shallots, finely chopped
- 2 garlic cloves, minced
- 1 (32-ounce) container fat-free, less-sodium chicken broth
- 1 (28-ounce) can roasted garlic diced tomatoes with onion and oregano, undrained
- 2 tablespoons dry white wine
- ½ teaspoon freshly ground black pepper
- 1 (9-ounce) package fresh mozzarella and herb tortellini
- ¾ cup shredded fresh spinach
- 1 (15-ounce) can cannellini beans, rinsed and drained
- 1 (14-ounce) can quartered artichoke hearts, rinsed and drained
- 8 tablespoons shaved Parmesan-Reggiano cheese

1. Place a Dutch oven coated with cooking spray over medium heat. Add bell pepper, shallots, and garlic; sauté 5 minutes or just until tender. Stir in chicken broth, tomatoes, wine, and black pepper. Bring to a boil; cover, reduce heat, and simmer 15 minutes.
2. Add tortellini; bring to a boil, and cook 3 minutes.
3. Stir in spinach, beans, and artichoke hearts. Cook over medium heat until thoroughly heated.
4. Ladle soup into bowls; top evenly with cheese. YIELD: 8 servings (1¼ cups soup and 1 tablespoon cheese).

POINTS: 4; **EXCHANGES:** 1 Starch, 2 Vegetable, 1 Medium-Fat Meat; **PER SERVING:** CAL 202 (22% from fat); PRO 12.4g; FAT 4.9g (sat 2.8g); CARB 28g; FIB 4.6g; CHOL 19mg; IRON 1.6mg; SOD 950mg; CALC 200mg

SHRIMP WON TON DUMPLING SOUP

- ¾ pound unpeeled large shrimp
- 6 cups fat free, less-sodium chicken broth
- ½ cup finely chopped bok choy
- ¼ cup finely chopped fresh bean sprouts
- 2 teaspoons grated peeled fresh ginger
- ¾ teaspoon dark sesame oil
- 2 garlic cloves, minced
- 12 won ton wrappers
- 20 snow peas
- 5 small mushrooms, sliced
- 3 tablespoons sliced green onions

1. Peel and devein shrimp; reserve shells. Rinse and drain shells; place in a Dutch oven. Add chicken broth. Bring to a boil; reduce heat, and simmer, uncovered, 10 minutes. Strain broth mixture through a sieve over a bowl; discard solids. Return broth to pan.
2. Stir together bok choy and next 4 ingredients. Working with 1 wrapper at a time (cover remaining wrappers with a damp towel to keep them from drying), spoon about 1 tablespoon of bok choy mixture into center of each wrapper. Moisten edges of wrapper with water; bring 2 opposite corners to center, pinching points to seal. Bring remaining 2 corners to center, pinching points to seal. Pinch 4 edges together to seal.
3. Add shrimp, snow peas, and mushrooms to pan; bring to a boil. Reduce heat to simmer; gently drop dumplings into pan, 2 at a time. Cook 3 to 4 minutes, or until dumplings are done.
4. Gently ladle soup into bowls; sprinkle with green onions. YIELD: 6 servings (1½ cups soup and 2 dumplings).

POINTS: 3; **EXCHANGES:** ½ Starch, 1 Vegetable, 2 Very Lean Meat; **PER SERVING:** CAL 141 (12% from fat); PRO 17.3g; FAT 1.9g (sat 0.3g); CARB 13.3g; FIB 0.9g; CHOL 88mg; IRON 2.4mg; SOD 801mg; CALC 54mg

VITAL VITAMINS

In addition to a healthy diet, taking a multivitamin each day is a great habit to start. Of course, the best way to get vitamins and minerals is through the foods you eat; no supplement can supply your body with all the components that food supplies, such as fiber and antioxidants. Don't skimp on eating nutrient-rich foods if you take a vitamin; think of vitamins as extra health insurance on the days you may not get 100% of each nutrient through your diet.

FOUR-WAY CINCINNATI CHILI

2 pounds ground round
2 cups chopped onion
1 cup chopped green bell pepper
1 (28-ounce) can diced tomatoes
  with basil, garlic, and oregano
1¼ cups water
2 tablespoons chili powder
1 teaspoon ground cumin
½ teaspoon salt
½ teaspoon ground cinnamon
¼ teaspoon ground allspice
¼ teaspoon pepper
1 (15-ounce) can light red kidney
  beans, rinsed and drained
1 (6-ounce) can no-salt-added
  tomato paste
5 cups hot cooked spaghetti
10 tablespoons reduced-fat
  shredded Cheddar cheese
10 tablespoons chopped red onion
2½ cups oyster crackers

1. Cook beef, onion, and green bell
pepper in a large nonstick skillet
over medium-high heat until
browned; stir to crumble. Stir in
diced tomatoes and next 9 ingredients. Bring to a boil; cover, reduce
heat, and simmer 30 minutes,
stirring occasionally.
2. Divide cooked spaghetti among
serving bowls. Spoon chili over pasta;
top each with 1 tablespoon each of
cheese and onion and ¼ cup crackers. YIELD: 10 servings (serving size: 1
cup chili and ½ cup pasta).

POINTS: 7; **EXCHANGES:** 3 Starch, 1 Vegetable,
2½ Lean Meat; **PER SERVING:** CAL 360
(16% from fat); PRO 29.7g; FAT 6.6g (sat 2.4g);
CARB 47.3g; FIB 5.5g; CHOL 51mg; IRON 5.3mg;
SOD 892mg; CALC 161mg

POT ROAST STEW

Cooking spray
1½ pounds boneless chuck roast,
  trimmed and cut into 1-inch
  cubes
1½ cups water
1 (14½-ounce) can beef broth
2½ cups cubed peeled red potato
1¾ cups sliced peeled carrot
1 tablespoon Worcestershire sauce
2 teaspoons olive oil
½ teaspoon salt
½ teaspoon freshly ground black
  pepper
3 garlic cloves, minced
1 large onion, cut into 1-inch pieces
¼ cup all-purpose flour
¼ cup water
1 tablespoon chopped fresh thyme
¼ cup minced fresh chives

1. Coat a large nonstick skillet with
cooking spray; place over high heat
until hot. Add beef; cook 5 minutes
or until browned. Remove beef; place
in a 4½-quart electric slow cooker.
2. Add water and broth to pan, scraping pan to loosen browned bits; pour
over beef in slow cooker. Add potato
and next 7 ingredients to slow cooker; stir well. Cover with lid; cook on
high-heat setting 6 to 8 hours.
3. Lightly spoon flour into a dry
measuring cup; level with a knife.
Combine flour and ¼ cup water in
a bowl; stir well with a whisk until
blended. Add flour mixture, thyme,
and chives to slow cooker; stir well.
Cover and cook on high-heat setting for 20 minutes. YIELD: 8 servings
(serving size: 1 cup).

POINTS: 5; **EXCHANGES:** 1 Starch, 2½ Lean Meat;
PER SERVING: CAL 234 (36% from fat); PRO 20.4g;
FAT 9.1g (sat 3.2g); CARB 16.9g; FIB 2g; CHOL 61mg;
IRON 3.1mg; SOD 406mg; CALC 32mg

LAMB STEW WITH SPRING VEGETABLES

(pictured on page 159)

Cooking spray
1½ pounds lamb stew meat, cut
  into ½-inch pieces
½ cup finely chopped onion
2 tablespoons all-purpose flour
½ cup dry white wine
2 (14½-ounce) cans fat-free,
  less-sodium chicken broth
½ pound small red potatoes,
  quartered
¼ pound baby carrots
¼ pound radishes, halved
4 thyme sprigs
1 cup frozen green peas
2 tablespoons chopped fresh
  parsley
½ teaspoon salt
¼ teaspoon pepper

1. Coat a Dutch oven with cooking
spray; place over medium-high heat
until hot. Add lamb and onion; cook
5 minutes or until browned on all
sides.
2. Add flour and cook, stirring
constantly, 1 minute. Stir in wine,
and simmer 2 minutes. Add chicken
broth; simmer, covered, 10 minutes
or until lamb is tender. Add potato,
carrots, radishes, and thyme; simmer,
uncovered, 12 minutes or until potato is tender. Add peas, and simmer
5 minutes. Stir in parsley, salt, and
pepper. Discard thyme sprigs before
serving. YIELD: 6 servings (serving
size: 1⅓ cups).

POINTS: 5; **EXCHANGES:** 1 Starch, 1 Vegetable,
3½ Lean Meat; **PER SERVING:** CAL 250
(24% from fat); PRO 28.5g; FAT 6.6g (sat 2.3g);
CARB 18.1g; FIB 3g; CHOL 77mg; IRON 3.3mg;
SOD 677mg; CALC 36mg

Making Time for Mom

KATHY LIESER • **HEIGHT** 5'4" • **BEFORE** 212 LBS. • **AFTER** 125 LBS.

Tip: "If I think I'm too busy to walk or to plan meals, I tell myself I'm worth it. It's my health and happiness. And if Mom's not happy, nobody's happy."

When Kathy Lieser's husband left his job to go to medical school, the responsibility of caring for their children fell squarely upon her shoulders. "I was too busy to plan healthful meals," recalls Kathy, now a mother of four. "At mealtime, I'd eat what the kids ate or grab a cookie and run." After getting the kids to bed, she rewarded herself with a big bowl of ice cream or popcorn.

With each pregnancy, Kathy kept 10 of the pounds she gained. She couldn't comfortably wear jeans anymore and chose jumpers over anything with a waistband. But in early 1998, she'd had enough.

"It was Jeans Day at my son's school, where I help out. I told Joey's teacher I didn't wear jeans because I'd never be able to get off the floor after the children's activities. The teacher, who wasn't wearing jeans for the same reason, asked if I would join Weight Watchers with her. I said yes immediately."

Just a week earlier, Kathy's mother had talked about Weight Watchers. "I was skeptical because I had tried to lose before, but gained the weight back every time. I didn't see why I should spend money if it wasn't going to work," she explains. "But my mother said she was going to do it. That and the teacher's invitation convinced me to try it."

Kathy began Weight Watchers *1•2•3 Success* plan and immediately liked the **POINTS** system. "Joey had started school full-time, so I had time to plan meals. Taking time for myself made me realize what I'd been eating." Kathy found keeping a food journal helpful. "That saved me," she says.

And she started walking. At first, she just went around the block, but eventually Kathy walked for 90 minutes straight. "I chose walking because it's easy and cheap," she explains. "I felt guilty at first, as if I should be doing something else, such as laundry. But I enjoyed it and learned to make time for myself. Now, I plan my life around my walks."

Reinforcement from family kept Kathy on track. There were calls from her mother. "Every

"I exercise . . . and count **POINTS** *every day."*

week after she weighed in, she'd call and tell me how much she'd lost," Kathy says. "When I weighed in, I'd call her. It helped us both." Kathy's husband, Thomas, offered unwavering support. "He wanted me to be happy, so he encouraged me to do it for myself," she says.

In 2001, Kathy is happy to report that she has maintained her goal weight of 125 pounds for more than two years. "I exercise, drink at least six glasses of water daily, and count **POINTS** every day," she says.

"I can't believe the change in my lifestyle," she says. "Instead of staying home all the time, I love to go out. I like to shop for clothes. I have energy. I can even ride a bike with Joey. You should have seen the look on his face when I did that." For Kathy, that look was the biggest compliment of all.

Weight-loss results not typical.

Beer-Cheese Soup
with Pretzel
Croutons, page 153

Berry Patch Soup,
page 153

Lamb Stew with
Spring Vegetables,
page 156

159

Butternut Squash-and-Caramelized Onion Soup with Pesto, page 154

Tortellini Fagioli, page 155

BAMA BURGOO

Cooking spray
2 (6-ounce) skinless bone-in
    chicken breast halves
¾ pound boneless pork loin roast,
    trimmed
1 teaspoon olive oil
2 cups chopped onion (about
    1 large)
1¾ cups sliced carrot
1½ cups chopped celery
1 cup chopped green bell pepper
3 garlic cloves, minced
2 (14½-ounce) cans diced
    tomatoes with basil, garlic,
    and oregano
1½ cups packaged angel hair
    coleslaw
1 teaspoon dried thyme
½ teaspoon salt
½ teaspoon black pepper
¼ teaspoon ground red pepper
1 (16-ounce) package frozen
    vegetable soup mix with
    tomatoes (such as McKenzie's)
2 (14½-ounce) cans fat-free,
    less-sodium chicken broth
1 (14½-ounce) can beef broth
2 (5.5-ounce) cans spicy-hot
    vegetable juice (such as V-8)
⅓ cup chopped fresh parsley

1. Preheat oven to 375°.
2. Arrange chicken and pork roast on a jelly-roll pan coated with cooking spray. Bake at 375° for 35 minutes or until done. Remove chicken and pork roast from pan; cool. Shred meat with 2 forks.
3. Heat oil over medium-high heat in a large Dutch oven coated with cooking spray. Add onion and next 4 ingredients; sauté 8 minutes or until tender. Stir in shredded meat, tomato, and next 9 ingredients. Bring to a

boil; cover, reduce heat, and simmer, 45 minutes. Stir in parsley. YIELD: 15 servings (serving size: 1 cup).

POINTS: 3; EXCHANGES: 3 Vegetable, 2 Very Lean Meat; PER SERVING: CAL 152 (% from fat); PRO 17.2g; FAT 2.9g (sat 0.9g); CARB 14.4g; FIB 2.7g; CHOL 37mg; IRON 1.8mg; SOD 741mg; CALC 65mg

BEAN-AND-BACON SOUP

1 pound dried navy beans
8 slices bacon
3 cups chopped onion
2½ cups chopped carrot
1½ cups chopped celery
1 tablespoon minced garlic
2 (14½-ounce) cans fat-free,
    less-sodium chicken broth
3 cups water
1 teaspoon salt
1 teaspoon dried thyme
¼ teaspoon pepper
1 bay leaf

1. Sort and wash beans; place in a large Dutch oven. Cover with water; bring to a boil, and cook, uncovered, 2 minutes. Remove from heat; cover and let stand 1 hour. Drain beans, and set aside.
2. Cook bacon in Dutch oven over medium-high heat until crisp. Remove bacon, reserving 2 teaspoons drippings in pan.
3. Add onion, carrot, celery, and garlic to drippings in pan; sauté 10 minutes or until tender. Add beans. Stir in chicken broth and remaining 5 ingredients. Crumble 6 slices bacon into soup. Bring to a boil; cover, reduce heat, and simmer 1 hour and 30 minutes or until beans are tender, stirring occasionally. Cool 10 minutes. Discard bay leaf.

4. Place 6 cups soup in a blender; process at low speed until smooth. Stir pureed soup into remaining soup in pan. Cook over medium heat, stirring occasionally, until heated. Ladle into bowls. Crumble remaining 2 slices bacon, and sprinkle evenly over soup. YIELD: 10 cups (serving size: 1 cup).

POINTS: 4; EXCHANGES: 2 Starch, 1 Vegetable, 1 Very Lean Meat, 1 Fat; PER SERVING: CAL 229 (17% from fat); PRO 12.8g; FAT 4.4g (sat 1.3g); CARB 36.3g; FIB 8.9g; CHOL 6mg; IRON 3.1mg; SOD 593mg; CALC 102mg

CHICKEN ALPHABET SOUP

2 teaspoons olive oil
1 cup sliced leek
1 cup sliced baby carrots
½ cup chopped green bell pepper
½ cup chopped celery
¾ cup water
3 (14½-ounce) cans fat-free,
    less-sodium chicken broth
⅔ cup uncooked alphabet pasta
2 cups chopped cooked chicken
2 tablespoons chopped fresh basil
1 tablespoon chopped fresh
    oregano
¼ teaspoon black pepper

1. Heat oil over medium heat in a Dutch oven. Add leek and next 3 ingredients; sauté until tender. Add water and broth. Bring to a boil; add pasta, and cook 5 minutes or until pasta is done. Stir in chicken and remaining ingredients. YIELD: 6 servings (serving size: 1½ cups).

POINTS: 4; EXCHANGES: ½ Starch, 1 Vegetable, 2 Lean Meat; PER SERVING: CAL 185 (26% from fat); PRO 18.4g; FAT 5.3g (sat 1.2g); CARB 15.6g; FIB 1.5g; CHOL 42mg; IRON 1.5mg; SOD 630mg; CALC 32mg

MULLIGATAWNY

1 teaspoon olive oil
3 cups cubed peeled sweet potato
1½ cups chopped onion
1 cup chopped green bell pepper
3 garlic cloves, minced
2 (14½-ounce) cans fat-free,
  less-sodium chicken broth
1 cup water
1 tablespoon curry powder
1 tablespoon grated peeled fresh
  ginger
1½ cups chopped roasted chicken
1 cup hot cooked basmati rice
½ cup light coconut milk
Lime wedges (optional)

1. Heat oil in a Dutch oven over medium-high heat. Add sweet potato, onion, and pepper; sauté 10 minutes or until almost tender; add garlic, and sauté 30 seconds. Add chicken broth and next 3 ingredients. Bring to a boil; reduce heat, and cook, uncovered, 20 minutes, stirring occasionally.
2. Place 2 cups soup mixture in a blender. With center cap of blender lid removed, process on low speed until smooth. Return pureed mixture to remaining soup mixture.
3. Stir in chicken; cook over medium heat 5 minutes. Stir in rice and coconut milk. Cook over medium-low heat 5 minutes or until thoroughly heated, stirring occasionally. Serve with lime wedges, if desired. YIELD: 4 servings (serving size: 1½ cups).

POINTS: 6; **EXCHANGES:** 2½ Starch, 2 Vegetable, 2 Very Lean Meat, ½ Fat; **PER SERVING:** CAL 321 (15% from fat); PRO 22.9g; FAT 5.3g (sat 1.8g); CARB 45.5g; FIB 4g; CHOL 45mg; IRON 2.7mg; SOD 826mg; CALC 55mg

OLD-FASHIONED CHICKEN-AND-RICE SOUP

1 cup water
1 (32-ounce) package fat-free,
  less-sodium chicken broth
3 (6-ounce) skinless bone-in
  chicken breast halves
4 parsley sprigs
2 celery stalks, halved
2 bay leaves
1 tablespoon olive oil
1⅓ cups chopped onion
½ cup chopped celery
3 carrots, halved lengthwise and
  sliced
2 garlic cloves, minced
⅓ cup uncooked long-grain rice
⅓ cup sliced green onions
¾ teaspoon salt
½ teaspoon dried basil
½ teaspoon freshly ground pepper

1. Combine first 6 ingredients in a Dutch oven; bring to a boil. Cover, reduce heat, and simmer 40 minutes or until chicken is tender. Remove chicken from cooking liquid; cool. Remove meat from bones, and chop. Strain mixture through a sieve into a large bowl; reserve 4½ cups. Reserve remaining broth for another use.
2. Heat oil in pan over medium-high heat. Add onion and next 3 ingredients; sauté 10 minutes or until tender. Stir in chicken, reserved broth, rice, and remaining ingredients; bring to a boil. Cover, reduce heat, and simmer 20 minutes or until rice is tender. YIELD: 5 servings (serving size: 1½ cups).

POINTS: 4; **EXCHANGES:** 1 Starch, 1 Vegetable, 2 Very Lean Meat, ½ Fat; **PER SERVING:** CAL 205 (21% from fat); PRO 20.6g; FAT 4.7g (sat 0.9g); CARB 19.5g; FIB 2.3g; CHOL 44mg; IRON 1.3mg; SOD 854mg; CALC 37mg

CREAMY TURKEY-AND-WILD RICE SOUP

1 tablespoon light butter
2 cups chopped celery
2 cups chopped onion
1 (8-ounce) package mushrooms,
  quartered
1 tablespoon chopped fresh
  rosemary
3 garlic cloves, minced
2 cups fat-free, less-sodium
  chicken broth
½ cup dry white wine
¼ cup all-purpose flour
3 cups 2% reduced-fat milk
2 cups cooked shredded turkey
  breast
1 cup hot cooked wild rice
2 tablespoons chopped fresh parsley
½ teaspoon salt
¼ teaspoon freshly ground black
  pepper

1. Melt butter in a large Dutch oven over medium-high heat. Add celery and onion; sauté 5 minutes. Add mushrooms, rosemary, and garlic; sauté 5 minutes. Add broth and wine; bring to a boil. Reduce heat, and simmer, uncovered, 10 minutes.
2. Lightly spoon flour into a dry measuring cup; level with a knife. Place flour in a small bowl. Gradually add milk, stirring well with a whisk; add to soup. Bring to a boil. Reduce heat, and simmer, uncovered, 8 minutes.
3. Add turkey and remaining ingredients; cook until heated. YIELD: 6 servings (serving size: 1½ cups).

POINTS: 5; **EXCHANGES:** 1 Starch, 1 Vegetable, ½ Low-Fat Milk, 2 Very Lean Meat, 1 Fat; **PER SERVING:** CAL 255 (26% from fat); PRO 23.3g; FAT 7.5g (sat 3.2g); CARB 24.6g; FIB 2.8g; CHOL 50mg; IRON 2mg; SOD 546mg; CALC 196mg

SPICY BLACK BEAN-AND-SAUSAGE SOUP

1 pound dried black beans
4 cups water
Cooking spray
8 ounces turkey kielbasa, thinly sliced
1 teaspoon olive oil
1½ cups chopped onion
1 cup chopped green bell pepper
3 garlic cloves, minced
2 large carrots, scraped and coarsely chopped
1 (8-ounce) package mushrooms, coarsely chopped
2 (14½-ounce) cans zesty jalapeño diced tomatoes
⅓ cup Madeira wine or water
1 teaspoon dried thyme
1 teaspoon ground cumin
½ teaspoon ground coriander
¼ teaspoon ground red pepper or ¾ teaspoon chipotle hot sauce
1 (10¾-ounce) can beef consommé
10 tablespoons reduced-fat sour cream
Fresh cilantro sprigs (optional)

1. Sort and wash beans; place in a large Dutch oven. Cover with water to 1 inch above beans. Let soak 8 hours.
2. Drain beans; add 4 cups water. Bring to a boil; cover, reduce heat, and simmer 1½ hours or until beans are tender.
3. Brown sausage in a large nonstick skillet coated with cooking spray over medium-high heat, stirring often. Remove from pan, and set aside.
4. Heat oil in pan over medium-high heat. Add onion and next 3 ingredients; sauté until tender. Add mushrooms, and cook 5 minutes.
5. Add vegetable mixture to Dutch oven when beans are tender. Stir in tomato and next 6 ingredients. Bring to a boil; cover; reduce heat, and simmer 30 minutes, stirring once. Ladle into individual bowls; top each with sour cream. Garnish with cilantro, if desired. YIELD: 10 cups (serving size: 1 cup soup and 1 tablespoon sour cream).

POINTS: 4; EXCHANGES: 2 Starch, 2 Vegetable, 1 Very Lean Meat; PER SERVING: CAL 240 (11% from fat); PRO 15.2g; FAT 2.9g (sat 1.2g); CARB 39.1g; FIB 11g; CHOL 14mg; IRON 3.3mg; SOD 920mg; CALC 103mg

HOLIDAY GUMBO

⅔ cup all-purpose flour
½ pound medium shrimp
5 cups fat-free, less-sodium chicken broth, divided
Cooking spray
½ pound turkey kielbasa, sliced
2 (4-ounce) skinless, boneless chicken breast halves, chopped
4 garlic cloves, minced
1 tablespoon tomato paste
1 (16-ounce) package frozen vegetable gumbo mix, thawed
½ teaspoon salt
¼ teaspoon dried thyme
¼ teaspoon dried oregano
¼ teaspoon ground red pepper
1 bay leaf
4 cups hot cooked long-grain rice
½ cup chopped green onions

1. Preheat oven to 350°.
2. Lightly spoon flour into a dry measuring cup; level with a knife. Place flour on a jelly-roll pan. Bake at 350° for 1 hour and 15 minutes or until very brown, stirring every 15 minutes. Set aside.
3. Peel and devein shrimp; reserve shells. Pour 3½ cups chicken broth into a large Dutch oven; bring to a boil. Add reserved shrimp shells; reduce heat, and simmer, uncovered, 15 minutes. Strain broth mixture through a sieve into a bowl; discard solids.
4. Coat pan with cooking spray. Add sausage and chicken; sauté 7 minutes. Add garlic; sauté 1 minute. Stir in tomato paste, vegetable gumbo mix, and strained broth.
5. Place browned flour in a bowl. Slowly add 1½ cups chicken broth to flour; add to chicken and vegetable mixture, stirring with a whisk. Bring to a boil; reduce heat, and simmer, uncovered, 1 hour. Skim froth from top of gumbo as necessary.
6. Add salt and next 4 ingredients; simmer 20 minutes. Remove and discard bay leaf. Serve gumbo over rice; sprinkle with green onions. YIELD: 8 servings (serving size: 1 cup gumbo and ½ cup rice).

POINTS: 5; EXCHANGES: 2 Starch, 2 Vegetable, 1 Very Lean Meat; PER SERVING: CAL 263 (6% from fat); PRO 19.3g; FAT 1.6g (sat 0.5g); CARB 40.9g; FIB 2.4g; CHOL 57mg; IRON 2.6mg; SOD 854mg; CALC 61mg

One day's menu provides at least two servings of milk and at least five servings of fruits and/or vegetables.

	MONDAY	TUESDAY	WEDNESDAY	THURSDAY
BREAKFAST	**waffles,** 2 fat-free frozen **maple syrup,** 2 tablespoons **fat-free milk,** 1 cup **banana,** 1	**bagel,** small **light cream cheese,** 2 tablespoons **blueberries,** 1 cup **cappuccino made with fat-free milk,** 1 small	**whole wheat English muffin,** 1 **light whipped butter,** 2 tablespoons **cranberry juice,** ½ cup **vanilla fat-free aspartame-sweetened yogurt,** 8 ounces	**bran flakes,** 1 cup **banana,** 1 **fat-free milk,** 1 cup
LUNCH	**Turkey Pasta Salad** (Combine 1 cup cooked penne pasta, 1 ounce diced cooked turkey breast, 2 tablespoons *each of* chopped green onions and light ranch dressing, 1 tablespoon plain fat-free yogurt, and a dash *each of* salt and pepper. Serve over 1 cup chopped romaine lettuce. [*POINTS:* 7]) **pineapple chunks,** 1 cup	**Stuffed Sweet Potato** (Split a large baked sweet potato, and top with 2 tablespoons vanilla fat-free aspartame-sweetened yogurt, 1 tablespoon *each of* brown sugar and chopped pecans, and 2 tablespoons raisins. [*POINTS:* 5]) **fat-free milk,** 1 cup	**canned vegetable soup,** 1 cup **saltine crackers,** 6 **apple,** 1 small **fat-free milk,** 1 cup	**Crunchy Chicken Wraps** (Heat 1 [8-inch] fat-free flour tortilla in microwave for 10 seconds; in a bowl, combine 3 ounces cooked chicken tenders, ¼ cup alfalfa sprouts, and 2 tablespoons *each of* sliced water chestnuts and low-fat creamy Italian dressing. Sprinkle with 1 tablespoon chopped roasted peanuts. Place a lettuce leaf on tortilla; top with chicken mixture, and roll up tortilla. [*POINTS:* 7]) **seedless red grapes,** 1 cup
DINNER	**Vegetarian Chili** (Saute ½ cup diced onion in 1 teaspoon olive oil until soft. Add ¾ cup cooked kidney beans, ½ cup Mexican-style stewed tomatoes, and 1 teaspoon chopped green chiles; simmer 15 minutes. Top with 2 tablespoons *each of* reduced-fat shredded Cheddar cheese and fat-free sour cream. [*POINTS:* 6]) **brown rice,** ½ cup **mixed salad greens,** 2 cups **light Italian dressing,** 2 tablespoons	**Chicken-and-Spinach Quesadilla** (Heat a large skillet coated with cooking spray over medium heat; melt 1 tablespoon light whipped butter. Sprinkle ½ cup *each of* cooked diced chicken and torn spinach leaves and ¼ cup reduced-fat shredded sharp Cheddar cheese onto a 10-inch fat-free flour tortilla; top with another tortilla, and cook until slightly browned, turning once. Cut into 4 wedges; serve with 2 tablespoons reduced-fat sour cream. [*POINTS:* 7]) **red seedless grapes,** 1 cup	**Rosemary Swordfish** (Combine 1 teaspoon *each of* crushed dried rosemary and minced garlic with ¼ teaspoon *each of* salt and pepper; rub over a 6-ounce swordfish steak. Pan-sear over medium-high heat 4 minutes on each side. [*POINTS:* 4]) **steamed new potatoes,** 1 cup **green beans,** 1 cup **papaya,** 1 cup	**Baked Ziti** (Combine 1 cup *each of* cooked ziti pasta and tomato sauce with ½ cup sliced zucchini. Spread in a non-stick baking pan; top with ⅓ cup fat-free ricotta and ¼ cup preshredded part-skim mozzarella cheese. Bake at 350° until bubbly, about 15 minutes. [*POINTS:* 8]) **soft breadstick,** 1 **Italian Salad** (Combine 2 cups shredded romaine lettuce and ¼ cup *each of* chopped tomato and fat-free croutons. Drizzle with 3 tablespoons fat-free red-wine vinaigrette. [*POINTS:* 1])
SNACK	**coconut cream pie fat-free aspartame-sweetened yogurt,** 8 ounces	**Peach-Banana Smoothie** (Combine 1 [8¼-ounce] can sliced peaches in juice, undrained; 1 [8-ounce] carton vanilla fat-free aspartame-sweetened yogurt; ½ cup fat-free milk; and 1 banana in a blender. Process until smooth. [*POINTS:* 7])	**S'mores** (Top 4 [2.5-inch] graham crackers with 1 medium marshmallow; broil until marshmallows are lightly browned. Top with 1 tablespoon fat-free hot fudge topping. [*POINTS:* 4]) **fat-free milk,** 1 cup	**reduced-fat vanilla wafers,** 6 **fat-free milk,** 1 cup
POINTS	*POINTS* for the day: 26 **Exchanges:** 6½ Starch, 3 Vegetable, 2 Fruit, 3 Very Lean Meat, ½ Medium-Fat Meat, 2 Skim Milk, 2 Fat	*POINTS* for the day: 27 **Exchanges:** 7 Starch, 1 Vegetable, 5 Fruit, 2 Very Lean Meat, 2 Medium-Fat Meat, 4 Skim Milk, 2 Fat	*POINTS* for the day: 27 **Exchanges:** 7 Starch, 2 Vegetable, 5 Fruit, 5 Very Lean Meat, 2 Skim Milk, 2 Fat	*POINTS* for the day: 28 **Exchanges:** 7½ Starch, 5 Vegetable, 2 Fruit, 4½ Very Lean Meat, 1 Medium-Fat Meat, 2 Skim Milk, 2 Fat

	FRIDAY	SATURDAY	SUNDAY
BREAKFAST	**Maple-Pecan Pancakes** (Top 2 [4-inch] pancakes with 2 tablespoons *each of* maple syrup and chopped pecans. [*POINTS:* 6]) **fat-free milk,** 1 cup	**bagel,** 1 small **light whipped butter,** 1 tablespoon **grape jelly,** 1 tablespoon **strawberries,** 1½ cups **fat-free milk,** 1 cup	**Cheese Toast** (Place ¼ cup reduced-fat shredded Cheddar cheese on 1 slice high-fiber bread; broil until bubbly. [*POINTS:* 3]) **peach fat-free aspartame-sweetened yogurt,** 8 ounces **orange juice,** ½ cup
LUNCH	**Three-Bean Salad** (Toss ¼ cup *each of* cooked black and red kidney beans with 1 cup steamed green beans; drizzle with 1 teaspoon *each of* olive oil and red wine vinegar and a dash *each of* dried oregano and garlic powder. [*POINTS:* 4]) **garlic bagel chips,** 3 **orange sections,** 1 cup	**low-fat lasagna with meat sauce,** 1 frozen entrée **tossed green salad,** 2 cups **light Italian dressing,** 2 tablespoons **soft breadstick,** 1 **fat-free milk,** 1 cup	**Veggie Wrap** (Spread 1 [10-inch] fat-free flour tortilla with ¼ cup prepared hummus; top tortilla with ¼ cup *each of* diced cucumber, shredded carrot, chopped plum tomato, and thinly sliced spinach. Roll up tortilla. Serve with ½ cup salsa. [*POINTS:* 5]) **key lime fat-free aspartame-sweetened yogurt,** 8 ounces
DINNER	**broiled lamb chop,** 3 ounces **Creamy Mashed Potatoes** (Mash 1 cup boiled cubed potato with 3 tablespoons reduced-fat sour cream and a dash *each of* salt and pepper. [*POINTS:* 4]) **steamed asparagus spears,** 12	**Chicken à la King** (Melt 1 tablespoon whipped butter in a nonstick skillet. Add 3 ounces cubed skinless, boneless chicken breast and 1 tablespoon chopped onion; sauté 4 minutes. Add ¼ cup sliced fresh mushrooms; sauté 1 minute. Stir in 1 tablespoon flour; sauté 1 minute. Add 2 tablespoons frozen green peas and a dash *each of* salt, pepper, and paprika; sauté until thick. Serve over 1 slice toasted whole wheat bread. [*POINTS:* 4]) **steamed broccoli,** 1 cup	**Blue Cheeseburger** (Shape 4 ounces lean ground beef into a patty; broil until cooked, about 10 minutes, turning once. Top patty with 1 tablespoon fat-free blue cheese dressing and 2 tablespoons crumbled blue cheese; serve on a 2-ounce whole wheat bun with 2 lettuce leaves and 2 tomato slices. [*POINTS:* 10]) **stewed zucchini,** 1 cup **corn-on-the-cob,** 1 ear **light whipped butter,** 1 tablespoon
SNACK	**nonfat chocolate pudding snack cup,** 1 **banana,** 1	**low-fat vanilla ice cream,** ½ cup **chocolate syrup,** 2 tablespoons	**raspberries,** 1 cup
POINTS	**POINTS** for the day: 27 **Exchanges:** 10 Starch, 3 Vegetable, 2 Fruit, 1 Very Lean Meat, 4 Lean Meat, 2 Skim Milk, 4 Fat	**POINTS** for the day: 28 **Exchanges:** 9½ Starch, 5 Vegetable, 1 Fruit, 2 Very Lean Meat, 4 Lean Meat, 2 Skim Milk, 5 Fat	**POINTS** for the day: 26 **Exchanges:** 6½ Starch, 4 Vegetable, 2 Fruit, 3 Very Lean Meat, 2 Medium-Fat Meat, 2 Skim Milk, 3 Fat

One day's menu provides at least two servings of milk and at least five servings of fruits and/or vegetables.

	MONDAY	TUESDAY	WEDNESDAY	THURSDAY
BREAKFAST	**fruit cereal bar,** 1 **orange juice,** ½ cup **strawberry fat-free aspartame-sweetened yogurt,** 8 ounces	**cooked oatmeal,** 1 cup **raisins,** 2 tablespoons **brown sugar,** 1 tablespoon **fat-free milk,** 1 cup	**Scrambled Eggs** (Whisk together 1 large egg with 3 large egg whites and 1 tablespoon fat-free milk. Pour into a hot skillet and scramble. [*POINTS:* 3]) **reduced-calorie toast,** 2 slices **light whipped butter,** 1 tablespoon **orange juice,** ½ cup	**crisped rice cereal,** 1¼ cups **strawberries,** 1 cup **fat-free milk,** 1 cup
LUNCH	**Broccoli- and Cheese-Stuffed Potato** (Split a large baked potato, and stuff with ¾ cup steamed broccoli florets, ¼ cup reduced-fat shredded sharp Cheddar cheese, and 1 tablespoon *each of* fat-free sour cream and chopped green onions. [*POINTS:* 6]) **peach,** 1 medium **fat-free milk,** 1 cup	**Sloppy Joe** (Cook 4 ounces ground round, ¼ cup chopped onion, and 1 minced garlic clove over medium-high heat until beef is browned, stirring to crumble. Stir in ½ cup tomato sauce and ½ teaspoon chili powder; cook until thoroughly heated. Serve on a 2-ounce hamburger bun. [*POINTS:* 7]) **celery and carrot sticks,** 1 cup	**Lentil Salad** (Combine ½ cup cooked lentils with ¼ cup *each of* chopped red bell pepper and garbanzo beans, 2 tablespoons chopped green onions, 1 teaspoon lemon juice, and a dash *each of* salt and pepper. Sprinkle with 3 tablespoons feta cheese. [*POINTS:* 5]) **raspberries,** 1 cup **lemon chiffon fat-free aspartame-sweetened yogurt,** 8 ounces	**Grilled Tomato-and-Cheese Sandwich** (Spread 2 teaspoons light mayonnaise on a slice of reduced-calorie bread; top with 3 tomato slices, ½ cup reduced-fat shredded Cheddar cheese, and another slice of bread. Cook over medium heat in a nonstick skillet coated with cooking spray, turning once, until bread is brown and cheese melts. [*POINTS:* 5]) **key lime pie fat-free aspartame-sweetened yogurt,** 8 ounces **apple,** 1 small
DINNER	**Chicken Kebabs** (Cut a 4-ounce skinless, boneless chicken breast into 1-inch pieces. Combine chicken; ¼ cup *each of* red bell pepper squares, onion chunks, small mushrooms, and cherry tomatoes; 1 tablespoon balsamic vinegar; 1 teaspoon olive oil; ¼ teaspoon soy sauce; and a dash of dried Italian seasoning. Marinate in refrigerator 1 hour. Thread on skewers, and grill or broil 6 minutes or until chicken is done. [*POINTS:* 5]) **steamed white rice,** 1 cup	**Fettuccine Alfredo Florentine** (Stir together 1 cup hot cooked fettuccine noodles, ½ cup steamed spinach, and ¼ cup refrigerated light Alfredo sauce. Sprinkle with 1 tablespoon grated fresh Parmesan cheese. [*POINTS:* 7]) **mixed salad greens,** 2 cups **light Italian dressing,** 2 tablespoons **orange and grapefruit sections,** 1 cup	**Southwestern Pork Chops** (Season 1 [4-ounce] lean boneless loin pork chop with a dash *each of* salt and pepper. Heat a nonstick skillet to medium-high, and brown one side of chop. Turn chop, add ½ cup salsa, and bring to a boil. Lower heat, cover, and simmer for 6 to 8 minutes. [*POINTS:* 5]) **roasted potato wedges,** 1 cup **steamed spinach,** ½ cup	**Lime-Marinated Sea Bass** (Combine 1 tablespoon *each of* dry white wine and fresh lime juice with minced fresh cilantro, 1 teaspoon soy sauce, and ½ teaspoon olive oil in a zip-lock bag; add 1 [4-ounce] sea bass filet, and marinate in refrigerator for 30 minutes. Coat grill rack with cooking spray; grill, covered, over hot coals 4 to 5 minutes on each side. [*POINTS:* 4]) **couscous,** 1 cup **steamed snow peas with 1 tablespoon light whipped butter,** 1 cup
SNACK	**Strawberry Smoothie** (Combine 1 cup sliced strawberries, ½ cup fat-free milk, and 8 ounces vanilla fat-free aspartame-sweetened yogurt in a blender; process until smooth. [*POINTS:* 3])	**blueberry fat-free aspartame-sweetened yogurt,** 8 ounces **gingersnaps,** 4	**reduced-fat chocolate sandwich cookies,** 3 **fat-free milk,** 1 cup	**Chocolate-Butterscotch Parfait** (Crumble 3 reduced-fat chocolate sandwich cookies. Place ¼ cup banana slices in bottom of a bowl; top with half of a fat-free butterscotch pudding snack cup bowl and half of crumbs. Repeat layers; top with 2 tablespoons lite whipped topping. [*POINTS:* 7])
POINTS	*POINTS* for the day: 27 **Exchanges:** 6 Starch, 3 Vegetable, 3 Fruit, 3 Very Lean Meat, 1 Medium-Fat Meat, 3½ Skim Milk, 1 Fat	*POINTS* for the day: 28 **Exchanges:** 6 Starch, 4 Vegetable, 2 Fruit, 3 Lean Meat, ½ Medium-Fat Meat, 2 Skim Milk, 3 Fat	*POINTS* for the day: 27 **Exchanges:** 5 Starch, 3 Vegetable, 2 Fruit, 3 Very Lean Meat, 2 Lean Meat, 2 Medium-Fat Meat, 2 Skim Milk, 4 Fat	*POINTS* for the day: 29 **Exchanges:** 5 Starch, 2 Vegetable, 3 Fruit, 5 Very Lean Meat, 2 Medium-Fat Meat, 2½ Skim Milk, 2 Fat

	FRIDAY	SATURDAY	SUNDAY	
BREAKFAST	**reduced-calorie toast,** 2 slices **grape jelly,** 2 tablespoons **fat-free milk,** 1 cup **grapefruit,** ½	**cooked grits,** 1 cup **light whipped butter,** 1 tablespoon **center-cut bacon,** 2 slices **orange juice,** ½ cup	**Belgian Waffles** (Top 2 toasted fat-free frozen waffles with ¾ cup sliced strawberries and ¼ cup lite whipped topping. Dust with 1 tablespoon powdered sugar. [*POINTS:* 5]) **fat-free milk,** 1 cup	
LUNCH	**Tuna Salad in Tomato** (Combine 4 ounces drained canned tuna in water with 1 tablespoon chopped celery, 2 teaspoons light mayonnaise, and 1 teaspoon Dijon mustard; stir well. Spoon into a tomato. [*POINTS:* 4]) **saltines,** 6 **peach,** 1 cup **fat-free milk,** 1 cup	**Peanut Butter-and-Jelly Sandwich** (Spread 2 tablespoons *each of* peanut butter and jelly between 2 slices of reduced-calorie bread. [*POINTS:* 7]) **fat-free milk,** 1 cup	**Chicken-Spinach Salad** (Drizzle 1 teaspoon *each of* lemon juice and olive oil over a 4-ounce skinless, boneless chicken breast. Sprinkle with a dash *each of* salt and garlic powder. Broil 5 minutes or until done; slice. Combine 2 cups torn spinach with ¼ cup *each of* diced tomato, red bell pepper, and red onion; top with sliced chicken and 2 tablespoons *each of* feta cheese and light balsamic vinaigrette. [*POINTS:* 7]) **saltines,** 6 **orange sections,** 1 cup	
DINNER	**Roast Beef Wrap** (Combine 1 tablespoon light cream cheese with 1 teaspoon horseradish mustard; spread evenly over 1 [8-inch] fat-free flour tortilla. Top with 3 ounces lean deli shaved roast beef and lettuce leaves; roll up tortilla. [*POINTS:* 7]) **fat-free raspberry yogurt with granola,** 8 ounces **carrot sticks,** 1 cup	**Chicken Parmesan** (Coat a 3-ounce skinless, boneless chicken breast with 3 tablespoons Italian-seasoned bread crumbs. Coat a nonstick skillet with cooking spray; add 1 teaspoon olive oil, and place over medium-high heat. Brown chicken in pan on both sides until done. Heat ½ cup reduced-fat tomato sauce in microwave, and spoon over chicken. Sprinkle with 1 teaspoon Parmesan cheese. [*POINTS:* 7]) **angel hair pasta,** 1 cup **sautéed zucchini,** 1 cup	**Blackened Shrimp Pasta** (Heat 1 teaspoon olive oil in a skillet over medium-high heat. Sprinkle ½ teaspoon blackening seasoning over 4 ounces peeled and deveined shrimp; add to skillet, and sauté until shrimp are pink. Stir in 2 teaspoons lemon juice and ½ cup diced tomatoes with roasted garlic. Serve over 1 cup hot cooked linguini. [*POINTS:* 6]) **steamed snow peas,** 1 cup	
SNACK	**part-skim mozzarella string cheese,** 1 stick **apple,** 1 small	**raspberries,** 1 cup **cappuccino fat-free aspartame-sweetened yogurt,** 8 ounces	**gingersnaps,** 4 **fat-free milk,** 1 cup	
POINTS	**POINTS** for the day: 28 **Exchanges:** 6 Starch, 2 Vegetable, 3 Fruit, 4 Very Lean Meat, 3 Lean Meat, 2 Medium-Fat Meat, 3 Skim Milk,	**POINTS** for the day: 29 **Exchanges:** 8 Starch, 3 Vegetable, 2 Fruit, 2 Very Lean Meat, 1 High-Fat Meat, 2 Skim Milk, 4 Fat	**POINTS** for the day: 27 **Exchanges:** 7 Starch, 5 Vegetable, 2 Fruit, 6 Very Lean Meat, ½ High-Fat Meat, 2 Skim Milk, 2 Fat	

One day's menu provides at least two servings of milk and at least five servings of fruits and/or vegetables.

	MONDAY	TUESDAY	WEDNESDAY	THURSDAY
BREAKFAST	**fruit cereal bar,** 1 **blueberry fat-free aspartame-sweetened yogurt,** 8 ounces	**French Toast** (Combine 3 tablespoons fat-free milk, 2 large egg whites, and a dash *each of* salt, cinnamon, and vanilla. Dip 2 slices high-fiber bread in mixture. Melt 1 tablespoon light whipped butter in a nonstick skillet over medium heat; add bread. Cook 7 minutes, turning after 3 minutes. Serve with 2 tablespoons maple syrup. [*POINTS:* 6]) **fat-free milk,** 1 cup	**cooked grits,** 1 cup **lean Canadian bacon,** 1 slice **orange juice,** ½ cup	**waffles,** 2 fat-free frozen **maple syrup,** 2 tablespoons **orange juice,** ½ cup
LUNCH	**Turkey-Swiss Sandwich** (Spread 2 teaspoons *each of* fat-free mayonnaise and Dijon mustard over 2 slices high-fiber bread. Place 2 ounces thinly sliced smoked deli turkey, 1 ounce reduced-fat Swiss cheese, 2 lettuce leaves, and 2 tomato slices on 1 bread slice; top with remaining slice. [*POINTS:* 6]) **baked chips,** 1 ounce **apple,** 1 small	**Chunky Garden Tomato Soup** (Heat 1 can tomato soup in a saucepan over medium heat. Add ½ cup *each of* canned black-eyed peas, rinsed and drained, and frozen spinach, thawed and patted dry. Stir in ¼ cup salsa. Heat until warm. [*POINTS:* 2]) **saltines,** 6 **orange-mango fat-free aspartame-sweetened yogurt,** 8 ounces	**Tuna Salad Pita** (Combine ½ cup canned tuna packed in water, drained; 4 teaspoons light mayonnaise; and ⅛ teaspoon *each of* dried dill and pepper; mix well. Cut 1 [2-ounce] pita in half; line each half with 2 lettuce leaves and 2 tomato slices. Stuff halves evenly with tuna mixture. [*POINTS:* 7]) **grapes,** 1 cup **fat-free milk,** 1 cup	**Stuffed Peppers** (Cut a large green pepper in half; discard seeds. Boil for 5 minutes, and drain. Sauté 4 ounces lean ground turkey until brown. Add ½ cup *each of* cooked rice and tomato sauce and a dash *each of* onion salt, garlic powder, and pepper. Spoon mixture into halves, and place in a baking dish; add hot water to a depth of 1 inch. Bake uncovered at 350° for 45 minutes. [*POINTS:* 6]) **strawberry cheesecake fat-free aspartame-sweetened yogurt,** 8 ounces
DINNER	**Roast Beef Salad with Blue Cheese** (Arrange 2 cups mixed greens on a plate; top with 2 ounces thinly sliced lean deli roast beef, 5 cherry tomatoes, and 1 tablespoon crumbled blue cheese. Drizzle 2 tablespoons fat-free raspberry vinaigrette over salad. [*POINTS:* 5]) **cherries,** 1 cup	**Stir-Fry Shrimp and Vegetables** (Heat 1 teaspoon sesame oil in a large nonstick skillet over medium-high heat. Sauté 1 teaspoon fresh ginger; add ¼ cup sliced white onion and ½ cup *each of* broccoli and snow peas. Cook 3 minutes; toss with 1 tablespoon hoisin sauce and 2 tablespoons reduced-sodium soy sauce. Add 3 ounces peeled and deveined shrimp; sauté 3 minutes or until shrimp turn pink. Serve over 1 cup oriental noodles. [*POINTS:* 6])	**Cheesy Bean Burritos** (Warm 1 [8-inch] fat-free flour tortilla for 10 seconds in the microwave. Spread ½ cup prepared fat-free refried beans in center of tortilla. Cover beans with ¼ cup reduced-fat shredded Cheddar cheese. Roll tortilla up; microwave at MEDIUM 35 to 45 seconds or until cheese melts. Top with ½ cup of shredded lettuce, ¼ cup salsa, and 1 tablespoon reduced-fat sour cream. [*POINTS:* 6]) **orange,** 1 whole cut into wedges	**Crispy Honey-Mustard Chicken** (Combine 1 tablespoon honey and 1½ teaspoons Dijon mustard; spread evenly over a 4-ounce skinless, boneless chicken breast. Dredge in ⅓ cup crushed cornflakes, and place on a baking sheet coated with cooking spray. Spray chicken with cooking spray; bake at 400° for 40 minutes. [*POINTS:* 5]) **mashed potatoes,** ½ cup **steamed broccoli,** 1 cup **fat-free milk,** 1 cup
SNACK	**graham crackers,** 4 (2.5-inch) squares **reduced-fat peanut butter,** 1 tablespoon **fat-free milk,** 1 cup	**peaches,** 1 cup sliced	**reduced-fat chocolate sandwich cookies,** 3 **fat-free milk,** 1 cup	**carrot sticks,** 1 cup **prepared hummus,** ¼ cup **pita bread,** 2 ounces
POINTS	**POINTS** for the day: 27 **Exchanges:** 5 Starch, 4 Vegetable, 2 Fruit, 2 Very Lean Meat, 2 Lean Meat, 2 High-Fat Meat, 2 Skim Milk	**POINTS** for the day: 25 **Exchanges:** 8 Starch, 5 Vegetable, 2 Fruit, 4 Very Lean Meat, 2 Skim Milk, 2 Fat	**POINTS** for the day: 27 **Exchanges:** 8 Starch, 2 Vegetable, 3 Fruit, 4 Very Lean Meat, 1 Lean Meat, 1 Medium-Fat Meat, 2 Skim Milk, 2 Fat	**POINTS** for the day: 27 **Exchanges:** 10 Starch, 4 Vegetable, 1 Fruit, 3 Very Lean Meat, 3 Lean Meat, 2 Skim Milk, 1 Fat

7-DAY MENU PLANNER

WEEK 3

	FRIDAY	SATURDAY	SUNDAY
BREAKFAST	**high-fiber toast,** 2 slices **grape jelly,** 2 tablespoons **light whipped butter,** 1 tablespoon **apple juice,** 1 cup	**Garlic-Cheese Grits** (Stir ¼ cup reduced-fat shredded Cheddar cheese and ¼ teaspoon garlic salt into 1 cup hot cooked grits; stir until smooth. [*POINTS:* 5]) **orange juice,** ½ cup **peach fat-free aspartame-sweetened yogurt,** 8 ounces	**Spiced Peach Waffles** (In a microwave-safe bowl, combine 1 [8¼-ounce] can sliced peaches, drained, with 2 tablespoons peach jam or preserves and ¼ teaspoon cinnamon. Heat on MEDIUM-HIGH for 1 minute or until jam melts. Top 2 warmed fat-free frozen waffles with peach mixture. [*POINTS:* 5]) **fat-free milk,** 1 cup
LUNCH	**hamburger,** fast food **side salad,** fast food with 2 tablespoons fat-free Italian dressing	**Grilled Chicken Salad** (Slice a 3-ounce grilled or broiled skinless, boneless chicken breast; place on a bed of 2 cups torn romaine lettuce. Top with ½ cup *each of* diced tomato and cucumber slices and ¼ cup fat-free croutons. Drizzle 2 tablespoons light ranch dressing, and sprinkle 1 tablespoon Parmesan cheese. [*POINTS:* 8]) **saltines,** 6	**Greek Salad** (Toss 2 cups torn romaine lettuce, ½ cup diced tomato, and 6 olives. Sprinkle with 3 tablespoons feta cheese. For dressing, combine 2 teaspoons white wine vinegar, 1 teaspoon olive oil, ½ teaspoon *each of* Dijon mustard and honey, and a dash *each of* salt and pepper. [*POINTS:* 5]) **toasted pita chips,** 1 ounce **blueberry fat-free aspartame-sweetened yogurt,** 8 ounces
DINNER	**Creamy Pesto Primavera** (Cook 3 ounces refrigerated cheese tortellini and 1 cup frozen broccoli stir-fry vegetables in 3 quarts boiling water 5 to 7 minutes; drain and return to pan. Combine 3 tablespoons reduced-fat sour cream, 2 teaspoons pesto, and a dash *each of* salt and pepper. Gently stir into pasta mixture. Sprinkle with 1 tablespoon grated Parmesan cheese. [*POINTS:* 8]) **steamed carrots,** 1 cup **fat-free milk,** 1 cup	**Quick Turkey Enchiladas** (Combine ½ cup shredded smoked turkey breast, ¼ cup salsa, and 2 tablespoons reduced-fat Mexican-blend cheese in a saucepan. Cook over medium heat until cheese melts. Spoon into a tortilla; roll up, and place, seam side down, in a microwave-safe baking dish. Top with ¼ cup salsa and 2 tablespoons cheese. Microwave at MEDIUM-HIGH 3 minutes or until cheese melts. Serve with 3 tablespoons reduced-fat sour cream. [*POINTS:* 7]) **grapes,** 1 cup	**Herb-Baked Trout** (Place 1 [6-ounce] rainbow trout fillet in a baking dish coated with cooking spray. Sprinkle fish with a dash *each of* salt and pepper; top with 2 lemon slices. Combine 1 teaspoon olive oil and 2 tablespoons *each of* minced fresh basil and lemon juice; pour over trout. Bake at 350° for 13 to 15 minutes. [*POINTS:* 7]) **wild rice,** 1 cup **steamed broccoli,** 1 cup
SNACK	**blackberry pie fat-free aspartame-sweetened yogurt,** 8 ounces	**crème caramel fat-free aspartame-sweetened yogurt,** 8 ounces	**cherries,** 1 cup
POINTS	**POINTS** for the day: 26 **Exchanges:** 8 Starch, 4 Vegetable, 2 Fruit, 1 Lean Meat, 2 Medium-Fat Meat, 2 Skim Milk, 3 Fat	**POINTS** for the day: 28 **Exchanges:** 6 Starch, 4 Vegetable, 2 Fruit, 6 Very Lean Meat, 2 Medium-Fat Meat, 2 Skim Milk, 2 Fat	**POINTS** for the day: 27 **Exchanges:** 6½ Starch, 5 Vegetable, 2 Fruit, 5 Very Lean Meat, 1 Medium-Fat Meat, 2 Skim Milk, 2 Fat

Turkeyfoot Reading Center
Confluence, PA

169

One day's menu provides at least two servings of milk and at least five servings of fruits and/or vegetables.

	MONDAY	TUESDAY	WEDNESDAY	THURSDAY
BREAKFAST	**cooked oatmeal**, 1 cup **light whipped butter**, 1 tablespoon **brown sugar**, 1 tablespoon **fat-free milk**, 1 cup	**Waffles with Apple Syrup** (Melt 1 teaspoon light butter in a nonstick skillet. Add ½ cup chopped apple; sauté 3 minutes. Stir in 2 tablespoons maple syrup and a dash of cinnamon. Spoon over 2 warmed fat-free frozen waffles. [*POINTS:* 6]) **fat-free milk**, 1 cup	**bagel**, 1 small **light cream cheese**, 2 tablespoons **orange juice**, ½ cup	**Cranberry Oatmeal** (Stir ¼ cup dried cranberries, 2 tablespoons fat-free milk, and 1 tablespoon brown sugar into 1 cup hot cooked oatmeal. [*POINTS:* 6]) **fat-free milk**, 1 cup
LUNCH	**Veggie Couscous** (Combine ⅓ cup *each of* cubed zucchini, yellow squash, and red bell pepper with 2 tablespoons fat-free balsamic vinaigrette in a baking dish. Bake at 400° for 25 minutes or until lightly browned. Toss with 1 cup cooked couscous, ½ cup *each of* torn spinach and chopped tomato, and 2 teaspoons olive oil; sprinkle with 1 tablespoon grated Parmesan cheese. [*POINTS:* 8]) **apple**, 1 **fat-free milk**, 1 cup	**Philly Swiss Melt** (Place a nonstick skillet coated with cooking spray over medium heat; sauté ½ cup *each of* sliced onion and red bell pepper for 4 minutes. Spread 2 teaspoons light mayonnaise over 2 cut sides of a 2-ounce whole wheat roll. Layer 2 ounces thinly sliced lean deli roast beef, sautéed vegetables, and 1 [¾-ounce] slice Swiss cheese; broil until cheese melts. Top with remaining bread slice. [*POINTS:* 7]) **baked chips**, 1 ounce	**Peanut Butter-and-Banana Sandwich** (Spread 2 tablespoons peanut butter over 1 slice high-fiber bread; top with 1 sliced banana and another slice of bread. [*POINTS:* 7]) **fat-free milk**, 1 cup **carrot sticks**, 1 cup	**Veggie Burger** (Heat veggie burger according to package directions. Spread 2 teaspoons *each of* fat-free mayonnaise, ketchup, and mustard on 1 cut side of hamburger bun. Layer with patty, 2 lettuce leaves, and 2 tomato slices. Top with remaining piece of bun. [*POINTS:* 3]) **fat-free milk**, 1 cup **blueberries**, 1 cup
DINNER	**Pork-and-Potato Skillet** (Coat a skillet with cooking spray, and place over medium-high heat. Add ½ cup chopped onion, ⅛ teaspoon *each of* salt and pepper, and 1 teaspoon minced garlic; sauté 3 minutes. Add 4 ounces cubed lean pork loin; sauté 3 minutes. Add 1 cup cubed potato, 1 cup broccoli florets, and ¼ cup fat-free chicken broth; cook over medium heat until potato is tender. [*POINTS:* 7]) **green beans**, 1 cup	**Tortellini Soup** (Combine 1½ cups *each of* canned stewed tomatoes and fat-free, reduced-sodium chicken broth and ⅛ teaspoon Italian seasoning in a saucepan; bring to a boil. Add 3 ounces fresh cheese tortellini, ½ cup sliced zucchini, and a dash of pepper; bring to a boil. Cover, reduce heat and simmer 5 to 7 minutes or until pasta and zucchini are tender. [*POINTS:* 3]) **romaine lettuce**, 1 cup **fat-free balsamic vinaigrette**, 2 tablespoons **fat-free milk**, 1 cup	**Sesame Chicken** (Toast 1 tablespoon sesame seeds in a nonstick skillet over medium-high heat; remove seeds, and set aside. Coat pan with cooking spray, and return to heat; add a 4-ounce skinless, boneless chicken breast, and cook 3 minutes on each side. Combine sesame seeds, 1 tablespoon *each of* honey and soy sauce, and a dash ground ginger; pour over chicken. Cook 1 minute, turning chicken to coat with sauce. [*POINTS:* 5]) **steamed white rice**, ½ cup **Garlicky Broccoli** (Sauté 1 cup steamed broccoli florets in 1 teaspoon *each of* olive oil and minced garlic 1 to 2 minutes. [*POINTS:* 1])	**Easy Parmesan Flounder** (Place a 6-ounce flounder fillet on rack of a broiler pan coated with cooking spray; brush fillet with 2 teaspoons lemon juice. Broil 5 to 6 minutes. Combine 1 tablespoon fat-free mayonnaise; 1 teaspoon light butter, softened; and 2 teaspoons *each of* grated Parmesan cheese and sliced green onions. Spread over 1 side of fillet. Broil 1 minute or until lightly browned and bubbly. [*POINTS:* 5]) **baked potato**, 1 small **light whipped butter**, 1 tablespoon **asparagus spears**, 12
SNACK	**low-fat graham crackers**, 2 (2.5-inch) squares **apple pie à la mode fat-free aspartame-sweetened yogurt**, 8 ounces	**vanilla fat-free ice cream**, ¾ cup **chocolate syrup**, 1 tablespoon	**Ice Cream Sandwich** (Place ¼ cup fat-free vanilla ice cream between 2 [2.5-inch] graham cracker squares; repeat procedure. Wrap sandwiches in plastic wrap, and place in freezer at least 1 hour before serving. [*POINTS:* 4]) **fat-free milk**, 1 cup	**Banana Split** (Place a peeled banana in a bowl; top with ¾ cup vanilla fat-free ice cream, ¼ cup fat-free whipped topping, and 1 tablespoon chocolate syrup. [*POINTS:* 6])
POINTS	*POINTS* for the day: 28 **Exchanges:** 8 Starch, 6 Vegetable, 1 Fruit, 3 Lean Meat, 3 Skim Milk, 3 Fat	*POINTS* for the day: 26 **Exchanges:** 10 Starch, 6 Vegetable, 1 Fruit, 2 Lean Meat, 1 High-Fat Meat, 2 Skim Milk, 2 Fat	*POINTS* for the day: 28 **Exchanges:** 9 Starch, 3 Vegetable, 2 Fruit, 3 Very Lean Meat, 2 High-Fat Meat, 2 Skim Milk	*POINTS* for the day: 28 **Exchanges:** 11 Starch, 2 Vegetable, 3 Fruit, 6 Very Lean Meat, 2 Skim Milk, 2 Fat

	FRIDAY	SATURDAY	SUNDAY
BREAKFAST	**scrambled eggs,** 1 large egg and 3 large egg whites **reduced-fat bacon,** 2 slices **orange juice,** ½ cup	**Honey-Cinnamon Bagel** (Mix together 2 tablespoons light cream cheese with 1 tablespoon honey and ¼ teaspoon cinnamon. Spread mixture over a small toasted bagel. [POINTS: 5]) **blueberries,** 1 cup **fat-free milk,** 1 cup	**poached egg,** 1 large **high-fiber bread,** 1 slice **light whipped butter,** 1 tablespoon **orange juice,** ½ cup
LUNCH	**Barbecue Chicken Pizza** (Spread 2 tablespoons barbecue sauce over a 4-ounce Italian cheese-flavored pizza crust [such as Boboli]. Top with 2 ounces chopped roasted chicken breast, 2 tablespoons chopped green onions, and 3 tablespoons preshredded part-skim mozzarella cheese. [POINTS: 8]) **carrot sticks,** 1 cup **fat-free milk,** 1 cup **peach,** 1 medium	**Spicy Shrimp Sandwich** (Combine 5 ounces peeled shrimp, 1 teaspoon lemon juice, and ½ teaspoon each of Cajun seasoning and olive oil; sauté 3 minutes or until done. Spread 2 teaspoons fat-free mayonnaise and 1 teaspoon Dijon mustard on 1 side of a 2-ounce whole wheat bun. Layer with shrimp, 2 lettuce leaves, 2 tomato slices, and 1 onion. Top with remaining piece of bun. [POINTS: 5]) **apple,** 1 small	**Hopping John** (Heat 1 teaspoon olive oil in a nonstick skillet over medium heat. Add ⅓ cup chopped onion and 1 minced garlic clove; sauté 5 minutes. Add 1 teaspoon white wine vinegar and ⅛ teaspoon each of dried oregano and hot sauce; stir well. Add ½ cup drained canned black-eyed peas and ¼ cup chopped lean ham. Toss with 1 cup cooked brown rice. [POINTS: 6]) **fresh tomato slices,** 1 cup **fat-free balsamic vinaigrette dressing,** 1 tablespoon
DINNER	**Tofu-and-Broccoli Stir-Fry** (Heat 2 teaspoons dark sesame oil in a nonstick skillet. Add ½ cup cubed firm tofu or chicken, ¼ cup sliced onion, and 1 cup broccoli florets; stir-fry until vegetables are crisp-tender. Stir in 2 teaspoons soy sauce. [POINTS: 5]) **cellophane or oriental noodles,** 1 cup	**Sausage-Vegetable Soup** (Brown 3 ounces reduced-fat turkey sausage [such as Healthy Choice] in a small sauce pan coated with cooking spray. Add 1 cup each of chicken broth and frozen mixed stew vegetables and ½ cup tomato juice; bring to a boil. Lower heat, cover, and simmer for 20 to 25 minutes. [POINTS: 4]) **Cheese Toast** (Place ¼ cup reduced-fat shredded Cheddar cheese on 1 slice high-fiber bread; broil until bubbly. [POINTS: 3])	**Greek Chicken Spaghetti** (Place 1 [4-ounce] skinless, boneless chicken breast in a skillet with ¼ cup chicken broth and ½ teaspoon dried oregano; bring to a boil. Cover, reduce heat, and simmer 10 minutes. Remove from heat; when cool, shred chicken with 2 forks. Coat a skillet with cooking spray, and place over medium heat; add 1 minced clove garlic, and cook 2 minutes. Add ½ cup canned chopped tomatoes, 1 teaspoon lemon juice, and chicken. Bring to a boil; reduce heat, and simmer 5 minutes. Serve over 1 cup hot cooked spaghetti. Top with 2 tablespoons crumbled feta cheese and 2 olives, pitted and chopped. [POINTS: 8]) **sautéed spinach,** 1 cup **fat-free milk,** 1 cup
SNACK	**strawberry fat-free aspartame-sweetened yogurt,** 8 ounces	**Peanut Butter-Fruit Squares** (Spread 2 tablespoons peanut butter evenly over 4 [2.5-inch] graham cracker squares. Top with ¼ cup dried cranberries. [POINTS: 4]) **fat-free milk,** 1 cup	**Honeyed Peach Yogurt** (Top 8 ounces peach fat-free aspartame-sweetened yogurt with ½ cup sliced fresh peaches and 1 tablespoon each of honey and toasted almonds. [POINTS: 5])
POINTS	**POINTS** for the day: 27 **Exchanges:** 4 Starch, 3 Vegetable, 2 Fruit, 3½ Lean Meat, 3 Medium-Fat Meat, 2 Skim Milk, 3½ Fat	**POINTS** for the day: 27 **Exchanges:** 6½ Starch, 3 Vegetable, 2 Fruit, 4 Very Lean Meat, 3 Lean Meat, 2½ Medium-Fat Meat, 2 Skim Milk	**POINTS** for the day: 26 **Exchanges:** 7 Starch, 3 Vegetable, 2 Fruit, 4 Very Lean Meat, 1 Medium-Fat Meat, 2 Skim Milk, 3 Fat

One day's menu provides at least two servings of milk and at least five servings of fruits and/or vegetables.

	MONDAY	TUESDAY	WEDNESDAY	THURSDAY
BREAKFAST	**Waffles with Blueberry Syrup** (In a microwave-safe bowl, heat 2 table-spoons blueberry jelly or jam at HIGH until melted; stir in 1 tablespoon maple syrup. Add ½ cup blueberries. Pour over 2 heated fat-free frozen waffles. [*POINTS:* 5]) **fat-free milk,** 1 cup	**poached egg,** 1 large **lean Canadian bacon,** 1 slice **high-fiber toast,** 1 slice **light whipped butter,** 1 tablespoon **orange juice,** ½ cup	**French Toast** (Combine 3 tablespoons fat-free milk, 2 large egg whites, and a dash *each of* salt, cinnamon, and vanil-la; stir well. Dip 2 slices high-fiber bread in mixture. Melt 1 tablespoon light whipped butter in a nonstick skillet over medium heat; add bread. Cook 7 min-utes, turning after 3 minutes. Serve with 2 tablespoons maple syrup. [*POINTS:* 6]) **fat-free milk,** 1 cup	**Cinnamon-Raisin Bread** (Spread 1½ teaspoons light whipped butter on *each of* two slices raisin bread. Sprinkle with cinnamon-sugar. Place under broiler 1 to 2 minutes or until toasted. [*POINTS:* 3]) **strawberries,** 1½ cups **fat-free milk,** 1 cup
LUNCH	**Egg-and-Cheese Bagel** (Combine 1 large egg and 3 tablespoons reduced-fat shredded Cheddar cheese. Cook in a nonstick skillet coated with cooking spray over medium heat until set, stirring occasionally. Place between 2 toasted halves of a small bagel. [*POINTS:* 6]) **grapes,** 1 cup	**canned chicken noodle soup,** 2 cups **saltines,** 6 **blueberries,** 1 cup **peach fat-free aspartame-sweetened yogurt,** 8 ounces	**Seafood-Orzo Salad** (Combine ½ cup drained cooked orzo pasta, 2 ounces imitation crab meat, 2 table-spoons crumbled feta cheese, 5 chopped small olives, and 2 tablespoons fat-free balsamic vinaigrette. Serve over 1 cup chopped lettuce. [*POINTS:* 7]) **grapes,** 1 cup	**Veggie Pizza** (Spread ¼ cup prepared low-fat tomato sauce over a 4-ounce thin-crust Italian bread shell [such as Boboli]. Top with ¼ cup fresh sliced mushrooms, 2 tablespoons diced green or red bell peppers, and 1 ounce preshredded part-skim mozzarella cheese. Bake at 450° for 6 minutes or until cheese melts. [*POINTS:* 8])
DINNER	**Barbecue Chicken** (Place a 4-ounce skinless, boneless chicken breast on a broiler pan coated with cooking spray; brush with ¼ cup barbecue sauce. Bake at 350° for 30 minutes or until done. [*POINTS:* 4]) **Dilled Potato Salad** (Toss together 1 cup diced cooked potato, ½ cup chopped green onions, ¼ cup plain fat-free yogurt, 2 teaspoons light mayon-naise, and 1 teaspoon chopped fresh dill. [*POINTS:* 5]) **green beans,** 1 cup	**Quick Jambalaya** (Place a skillet over medium-high heat. Add 1 ounce sliced turkey kielbasa, ½ cup *each of* chopped onion and green bell pepper, and 1 minced garlic clove. Stir in 1 cup cooked rice, ¾ cup undrained canned diced tomatoes, ½ teaspoon Cajun sea-soning, and a dash of hot sauce; cook 5 minutes. [*POINTS:* 5])	**Macaroni and Cheese with Bacon** (Combine ⅓ cup reduced-fat shredded sharp Cheddar cheese and ¼ fat-free ricotta cheese. Fold ¾ cup hot cooked elbow pasta into cheese mixture. Add 1 ounce Canadian bacon, chopped, and a dash of pepper; toss to combine. Place in a small baking dish; bake at 350° for 10 to 15 minutes or until cheese melts. [*POINTS:* 7]) **steamed broccoli,** 1 cup **fat-free milk,** 1 cup	**Curried Lamb Kebabs** (Cut 3 ounces lean, boneless trimmed lamb into 1¼-inch cubes. Combine ¼ cup plain fat-free yogurt, 2 teaspoon soy sauce, and 1 teaspoon curry; add lamb, stirring to coat. Cover and marinate in refrigerator 2 hours. Thread lamb, ½ cup *each of* onion chunks and green bell pepper, and 4 mushrooms onto 2 skewers. Grill over hot coals, covered, 10 minutes, turning kebabs once. [*POINTS:* 4]) **couscous,** 1 cup **Mediterranean Green Salad** (Toss 2 cups torn romaine lettuce with 2 table-spoons *each of* feta cheese, diced toma-to, and fat-free balsamic vinaigrette. [*POINTS:* 1])
SNACK	**Banana Pudding** (Place ½ of a sliced banana in a small bowl. Top with ½ [8-ounce] carton banana cream fat-free aspartame-sweetened yogurt. Place 3 reduced-fat vanilla wafers in yogurt against sides of bowl. Top with remain-ing ½ of banana slices and yogurt. Chill until serving. [*POINTS:* 4])	**Peanut Butter-Raisin Toast** (Spread 1 tablespoon reduced-fat peanut butter over 1 slice toasted raisin bread. [*POINTS:* 3]) **fat-free milk,** 1 cup	**pretzels,** 15 small **apple,** 1 small	**angel food cake,** 2 ounces **fat-free milk,** 1 cup
POINTS	***POINTS* for the day: 27** **Exchanges:** 10 Starch, 3 Vegetable, 3 Fruit, 3 Very Lean Meat, 2 Medium-Fat Meat, 2 Skim Milk, 1 Fat	***POINTS* for the day: 25** **Exchanges:** 7 Starch, 3 Vegetable, 2 Fruit, 2 Lean Meat, 2 Medium-Fat Meat, 2 Skim Milk, 2 Fat	***POINTS* for the day: 28** **Exchanges:** 7½ Starch, 4 Vegetable, 2 Fruit, 4 Very Lean Meat, 3 Medium-Fat Meat, 2 Skim Milk, 1 Fat	***POINTS* for the day: 26** **Exchanges:** 8 Starch, 5 Vegetable, 1 Fruit, 2 Lean Meat, 1½ Medium-Fat Meat, 2 Skim Milk, 2 Fat

FRIDAY	SATURDAY	SUNDAY	
bagel, 1 small **light cream cheese,** 2 tablespoons **blueberries,** 1 cup	**Banana-Walnut Oatmeal** (Stir 1 sliced banana and 2 tablespoons chopped walnuts into 1 cup cooked oatmeal. [*POINTS:* 7]) **fat-free milk,** 1 cup	**Peanut Butter-Raisin Toast** (Spread 1 tablespoon reduced-fat peanut butter over 1 slice toasted raisin bread. [*POINTS:* 3]) **fat-free milk,** 1 cup	**BREAKFAST**
Greek Pasta Salad (Combine ½ cup *each of* cannellini beans and chopped tomato; add ½ cup *each of* shredded romaine lettuce and cooked penne pasta and 2 tablespoons light olive oil vinaigrette. Top with 1 tablespoon grated Parmesan cheese. [*POINTS:* 8]) **saltines,** 6 **fat-free milk,** 1 cup	**canned minestrone soup,** 1 cup **Grilled Cheese Sandwich** (Place ½ cup reduced-fat shredded Cheddar cheese between 2 slices high-fiber bread. Cook sandwich over medium heat until browned in a nonstick skillet coated with butter-flavored cooking spray. [*POINTS:* 6]) **fat-free milk,** 1 cup	**Chicken Caesar Salad** (Top 2 cups torn lettuce with a 3-ounce baked skinless, boneless chicken breast cut into thin strips, ½ cup diced tomato, ½ cup fat-free croutons, and 2 tablespoons *each of* grated Parmesan cheese and fat-free Caesar dressing. [*POINTS:* 8]) **fresh strawberries,** 1.5 cups **tangerine chiffon fat-free aspartame-sweetened yogurt,** 8 ounces	**LUNCH**
Western Omelet (Combine 2 large egg whites, 1 large egg, 1 tablespoon fat-free milk, and a dash *each of* salt and pepper. Cook in a small nonstick skillet coated with cooking spray over medium heat 4 minutes or until set. [Do not stir.] Top with ¼ cup *each of* chopped red bell pepper, chopped green bell pepper, chopped lean ham and 3 tablespoons reduced-fat shredded Cheddar cheese. Fold omelet in half. Serve with ½ cup salsa and 2 tablespoons reduced-fat sour cream. [*POINTS:* 7]) **grapes,** 1 cup **high-fiber toast,** 1 slice	**Lemon-Pepper Chicken** (Coat a nonstick skillet with cooking spray; heat over medium-high heat until hot. Sprinkle a 4-ounce skinless, boneless chicken breast with lemon-pepper seasoning; add to pan, and cook 4 to 5 minutes on each side or until done. [*POINTS:* 3]) **risotto,** 1 cup **Creamy Spinach** (Sauté 1 cup thawed frozen spinach in 1 teaspoon minced garlic for 3 to 4 minutes in a skillet coated with cooking spray. Remove from heat, and stir in 3 tablespoons reduced-fat sour cream. Sprinkle with 1 tablespoon Parmesan cheese. [*POINTS:* 1])	**Beef Stroganoff** (Cook 4 ounces lean ground beef and ¼ cup *each of* chopped onion and sliced mushrooms in a nonstick skillet until meat is browned. Stir in ⅓ cup fat-free beef gravy, ¼ cup fat-free sour cream, and a dash *each of* garlic salt and pepper. Serve over 1 cup hot cooked egg noodles. [*POINTS:* 8]) **green peas,** 1 cup	**DINNER**
Tropical Smoothie (Combine 1 cup fat-free milk, ¾ cup cubed peeled ripe mango, and 1 peeled banana; process until smooth. [*POINTS:* 5])	**Strawberry Shortcake** (Top a 1-ounce slice angel food cake with ¾ cup sliced strawberries and ¼ cup lite whipped topping. [*POINTS:* 2])	**reduced-fat vanilla wafers,** 6	**SNACK**
POINTS for the day: 28 **Exchanges:** 6 Starch, 3 Vegetable, 4 Fruit, 3 Very Lean Meat, 3 Medium-Fat Meat, 2 Skim Milk, 2 Fat	***POINTS*** for the day: 28 **Exchanges:** 9 Starch, 3 Vegetable, 1½ Fruit, 3 Very Lean Meat, 2 Medium-Fat Meat, 2 Skim Milk, 2 Fat	***POINTS*** for the day: 28 **Exchanges:** 9 Starch, 4 Vegetable, 1 Fruit, 3 Very Lean Meat, 3 Lean Meat, 1 High-Fat Meat, 2 Skim Milk	**POINTS**

7-DAY MENU PLANNER

WEEK 5

173

One day's menu provides at least two servings of milk and at least five servings of fruits and/or vegetables.

	MONDAY	TUESDAY	WEDNESDAY	THURSDAY
BREAKFAST	**low-fat granola,** ½ cup **fat-free milk,** 1 cup **peach,** 1 medium	**Breakfast Burrito** (Scramble 2 large egg whites and 1 large egg. Place in the center of a warmed 10-inch fat-free flour tortilla. Sprinkle 3 tablespoons reduced-fat shredded Cheddar cheese on eggs; roll up. [*POINTS:* 6]) **orange juice,** 1 cup	**high-fiber toast,** 1 slice **peanut butter,** 1 tablespoon **banana,** 1 **fat-free milk,** 1 cup	**low-fat granola,** ½ cup **fat-free milk,** 1 cup **blueberries,** 1 cup
LUNCH	**Chicken Salad** (Combine ½ cup chopped cooked chicken, ¼ cup *each of* finely diced celery and onion, 3 tablespoons low-fat mayonnaise, and a dash *each of* salt and pepper. Chill until serving. [*POINTS:* 4]) **fresh tomato slices,** 1 cup **saltines,** 6	**canned reduced-fat, reduced-sodium New England clam chowder,** 1 cup **oyster crackers,** ½ cup **seedless grapes,** 1 cup **carrot sticks,** 1 cup **fat-free milk,** 1 cup	**frozen low-fat French bread pepperoni pizza,** 1 (6-ounce) boxed entrée **fat-free milk,** 1 cup **strawberries,** 1½ cups	**Tomato-Avocado Sandwich** (Top 1 slice high-fiber whole wheat bread with 2 tablespoons mashed avocado; 3 tablespoons reduced-fat shredded sharp Cheddar cheese; 1 small tomato, sliced; ⅛ teaspoon *each of* salt and pepper; and another slice of bread. [*POINTS:* 5]) **orange sections,** 1 cup
DINNER	**Pesto-Cheese Tortellini** (Cook ¾ cup reduced-fat fresh cheese tortellini according to package directions; drain, reserving 1 tablespoon cooking water. Combine reserved cooking water, 2 teaspoons prepared pesto, and cooked tortellini; toss well. [*POINTS:* 7]) **salad greens,** 2 cups **fat-free balsamic vinaigrette,** 2 tablespoons	**Crispy-Baked Pork Chop** (Combine 1 large egg white and ¼ cup fat-free milk. Place a 4-ounce lean pork chop in milk mixture; let stand for 5 minutes, turning chop once. Combine 2 tablespoons cornflake crumbs, 1 tablespoon plain bread crumbs, and a dash *each of* salt and pepper. Remove chops from milk mixture, and coat thoroughly with crumb mixture. Bake at 350° in pan coated with cooking spray for 30 to 35 minutes or until no pink remains, turning once. [*POINTS:* 6]) **yellow saffron rice,** ½ cup **steamed broccoli,** 1 cup	**Grilled Chicken Sandwich** (Combine 2 tablespoons dry white wine, 1 teaspoon lemon juice, ½ teaspoon *each of* olive oil and Italian seasoning, and a dash *each of* salt and pepper. Brush over a 4-ounce skinless, boneless chicken breast. Coat grill rack with cooking spray, and heat over medium-hot coals. Grill chicken, covered, 5 minutes; turn and grill 5 minutes or until done. Serve on a hamburger bun with 2 teaspoons fat-free mayonnaise, 2 lettuce leaves, and 2 slices tomato. [*POINTS:* 6]) **carrot sticks,** 1 cup	**grilled filet mignon,** 3 ounces **Blue Cheese Mashed Potatoes** (Combine 1 cup mashed cooked peeled baking potato; 2 tablespoons *each of* reduced-fat sour cream, fat-free milk, and blue cheese; and a dash *each of* salt and pepper; mix well. [*POINTS:* 4]) **Sautéed Spinach** (Heat 1 teaspoon olive oil in a nonstick skillet. Add 1 garlic clove, minced, and 2 cups fresh torn spinach; sauté 3 minutes or until spinach wilts. Toss with 2 teaspoons lemon juice and a dash of salt. [*POINTS:* 1])
SNACK	**Banana-Strawberry Sundae** (Top ½ cup strawberry fat-free ice cream with 1 sliced banana, ¼ cup lite whipped topping, and 1 tablespoon chocolate syrup. [*POINTS:* 6])	**reduced-fat chocolate sandwich cookies,** 3 **fat-free milk,** 1 cup	**prepared hummus,** ⅓ cup **Pita Chips** (Cut a 10-inch fat-free flour tortilla into 8 wedges. Coat wedges with cooking spray. Place on a baking sheet, and bake at 400° for 6 to 8 minutes or until toasted. [*POINTS:* 2]) **orange juice,** ½ cup	**Quick Hot Chocolate** (Combine 1 cup fat-free milk with 2 tablespoons chocolate syrup; stir well. Heat in microwave 1 minute or until hot. [*POINTS:* 4]) **apple,** 1 small
POINTS	*POINTS* for the day: 28 **Exchanges:** 8 Starch, 5 Vegetable, 2 Fruit, 2 Very Lean Meat, 1 Medium-Fat Meat, 2 Skim Milk, 2 Fat	*POINTS* for the day: 28 **Exchanges:** 6 Starch, 2 Vegetable, 3 Fruit, 2 Medium-Fat Meat, 1 Very Lean Meat, 3 Lean Meat, 2 Skim Milk, 1 Fat	*POINTS* for the day: 28 **Exchanges:** 7 Starch, 2 Vegetable, 3 Fruit, 3 Very Lean Meat, 1 Medium-Fat Meat, 2 Skim Milk, 1 Fat	*POINTS* for the day: 28 **Exchanges:** 7 Starch, 2 Vegetable, 3 Fruit, 5 Medium-Fat Meat, 2 Skim Milk, 2 Fat

	FRIDAY	SATURDAY	SUNDAY
BREAKFAST	**Ham, Egg, and Cheese Bagelwich** (Cook 1 large egg in a nonstick skillet coated with cooking spray until firm, stirring constantly. Place 1 ounce sliced lean ham on the bottom half of a small toasted bagel; top with egg, a ¾-ounce slice low-fat American cheese, and remaining bagel half. [*POINTS:* 7]) **orange juice,** ½ cup	**reduced-fat biscuit,** 1 large (such as Pillsbury Grands!) **grape jelly,** 1 tablespoon **fat-free milk,** 1 cup	**bagel,** 1 small **light whipped butter,** 1 tablespoon **cranberry juice,** ½ cup
LUNCH	**chili,** small fast food **side salad,** fast food, with 2 table-spoons fat-free French or vinaigrette dressing **fat-free milk,** 1 cup	**Chef Salad** (Top 2 cups torn romaine lettuce with 1 ounce *each of* julienne-cut deli turkey, deli ham, and reduced-fat shredded Cheddar cheese and ⅓ cup *each of* chopped tomato, shredded carrot, sliced cucumber, and fat-free croutons. Serve with 3 tablespoons fat-free ranch dressing. [*POINTS:* 6]) **saltines,** 6	**Hummus-Veggie Pita** (Spread ¼ cup prepared hummus on a 10-inch fat-free flour tortilla; top with ⅓ cup *each of* sliced red bell pepper, zucchini, and yellow squash. Sprinkle with 3 table-spoons crumbled feta cheese. [*POINTS:* 6]) **mixed berry fat-free aspartame-sweetened yogurt,** 8 ounces
DINNER	**Shrimp Fried Rice** (Heat 1 teaspoon sesame oil in a nonstick skillet over medium-high heat. Add 2 large egg whites; stir-fry 30 seconds. Add 4 ounces peeled shrimp and 1 cup chilled cooked brown rice; stir-fry 4 minutes. Add ¼ cup frozen green peas, thawed; 2 tablespoons chopped green onions; 1 teaspoon soy sauce; and dash of pepper. Stir-fry until heated. [*POINTS:* 8]) **steamed broccoli and carrots,** 1 cup	**Veggie Quesadilla** (Combine ½ cup *each of* quartered onion, yellow squash, and sliced zucchini with 2 tablespoons balsamic vinegar in a baking dish coated with cooking spray; toss well. Bake at 400° for 20 minutes or until lightly browned. Spoon onto 1 side of a 10-inch fat-free flour tortilla; sprinkle with 3 tablespoons reduced-fat shredded Cheddar cheese. Fold tortilla half over onto vegetables; gently place in a hot nonstick skillet coated with cooking spray. Cook for 2 minutes on each side or until golden and toasted. [*POINTS:* 4]) **fat-free milk,** 1 cup	**Chicken Cacciatore** (Heat a nonstick skillet over medium-high heat until hot; add 4 ounces skinless, boneless chicken tenders and ½ cup sliced green bell pepper. Cook, stirring constantly, 5 minutes. Add ½ cup chunky tomato pasta sauce, 2 tablespoons water, and a dash of salt; bring to a boil. Cover, reduce heat, and simmer 5 minutes. Serve over 1 cup hot cooked rice. [*POINTS:* 6]) **Spinach-Strawberry Salad** (Combine 2 cups torn spinach leaves and ¾ cup sliced strawberries; toss with 2 tablespoons fat-free balsamic vinaigrette. [*POINTS:* 1]) **fat-free milk,** 1 cup
SNACK	**lemon chiffon fat-free aspartame-sweetened yogurt,** 8 ounces	**Strawberry-Granola Parfait** (In a tall glass, layer ½ cup *each of* peach fat-free yogurt and sliced strawberries and ¼ cup low-fat granola. Repeat layers once. Top with 2 tablespoons lite whipped topping. [*POINTS:* 6])	**Cookies and Cream** (Let ¾ cup vanilla low-fat ice cream soften at room temperature. Crumble 2 reduced-fat chocolate sandwich cookies, and sprinkle on softened ice cream. Stir until well blended. Return to freezer until serving. [*POINTS:* 5])
POINTS	**POINTS** for the day: 27 **Exchanges:** 5 Starch, 4 Vegetable, 1 Fruit, 3 Very Lean Meat, 2 Lean Meat, 2 Medium-Fat Meat, 2 Skim Milk, 2 Fat	**POINTS** for the day: 27 **Exchanges:** 8 Starch, 4 Vegetable, 1 Fruit, 1 Very Lean Meat, 1 Lean Meat, 2 Medium-Fat Meat, 3 Skim Milk, 1 Fat	**POINTS** for the day: 27 **Exchanges:** 10 Starch, 5 Vegetable, 2 Fruit, 3 Very Lean Meat, 1 Medium-Fat Meat, 2 Skim Milk, 3 Fat

One day's menu provides at least two servings of milk and at least five servings of fruits and/or vegetables.

	MONDAY	TUESDAY	WEDNESDAY	THURSDAY
BREAKFAST	**bran flakes,** 1 cup **fat-free milk,** 1 cup **banana,** 1 medium	**waffles,** 2 fat-free frozen **maple syrup,** 2 tablespoons **fat-free milk,** 1 cup **blueberries,** 1 cup	**Extra Cheesy Toast** (Place ½ cup reduced-fat shredded Cheddar cheese on 1 slice high-fiber bread; broil until bubbly. [*POINTS:* 5]) **strawberry-banana fat-free aspartame-sweetened yogurt,** 8 ounces	**scrambled eggs,** 1 large egg and 2 large egg whites **high-fiber toast,** 1 piece **light whipped butter,** 1 tablespoon **grapefruit,** ½
LUNCH	**Potato, Broccoli, and Ham Soup** (Heat 1 teaspoon olive oil in a small saucepan. Add ½ cup chopped onion; sauté 3 minutes. Add 1 cup cubed peeled baking potato; sauté 5 minutes. Add 1 cup steamed broccoli florets and 1 ounce chopped lean ham. Stir in 1 cup fat-free milk and ⅛ teaspoon *each of* salt and pepper; cook until thoroughly heated. [*POINTS:* 7]) **saltines,** 6	**Pepper-and-Beef Sandwich** (Heat a skillet coated with cooking spray over medium-high heat; sauté ½ cup *each of* sliced red and green bell peppers until limp. Place 2 ounces lean roast beef on the bottom half of a toasted 2-ounce hoagie roll; top with peppers and a 1-ounce slice Swiss cheese. Broil sandwich until cheese melts; top with remaining half of roll. [*POINTS:* 6]) **green salad,** 2 cups **fat-free ranch dressing,** 2 tablespoons	**Hot Ham-and-Swiss Sandwich** (Spread 2 teaspoons *each of* light mayonnaise and Dijon mustard evenly over 2 slices high-fiber bread. Place 2 ounces thinly sliced lean deli ham, 1 [¾-ounce] slice reduced-fat Swiss cheese, 2 lettuce leaves, 2 tomato slices, and remaining bread slice. Cook sandwich until browned in a nonstick skillet coated with butter-flavored cooking spray over medium heat, turning once. [*POINTS:* 6]) **apple,** 1 small	**cheese pizza,** ⅛ of 12-inch hand-tossed crust pizza **green salad,** 2 cups with 2 table-spoons fat-free Italian dressing **fat-free milk,** 1 cup **apple wedges,** 1 small
DINNER	**Lemon-Dill Scallops with Snow Peas** (Coat a nonstick skillet with cooking spray; add 1 tablespoon light whipped butter, and place over high heat until melted. Add 4 ounces bay scallops; cook 2 minutes, stirring often. Add 1 cup trimmed fresh snow peas, ½ teaspoon *each of* chopped fresh dill and lemon juice, and dash of salt; cook 2 minutes, stirring often. Serve over 1 cup hot cooked angel hair pasta. [*POINTS:* 6]) **mixed fruit salad,** 1½ cups cut-up fruit	**Grilled Chicken with Basil** (Combine 2 teaspoons lemon juice, 1 tablespoon chopped fresh basil, 1 teaspoon minced garlic, and 2 teaspoons olive oil; spread mixture over a 4-ounce skinless, boneless chicken breast. Marinate in refrigerator 30 minutes. Grill chicken, covered with grill lid, over hot coals, 30 minutes or until done. [*POINTS:* 5]) **Pesto Pasta** (Toss together 1 cup hot cooked angel hair pasta and 1 tablespoon pesto sauce; sprinkle with 2 teaspoons Parmesan cheese. [*POINTS:* 6]) **sauteed zucchini,** 1 cup	**Penne with Vegetable Marinara** (Heat 1 teaspoon olive oil in nonstick skillet. Sauté 1 cup *each of* diced yellow squash and diced zucchini and 1 garlic clove 4 minutes. Add 1 cup low-fat marinara sauce; cook over medium heat for 5 minutes. Serve over 1 cup hot cooked penne noodles. Sprinkle with 1 tablespoon grated Parmesan cheese. [*POINTS:* 7])	**Cajun Grilled Snapper** (Combine 1 teaspoon *each of* light butter and lemon juice; brush over a 6-ounce snapper fillet. Sprinkle with ¼ teaspoon Cajun seasoning. Grill 6 minutes on each side or until fish flakes easily when tested with a fork. [*POINTS:* 4]) **grilled corn,** 1 small ear **light whipped butter,** 1 tablespoon **Spicy Coleslaw** (Combine 1 tablespoon *each of* light mayonnaise and plain fat-free yogurt with 1 teaspoon minced seeded jalapeño pepper; toss with ¾ cup chopped cabbage and ¼ cup shredded carrot. [*POINTS:* 2])
SNACK	**fruit-filled cereal bar,** 1 **fat-free milk,** 1 cup	**crème caramel fat-free aspartame-sweetened yogurt,** 8 ounces	**Sugared Pineapple** (Sprinkle 1 tablespoon brown sugar over 2 pineapple slices; broil. Top with ½ cup vanilla fat-free ice cream. [*POINTS:* 4]) **fat-free milk,** 1 cup	**Cinnamon-Sugar Toasted Tortilla** (Lightly coat 1 [10-inch] fat-free flour tortilla with cooking spray. Sprinkle with 2 teaspoons cinnamon-sugar. Bake at 350° for 5 minutes or until crisp. [*POINTS:* 3]) **fat-free milk,** 1 cup
POINTS	*POINTS* for the day: 26 **Exchanges:** 7 Starch, 3 Vegetable, 3 Fruit, 3 Very Lean Meat, 1 Lean Meat, 3 Skim Milk, 2 Fat	*POINTS* for the day: 26 **Exchanges:** 7 Starch, 5 Vegetable, 1 Fruit, 3 Very Lean Meat, 2 Lean Meat, 1 Medium-Fat Meat, 2 Skim Milk, 3 Fat	*POINTS* for the day: 27 **Exchanges:** 7 Starch, 4 Vegetable, 2 Fruit, 2 Lean Meat, 3 Medium-Fat Meat, 2 Skim Milk, 2 Fat	*POINTS* for the day: 28 **Exchanges:** 6 Starch, 3 Vegetable, 2 Fruit, 6 Very Lean Meat, 2 Medium-Fat Meat, 2 Skim Milk, 3 Fat

	FRIDAY	SATURDAY	SUNDAY
BREAKFAST	**bran flakes,** 1 cup **blueberries,** 1 cup **fat-free milk,** 1 cup	**Waffles with Blueberry Syrup** (In a microwave-safe bowl, heat 2 tablespoons blueberry jelly or jam at HIGH until melted; stir in 1 tablespoon maple syrup. Add ½ cup blueberries. Pour over 2 heated fat-free frozen waffles. [POINTS: 5]) **fat-free milk,** 1 cup	**fruit-filled cereal bar,** 1 **fat-free milk,** 1 cup **grapefruit,** ½
LUNCH	**Onion-Pepper Frittata** (Sauté ½ cup *each of* chopped onion and red or green bell pepper in a small nonstick skillet over medium heat until tender. Combine 1 large egg, 2 large egg whites, 1 tablespoon fat-free milk, and ⅛ teaspoon *each of* salt and pepper; stir well. Pour over vegetables; cover and cook until firm. Sprinkle with 3 tablespoons reduced-fat shredded sharp Cheddar cheese. (POINTS: 5) **blueberry fat-free aspartame-sweetened yogurt,** 8 ounces	**reduced-fat hot dog,** 1 on 1 hot dog bun **baked potato chips,** 1 ounce **celery or carrot sticks,** 1 cup **grapes,** 1 cup	**French Onion Soup** (Heat 1 can prepared French onion soup on the stovetop; top a 1-ounce slice toasted French bread with ¼ cup shredded Swiss cheese. Broil until cheese melts. To serve, ladle soup into bowl; top with slice of cheese toast. [POINTS: 8]) **pineapple chunks,** 1 cup **fat-free milk,** 1 cup
DINNER	**Black Beans and Rice** (Cook 2 ounces sliced turkey kielbasa and ¼ cup *each of* chopped onion and red bell pepper over medium heat until sausage is browned. Stir in ½ cup drained canned black beans, 2 tablespoons water, and a dash of hot sauce; cook until thoroughly heated. Serve over 1 cup hot cooked white rice. [POINTS: 6]) **Red-and-Green Salad** (Toss together 1½ cups chopped romaine lettuce, ½ cup diced red bell pepper, and 2 tablespoons crumbled feta cheese. Drizzle with 2 tablespoons fat-free balsamic vinaigrette. [POINTS: 2]) **fat-free milk,** 1 cup	**Curried Chicken Salad** (Chop half of a peeled apple, and toss with ½ teaspoon lemon juice; add 3 ounces chopped cooked chicken breast, 2 tablespoons sliced celery, and 1 tablespoon raisins. In a small bowl, combine 1 tablespoon *each of* low-fat mayonnaise and nonfat sour cream, ½ teaspoon sugar, and ⅛ teaspoon curry powder; add to chicken mixture, tossing well. Cover and chill at least 1 hour. Serve on 1 cup shredded lettuce. [POINTS: 5]) **soft breadstick,** 1	**Oven-Fried Catfish** (Combine ¼ cup crushed cornflakes, ½ teaspoon Creole seasoning, and a dash of salt. Combine 1 tablespoon fat-free mayonnaise, 1 teaspoon lemon juice, and a dash of hot sauce. Brush a 6-ounce catfish fillet with mayonnaise mixture; dredge in cereal mixture. Place fillet on rack of a broiler pan coated with cooking spray. Bake at 450° for 18 minutes. [POINTS: 5]) **baked potato,** 1 medium **reduced-fat sour cream,** 3 tablespoons **green beans,** 1 cup
SNACK	**Banana Split** (Place a peeled banana in a bowl; top with ¾ cup vanilla fat-free ice cream, ¼ cup fat-free whipped topping, and 1 tablespoon chocolate syrup. [POINTS: 6])	**Mediterranean Snack Sandwich** (Spread ⅓ cup prepared hummus inside a pita half; stuff with ⅓ cup *each of* chopped tomato, diced bell pepper, and sprouts. [POINTS: 4]) **fat-free milk,** 1 cup	**fat-free vanilla ice cream,** ½ cup
POINTS	*POINTS* for the day: 27 **Exchanges:** 8 Starch, 4 Vegetable, 1 Fruit, 2 Very Lean Meat, 2 Lean Meat, 3 Medium-Fat Meat, 2 Skim Milk	*POINTS* for the day: 27 **Exchanges:** 7 Starch, 3 Vegetable, 2 Fruit, 3 Very Lean Meat, 1 Lean Meat, 2 Skim Milk, 1 Fat	*POINTS* for the day: 28 **Exchanges:** 6 Starch, 4 Vegetable, 1 Fruit, 5 Lean Meat, 1 Medium-Fat Meat, 2 Skim Milk, 1 Fat

One day's menu provides at least two servings of milk and at least five servings of fruits and/or vegetables.

	MONDAY	TUESDAY	WEDNESDAY	THURSDAY
BREAKFAST	**Sunrise Smoothie** (Place ½ cup orange juice, 1 [8-ounce] carton strawberry fat-free aspartame-sweetened yogurt, and 1 banana in a blender; process until smooth. [*POINTS:* 4])	**fruit-filled cereal bar**, 1 **fat-free milk**, 1 cup **banana**, 1	**oatmeal**, 1 cup **raisin**, 2 tablespoons **fat-free milk**, 1 cup	**Cheese Toast** (Place ¼ cup reduced-fat shredded Cheddar cheese on 1 slice high-fiber bread; broil until bubbly. [*POINTS:* 3]) **orange juice**, ½ cup **vanilla fat-free aspartame-sweetened yogurt**, 8 ounces
LUNCH	**Lamb-Vegetable Salad** (Cut 4 ounces lean leg of lamb into ½-inch cubes. Place a nonstick skillet over medium-high heat until hot. Add lamb; sauté 3 minutes or until browned. Combine lamb; 2 cups sliced romaine lettuce; 1 cup sliced cucumber; 2 steamed small new potatoes, quartered; and 1 plum tomato, chopped. Drizzle with 3 tablespoons fat-free creamy Italian dressing. [*POINTS:* 7]) **pretzels**, 15 small	**Red Beans and Rice** (Cook ¼ cup *each of* chopped onion and chopped green bell pepper over medium heat until vegetables are tender. Stir in ½ cup drained and rinsed red kidney beans, 2 tablespoons water, ½ teaspoon chili powder, and dash of hot sauce. Serve over ½ cup cooked rice. [*POINTS:* 4]) **corn bread**, 1 (2-inch) square **green salad**, 2 cups **fat-free Italian dressing**, 2 tablespoons	**Ham-and-Cheese Sandwich** (Top a slice of high-fiber bread with 3 ounces lean ham and ¼ cup reduced-fat shredded Cheddar cheese. Broil until cheese is melted and bubbly. Top with 2 lettuce leaves, 2 tomato slices, and another slice of bread. [*POINTS:* 6]) **strawberry fat-free aspartame-sweetened yogurt**, 8 ounces	**White Bean-and-Tomato Salad** (Combine 1 cup of navy or white beans with ½ cup chopped tomato. Add 2 tablespoons *each of* light balsamic vinaigrette and crumbled feta cheese; mix well. Sprinkle with pepper, serve over lettuce. [*POINTS:* 7]) **pretzels**, 15 small **peach**, 1 **fat-free milk**, 1 cup
DINNER	**Greek Grouper** (Sprinkle a 6-ounce grouper filet with ½ teaspoon Greek seasoning. Coat a nonstick skillet with cooking spray, and place over medium-high heat until hot. Add fish, and cook 3 minutes; remove from heat. Turn fish; top with ¼ cup *each of* thawed frozen spinach and chopped tomato and 2 tablespoons crumbled feta cheese. [*POINTS:* 5]) **couscous**, 1 cup **Spinach with Walnuts** (Sauté 1 cup fresh spinach in a skillet coated with olive oil-flavored cooking spray until limp; sprinkle with 2 teaspoons chopped walnuts. [*POINTS:* 1])	**baked lean ham**, 3 ounces **Mashed Sweet Potato** (Combine ½ cup mashed cooked sweet potato, 2 tablespoons fat-free milk, 1 tablespoon chopped pecans, 1 teaspoon *each of* brown sugar and margarine, and a dash of salt; stir well. [*POINTS:* 6]) **steamed broccoli**, 1 cup	**Eggplant Parmesan** (Brush 1 teaspoon *each of* olive oil and balsamic vinegar over 3 eggplant slices; sprinkle with ⅛ teaspoon *each of* salt and pepper. Broil 3 minutes, turning once. Top with ½ cup bottled marinara sauce; sprinkle with 3 tablespoons grated Parmesan cheese. [*POINTS:* 5]) **fettuccine noodles**, 1 cup **Traditional Spinach Salad** (Top 2 cups torn spinach leaves with 1 hard-boiled egg, chopped; 1 slice reduced-fat bacon, crumbled; ½ cup diced tomato; and 2 tablespoons fat-free Italian dressing. [*POINTS:* 3])	**Chicken Teriyaki** (Combine 2 tablespoons low-sodium soy sauce; 1 tablespoon *each of* dry white wine and honey; 1 garlic clove, minced; and ⅛ teaspoon ground ginger in a large zip-top plastic bag. Add 1 [6-ounce] skinless, boneless chicken breast. Marinate in refrigerator 8 hours. Remove chicken from marinade. Coat grill rack with cooking spray; place over medium-hot coals. Grill chicken, covered, 20 to 25 minutes or until tender. [*POINTS:* 5]) **cooked white rice**, 1 cup **steamed snow peas**, 1 cup
SNACK	**cherry-vanilla fat-free aspartame-sweetened yogurt**, 8 ounces	**reduced-fat chocolate sandwich cookies**, 3 **fat-free milk**, 1 cup	**pretzels**, 15 small **apple**, 1	**vanilla reduced-fat ice cream**, ½ cup
POINTS	*POINTS* for the day: 25 **Exchanges:** 5 Starch, 5 Vegetable, 2 Fruit, 5 Very Lean Meat, 3 Lean Meat, 2 Skim Milk, 1 Fat	*POINTS* for the day: 28 **Exchanges:** 8 Starch, 4 Vegetable, 1 Fruit, 1 Very Lean Meat, 3 Lean Meat, 2 Skim Milk, 2 Fat	*POINTS* for the day: 28 **Exchanges:** 8 Starch, 5 Vegetable, 1 Fruit, 3 Lean Meat, 3 Medium-Fat Meat, 2 Skim Milk, 1½ Fat	*POINTS* for the day: 29 **Exchanges:** 8 Starch, 3 Vegetable, 2 Fruit, 5 Very Lean Meat, 1½ Medium-Fat Meat, 2 Skim Milk, 2 Fat

7-DAY MENU PLANNER

WEEK 8

	FRIDAY	SATURDAY	SUNDAY
BREAKFAST	**oatmeal,** 1 cup **raisins,** 2 tablespoons **fat-free milk,** 1 cup	**high-fiber toast,** 2 slices **grape jelly,** 2 tablespoons **fat-free milk,** 1 cup **banana,** 1	**fruit-filled cereal bar,** 1 **fat-free milk,** 1 cup
LUNCH	**Turkey-Spinach Roll-Up** (Spread 2 teaspoons light mayonnaise over 1 [8-inch] fat-free flour tortilla; layer 2 ounces shaved deli turkey breast, ½ cup fresh spinach leaves, ¼ cup diced tomato, and 3 tablespoons crumbled blue cheese. Roll up tightly. [*POINTS:* 6]) **peach,** 1 medium	**grilled chicken sandwich,** 1 fast-food sandwich without mayonnaise **vanilla reduced-fat ice cream cone,** 1 fast-food cone **apple,** 1	**Mexican Pizza** (Top 1 [10-inch] fat-free flour tortilla with ⅓ cup *each of* fat-free refried beans, chopped tomato, and reduced-fat shredded sharp Cheddar cheese. Broil 2 minutes or until cheese melts. Top with 1 cup shredded lettuce, 2 tablespoons salsa, and 1 tablespoon *each of* chopped fresh cilantro, sliced ripe olives, and fat-free sour cream. [*POINTS:* 6])
DINNER	**Beef with Asparagus** (Combine 1 teaspoon *each of* sesame oil, soy sauce, and minced garlic and ½ teaspoon *each of* cornstarch and rice wine in a zip-top plastic bag. Add 4 ounces thinly sliced flank steak; marinate overnight. Coat skillet with cooking spray; add beef marinade and ¾ cup *each of* sliced water chestnuts and chopped asparagus. Stir-fry 8 minutes, or until cooked. [*POINTS:* 7]) **oriental noodles,** 1 cup	**Cilantro-Lime Shrimp** (Toss 4 ounces peeled and deveined shrimp with 2 teaspoons lime juice, a dash of cumin, 1 tablespoon fresh chopped cilantro, and 1 garlic clove, minced, in a bowl. Heat 2 teaspoons olive oil over medium-high heat. Add shrimp, and sauté for 4 minutes. [*POINTS:* 4]) **steamed spinach,** 1 cup **olive oil and garlic-flavored couscous,** 1 cup	**Peppered Filet with Mushroom Sauce** (Melt 1 teaspoon light whipped butter in a nonstick skillet over medium-high heat. Add ¾ cup sliced fresh mushrooms and 2 tablespoons chopped shallot; sauté 4 minutes. Add ¼ cup *each of* dry red wine and fat-free beef broth; cook 5 minutes. Place mushroom-wine mixture in a bowl. Sprinkle a 4-ounce filet mignon steak with a dash *each of* salt and pepper; add to skillet. Add mushroom mixture, ½ teaspoon cornstarch, and a dash of dried thyme to pan. Boil 1 minute, stirring constantly. [*POINTS:* 9]) **baked potato,** 1 medium **steamed asparagus,** 12 spears
SNACK	**Berry-Yogurt Parfait** (Place ⅓ cup blueberries in the bottom of a tall glass; top with half of an 8-ounce carton of raspberry fat-free aspartame-sweetened yogurt. Add another ⅓ cup blueberries and remaining yogurt. Top parfait with ⅓ cup blueberries. [*POINTS:* 3])	**fat-free milk,** 1 cup **blueberries,** 1 cup	**Cinnamon-Banana Smoothie** (Process 8 ounces vanilla fat-free aspartame-sweetened yogurt, 1 banana, and 1 teaspoon cinnamon-sugar in a blender until smooth. [*POINTS:* 4])
POINTS	**POINTS** for the day: 26 **Exchanges:** 5 Starch, 2 Vegetable, 3 Fruit, 2 Very Lean Meat, 3 Lean Meat, 1 Medium-Fat Meat, 2 Skim Milk, 2 Fat	**POINTS** for the day: 27 **Exchanges:** 9 Starch, 2 Vegetable, 3 Fruit, 7 Very Lean Meat, 2 Skim Milk, 4 Fat	**POINTS** for the day: 26 **Exchanges:** 5 Starch, 4 Vegetable, 1 Fruit, 1 Very Lean Meat, 4 Medium-Fat Meat, 2 Skim Milk, 1 Fat

One day's menu provides at least two servings of milk and at least five servings of fruits and/or vegetables.

	MONDAY	TUESDAY	WEDNESDAY	THURSDAY
BREAKFAST	**fruit-filled cereal bar,** 1 **cappuccino fat-free aspartame-sweetened yogurt,** 8 ounces	**Garlic-Cheese Grits** (Stir ¼ cup reduced-fat shredded Cheddar cheese and ¼ teaspoon garlic salt into 1 cup hot cooked grits; stir until smooth. [*POINTS:* 5]) **peach fat-free aspartame-sweetened yogurt,** 8 ounces	**bran cereal,** 1 cup **strawberries,** 1½ cups **fat-free milk,** 1 cup	**Cinnamon Toast** (Spread 1 tablespoon light whipped butter on 2 slices high-fiber bread. Sprinkle each with 2 teaspoons cinnamon-sugar; broil until toasted. [*POINTS:* 4]) **banana,** 1 **fat-free milk,** 1 cup
LUNCH	**Pimiento Cheese-Veggie Sandwich** (Combine ¼ cup reduced-fat shredded Cheddar cheese and 4 teaspoons *each of* light mayonnaise and diced pimiento; spread over 1 slice high-fiber bread. Top with 2 lettuce leaves, 2 tomato slices, and another slice of bread. [*POINTS:* 6]) **fat-free milk,** 1 cup **apple,** 1 small	**Broccoli Salad** (Combine 1 cup steamed broccoli florets, 1 cup cooked rice, 2 teaspoons *each of* light mayonnaise, lemon juice, and walnuts; toss well. [*POINTS:* 6]) **soft breadstick,** 1 **cantaloupe chunks,** 1 cup	**Roast Beef-and-Feta Sandwich** (Spread 2 teaspoons light mayonnaise and 1 teaspoon Dijon mustard over 1 slice toasted whole-grain, high-fiber bread. Layer 2 lettuce leaves, 2 tomato slices, 2 ounces thinly sliced lean deli roast beef, and 2 tablespoons crumbled feta cheese. Top with 1 slice toasted bread. [*POINTS:* 6]) **baked chips,** 1 ounce **fat-free milk,** 1 cup	**low-fat macaroni-and-cheese,** 1 frozen boxed entrée **fat-free fat-free milk,** 1 cup
DINNER	**Spaghetti with Meat Sauce** (Sauté ¼ cup diced onion and 1 teaspoon minced garlic in a skillet coated with cooking spray. Add 3 ounces lean ground beef, and cook until beef is no longer pink. Stir in ½ cup tomato sauce; serve over 1 cup cooked spaghetti. Top with 2 tablespoons grated Parmesan cheese. [*POINTS:* 8]) **tossed salad,** 2 cups **fat-free Italian dressing,** 2 tablespoons **soft breadstick,** 1	**Grilled Herbed Chicken** (Combine 1 teaspoon dried Italian seasoning, a dash of ground pepper, 2 tablespoons dry white wine, 2 teaspoons lemon juice, ½ teaspoon olive oil, and 1 teaspoon minced garlic; coat a 4-ounce skinless, boneless chicken breast with mixture. Coat grill rack with cooking spray; grill chicken over medium-hot coals, covered, 5 minutes on each side. [*POINTS:* 3]) **Tomato, Basil, and Corn Couscous** (Combine 1 cup hot cooked couscous, ¼ cup *each of* diced tomato and whole-kernel corn, 1 tablespoon chopped fresh basil, ½ teaspoon olive oil, and a dash *each of* salt and pepper. [*POINTS:* 4]) **steamed spinach,** 1 cup	**South-of-the-Border Snapper** (Coat a nonstick skillet with cooking spray, and place over medium heat. Sprinkle ¼ teaspoon cumin on one side of a 6-ounce snapper filet. Place seasoned side of fish down in skillet; cook 3 minutes. Turn fish; top with ½ cup Mexican-style stewed tomatoes and 2 tablespoons salsa. Reduce heat, and simmer, uncovered, 5 minutes or until fish flakes with a fork. Sprinkle with cilantro, if desired. [*POINTS:* 4]) **yellow saffron rice,** 1 cup **Garlicky Broccoli** (Sauté 1 cup steamed broccoli florets in 1 teaspoon *each of* olive oil and minced garlic 1 to 2 minutes. [*POINTS:* 1])	**baked chicken,** 3 ounces **Squash Casserole** (Combine 1 large egg, 1 [1-ounce] slice chopped French bread, and 1 tablespoon light whipped butter, melted. Add 1 cup chopped cooked yellow squash and a dash *each of* salt and pepper. Spoon into a small baking dish coated with cooking spray; sprinkle with 3 tablespoons reduced-fat shredded Cheddar cheese, and bake at 350° for 30 minutes. [*POINTS:* 6]) **steamed green beans,** 1 cup
SNACK	**prepared hummus,** ¼ cup **pita bread,** 1 small	**coconut cream pie fat-free aspartame-sweetened yogurt,** 8 ounces **reduced-fat chocolate graham crackers,** 2 (2.5-inch) crackers	**Frozen Dessert Sandwiches** (Spread ¼ cup lite whipped topping between 2 [2.5-inch] reduced-fat chocolate graham cracker squares. Wrap sandwich in plastic wrap, and place in freezer until frozen. [*POINTS:* 3])	**cantaloupe chunks,** 1 cup **cherry-vanilla fat-free yogurt,** 8 ounces
POINTS	***POINTS* for the day: 28** **Exchanges:** 8 Starch, 4 Vegetable, 1 Fruit, 3 Lean Meat, 1 Medium-Fat Meat, 2 Skim Milk, 2 Fat	***POINTS* for the day: 27** **Exchanges:** 8 Starch, 4 Vegetable, 1 Fruit, 3 Very Lean Meat, 1 Medium-Fat Meat, 2 Skim Milk, 2 Fat	***POINTS* for the day: 26** **Exchanges:** 8 Starch, 4 Vegetable, 1 Fruit, 5 Very Lean Meat, 2 Lean Meat, 2 Skim Milk, 2 Fat	***POINTS* for the day: 25** **Exchanges:** 7 Starch, 4 Vegetable, 2 Fruit, 3 Very Lean Meat, 1 Lean Meat, 2 Medium-Fat Meat, 3 Skim Milk, 2 Fat

	FRIDAY	SATURDAY	SUNDAY
BREAKFAST	**cooked grits,** 1 cup **cranberry juice,** ½ cup	**fruit-filled cereal bar,** 1 **fat-free milk,** 1 cup	**bran cereal,** 1 cup **blueberries,** 1 cup **fat-free milk,** 1 cup
LUNCH	**Portobello Sandwich** (Brush 1 teaspoon *each of* olive oil, balsamic vinegar, and soy sauce over 1 large portobello mushroom cap. Broil 2 minutes on each side. Place mushroom, 2 tomato slices, 1 red onion slice, and a 1-ounce slice reduced-fat Swiss cheese on a 2-ounce whole wheat bun. [*POINTS:* 6]) **fat-free milk,** 1 cup	**Mediterranean Chicken Pita** (Broil a 4-ounce skinless, boneless chicken breast for 5 minutes on each side or until done, basting frequently with 2 tablespoons fat-free Italian dressing. Cut into strips. Cut a pita in half crosswise. Spread 1 tablespoon prepared hummus on inside of each pita half. Stuff each half with a lettuce leaf, a tomato slice, half of chicken, and 1 tablespoon crumbled feta. [*POINTS:* 8]) **baked chips,** 1 ounce **strawberry-kiwi fat-free aspartame-sweetened yogurt,** 8 ounces	**Pasta Primavera** (Heat 1 teaspoon olive oil in a nonstick skillet over medium heat. Add 1 minced garlic clove and ¼ cup *each of* broccoli florets, chopped green onions, red bell pepper, and tomato; sauté 3 minutes. Stir in ¼ cup chopped fresh basil, 2 tablespoons grated Parmesan cheese, 1 teaspoon lemon juice, and a dash *each of* salt and pepper; toss with 1 cup hot cooked spaghetti. [*POINTS:* 7]) **strawberries,** 1 cup
DINNER	**Mustard-Garlic Lamb Chops** (Combine 1 teaspoon minced garlic, ⅛ teaspoon dried thyme, dash *each of* salt and pepper, and ½ teaspoon *each of* lemon juice, Dijon mustard, and olive oil. Spread mixture over both sides of a trimmed 5-ounce lean lamb chop; broil 6 to 7 minutes on each side. [*POINTS:* 5]) **mashed potatoes,** 1 cup **green peas,** 1 cup **fat-free milk,** 1 cup	**Beef-Vegetable Soup** (Brown 4 ounces raw lean ground beef. Combine ¼ cup beef broth and 1 tablespoon flour, blending well. Add flour mixture, ¾ cup beef broth, ½ cup canned stewed Mexican tomatoes, 1 cup frozen mixed soup vegetables, and a dash *each of* salt and pepper. Bring to a boil; cover, reduce heat to medium, and cook 20 minutes. [*POINTS:* 6]) **saltine crackers,** 6	**Baked Pesto Salmon** (Brush 2 teaspoons prepared pesto over 1 [4-ounce] skinless salmon fillet; bake at 350° for 20 minutes or until fish flakes when tested with a fork. [*POINTS:* 7]) **baked potato,** 1 large **low-fat sour cream,** 3 tablespoons **steamed asparagus,** 12 spears
SNACK	**part-skim mozzarella cheese snack stick,** 1 **blueberries,** 1 cup	**Wild Fruit Smoothie** (Blend together ½ cup cranberry juice, ½ cup blueberries, 1 banana, and ice. Serve immediately. [*POINTS:* 4])	**chocolate graham crackers,** 2 (2½-inch) squares **peanut butter,** 1 tablespoon **fat-free milk,** 1 cup
POINTS	***POINTS*** for the day: 28 **Exchanges:** 7 Starch, 3 Vegetable, 2 Fruit, 3 Lean Meat, 2 Medium-Fat Meat, 2 Skim Milk, 1½ Fat	***POINTS*** for the day: 29 **Exchanges:** 5 Starch, 3 Vegetable, 2½ Fruit, 3 Very Lean Meat, 3½ Lean Meat, 2 Skim Milk, 1 Fat	***POINTS*** for the day: 29 **Exchanges:** 6 Starch, 3 Vegetable, 2 Fruit, 4½ Lean Meat, ½ High-Fat Meat, 2 Skim Milk, 2 Fat

181

General Recipe Index

Appetizers. *See also* Snacks.
  Baba Ghanoush with Pita Chips, 13
  Caponata, 13
  Chicken Bites with Creamy Parmesan Dip, 14
  Crostini with Roasted Pepper and Goat Cheese, Pesto, 13
  Dip, Roasted Red Pepper, 12
  Dip with Feta, Spinach, 12
  Meatballs, Swedish, 14
  Mushroom Tartlets, 15
  Shrimp, Party, 14
  Spread, Goat Cheese and Anchovy, 12
Apples. *See also* Desserts.
  Compote, Thyme Pork with Apple-Cherry, 96
  Muffins, Apple-Ginger, 29
  Salad, Turkey Waldorf, 125
  Syrup, Waffles with Apple, 170
Apricot Butter, 29
Apricot-Ginger Sauce, Turkey Scaloppine with, 108
Artichokes, Valencia, 142
Asparagus and Carrots, Stir-Fried, 142
Asparagus, Lemon Roasted, 142
Avocado Picadillo, 131

Bananas. *See also* Beverages, Desserts.
  Bread, Banana-Date, 32
  Butter-Rum Sauce and Bananas, Deep, 37
  Oatmeal, Banana-Walnut, 173
  Pancakes, Banana-Buttermilk, 20
Barbecue
  Chicken, Barbecue, 172
  Chicken, Cheater's Deep-Flavored Barbecued, 105
  Chicken Pizza, Barbecue, 171
Barley Pilaf with Toasted Almonds and Raisins, 149
Barley Salad with Black Beans and Corn, Mexican, 121
Beans. *See also* Salads, Soups.
  Baby Limas with Tarragon Mustard, Buttery, 142
  Black Bean-and-Corn Ravioli with Red Pepper Sauce, 82
  Black Bean Quesadillas, Spinach-and-, 77
  Black Beans and Rice, 177
  Black Beans and Rice, Chipotle, 75
  Burritos, Cheesy Bean, 168
  Chickpeas, Ratatouille with, 76

Chile Beans, Cornbread-Crusted, 78
Fagioli, Tortellini, 155
Pinto Beans, Smothered Squash and, 76
Red Beans and Rice, 178
Red Beans and Rice, Kicked-Up, 108
Tostada, Chili Bean, 78
White Bean Rice, Kalamata-, 75
White Bean-and-Wilted Spinach Penne, 81
White Bean Spread, Caramelized Onion-and-, 12
Beef. *See also* Beef, Ground; Sandwiches; Stir-Fry.
  Pot Roast Stew, 156
  Roast Beef Salad with Blue Cheese, 168
  Slow-Roasted Beef and Gravy, 94
  Steaks
    Asparagus, Beef with, 179
    Filet with Mushroom Sauce, Peppered, 179
    Flank Steak, Greek Stuffed, 88
    Salad, Thai Beef, 124
    Sirloin Stroganoff, 88
    Sirloin with Sweet Marinade, Skillet, 93
  Tenderloin with Horseradish-Mustard Crust, Beef, 94
  Tenderloin with Marsala-Mushroom Sauce, Beef, 93
Beef, Ground
  Burgers, Stuffed Blue Cheese, 130
  Cheeseburger, Blue, 165
  Chili, Four-Way Cincinnati, 156
  Meatball Subs, 130
  Meat Loaf with Browned Gravy, Café-Style, 87
  Sauce, Spaghetti with Meat, 180
  Sloppy Joe, 166
  Soup, Beef-Vegetable, 181
  Stroganoff, Beef, 173
  Tacos, Beef, Bean, and Vegetable, 87
Beets and Sweet Potatoes, Roasted, 143
Beverages
  Cocoa, Mocha, 17
  Coolers, Wine, 16
  Fizz, Peach, 16
  Hot Chocolate, Quick, 174
  Milkshake, Strawberry, 17
  Punch, Lemony Gingerale, 16
  Shake, Fudgy Peanut Butter, 17
  Smoothie, Cinnamon-Banana, 179
  Smoothie, Mango, 16

Smoothie, Peach-Banana, 164
Smoothie, Strawberry, 166
Smoothie, Strawberry-Banana Soy, 17
Smoothie, Sunrise, 178
Smoothie, Tropical, 173
Smoothie, Wild Fruit, 181
Blueberries
  Muffins, Blueberry-Bran, 30
  Parfait, Berry-Yogurt, 179
  Sauce, Buttermilk Panna Cotta with Blueberry, 39
  Syrup, Waffles with Blueberry, 172, 177
Bok Choy-Tofu Stir-Fry, 85
Breads
  Anadama Raisin Bread, 34
  Banana-Date Bread, 32
  Breadsticks, Herb-and-Garlic, 19
  Breadsticks, Rosemary-Garlic, 19
  Cinnamon-Raisin Bread, 172
  Cinnamon Swirl Loaf, 34
  Cornbread, Buttermilk, 32
  Crostini with Roasted Pepper and Goat Cheese, Pesto, 13
  Focaccia, Herbed Tomato, 19
  French Toast, 168, 172
  Muffins, Apple-Ginger, 29
  Muffins, Blueberry-Bran, 30
  Muffins, Cinnamon-Kissed Raspberry, 30
  Muffins, Mixed Fruit, 31
  Muffins, Sweet Potato-Bran, 31
  Muffins with Jalapeños, Country Cornbread, 30
  Pinwheels, Mediterranean, 19
  Popovers, Hot, 29
  Pudding with Rum-Raisin Caramel Sauce, Bread, 54
  Pumpkin-Oat Bread with Walnut Streusel Topping, 33
  Rolls, Cheddar-Herb, 20
  Rolls, Whole Wheat, 33
  Scones, Cinnamon-Raisin, 32
  Scones, Cranberry-Orange, 31
  Toast, Cheese, 165, 171, 178
  Toast, Cinnamon, 180
  Toast, Extra Cheesy, 176
  Toast, Peanut Butter-Raisin, 172, 173
Broccoli. *See also* Salads.
  Almond-Breadcrumb Topping, Broccoli with, 143
  Calzones, Broccoli-and-Two Cheese, 128
  Casserole, Broccoli-Rotini, 82

Garlicky Broccoli, 170, 180
Soup, Potato, Broccoli, and Ham, 176
Stir-Fry, Beef-and-Broccoli, 93
Stir-Fry, Tofu-and-Broccoli, 171
Bulgur with Zucchini and Peas, 121
Burrito, Breakfast, 174
Burritos, Cheesy Bean, 168
Butter, Apricot, 29

Cabbage. See also Salads and Salad
    Dressings.
    Onions with Bacon, Old-World
        Cabbage and, 143
    Parmesan, Cabbage and Carrots, 144
Cakes
    Angel Food Cake with Lemon Sauce,
        Molasses, 44
    Apple Cake, Warm Fresh, 42
    Chocolate Bundt Cake, Double, 44
    Fig Spice Cake, 42
    Gingerbread-Pineapple Cake,
        Quick, 43
    Lemon Loaf Cake, Glazed, 43
    Shortcake, Strawberry, 173
    Shortcake, Very Berry, 37
Carrots
    Curried Lentils and Carrots on
        Couscous, 76
    Gingered Carrots and Peas, 144
    Parmesan, Cabbage and Carrots, 144
    Stir-Fried Asparagus and Carrots, 142
Casseroles. See also Lasagna.
    Broccoli-Rotini Casserole, 82
    Chicken-and-Dressing Casserole,
        Farmhouse, 101
    Chicken-and-Pasta Bake with Basil, 101
    Corn-and-Green Chile Casserole, 78
    Crab Casseroles, Individual, 65
    Hash Brown Casserole, 145
    Macaroni and Cheese with Carrots
        and Roasted Pepper, 80
    Squash Casserole, 180
    Tortilla Casserole, Mexican, 77
    Ziti, Baked, 164
Cauliflower
    Puttanesca, Cauliflower, 144
    Salad with Blue Cheese Dressing,
        Broccoli-and-Cauliflower, 119
    Soup, Cream of Cauliflower, 153
Cheese. See also Sandwiches.
    Blue Cheese Burgers, Stuffed, 130
    Burrito, Breakfast, 174
    Cheeseburger, Blue, 165
    Chicken Cordon Bleu, 103
    Chicken Parmesan, 167
    Dressing, Blue Cheese, 125
    Dressing, Broccoli-and-Cauliflower
        Salad with Blue Cheese, 119

Dressing, Creamy Feta, 125
Eggplant Parmesan, 178
Flounder, Easy Parmesan, 170
Grits, Garlic-Cheese, 169, 180
Macaroni and Cheese with Bacon, 172
Macaroni and Cheese with Carrots
    and Roasted Pepper, 80
Mashed Potatoes, Blue Cheese, 174
Penne Toss, Feta-and-, 81
Potatoes with Spinach and Cheese,
    Scalloped, 146
Rolls, Cheddar-Herb, 20
Soup with Pretzel Croutons, Beer-
    Cheese, 153
Tabbouleh with Feta, 122
Toast, Cheese, 165, 171, 178
Toast, Extra Cheesy, 176
Tortellini, Pesto-Cheese, 174
Chicken. See also Salads/Chicken;
    Sandwiches.
    à la King, Chicken, 165
    Bake with Basil, Chicken-and-
        Pasta, 101
    Barbecue Chicken, 172
    Barbecue Chicken Pizza, 171
    Barbecued Chicken, Cheater's
        Deep-Flavored, 105
    Bites with Creamy Parmesan Dip,
        Chicken, 14
    Burgoo, Bama, 161
    Cacciatore, Chicken, 175
    Casserole, Farmhouse Chicken-and-
        Dressing, 101
    Coq au Vin, 104
    Cordon Bleu, Chicken, 103
    Curried Chicken, Creamy, 102
    Fajitas, Spicy Chipotle Chicken-and-
        Pepper, 102
    Greek Chicken with Lemon and
        Mint, 104
    Grilled Chicken with Basil, 176
    Grilled Herbed Chicken, 180
    Gumbo, Holiday, 163
    Honey-Mustard Chicken, Crispy, 168
    Kebabs, Chicken, 166
    Kiev, Chicken, 104
    Lemon, Figs, and Olives, Chicken
        with, 106
    Lemon-Pepper Chicken, 173
    Mexican Chicken, Skillet, 105
    Mulligatawny, 162
    Parmesan, Chicken, 167
    Quesadilla, Chicken-and-
        Spinach, 164
    Roasted Chicken and Vegetables,
        Lemon-Sage, 106
    Sesame Chicken, 170
    Smothered Chicken in Mushroom
        Ragoût, 103

Soup, Chicken Alphabet, 161
Soup, Old-Fashioned Chicken-and-
    Rice, 162
Spaghetti, Greek Chicken, 171
Sweet-and-Sour Chicken, 101
Tandoori Chicken, Broiled, 102
Tarragon Chicken, Buttery, 103
Teriyaki, Chicken, 178
Chili, Four-Way Cincinnati, 156
Chili, Vegetarian, 164
Chocolate. See also Beverages.
    Brownies, Frozen Chocolate
        Decadence, 40
    Cake, Double Chocolate Bundt, 44
    Crêpes, Chocolate-Raspberry, 38
    Ice Cream, Milk Chocolate, 40
    Parfait, Chocolate-Butterscotch, 166
    Pie, Brownie Sundae, 41
    S'mores, 164
Clam-and-Mushroom Linguine,
    Garlicky, 65
Cookies
    Bars and Squares
        Brownies, Frozen Chocolate
            Decadence, 40
        Oatmeal Energy Bars, 15
        Peanut Butter S'mores Bars, 56
        Raspberry-Lemon Squares, 56
    Biscotti, Almond, 56
    Brown Sugar Icebox Cookies, 55
    Gingerbread-Raisin Cookies, 55
Corn. See also Salads.
    Cakes with Creamy Cumin Sauce,
        Rustic Corn, 79
    Casserole, Corn-and-Green Chile, 78
    Couscous, Tomato, Basil, and
        Corn, 180
    Ravioli with Red Pepper Sauce, Black
        Bean-and-Corn, 82
    Roasted Peppers and Corn, 145
    Sauté, Zucchini-and-Corn, 148
    Succotash Quesadillas, 77
Cornish Hens, Grilled Spice-
    Rubbed, 107
Couscous
    Confetti Couscous, 149
    Tomato, Basil, and Corn
        Couscous, 180
    Veggie Couscous, 170
Crab Cakes, Maryland, 65
Crab Casseroles, Individual, 65
Cranberries
    Oatmeal, Cranberry, 170
    Pears with Cranberries, Spiced, 37
    Scones, Cranberry-Orange, 31
Crêpes, Chocolate-Raspberry, 38
Cucumber Party Sandwiches,
    Kalamata-, 127
Cucumber Salad, Sliced, 120

Desserts. *See also* specific types.
  Apples with Caramel Dipping
    Sauce, 36
  Bananas Foster, 36
  Banana Split, 170, 177
  Crêpes, Chocolate-Raspberry, 38
  Frozen
        Brownies, Frozen Chocolate
          Decadence, 40
        Cookies and Cream, 175
        Dessert Sandwiches, 180
        Ice Cream, Milk Chocolate, 40
        Ice Cream Sandwich, 170
        Ice, Strawberry-Merlot, 40
  Fruit Medley with Orange-Yogurt
    Sauce, 36
  Grapefruit Ambrosia Coupes, 36
  Panna Cotta with Blueberry Sauce,
    Buttermilk, 39
  Parfait, Berry-Yogurt, 179
  Parfait, Chocolate-Butterscotch, 166
  Parfait, Strawberry-Granola, 175
  Pears with Cranberries, Spiced, 37
  Pineapple, Sugared, 176
  Sauces
        Butter-Rum Sauce and Bananas,
          Deep, 37
        Lemon Sauce, 44
        Rum-Raisin Caramel Sauce, 55
  S'mores, 164
  Sundae, Banana-Strawberry, 174
  Tiramisu, Angelic, 39
  Yogurt, Greek Honey, 38

Eggplant Parmesan, 178
Eggs. *See also* Sandwiches.
  Frittata, Cheesy Zucchini, 85
  Frittata, Onion-Pepper, 177
  Omelet, Western, 173
  Scrambled Eggs, 166
Enchiladas, Quick Turkey, 169

Fajitas, Spicy Chipotle Chicken-and-
  Pepper, 102
Fettuccine Alfredo Florentine, 166
Figs, and Olives, Chicken with
  Lemon, 106
Fig Spice Cake, 42
Fish. *See also* specific types and Seafood.
  Breaded Fish Italian Style, 59
  Broiled Fish with Tapenade, 61
  Catfish, Oven-Fried, 177
  Flounder, Easy Parmesan, 170
  Flounder Florentine, 58
  Grouper, Greek, 178
  Grouper, Pecan-Crusted, 58
  Halibut Fillets with Teriyaki Sauce, 59

Mahimahi, Caesar, 60
Mahimahi, Glazed, 60
Oven-Fried Fish, 60
Sea Bass, Lime-Marinated, 166
Sea Bass with Jalapeño-Lime Oil, Pan-
  Seared, 58
Seared Fish with Yucatan Vegetables,
  Chili-, 61
Snapper, Cajun Grilled, 176
Snapper, Creole Baked, 63
Snapper, Greek, 63
Snapper, South-of-the-Border, 180
Snapper, Tarragon, 63
Swordfish, Rosemary, 164
Tilapia, Caribbean Mango, 64
Trout, Herb-Baked, 169
Fruit. *See also* specific types and
  Beverages, Salads.
  Medley with Orange-Yogurt Sauce,
    Fruit, 36
  Muffins, Mixed Fruit, 31
  Pork Tenderloin with Orange-Mustard
    Sauce, Fruit-Stuffed, 99
  Soup, Berry Patch, 153
  Squares, Peanut Butter-Fruit, 171

Garlic
  Coq au Vin, 104
  Couscous, Confetti, 149
  Gumbo, Holiday, 163
  Linguine, Garlicky Clam-and-
    Mushroom, 65
  Mahimahi, Caesar, 60
  Mahimahi, Glazed, 60
  Mashed Potatoes with Rosemary,
    Garlic, 145
  Pilaf, Lentils-and-Brown Rice, 74
  Pork Roast with Hopping John
    Stuffing, 98
  Portobellos, Yukon Gold-Stuffed, 84
  Ratatouille with Chickpeas, 76
  Red Beans and Rice, Kicked-Up, 108
  Rice, Vegetable Creole, 151
  Soup, Bean-and-Bacon, 161
  Spinach-Rice Skillet, Cheesy, 74
  Spinach with Rustic Mashed Potatoes,
    Sautéed, 84
  Stuffed Potatoes, Garlic- and Green
    Onion-, 146
  Vegetables, Roasted Fall, 149
Grapefruit Ambrosia Coupes, 36
Gravies
  Beef and Gravy, Slow-Roasted, 94
  Browned Gravy, 87
  Onion Gravy, Turkey with
    Golden, 108
Grits, Garlic-Cheese, 169, 180
Gumbo, Holiday, 163

Ham. *See also* Sandwiches.
  Hopping John, 171
  Omelet, Western, 173
  Skillet Ham with Spicy Peach Salsa, 99
  Soup, Potato, Broccoli, and Ham, 176

Jambalaya, Delta Shrimp-and-Sausage, 68
Jambalaya, Quick, 172

Kebabs, Chicken, 166
Kebabs, Curried Lamb, 172

Lamb
  Chops, Mustard-Garlic Lamb, 181
  Grilled Lamb, Mediterranean, 96
  Kebabs, Curried Lamb, 172
  Salad, Lamb-Vegetable, 178
  Shanks on Lentil-Spinach Ragoût,
    Lamb, 95
  Stew with Spring Vegetables, Lamb, 156
  Vegetables, Middle Eastern Sweet
    Spiced Lamb and, 95
Lasagna, Skillet Roasted Pepper, 80
Leeks and Mushrooms, Risotto with, 151
Leek Soup, Potato-and-, 154
Lemon. *See also* Chicken.
  Asparagus, Lemon Roasted, 142
  Basmati Rice with Pine Nuts,
    Lemon, 150
  Cake, Glazed Lemon Loaf, 43
  Crust, Roast Pork with Lemon-
    Pepper, 98
  Dressing, Salmon-Potato Salad with
    Lemon-Dill, 62
  Pie, Lemon Meringue, 41
  Punch, Lemony Gingerale, 16
  Sauce, Lemon, 44
  Scallops with Snow Peas, Lemon-
    Dill, 176
  Squares, Raspberry-Lemon, 56
Lentils
  Curried Lentils and Carrots on
    Couscous, 76
  Pilaf, Lentils-and-Brown Rice, 74
  Ragoût, Lamb Shanks on Lentil-
    Spinach, 95
  Salad, Lentil, 166
Linguine, Garlicky Clam-and-
  Mushroom, 65

Macaroni and Cheese with Bacon, 172
Macaroni and Cheese with Carrots and
  Roasted Pepper, 80
Mango Smoothie, 16
Mango Tilapia, Caribbean, 64

Mushrooms
  Gratin of Noodles and Mushrooms, 150
  Linguine, Garlicky Clam-and-
    Mushroom, 65
  Portobello-and-Caramelized Onion
    Sandwiches, 127
  Portobello Sandwich, 181
  Portobellos, Yukon Gold-Stuffed, 84
  Ragoût, Smothered Chicken in
    Mushroom, 103
  Tartlets, Mushroom, 15

Noodle Salad with Chicken and Sugar
  Peas, Asian, 124
Noodles and Mushrooms, Gratin of, 150

Oatmeal
  Banana-Walnut Oatmeal, 173
  Bars, Oatmeal Energy, 15
  Bread with Walnut Streusel Topping,
    Pumpkin-Oat, 33
  Cranberry Oatmeal, 170
Onions
  Cabbage and Onions with Bacon,
    Old-World, 143
  Caramelized Onion-and-White Bean
    Spread, 12
  Caramelized Onion Sandwiches,
    Portobello-and-, 127
  Caramelized Onion Soup with Pesto,
    Butternut Squash-and-, 154
  Caramelized Onions, Pork with
    Sweet, 97
  Frittata, Onion-Pepper, 177
  Gravy, Turkey with Golden
    Onion, 108
  Green Onion-Stuffed Potatoes, Garlic-
    and, 146
  Panzanella, 121
  Roasted Onions, Balsamic, 144
  Soup, French Onion, 177
Oranges. See also Salsas, Sauces.
  Mandarin Beef Stir-Fry, 88
  Scones, Cranberry-Orange, 31
  Valencia Artichokes, 142
  Vinaigrette, Citrus, 125
Orzo Salad, Seafood-, 172
Orzo with Pesto Mayonnaise and
  Broccoli, 122
Oysters with Spicy Cocktail Sauce,
  Cajun Oven-Fried, 66

Pancakes, Banana-Buttermilk, 20
Pancakes, Maple-Pecan, 165
Pastas. See also specific types and Salads.
  Bake with Basil, Chicken-and-Pasta, 101

Blackened Shrimp Pasta, 167
Penne Toss, Feta-and-, 81
Penne, White Bean-and-Wilted
  Spinach, 81
Penne with Vegetable Marinara, 176
Pesto Pasta, 176
Primavera, Creamy Pesto, 169
Primavera, Pasta, 181
Rotini Casserole, Broccoli-, 82
Skillet, Quick Pasta, 81
Tortellini Fagioli, 155
Tortellini, Pesto-Cheese, 174
Tortellini Soup, 170
Ziti, Baked, 164
Ziti, Hot Monterey, 82
Peaches. See also Beverages.
  Crisp, Almond-Peach, 53
  Pie with Sugared Oat Topping,
    Peach, 42
  Pork with Ginger-Peach Sauce,
    Braised, 97
  Salsa, Skillet Ham with Spicy Peach, 99
  Waffles, Spiced Peach, 169
  Yogurt, Honeyed Peach, 171
Peanut Butter. See also Sandwiches.
  Bars, Peanut Butter S'mores, 56
  Pie, Frozen Peanut Butter Brittle, 40
  Shake, Fudgy Peanut Butter, 17
  Squares, Peanut Butter-Fruit, 171
  Toast, Peanut Butter-Raisin, 172, 173
Pear-Berry Granola Crisp, Crunchy, 54
Pears with Cranberries, Spiced, 37
Peas
  Gingered Carrots and Peas, 144
  Hopping John, 171
  Hopping John Stuffing, Pork Roast
    with, 98
  Snow Peas, Lemon-Dill Scallops
    with, 176
  Sugar Peas, Asian Noodle Salad with
    Chicken and, 124
Peppers
  Chipotle Black Beans and Rice, 75
  Chipotle Chicken-and-Pepper Fajitas,
    Spicy, 102
  Chipotle-Glazed Pork Sandwiches, 131
  Frittata, Onion-Pepper, 177
  Green Chile Casserole, Corn-and-, 78
  Jalapeño-Lime Oil, Pan-Seared Sea
    Bass with, 58
  Jalapeño Mayonnaise, Coleslaw with, 119
  Jalapeños, Country Cornbread Muffins
    with, 30
  Red Pepper Sauce, Black Bean-and-
    Corn Ravioli with, 82
  Red Pepper Stir-Fry, Shrimp-and-, 68
  Roasted Pepper and Goat Cheese,
    Pesto Crostini with, 13
  Roasted Pepper Lasagna, Skillet, 80

Roasted Pepper, Macaroni and Cheese
    with Carrots and, 80
  Roasted Peppers and Corn, 145
  Roasted Red Pepper Dip, 12
  Salad, Red-and-Green, 177
  Sandwich, Pepper-and-Beef, 176
  Stuffed Peppers, 168
Pies and Pastries
  Brownie Sundae Pie, 41
  Cobblers
    Almond-Peach Crisp, 53
    Apple-Berry Cobbler, 53
    Berry Crisp, Summer, 53
    Pear-Berry Granola Crisp,
      Crunchy, 54
  Frozen Peanut Butter Brittle Pie, 40
  Lemon Meringue Pie, 41
  Peach Pie with Sugared Oat
    Topping, 42
  Pot Pie, Vegetarian Comfort, 85
  Tartlets, Lime, 39
  Tartlets, Mushroom, 15
Pineapple Cake, Quick Gingerbread-, 43
Pineapple, Sugared, 176
Pizza
  Barbecue Chicken Pizza, 171
  Mexican Pizza, 179
  Veggie Pizza, 172
Polenta with Roasted Vegetables, Cheesy
  Soft, 79
Pork
  Burgoo, Bama, 161
  Caramelized Onions, Pork with
    Sweet, 97
  Chops
    Baked Pork Chop, Crispy-, 174
    Plum-Berry Sauce, Pork Chops
      with, 96
    Southwestern Pork Chops, 166
    Thyme Pork with Apple-Cherry
      Compote, 96
  Indian-Style Pork, Fruited, 97
  Roast with Hopping John Stuffing,
    Pork, 98
  Skillet, Pork-and-Potato, 170
  Tenderloin
    Braised Pork with Ginger-Peach
      Sauce, 97
    Herb-Crusted Pork with
      Pineapple Sauce, 98
    Roast Pork with Lemon-Pepper
      Crust, 98
    Sandwiches, Chipotle-Glazed
      Pork, 131
    Stuffed Pork Tenderloin with
      Orange-Mustard Sauce,
      Fruit-, 99
Potatoes. See also Salads, Sweet Potatoes.
  Fireside Potatoes and Vegetables, 83

Potatoes *(continued)*

Hash Brown Casserole, 145
Mashed Potatoes, Blue Cheese, 174
Mashed Potatoes, Creamy, 165
Mashed Potatoes, Sautéed Spinach
with Rustic, 84
Mashed Potatoes with Rosemary,
Garlic, 145
Salad with Lemon-Dill Dressing,
Salmon-Potato, 62
Scalloped Potatoes with Spinach and
Cheese, 146
Skillet, Pork-and-Potato, 170
Soup, Potato-and-Leek, 154
Soup, Potato, Broccoli, and Ham, 176
Stuffed Potato, Broccoli- and
Cheese-, 166
Stuffed Potatoes, Garlic- and Green
Onion-, 146
Yukon Gold-Stuffed Portobellos, 84
Puddings
Banana Pudding, 172
Bread Pudding with Rum-Raisin
Caramel Sauce, 54
Rice Pudding with Toasted Almonds,
Scandinavian, 54
Pumpkin-Oat Bread with Walnut
Streusel Topping, 33

Quesadillas
Chicken-and-Spinach Quesadilla, 164
Spinach-and-Black Bean
Quesadillas, 77
Succotash Quesadillas, 77
Veggie Quesadilla, 175

Ragoût, Lamb Shanks on Lentil-
Spinach, 95
Ragoût, Smothered Chicken in
Mushroom, 103
Raspberries
Crêpes, Chocolate-Raspberry, 38
Muffins, Cinnamon-Kissed
Raspberry, 30
Squares, Raspberry-Lemon, 56
Ravioli, Peasant Spinach, 83
Ravioli with Red Pepper Sauce, Black
Bean-and-Corn, 82
Relish, Tomato-Basil, 59
Rice. *See also* Beans, Soups.
Basmati Rice with Pine Nuts,
Lemon, 150
Brown Rice Pilaf, 150
Brown Rice Pilaf, Lentils-and-, 74
Fiesta Rice, Cumin Scallops on, 67
Fried Rice, Shrimp, 175

Fried Rice, Vegetable, 151
Pudding with Toasted Almonds,
Scandinavian Rice, 54
Risotto with Leeks and
Mushrooms, 151
Salad with Mango and Shrimp,
Coconut-Rice, 123
Skillet, Cheesy Spinach-Rice, 74
Vegetable Creole Rice, 151

Salads and Salad Dressings
Asian Noodle Salad with Chicken and
Sugar Peas, 124
Barley Salad with Black Beans and
Corn, Mexican, 121
Bean Salad, Three-, 165
Beef Salad, Thai, 124
Blue Cheese Dressing, 125
Broccoli-and-Cauliflower Salad with
Blue Cheese Dressing, 119
Broccoli Salad, 180
Bulgur with Zucchini and Peas, 121
Chef Salad, 175
Chicken
Asparagus, Chicken Salad
with, 124
Caesar Salad, Chicken, 173
Chicken Salad, 174
Curried Chicken Salad, 177
Grilled Chicken Salad, 169
Sandwiches, Homemade Chicken
Salad, 131
Spinach Salad, Chicken-, 167
Citrus Vinaigrette, 125
Coconut-Rice Salad with Mango and
Shrimp, 123
Coleslaw, Spicy, 176
Coleslaw with Jalapeño
Mayonnaise, 119
Corn-and-Basil Salad, Fresh, 119
Cucumber Salad, Sliced, 120
Egg Salad Sandwiches, Curried, 128
Feta Dressing, Creamy, 125
Field Salad with Mushrooms and
Feta, 118
Fruit Salad, Frozen, 118
Fruit Salad with Citrus-Cilantro
Dressing, Fresh, 118
Grapefruit-and-Greens Salad, 118
Greek Salad, 169
Honey-Mustard Dressing, 125
Italian Salad, 164
Lamb-Vegetable Salad, 178
Lentil Salad, 166
Mediterranean Green Salad, 172
Orzo with Pesto Mayonnaise and
Broccoli, 122
Panzanella, 121

Pasta Salad, Greek, 173
Pasta Salad, Primavera, 122
Potato Salad, Chunky, 120
Potato Salad, Dilled, 172
Red-and-Green Salad, 177
Roast Beef Salad with Blue
Cheese, 168
Salmon-Potato Salad with Lemon-Dill
Dressing, 62
Seafood-Orzo Salad, 172
Slaw, French Vinaigrette, 119
Slaw, Shrimp Po'boys with
Remoulade, 129
Spinach Salad, Traditional, 178
Spinach-Strawberry Salad, 175
Tabbouleh with Feta, 122
Tomatillo Salsa Salad, 120
Tomato Salad, Marinated Three-, 120
Tuna-and-White Bean Salad, 123
Tuna Salad in Tomato, 167
Tuna Salad Pita, 168
Turkey Pasta Salad, 164
Turkey Waldorf Salad, 125
White Bean-and-Tomato Salad, 178
White Bean-Pasta Salad, 123
Salmon
Baked Pesto Salmon, 181
Glazed Salmon with Fresh Ginger, 61
Mango Salsa, Salmon with Sweet, 62
Salad with Lemon-Dill Dressing,
Salmon-Potato, 62
Smoked Salmon-and-Watercress
Sandwiches, 129
Salsas. *See also* Relish, Sauces.
Mango Salsa, Salmon with Sweet, 62
Orange-Zested Salsa, Blackened Tuna
with, 64
Peach Salsa, Skillet Ham with
Spicy, 99
Sandwiches
Bagel, Egg-and-Cheese, 172
Bagel, Honey-Cinnamon, 171
Bagelwich, Ham, Egg, and
Cheese, 175
Calzones, Broccoli-and-Two
Cheese, 128
Chicken Salad Sandwiches,
Homemade, 131
Chicken Sandwiches, Open-Faced
Mediterranean Grilled, 132
Egg Salad Sandwiches, Curried, 128
Fried Egg Sandwiches with Toasted
Mustard Seed Aïoli, 128
Grilled Cheese Sandwich, 173
Grilled Chicken Sandwich, 174
Grilled Tomato-and-Cheese
Sandwich, 166
Ham-and-Cheese Sandwich, 178
Hot Ham-and-Swiss Sandwich, 176

Kalamata-Cucumber Party
    Sandwiches, 127
Peanut Butter-and-Banana
    Sandwich, 170
Peanut Butter-and-Jelly
    Sandwich, 167
Pepper-and-Beef Sandwich, 176
Philly Swiss Melt, 170
Pimiento Cheese-Veggie
    Sandwich, 180
Pita, Hummus-Veggie, 175
Pita, Mediterranean Chicken, 181
Pita, Tuna Salad, 168
Pita Wraps, Turkey-and-Chutney, 132
Po'boys with Remoulade Slaw,
    Shrimp, 129
Pork Sandwiches, Chipotle-Glazed, 131
Portobello-and-Caramelized Onion
    Sandwiches, 127
Portobello Sandwich, 181
Roast Beef-and-Feta Sandwich, 180
Roast Beef Sandwiches with
    Horseradish Cream, 129
Roll-Up, Turkey-Spinach, 179
Shrimp Sandwich, Spicy, 171
Sloppy Joe, 166
Smoked Salmon-and-Watercress
    Sandwiches, 129
Snack Sandwich, Mediterranean, 177
Subs, Meatball, 130
Tomato-Avocado Sandwich, 174
Turkey Cobb Sandwiches, 132
Turkey-Swiss Sandwich, 168
Veggie Burger, 170
Veggie Melts, 127
Wrap, Roast Beef, 167
Wraps, Crunchy Chicken, 164
Wraps with Avocado Picadillo, Grilled
    Steak, 130
Wrap, Veggie, 165
Sauces. See also Desserts/Sauces; Relish;
    Salsas; Topping.
    Apricot-Ginger Sauce, Turkey
        Scaloppine with, 108
    Butter Sauce, Sea Scallops with
        Lemony, 66
    Cocktail Sauce, Cajun Oven-Fried
        Oysters with Spicy, 66
    Cumin Sauce, Creamy, 79
    Ginger-Peach Sauce, Braised Pork
        with, 97
    Horseradish Sauce, Grilled Tuna Steaks
        with, 64
    Marinara, Penne with Vegetable, 176
    Marsala-Mushroom Sauce, Beef
        Tenderloin with, 93
    Meat Sauce, Spaghetti with, 180
    Mushroom Sauce, Peppered Filet
        with, 179

Orange-Mustard Sauce, Fruit-Stuffed
    Pork Tenderloin with, 99
Orange-Yogurt Sauce, Fruit Medley
    with, 36
Pineapple Sauce, Herb-Crusted Pork
    with, 98
Plum-Berry Sauce, Pork Chops
    with, 96
Red Pepper Sauce, Black Bean-and-
    Corn Ravioli with, 82
Tapenade, Broiled Fish with, 61
Teriyaki Sauce, Halibut Fillets
    with, 59
Sausage
    Gumbo, Holiday, 163
    Jambalaya, Delta Shrimp-and-
        Sausage, 68
    Jambalaya, Quick, 172
    Soup, Sausage-Vegetable, 171
    Soup, Spicy Black Bean-and-
        Sausage, 163
Scallops
    Cumin Scallops on Fiesta Rice, 67
    Lemon-Dill Scallops with Snow
        Peas, 176
    Sea Scallops with Lemony Butter
        Sauce, 66
Seafood. See also specific types and Fish.
    Salad, Seafood-Orzo, 172
Shrimp. See also Sandwiches.
    Blackened Shrimp Pasta, 167
    Cilantro-Lime Shrimp, 179
    Curried Shrimp, Sweet, 68
    Curry, Mild Shrimp-and-
        Vegetable, 67
    Fried Rice, Shrimp, 175
    Gumbo, Holiday, 163
    Jambalaya, Delta Shrimp-and-
        Sausage, 68
    Party Shrimp, 14
    Remoulade, Shrimp, 67
    Salad with Mango and Shrimp,
        Coconut-Rice, 123
    Soup, Shrimp Won Ton
        Dumpling, 155
    Stir-Fry, Shrimp-and-Red Pepper, 68
    Stir-Fry Shrimp and Vegetables, 168
Snacks
    Chips, Pita, 174
    Popcorn, Curried, 15
    Sandwich, Mediterranean Snack, 177
    S'mores, 164
    Tortilla, Cinnamon-Sugar Toasted, 176
Soups. See also Chili, Gumbo, Ragoût,
    Stews.
    Bean-and-Bacon Soup, 161
    Beef-Vegetable Soup, 181
    Beer-Cheese Soup with Pretzel
        Croutons, 153

Berry Patch Soup, 153
Black Bean-and-Sausage Soup,
    Spicy, 163
Butternut Squash-and-Caramelized
    Onion Soup with Pesto, 154
Cauliflower Soup, Cream of, 153
Chicken Alphabet Soup, 161
Chicken-and-Rice Soup, Old-
    Fashioned, 162
French Onion Soup, 177
Mulligatawny, 162
Posole with Summer Squash, 154
Potato-and-Leek Soup, 154
Potato, Broccoli, and Ham Soup, 176
Sausage-Vegetable Soup, 171
Shrimp Won Ton Dumpling
    Soup, 155
Tomato Soup, Chunky Garden, 168
Tortellini Fagioli, 155
Tortellini Soup, 170
Turkey-and-Wild Rice Soup,
    Creamy, 162
Spaghetti
    Chicken Spaghetti, Greek, 171
    Meat Sauce, Spaghetti with, 180
    Primavera, Pasta, 181
Spinach. See also Salads.
    Creamy Spinach, 173
    Dip with Feta, Spinach, 12
    Florentine, Fettuccine Alfredo, 166
    Florentine, Flounder, 58
    Quesadilla, Chicken-and-Spinach, 164
    Quesadillas, Spinach-and-Black
        Bean, 77
    Ragoût, Lamb Shanks on Lentil-
        Spinach, 95
    Ravioli, Peasant Spinach, 83
    Roll-Up, Turkey-Spinach, 179
    Sautéed Spinach, 174
    Sautéed Spinach with Rustic Mashed
        Potatoes, 84
    Skillet, Cheesy Spinach-Rice, 74
    Stuffed Tomatoes, Spinach- and
        Feta, 147
    Walnuts, Spinach with, 178
    Wilted Spinach Penne, White Bean-
        and-, 81
Spreads
    Aïoli, Toasted Mustard Seed, 128
    Caramelized Onion-and-White Bean
        Spread, 12
    Goat Cheese-and-Anchovy Spread, 12
    Horseradish Cream, Roast Beef
        Sandwiches with, 129
Squash. See also Zucchini.
    Butternut Squash-and-Caramelized
        Onion Soup with Pesto, 154
    Casserole, Squash, 180
    Smothered Squash and Pinto Beans, 76

Squash *(continued)*

Summer Squash, Posole with, 154
Yellow Squash, Stuffed Zucchini
and, 148
Stews. *See also* Chili, Gumbo, Jambalaya,
Ragoût, Soups.
Burgoo, Bama, 161
Lamb Stew with Spring
Vegetables, 156
Pot Roast Stew, 156
Stir-Fry
Asparagus and Carrots, Stir-Fried, 142
Beef-and-Broccoli Stir-Fry, 93
Beef Stir-Fry, Mandarin, 88
Bok Choy-Tofu Stir-Fry, 85
Shrimp-and-Red Pepper Stir-Fry, 68
Shrimp and Vegetables, Stir-Fry, 168
Tofu-and-Broccoli Stir-Fry, 171
Vegetable Stir-Fry, Asian, 148
Strawberries. *See also* Beverages, Desserts.
Salad, Spinach-Strawberry, 175
Shortcake, Strawberry, 173
Waffles, Belgian, 167
Stuffing, Pork Roast with Hopping
John, 98
Sweet Potatoes
Mashed Sweet Potato, 178
Muffins, Sweet Potato-Bran, 31
Roasted Beets and Sweet
Potatoes, 143
Stuffed Sweet Potato, 164
Whipped Spiced Sweet Potatoes, 146

Tabbouleh with Feta, 122
Tacos, Beef, Bean, and Vegetable, 87
Tips on Food and Nutrition
Asparagus, Preparing, 142
Bananas, Mashing, 32
Beans, The Power of, 76
Beef, The Bonuses of, 87
Broccoli, Bravo for, 143
Caffeine Basics, 17
Carbohydrate Concerns, 20
Choose the Right Rice, 150
Citrus, Sectioning, 118
Crêpes, Making, 38
Dessert Dilemma, 43
Fish, Quick Substitutions, 59
Ginger, Grating, 29
Herbs, Fresh or Dried—You
Pick!, 145
Iron, Don't Ignore, 95
Meatless Merits, 84
Milk, The Skinny on, 55
Oven-Frying the Low-Fat Way, 66
Pasta Myths, 75
Peanut Butter, A Sticky Situation, 15

Pork Perks, 98
Portobellos, Preparing, 127
Poultry Possibilities, 105
Ravioli, Making, 83
Salmon, Sneaky, 62
Smoothie Smarts, 16
Spinach, Super, 81
Tomato Tips, 147
Vegetables, Is Fresh the Best?, 121
Vitamins, Vital, 155
Water, boiling, 123
Tofu-and-Broccoli Stir-Fry, 171
Tofu Stir-Fry, Bok Choy-, 85
Tomatillo Salsa Salad, 120
Tomatoes. *See also* Salads, Sandwiches.
Baked Tomatoes Tapenade, 147
Chard with Tomatoes and Roasted
Garlic, Stewed, 147
Couscous, Tomato, Basil, and
Corn, 180
Focaccia, Herbed Tomato, 19
Panzanella, 121
Pinwheels, Mediterranean, 19
Relish, Tomato-Basil, 59
Soup, Chunky Garden Tomato, 168
Stuffed Tomatoes, Spinach- and
Feta, 147
Topping, Streusel, 33
Tortillas. *See also* Sandwiches/Wraps.
Casserole, Mexican Tortilla, 77
Cinnamon-Sugar Toasted Tortilla, 176
Pizza, Mexican, 179
Tostada, Chili Bean, 78
Tuna. *See also* Salads.
Blackened Tuna with Orange-Zested
Salsa, 64
Grilled Tuna Steaks with Horseradish
Sauce, 64
Turkey. *See also* Salads, Sandwiches.
Enchiladas, Quick Turkey, 169
Lo Mein, Turkey, 107
Meatballs, Swedish, 14
Onion Gravy, Turkey with
Golden, 108
Parmesan, Turkey-Vegetable, 107
Roll-Up, Turkey-Spinach, 179
Scaloppine with Apricot-Ginger
Sauce, Turkey, 108
Soup, Creamy Turkey-and-Wild
Rice, 162

Veal Chops with Grapes, Glazed, 94
Vegetables. *See also* specific types and
Salads, Sandwiches, Soups.
Alfredo, Vegetable, 80
Burger, Veggie, 170
Caponata, 13
Couscous, Confetti, 149

Couscous, Veggie, 170
Curry, Mild Shrimp-and-
Vegetable, 67
Fireside Potatoes and Vegetables, 83
Fried Rice, Vegetable, 151
Lamb and Vegetables, Middle Eastern
Sweet Spiced, 95
Marinara, Penne with Vegetable, 176
Mulligatawny, 162
Paella, Grilled Vegetable, 74
Parmesan, Turkey-Vegetable, 107
Pasta Skillet, Quick, 81
Pizza, Veggie, 172
Pot Pie, Vegetarian Comfort, 85
Primavera, Creamy Pesto, 169
Primavera, Pasta, 181
Quesadilla, Veggie, 175
Ratatouille with Chickpeas, 76
Rice, Vegetable Creole, 151
Roasted Chicken and Vegetables,
Lemon-Sage, 106
Roasted Fall Vegetables, 149
Roasted Vegetables, Cheesy Soft
Polenta with, 79
Spring Vegetables, Lamb Stew
with, 156
Stir-Fry, Asian Vegetable, 148
Stir-Fry Shrimp and Vegetables, 168
Turkey Lo Mein, 107
Yucatan Vegetables, Chili-Seared Fish
with, 61

Waffles
Apple Syrup, Waffles with, 170
Belgian Waffles, 167
Blueberry Syrup, Waffles with, 172,
177
Spiced Peach Waffles, 169

Yogurt, Greek Honey, 38
Yogurt, Honeyed Peach, 171

Zucchini
Bulgur with Zucchini and Peas, 121
Frittata, Cheesy Zucchini, 85
Sauté, Zucchini-and-Corn, 148
Stuffed Zucchini and Yellow
Squash, 148

POINTS® Recipe Index

All recipes, including those in the Weekly Menu Planners,
are listed under the **POINTS** value for the recipe.

0 POINTS

Caponata, 13
Caramelized Onion-and-White Bean
    Spread, 12
Lemon Roasted Asparagus, 142
Mushroom Tartlets, 15
Sliced Cucumber Salad, 120

1 POINT

Almond Biscotti, 56
Apricot Butter, 29
Balsamic Roasted Onions, 144
Blue Cheese Dressing, 125
Broccoli-and-Cauliflower Salad with
    Blue Cheese Dressing, 119
Brown Sugar Icebox Cookies, 55
Buttery Baby Limas with Tarragon
    Mustard, 142
Cabbage and Carrots Parmesan, 144
Cauliflower Puttanesca, 144
Citrus Vinaigrette, 125
Coleslaw with Jalapeño
    Mayonnaise, 119
Creamy Spinach, 173
Curried Popcorn, 15
French Vinaigrette Slaw, 119
Garlicky Broccoli, 170, 180
Gingerbread-Raisin Cookies, 55
Goat Cheese-and-Anchovy
    Spread, 12
Grapefruit-and-Greens Salad, 118
Honey-Mustard Dressing, 125
Hot Popovers, 29
Italian Salad, 164
Kalamata-Cucumber Party
    Sandwiches, 127
Lemon Sauce, 44
Lime Tartlets, 39
Marinated Three-Tomato Salad, 120
Mediterranean Green Salad, 172
Mediterranean Pinwheels, 19
Party Shrimp, 14
Posole with Summer Squash, 154
Roasted Red Pepper Dip, 12
Rum-Raisin Caramel Sauce, 55
Sautéed Spinach, 174

Spinach Dip with Feta, 12
Spinach-Strawberry Salad, 175
Spinach with Walnuts, 178
Stewed Chard with Tomatoes and
    Roasted Garlic, 147
Stir-Fried Asparagus and
    Carrots, 142
Toasted Mustard Seed Aïoli, 128
Tomatillo Salsa Salad, 120
Valencia Artichokes, 142
Whole Wheat Rolls, 33
Zucchini-and-Corn Sauté, 148

2 POINTS

Asian Vegetable Stir-Fry, 148
Butternut Squash-and-Caramelized
    Onion Soup with Pesto, 154
Cheddar-Herb Rolls, 20
Chicken Bites with Creamy Parme-
    san Dip, 14
Chunky Garden Tomato Soup, 168
Chunky Potato Salad, 120
Cinnamon-Kissed Raspberry
    Muffins, 30
Confetti Couscous, 149
Cream of Cauliflower Soup, 153
Creamy Feta Dressing, 125
Field Salad with Mushrooms and
    Feta, 118
Fresh Fruit Salad with Citrus-
    Cilantro Dressing, 118
Fruit Medley with Orange-Yogurt
    Sauce, 36
Gingered Carrots and Peas, 144
Herb-and-Garlic Breadsticks, 19
Herbed Tomato Focaccia, 19
Lemony Gingerale Punch, 16
Old-World Cabbage and Onions
    with Bacon, 143
Panzanella, 121
Peach Fizz, 16
Pesto Crostini with Roasted Pepper
    and Goat Cheese, 13
Pita Chips, 174
Raspberry-Lemon Squares, 56
Red-and-Green Salad, 177

Roasted Peppers and Corn, 145
Rosemary-Garlic Breadsticks, 19
Smoked Salmon-and-Watercress
    Sandwiches, 129
Spicy Coleslaw, 176
Strawberry-Merlot Ice, 40
Strawberry Shortcake, 173
Vegetable Creole Rice, 151
Vegetable Fried Rice, 151

3 POINTS

Anadama Raisin Bread, 34
Apples with Caramel Dipping
    Sauce, 36
Baba Ghanoush with Pita Chips, 13
Baked Tomatoes Tapenade, 147
Bama Burgoo, 161
Banana-Buttermilk Pancakes, 20
Banana-Date Bread, 32
Barley Pilaf with Toasted Almonds
    and Raisins, 149
Berry Patch Soup, 153
Berry-Yogurt Parfait, 179
Blueberry-Bran Muffins, 30
Broccoli with Almond-Breadcrumb
    Topping, 143
Broiled Tandoori Chicken, 102
Brown Rice Pilaf, 150
Bulgur with Zucchini
    and Peas, 121
Buttermilk Cornbread, 32
Cheese Toast, 165, 171, 178
Chicken Salad with Asparagus, 124
Chili-Seared Fish with Yucatan
    Vegetables, 61
Cinnamon-Raisin Bread, 172
Cinnamon-Sugar Toasted
    Tortilla, 176
Cinnamon Swirl Loaf, 34
Country Cornbread Muffins with
    Jalapeños, 30
Crunchy Pear-Berry Granola
    Crisp, 54
Fresh Corn-and-Basil Salad, 119
Frozen Dessert Sandwiches, 180
Frozen Fruit Salad, 118

Garlic Mashed Potatoes with
  Rosemary, 145
Grapefruit Ambrosia Coupes, 36
Gratin of Noodles and
  Mushrooms, 150
Grilled Herbed Chicken, 180
Grilled Spice-Rubbed Cornish
  Hens, 107
Hash-Brown Casserole, 145
Lemon Basmati Rice with Pine
  Nuts, 150
Lemon-Pepper Chicken, 173
Mango Smoothie, 16
Mediterranean Grilled Lamb, 96
Milk Chocolate Ice Cream, 40
Mocha Cocoa, 17
Oatmeal Energy Bars, 15
Orzo with Pesto Mayonnaise and
  Broccoli, 122
Peanut Butter-Raisin Toast, 172, 173
Peanut Butter S'mores Bars, 56
Pumpkin-Oat Bread with Walnut
  Streusel Topping, 33
Roasted Beets and Sweet
  Potatoes, 143
Roasted Fall Vegetables, 149
Roast Pork with Lemon-Pepper
  Crust, 98
Scrambled Eggs, 166
Shrimp Remoulade, 67
Shrimp Won Ton Dumpling
  Soup, 155
Spiced Pears with Cranberries, 37
Spinach- and Feta-Stuffed
  Tomatoes, 147
Strawberry-Banana Soy Smoothie, 17
Strawberry Smoothie, 166
Stuffed Zucchini and Yellow
  Squash, 148
Swedish Meatballs, 14
Sweet Potato-Bran Muffins, 31
Tabbouleh with Feta, 122
Tortellini Soup, 170
Traditional Spinach Salad, 178
Veggie Burger, 170
Whipped Spiced Sweet
  Potatoes, 146
White Bean-Pasta Salad, 123
Wine Coolers, 16

4 POINTS
Almond-Peach Crisp, 53
Apple-Berry Cobbler, 53

Apple-Ginger Muffins, 29
Banana Pudding, 172
Barbecue Chicken, 172
Bean-and-Bacon Soup, 161
Beer-Cheese Soup with Pretzel
  Croutons, 153
Blackened Tuna with Orange-Zested
  Salsa, 64
Blue Cheese Mashed Potatoes, 174
Broiled Fish with Tapenade, 61
Buttermilk Panna Cotta with Blue-
  berry Sauce, 39
Caesar Mahimahi, 60
Cajun Grilled Snapper, 176
Cheesy Zucchini Frittata, 85
Chicken à la King, 165
Chicken Alphabet Soup, 161
Chicken Salad, 174
Cilantro-Lime Shrimp, 179
Cinnamon-Banana Smoothie, 179
Cinnamon-Raisin Scones, 32
Cinnamon Toast, 180
Cranberry-Orange Scones, 31
Creamy Mashed Potatoes, 165
Curried Egg Salad Sandwiches, 128
Curried Lamb Kebabs, 172
Deep Butter-Rum Sauce and
  Bananas, 37
Fig Spice Cake, 42
Fudgy Peanut Butter Shake, 17
Garlic- and Green Onion-Stuffed
  Potatoes, 146
Glazed Lemon Loaf Cake, 43
Glazed Mahimahi, 60
Greek Chicken with Lemon and
  Mint, 104
Herb-Crusted Pork with Pineapple
  Sauce, 98
Ice Cream Sandwich, 170
Lime-Marinated Sea Bass, 166
Mediterranean Snack Sandwich, 177
Mixed Fruit Muffins, 31
Old-Fashioned Chicken-and-Rice
  Soup, 162
Peanut Butter-Fruit Squares, 171
Potato-and-Leek Soup, 154
Quick Hot Chocolate, 174
Red Beans and Rice, 178
Risotto with Leeks and
  Mushrooms, 151
Rosemary Swordfish, 164
Sausage-Vegetable Soup, 171
Scalloped Potatoes with Spinach and
  Cheese, 146

Scandinavian Rice Pudding with
  Toasted Almonds, 54
S'mores, 164
South-of-the-Border Snapper, 180
Spicy Black Bean-and-Sausage
  Soup, 163
Strawberry Milkshake, 17
Sugared Pineapple, 176
Sunrise Smoothie, 178
Three-Bean Salad, 165
Tomato, Basil, and Corn
  Couscous, 180
Tortellini Fagioli, 155
Tuna Salad in Tomato, 167
Turkey Waldorf Salad, 125
Veggie Quesadilla, 175
Wild Fruit Smoothie, 181

5 POINTS
Beef Tenderloin with Horseradish-
  Mustard Crust, 94
Beef Tenderloin with Marsala-
  Mushroom Sauce, 93
Belgian Waffles, 167
Black Bean-and-Corn Ravioli with
  Red Pepper Sauce, 82
Café-Style Meat Loaf with Browned
  Gravy, 87
Cajun Oven-Fried Oysters with
  Spicy Cocktail Sauce, 66
Cheesy Soft Polenta with Roasted
  Vegetables, 79
Chicken Cordon Bleu, 103
Chicken Kebabs, 166
Chicken Teriyaki, 178
Cookies and Cream, 175
Creamy Turkey-and-Wild Rice
  Soup, 162
Creole Baked Snapper, 63
Crispy Honey-Mustard
  Chicken, 168
Curried Chicken Salad, 177
Dilled Potato Salad, 172
Easy Parmesan Flounder, 170
Eggplant Parmesan, 178
Extra Cheesy Toast, 176
Fireside Potatoes and Vegetables, 83
Fried Egg Sandwiches with Toasted
  Mustard Seed Aïoli, 128
Frozen Chocolate Decadence
  Brownies, 40
Fruit-Stuffed Pork Tenderloin with
  Orange-Mustard Sauce, 99

Garlic-Cheese Grits, 169, 180
Greek Grouper, 178
Greek Honey Yogurt, 38
Greek Salad, 169
Greek Snapper, 63
Greek Stuffed Flank Steak, 88
Grilled Chicken with Basil, 176
Grilled Tomato-and-Cheese
    Sandwich, 166
Holiday Gumbo, 163
Honey-Cinnamon Bagel, 171
Honeyed Peach Yogurt, 171
Hot Monterey Ziti, 82
Individual Crab Casseroles, 65
Lamb Shanks on Lentil-Spinach
    Ragoût, 95
Lamb Stew with Spring
    Vegetables, 156
Lemon-Sage Roasted Chicken and
    Vegetables, 106
Lentil Salad, 166
Mexican Tortilla Casserole, 77
Molasses Angel Food Cake with
    Lemon Sauce, 44
Mustard-Garlic Lamb Chops, 181
Onion-Pepper Frittata, 177
Oven-Fried Catfish, 177
Pan-Seared Sea Bass with Jalapeño-
    Lime Oil, 58
Peasant Spinach Ravioli, 83
Pork with Sweet Caramelized
    Onions, 97
Pot Roast Stew, 156
Quick Jambalaya, 172
Roast Beef Salad with Blue
    Cheese, 168
Roast Beef Sandwiches with Horse-
    radish Cream, 129
Sesame Chicken, 170
Shrimp Po'boys with Remoulade
    Slaw, 129
Skillet Ham with Spicy Peach
    Salsa, 99
Skillet Mexican Chicken, 105
Skillet Sirloin with Sweet
    Marinade, 93
Slow-Roasted Beef and Gravy, 94
Southwestern Pork Chops, 166
Spiced Peach Waffles, 169
Spicy Shrimp Sandwich, 171
Stuffed Sweet Potato, 164
Succotash Quesadillas, 77
Tarragon Snapper, 63
Tofu-and-Broccoli Stir-Fry, 171

Tomato-Avocado Sandwich, 174
Tropical Smoothie, 173
Turkey Cobb Sandwiches, 132
Veggie Wrap, 165
Very Berry Shortcake, 37
Waffles with Blueberry Syrup, 172,
    177
Warm Fresh Apple Cake, 42

6 POINTS
Angelic Tiramisu, 39
Bananas Foster, 36
Banana Split, 170, 177
Banana-Strawberry Sundae, 174
Beef-Vegetable Soup, 181
Black Beans and Rice, 177
Blackened Shrimp Pasta, 167
Braised Pork with Ginger-Peach
    Sauce, 97
Breaded Fish Italian Style, 59
Bread Pudding with Rum-Raisin
    Caramel Sauce, 54
Breakfast Burrito, 174
Broccoli-and-Cheese Stuffed
    Potato, 166
Broccoli Salad, 180
Brownie Sundae Pie, 41
Caribbean Mango Tilapia, 64
Cheesy Bean Burritos, 168
Cheesy Spinach-Rice Skillet, 74
Chef Salad, 175
Chicken Cacciatore, 175
Chicken Kiev, 104
Chili Bean Tostada, 78
Chocolate-Raspberry Crêpes, 38
Cranberry Oatmeal, 170
Crispy-Baked Pork Chop, 174
Curried Lentils and Carrots on
    Couscous, 76
Double Chocolate Bundt Cake, 44
Egg-and-Cheese Bagel, 172
Farmhouse Chicken-and-Dressing
    Casserole, 101
Flounder Florentine, 58
French Toast, 168, 172
Frozen Peanut Butter Brittle Pie, 40
Garlicky Clam-and-Mushroom
    Linguine, 65
Glazed Veal Chops with Grapes, 94
Grilled Cheese Sandwich, 173
Grilled Chicken Sandwich, 174
Grilled Steak Wraps with Avocado
    Picadillo, 130

Grilled Tuna Steaks with Horseradish
    Sauce, 64
Halibut Fillets with Teriyaki
    Sauce, 59
Ham-and-Cheese Sandwich, 178
Homemade Chicken Salad
    Sandwiches, 131
Hopping John, 171
Hot Ham-and-Swiss Sandwich, 176
Hummus-Veggie Pita, 175
Lemon-Dill Scallops with Snow
    Peas, 176
Lentils-and-Brown Rice Pilaf, 74
Mandarin Beef Stir-Fry, 88
Maple-Pecan Pancakes, 165
Maryland Crab Cakes, 65
Mashed Sweet Potato, 178
Mexican Barley Salad with Black
    Beans and Corn, 121
Mexican Pizza, 179
Mulligatawny, 162
Open-Faced Mediterranean Grilled
    Chicken Sandwiches, 132
Oven-Fried Fish, 60
Peach Pie with Sugared Oat
    Topping, 42
Pecan-Crusted Grouper, 58
Pepper-and-Beef Sandwich, 176
Pesto Pasta, 176
Pimiento Cheese-Veggie
    Sandwich, 180
Pork Roast with Hopping John
    Stuffing, 98
Portobello-and-Caramelized Onion
    Sandwiches, 127
Portobello Sandwich, 181
Primavera Pasta Salad, 122
Quick Gingerbread-Pineapple
    Cake, 43
Ratatouille with Chickpeas, 76
Roast Beef-and-Feta
    Sandwich, 180
Sautéed Spinach with Rustic Mashed
    Potatoes, 84
Squash Casserole, 180
Stir-Fry Shrimp and Vegetables, 168
Strawberry-Granola Parfait, 175
Stuffed Peppers, 168
Summer Berry Crisp, 53
Sweet Curried Shrimp, 68
Thai Beef Salad, 124
Thyme Pork with Apple-Cherry
    Compote, 96
Tuna-and-White Bean Salad, 123

Turkey-and-Chutney Pita
    Wraps, 132
Turkey-Spinach Roll-Up, 179
Turkey-Swiss Sandwich, 168
Vegetable Alfredo, 80
Vegetarian Chili, 164
Vegetarian Comfort Pot Pie, 85
Veggie Melts, 127
Waffles with Apple Syrup, 170
Yukon Gold-Stuffed Portobellos, 84

7 POINTS
Asian Noodle Salad with Chicken
    and Sugar Peas, 124
Baked Pesto Salmon, 181
Banana-Walnut Oatmeal, 173
Beef, Bean, and Vegetable Tacos, 87
Beef with Asparagus, 179
Bok Choy-Tofu Stir-Fry, 85
Broccoli-and-Two Cheese
    Calzones, 128
Buttery Tarragon Chicken, 103
Chicken-and-Spinach
    Quesadilla, 164
Chicken Parmesan, 167
Chicken-Spinach Salad, 167
Chipotle-Glazed Pork
    Sandwiches, 131
Chocolate-Butterscotch Parfait, 166
Corn-and-Green Chile
    Casserole, 78
Crunchy Chicken Wraps, 164
Cumin Scallops on Fiesta Rice, 67
Delta Shrimp-and-Sausage
    Jambalaya, 68
Feta-and-Penne Toss, 81
Fettuccine Alfredo Florentine, 166
Four-Way Cincinnati Chili, 156
Glazed Salmon with Fresh
    Ginger, 61
Grilled Vegetable Paella, 74
Ham, Egg, and Cheese
    Bagelwich, 175
Herb-Baked Trout, 169
Kalamata-White Bean Rice, 75
Kicked-Up Red Beans and
    Rice, 108
Lamb-Vegetable Salad, 178
Lemon Meringue Pie, 41
Macaroni and Cheese with
    Bacon, 172
Macaroni and Cheese with Carrots
    and Roasted Pepper, 80

Meatball Subs, 130
Middle Eastern Sweet Spiced Lamb
    and Vegetables, 95
Mild Shrimp-and-Vegetable
    Curry, 67
Pasta Primavera, 181
Peach-Banana Smoothie, 164
Peanut Butter-and-Banana
    Sandwich, 170
Peanut Butter-and-Jelly
    Sandwich, 167
Penne with Vegetable Marinara, 176
Pesto-Cheese Tortellini, 174
Philly Swiss Melt, 170
Pork-and-Potato Skillet, 170
Pork Chops with Plum-Berry
    Sauce, 96
Potato, Broccoli, and Ham
    Soup, 176
Quick Turkey Enchiladas, 169
Roast Beef Wrap, 167
Rustic Corn Cakes with Creamy
    Cumin Sauce, 79
Salmon with Sweet Mango Salsa, 62
Seafood-Orzo Salad, 172
Sea Scallops with Lemony Butter
    Sauce, 66
Shrimp-and-Red Pepper Stir-
    Fry, 68
Skillet Roasted Pepper Lasagna, 80
Sloppy Joe, 166
Smothered Squash and Pinto
    Beans, 76
Stuffed Blue Cheese Burgers, 130
Sweet-and-Sour Chicken, 101
Tuna Salad Pita, 168
Turkey Pasta Salad, 164
Turkey Scaloppine with Apricot-
    Ginger Sauce, 108
Turkey-Vegetable Parmesan, 107
Turkey with Golden Onion
    Gravy, 108
Western Omelet, 173
White Bean-and-Tomato Salad, 178
White Bean-and-Wilted Spinach
    Penne, 81

8 POINTS
Baked Ziti, 164
Barbecue Chicken Pizza, 171
Beef-and-Broccoli Stir-Fry, 93
Beef Stroganoff, 173
Broccoli Rotini Casserole, 82

Cheater's Deep-Flavored Barbecued
    Chicken, 105
Chicken-and-Pasta Bake with
    Basil, 101
Chicken Caesar Salad, 173
Chipotle Black Beans and Rice, 75
Coconut-Rice Salad with Mango
    and Shrimp, 123
Cornbread-Crusted Chile Beans, 78
Creamy Curried Chicken, 102
Creamy Pesto Primavera, 169
French Onion Soup, 177
Greek Chicken Spaghetti, 171
Greek Pasta Salad, 173
Grilled Chicken Salad, 169
Mediterranean Chicken Pita, 181
Quick Pasta Skillet, 81
Salmon-Potato Salad with Lemon-
    Dill Dressing, 62
Shrimp Fried Rice, 175
Sirloin Stroganoff, 88
Smothered Chicken in Mushroom
    Ragoût, 103
Spaghetti with Meat Sauce, 180
Spicy Chipotle Chicken-and-Pepper
    Fajitas, 102
Spinach-and-Black Bean
    Quesadillas, 77
Turkey Lo Mein, 107
Veggie Couscous, 170
Veggie Pizza, 172

9 POINTS
Chicken with Lemon, Figs, and
    Olives, 106
Coq au Vin, 104
Fruited Indian-Style Pork, 97
Peppered Filet with Mushroom
    Sauce, 179

10 POINTS
Blue Cheeseburger, 165

VEGETABLE COOKING CHART

Vegetable	Servings	Preparations	Cooking Instructions
Asparagus	3 to 4 per pound	Snap off tough ends. Remove scales, if desired.	To steam: Cook, covered, on a rack above boiling water 8 to 12 minutes. To boil: Cook, covered, in a small amount of boiling water 6 to 8 minutes or until crisp-tender.
Broccoli	3 to 4 per pound	Remove outer leaves and tough ends of lower stalks. Wash; cut into spears.	To steam: Cook, covered, on a rack above boiling water 15 to 18 minutes.
Carrots	4 per pound	Scrape; remove ends, and rinse. Leave tiny carrots whole; slice large carrots, or cut into strips.	Cook, covered, in a small amount of boiling water 8 to 10 minutes (slices) or 12 to 15 minutes (strips).
Cauliflower	4 per medium head	Remove outer leaves and stalk. Wash. Leave whole, or break into florets.	Cook, covered, in a small amount of boiling water 10 to 12 minutes (whole) or 8 to 10 minutes (florets).
Corn	4 per 4 large ears	Remove husks and silks. Leave corn on the cob, or cut off tips of kernels, and scrape cob with dull edge of knife.	Cook, covered, in boiling water to cover 10 minutes (on cob) or in a small amount of boiling water 8 to 10 minutes (cut).
Green beans	4 per pound	Wash; trim ends, and remove strings. Cut into 1½-inch pieces.	Cook, covered, in a small amount of boiling water 12 to 15 minutes.
Potatoes	3 to 4 per pound	Scrub; peel, if desired. Leave whole, slice, or cut into chunks.	To cook: Cook, covered, in a small amount of boiling water 30 to 40 minutes (whole) or 15 to 20 minutes (slices or chunks). To bake: Bake at 400° for 1 hour or until done.
Snow peas	4 per pound	Wash; trim ends, and remove tough strings.	Cook, covered, in a small amount of boiling water 3 to 5 minutes. Or cook over high heat in reduced-calorie margarine or in pan coated with cooking spray 3 to 5 minutes, stirring constantly.
Squash, summer	3 to 4 per pound	Wash; trim ends. Leave whole, slice, or chop.	To steam: Cook, covered, on a rack over boiling water 10 to 12 minutes (sliced or chopped). To boil: Cook, covered, in a small amount of boiling water 8 to 10 minutes (slices) or 15 minutes (whole).
Squash, winter (including acorn, butternut, hubbard, and spaghetti)	2 per pound	Rinse; cut in half, and remove all seeds.	To boil: Cook, covered, in boiling water 20 to 25 minutes. To bake: Place cut side down in shallow baking dish; add ½ inch water. Bake, uncovered, at 375° for 30 minutes. Turn and season, or fill; bake 20 to 30 minutes or until tender.